FULFILLING THE PROMISE

FULFILLING THE PROMISE

Virginia Commonwealth University
and the City of Richmond, 1968-2009

John T. Kneebone
and Eugene P. Trani

University of Virginia Press • *Charlottesville and London*

University of Virginia Press
© 2020 by the Rector and Visitors of the University of Virginia
All rights reserved
Printed in the United States of America on acid-free paper

First published 2020

ISBN 978-0-8139-4482-1 (hardcover)
ISBN 978-0-8139-4483-8 (ebook)

9 8 7 6 5 4 3 2 1

Library of Congress Cataloging-in-Publication Data is available for this title.

Publication of this volume was supported by Virginia Commonwealth University.
All authors' royalties resulting from this publication will be paid directly to the
VCU Foundation.

For our wives,
Elizabeth Roderick and Lois E. Trani,
with deep appreciation for their support and understanding

CONTENTS

ILLUSTRATIONS

FOREWORD

WHEN I MOVED to Virginia to get married in 1984, Richmond was losing population to surrounding suburbs and was generally cited as one among many examples of American central cities in decline. Frustration with a lack of progress in our city led me to begin my career in elected office ten years later when I sought a seat on the Richmond City Council. My councilmanic district included the main academic campus of Virginia Commonwealth University, as well as many neighborhoods adjoining the university. And so I began what has now become a quarter century in public life—at the local, state, and federal levels—where I have observed, represented, and partnered with VCU.

I worked with VCU to cooperate with surrounding neighborhoods who have felt both threatened and excited by the university's dynamic growth. I helped the city collaborate with VCU to build an engineering school, biotech research park, and major sporting arena. I assisted VCU with ambitious efforts to expand its hospital campus and medical school. As a senator serving on the Health, Education, Labor and Pensions Committee, I am in frequent contact with VCU over national health and education policy, and VCU professors testify often before our committee on a myriad of topics.

I have also seen VCU in the life of my constituents—the college students attending classes, the community leaders who hash out the details of development plans so that VCU's presence can complement their own efforts without swamping them, the neighbors who work for the university, the area residents who benefit from the top-notch research hospital right in the heart of our city, the friends who pack the Siegel Center to cheer on the VCU Rams. And the university is personal to my family—all three of my children were born at the VCU hospital.

So I am not a disinterested party as I offer introductory thoughts on John Kneebone and Eugene Trani's history of VCU's progress from 1968 through 2009. I have seen it, participated in it, and benefited by it.

Let me get to the punch line—Richmond is a dramatically different city in 2020 than it was in 1984. We are not shrinking, we are growing. We are not aging, we are getting younger. We are not a backward-looking southern museum piece; we are a dynamic, forward-focused city. We are not economically stagnant; we are a hub of innovation. We are not culturally staid, we are creative and diverse. We are not a city of decaying brownfields or razed urban renewal projects; we are a community with uniquely preserved natural beauty and a carefully tended built environment.

We used to make top 10 lists only for tragedies like our homicide or violent crime rates. Now Richmond is celebrated often for its achievements, quality of life, natural beauty, and cultural vibe. We have our problems, to be sure. But we have had enough success in overcoming obstacles that once seemed insurmountable that we have developed a renewed sense of pride and confidence that we can overcome any challenge before us.

As I think about the trends that have led to a powerful transformation in Richmond during the last decades, the three that seem most obvious to me are the progress of VCU, the desire of our citizens to break out of long-standing patterns of discrimination, and the concerted effort by so many Richmonders to reclaim, preserve, and promote our city's natural beauty, particularly our proximity to the James River. *Fulfilling the Promise* tells the story of the first of these fundamental pillars that have produced such success.

The history told here is that of the first forty years of VCU—the product of a 1968 merger between the Medical College of Virginia (founded in 1838) and the Richmond Professional Institute (founded in 1917). It is actually multiple stories—how the two institutions came together to become one, how the newly founded VCU served its student populations, how VCU interacted with Virginia state government, how VCU interacted with the city of Richmond and its diverse neighborhoods. And the story—while particular to VCU—is also an exemplary story of how an urban university strives, struggles, and succeeds in its quest to educate young people and contribute to the broader economic and cultural life of a metropolitan area.

The book will be most appreciated by university leaders—presidents, administrators, board members—and VCU alumni. But reading it, I am struck by how much value it has for elected officials, state budget officials, and urban planners. The most vivid stories are about VCU's external relations—with policymakers, planners, neighborhood leaders, the business community, the media. I have been active long enough to see VCU make missteps in these relationships, but then learn and improve. The fact that Richmond's recent successes have been so connected with VCU's growth is a tribute to the university's understanding that the complex web of relationships needed for the success of an urban university cannot be taken for granted or delegated down. And it is also a two-way street—state and local policymakers, along with Richmond private sector leadership, have grown in their appreciation for the role that VCU plays in our metropolitan area and Commonwealth.

And VCU has played a role in the other developments that have hastened Richmond's successes. The diverse student body and faculty, with many VCU graduates choosing to stay in Richmond, has helped our city embrace beautiful differences rather than cling to an artificial aristocracy of white privilege that so defined us for so long. And the university's commitment to environmental education has been part of our city's rediscovery of our natural assets as defining features to be cherished.

I applaud Gene Trani and John Kneebone for telling this story so well. And I applaud Gene Trani, and so many others, whose advocacy for VCU has added such positive momentum to my hometown, a city with a magnificent and turbulent past, whose future is brighter because of VCU.

TIM KAINE

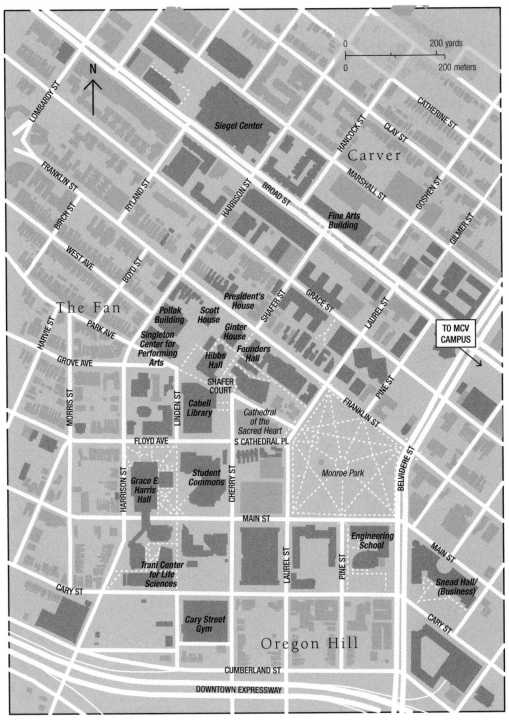

Monroe Park Campus. (Map by Nat Case, INCase, LLC; Underlying street and building data © OpenStreetMap contributors)

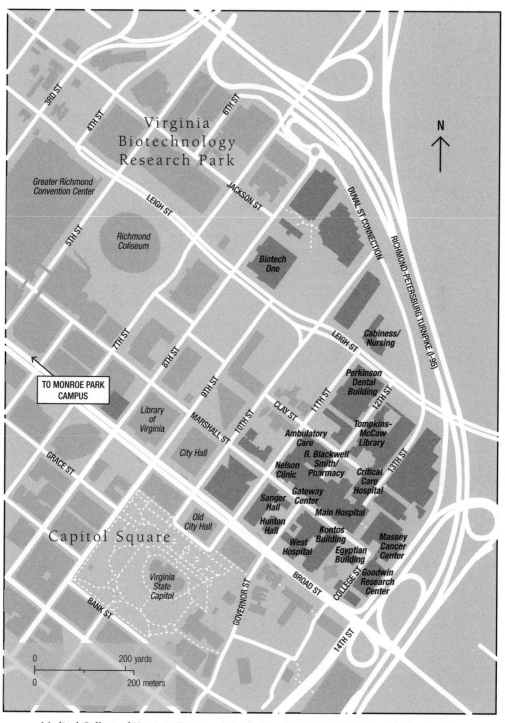

N

Virginia
Biotechnology
Research Park

Greater Richmond
Convention Center

3RD ST
4TH ST
6TH ST
JACKSON ST
LEIGH ST
5TH ST

Richmond
Coliseum

DUVAL ST CONNECTION
RICHMOND-PETERSBURG TURNPIKE (I-95)

Biotech
One

7TH ST
8TH ST

LEIGH ST

Cabiness/
Nursing

TO MONROE PARK
CAMPUS

9TH ST
10TH ST
11TH ST
12TH ST
13TH ST

Perkinson
Dental
Building

Library
of
Virginia

MARSHALL ST

CLAY ST

Tompkins-
McCaw
Library

Ambulatory
Care

City Hall

GRACE ST

Nelson
Clinic

R. Blackwell
Smith/
Pharmacy

Critical
Care
Hospital

Gateway
Center

Sanger
Hall

Main Hospital

Old
City Hall

Hunton
Hall

Kontos
Building

West
Hospital

Massey
Cancer
Center

Egyptian
Building

COLLEGE ST

Goodwin
Research
Center

Capitol Square

Virginia
State
Capitol

GOVERNOR ST

BROAD ST

14TH ST

BANK ST

| 0 | | 200 yards |
| 0 | | 200 meters |

Medical College of Virginia Campus. (Map by Nat Case, INCase, LLC; Underlying street
and building data © OpenStreetMap contributors)

Introduction

As THE TITLE declares, this book tells a success story, albeit one not unique to Virginia Commonwealth University, the subject of this history. Rather, VCU's history parallels general developments in American higher education and, specifically, the fall and rise of urban universities. Colleges and universities in cities, serving commuter students and engaged through teaching, research, and service with their communities, have become the norm for higher education in the United States. "Going to college in the city seems so normal now," writes historian Steven J. Diner, "that it's difficult to comprehend that it once represented a radical shift not only in the location of universities, but also in their ideals."[1] Leaders of higher education and the general public both long believed that schools in rural locations with bucolic residential campuses better served the character building they perceived as the center of normal college life. For example, Richmond College, now the University of Richmond, relocated after the Civil War to a site just a few blocks west of VCU's present-day Monroe Park Campus, then on the rural edge of the city. The city expanded westward and the college moved again in 1914 to its present campus, a park-like setting away from the city center and a location deemed better suited for higher education.

By contrast, at its founding in 1968, Virginia Commonwealth University was designated with a mission to serve the state of Virginia and city of Richmond as an urban university. The two institutions that merged to form VCU, the Medical College of Virginia (1838) and the Richmond Professional Institute (1917), were certainly urban in location, although in the decades just before their merger neither one had been on course to become an urban university. The term itself has long been a subject of debate, as indicated by the Association of Urban Universities, founded in 1914 (the year that Richmond College departed the city), which included members ranging from highly selective, research-oriented private schools to non-selective, service-oriented public commuter schools. That diversity notwithstanding, for many, the term "urban university" signified the stigma of

1

an institution with low admission standards, focused on educating nonresident students, usually of immigrant, working-class, and minority origins, who sought merely practical preparation for employment rather than engagement with the liberal arts.

After World War II, competition among institutions for status and resources, backed by the funding priorities of the federal government and other agencies, encouraged a focus on research and graduate education. The Medical College of Virginia, as an independent medical center, strove to demonstrate the same qualities found at university-affiliated medical schools, including full-time faculty engaged in grant-funded research programs. Simultaneously, the Richmond Professional Institute grew into the state's largest student body by the mid-1960s. Expanded tuition income coupled with more generous state financial support inspired university ambitions at that school, too.

Coinciding with VCU's founding, however, was the national awareness of an "urban crisis," brought on by suburbanization, desegregation, white flight, rising rates of violent crime, and numerous other problems associated with declining cities. If urban universities lacked status in higher education before, the urban crisis made that worse, while paradoxically reinforcing calls for higher education to democratize access and to address urban problems. VCU was not alone, however, in struggling with the tensions between the demands on urban universities and institutional aspirations to comprehensive and research university status. In 1977 the members of the Association of Urban Universities gave up and dissolved the association.

Then, as historian Steven Diner shows, during the last decades of the twentieth century a transformation occurred. Cities began to revitalize, middle- and upper-middle-class people moved back from the suburbs, and suburban-bred students looked to cities as stimulating environments and opportunities for experiential learning. Meanwhile, higher education in general committed to the democratization of access long associated with urban universities, while students of all backgrounds now focused more on occupational preparation than on the extracurricular activities associated with traditional college life. "At the start of the twenty-first century," writes Diner, "central cities and their surroundings housed 1,900 higher education institutions, more than half the nation's colleges and universities," and commuter students constituted the majority of university students in the country. The new attractiveness of both cities and civic engagement as means for research and teaching led the University of Richmond to formalize a closer relationship to the city with its own urban outpost, the University of Richmond Downtown, on Broad Street about midway between VCU's two campuses. Rejected in the past as shabby and second-rate, urban universities had become the cornerstone of U.S. higher education.[2]

This book is about VCU and the city of Richmond, with all the particularities of a specific tale, but it also echoes that larger narrative about higher education in the urban United States. What makes VCU's story especially appealing as a case study is that its origins came late in that narrative, arriving in the midst of the urban crisis and at the end of the postwar "golden age" of higher education. VCU arose out of the conflicts and tensions of that era, and the course of its aspirations—from urban university to comprehensive university to research university and back to urban university, yet with a residential campus and strong research programs—illuminates the general pattern of higher education at the time. This narrative differs from others, though, in treating the VCU Health System as an integral part of the urban university, whereas more often historians have set aside academic medical centers, with "eds and meds" both anchoring their cities but independently of one another.[3] VCU began with a merger of medical college and professional institute, and the success of that merger was crucial to fulfilling the promise of an urban university.

As important, this case study, focused on one university in its state's capital city, provides a close examination of the interactions between the university, city government, and state government. VCU emerged in the midst of the demise of the backward-looking political organization of Harry Flood Byrd and rose in tandem with new competitive two-party politics in state government. The city of Richmond saw desperate attempts by white elites to retain political power by way of annexations and other machinations, leading to court cases and eventually the election of a black majority in city government, followed by economic hard times and then revitalization in the 1990s. What happened in state and local government mattered to VCU, and what VCU did mattered for state and city.

IN FACT, the years since about 1970 have been both tumultuous and innovative for higher education as well as for cities. A confluence of unanticipated national issues—social and political conflicts, economic pressures, and declines in enrollments—exposed universities in the 1970s as overextended, forcing all to seek cost-reducing measures. Hannah Holborn Gray proposes that these pressures have had the long-term effect of making institutions "more rather than less similar to one another."[4]

To be sure, as a new university, VCU's experiences did not fit exactly with the national patterns in higher education. For instance, as enrollments suddenly declined after 1970, a host of prospective faculty members, just graduating from recently ramped-up doctoral programs, sought suddenly scarce opportunities in academe. With many in that cohort settling for work as untenured adjuncts and itinerant visiting assistant professors, the historians argue, power in higher education shifted away from faculty toward administrators. VCU then was still hiring new faculty and probably benefited from the suddenly larger pool of applicants. Even so, as chapters 3 and 5 show, issues of faculty tenure and governance roiled at VCU, too.[5]

A simultaneous aspect of VCU's early years after the merger of two independent institutions was the necessary and arduous effort to make administration more centralized and more efficient. As historian John Thelin argues, the economic downturn after 1970 exposed precarious finances at colleges and universities across the country. Consequently, he writes, "colleges and universities underwent a managerial revolution" as "administrative offices went from being passive to being active and systematic, from amateur to professional," a transformation that coincided with implementation of computer technologies and databases. The process at VCU was hardly as smooth and unproblematic as Thelin's summary suggests, but it was central to VCU's organizational development. Conflicts arose over and over between presidents seeking centralized management systems and employees at the two campuses seeking to retain the separate systems of the past, and this narrative gives attention to them.[6]

Indeed, debates in the Virginia legislature in the early 1970s about state governance of higher education showed a similar concern with organization and efficiency. The swift expansion of higher education in Virginia following the implementation of the Bird Commission's recommendations in the mid-1960s, as described in chapter 1, worried some legislators that the State Council of Higher Education for Virginia (SCHEV) lacked sufficient authority to manage the expanded system efficiently. The legislature created a commission to study Virginia's higher education, and the commission hired a Chicago management consulting firm, Donald Shaner and Associates, to conduct the study.[7]

The Shaner Report, as it was called, finally appeared in January 1974, in time for the next session of the legislature. The report's conclusion—that

Virginia needed a powerful statewide board of regents with control over all the institutions' budgets—did not fly, for after much debate and push-back from the universities, the commission instead recommended legislation that the existing SCHEV be given powers to coordinate higher education in Virginia but also that each school, through its board of visitors, should retain its autonomy. Senator Edward Willey, the commission's chair, explained that the legislators were disinclined to hand over their control of university budgets to a board of regents. The commission's compromise seemed to satisfy most parties, and SCHEV took on new powers.[8]

A decade and a half later, in 1987, Donald Finley, secretary of education for Governor Gerald Baliles, declared that Virginia was fortunate to have a system of coordination, not centralization, whose "strength is in its pluralism and diversity." VCU's president Eugene Trani and John Casteen, his contemporary at the University of Virginia, carried on a friendly debate in the 1990s about whether Virginia's higher education might have been better off with a board of regents, as in North Carolina. Trani, who had worked with such a board at the University of Wisconsin System, remains of the opinion that boards of regents better represented the established schools than the newcomers, and under such a system an upstart like VCU might never have developed as it did.[9]

Relative autonomy for universities (and their boards of visitors) in Virginia, however, also meant that economic ups and downs and political changes directly affected universities, for the legislature and governor readily cut away from budgets in hard times and only grudgingly expanded them in good times. Virginia's transformation from conservative one-party government to two-party politics, underway by the mid-1960s, with Republican governors followed by Democratic governors followed by Republican governors followed by Democratic governors, made nearly every legislative session an adventure for VCU and other state institutions. Ultimately, as discussed in chapter 11, in 2005 sweeping legislation intended to reduce this political and budgetary instability for Virginia higher education became law, but even then, state government still mattered.[10]

For much of the period after 1968, however, it was developments in the city of Richmond that most directly affected VCU. As elsewhere in the United States, urban problems of discrimination in housing and jobs, along with the flight of commerce and taxpayers to the suburbs, antedated the 1960s. Just as VCU got underway, the federal courts ordered the city finally to desegregate public schools and to accept the black majority's political power. The consequence was a long period of conflict, in the midst of economic decline driven by suburbanization. Richmond is an independent city, a quirk of Virginia governance, surrounded by suburban counties, with all entities aware of the need for cooperation but with high barriers to doing that.

Numerous scholars, many of them affiliated with VCU, have examined policy aspects of Richmond's post-1970 development, and most have lamented the limited results of political change and the persistence of poverty in the city's neighborhoods. Yet, like other cities, Richmond has stabilized after the hard blows of out-migration and disinvestment, with VCU as an economic anchor through all the changes. The city of Richmond's travails and its survival to new vigor under the proud logo of RVA are important themes in the narrative.[11]

THE AUTHORS hope that this book will not be associated with what the pioneer historian of American higher education, Lawrence Veysey, lamented as the custom of "aging professors writing celebratory histories of their local campuses." Both authors are aging, to be sure, and we are proud to be associated with VCU, but we are historians by training and profession. Kneebone has researched and taught the history of Richmond and Virginia, and Trani continued to publish in his field of U.S. diplomatic history during and after his presidency of Virginia Commonwealth University.[12]

One purpose for telling a university's story, to use Burton Clark's concept, is to provide it with a "saga" to reinforce the culture and identity of a distinctive institution. Certainly, VCU needs a proper history. An earlier history, Virginius Dabney's 1987 narrative, focuses mostly on the histories of the Medical College of Virginia and the Richmond Professional Institute prior to their 1968 merger that created VCU. Not only did he scant the school's more recent years, but at times the book rather resembled the sort of university history that Veysey condemned, with, as one reviewer put it, "a blizzard of names, publications, grants, and honors."[13]

This book intends to tell VCU's saga, but its authors also understand that there is truth to the charge that today imitation is the highest form of higher education, with accreditors and rankers imposing common standards, put into action by the national circulation of upwardly mobile administrators borrowing and applying one another's best methods. Clark's "distinctive college" is also Gaye Tuchman's *Wannabe U.*[14] VCU's history is distinctly its own, but it is also a history that reflects larger trends in higher education and American society.

Historian Paul Mattingly recently restated Veysey's complaint, saying that "so much of current scholarship seems to arise out of particularly local interests, narrow specializations, or anniversary celebrations." It seems right, then, that we should explain the origins of this book. In late spring 2009, as Eugene Trani prepared to retire as president, he invited John Kneebone, a member of the VCU History Department, to collaborate on a history of the university. Aware of Trani's transformative administration and VCU's role in Richmond's revitalization, Kneebone proposed instead a biographical study of Trani as president. The latter declined; biography was too narrow to tell the VCU story. Moreover, he went on, VCU needed a proper history from its founding. Kneebone warned that his own research and teaching concerned Richmond's and Virginia's history, not higher education. Trani responded that VCU's history was bound up with Richmond's history. The context of local and state developments mattered to the history of an urban university located in the state's capital. We agreed, then, to tell the history of VCU in Richmond and in Virginia.[15]

A word about our collaboration on this book is appropriate also. Kneebone researched and drafted the six chapters to 1990 and the beginning of Trani's presidency, although we consulted regularly throughout the process, with Trani sharing insights from his experiences as well as editorial comments on the draft chapters. We also began early on a series of oral history interviews about VCU after Trani arrived in 1990. Through those interviews we identified other people to interview and leads for further research. When Kneebone began drafting the chapters on the period after 1990, he and Trani met regularly for a new, yearlong round of interviews based on subject areas that Trani identified as significant. For each of these interviews, Trani developed a detailed written outline, which he then used to craft a spoken narrative about that subject. Kneebone researched those several narratives and organized them into roughly chronological chapters. Both authors collaborated on editing the entire manuscript. We consider this book a jointly coauthored project.

Around when the story reaches Trani's presidency there is a change in tone, which reflects a change in the nature of the available sources. To be sure, university archives, in general and for all periods, are not what a researcher might wish. As two scholars of higher education recently observed, "Anyone who has read, much less tried to write, a standard college or university history soon realizes the limits of public sources, including those stored within an institution's archives and special collections."

Recent history is usually underdocumented, but after the rise in the mid-1980s of swiftly outmoded word-processing systems and easily deleted email correspondence, archivists have struggled to retain the sorts of records once saved on paper. After that date, from about the middle of Edmund Ackell's presidency, the archives at VCU and about VCU grow thinner and scattered. Thus, the second part of the book is based largely on contemporary news stories and later oral history interviews, many of them conducted for this book. Even with that change in documentation, we have strived to tell a continuing history of VCU from its founding in 1968.[16]

A SPECIAL word of thanks goes to Gary Robertson, who covered higher education for the *Richmond Times-Dispatch* and then was director of special projects for VCU's University Relations. As such, he gathered documentation for commemoration of VCU's fortieth anniversary in 2008 and Trani's retirement in 2009. Not only was he generous in sharing those materials, but he also shared many insights into the university, the city, and the news media.

Thanks also to archivists and librarians everywhere, with special appreciation for Curtis Lyons and Wesley Chenault, former heads of Special Collections for VCU Libraries, and to Senior Research Associate Ray Bonis and Archivist and Head, TML, Special Collections Jodi L. Koste. Bonis and Koste have generously aided in the research for this book in a myriad of ways. They suggested materials, found new materials, and made all accessible.

Thanks to all those who sat for oral history interviews, listed in the bibliography, as well as the colleagues and friends who made suggestions along the way. Gloria Carnes, executive assistant to the president emeritus, aided in innumerable ways, and Sue Ann "SAM" Messmer, former chief of staff, Office of the President, and vice president for University Relations, not only contributed an oral history but also aided in selection of illustrations. Thanks also to Leigh Gutches for transcriptions of interviews and Margaret Acquarulo for editorial scrutiny of the manuscript.

1

The Merger

THE CREATION of Virginia Commonwealth University with a mission as an urban university was one part of a broader government-initiated program to expand and modernize higher education in Virginia, and thus was the result of a political process. Both of VCU's constituent institutions—the Medical College of Virginia, founded in 1838, and the Richmond Professional Institute, founded in 1917—had already set out on their own modernization programs by the 1960s. Neither had in mind a connection with the other, nor, despite themselves, a future identity as an urban university.

The Medical College of Virginia (MCV), as an independent school without connection to a university, had become an outlier in U.S. medical education by the end of World War II. Even so, the school's shift to full-time faculty (from 175 in 1956 to 407 in 1969), expanded building program (what became known as North Hospital opened in 1956, and the Medical Education Building, later Sanger Hall, in 1963), and commitment to seeking research funding was progress enough for the American Medical Association's Council on Education to remove MCV's probationary accreditation in 1953. To the consternation of some old-timers and a good number of local physicians, MCV then made "a head-long rush into a new era of medicine"—new faculty trained outside Virginia, new drugs, new clinical procedures, and new devotion to research and research funding. Yet, the school's ambitions brought reminders that the lack of a university affiliation hampered MCV in competition with other medical schools, and by the 1960s there was some thought of seeking an affiliation with the College of William and Mary, a state-supported liberal arts school located some forty miles east of Richmond in Williamsburg.[1]

At the same time, the Richmond Professional Institute sought to escape its affiliation with the College of William and Mary. Founded as the Richmond School of Social Work and Public Health, the school moved in 1924 from quarters adjacent to the Medical College of Virginia to a one-time elite suburb, now a city neighborhood of fine houses in decline. Also in that year, the school secured a connection—in name only, for no state funds came with it—with William and Mary. Art instruction began just before the Great Depression, through which hard times founder Henry H. Hibbs's ingenuity enabled the school to survive. At W&M's suggestion, the name was changed to Richmond Professional Institute (RPI) in 1939, to identify it as a school "of the occupational, technological or professional type." That resulted a year later in the first-ever state funds for RPI.

The GI Bill after World War II doubled the size of RPI's student body and transformed it from being almost entirely female to almost half male. The enrollment of males expecting to become family breadwinners actually reinforced Hibbs's commitment to preparing students to earn a living after their studies, and the School of Business, soon to become RPI's largest department, started in the 1946–47 school year. Talk of separation from William and Mary also began then, but independence did not finally arrive until 1962. With independent status came plans for building up the liberal arts and becoming a proper university.[2]

Both schools were bound to the city, as their leaders knew, yet ambitions made that location seem a liability, too. Henry H. Hibbs described concerns in the 1950s that the school's urban campus, occupying a mix of several renovated houses and a few new academic buildings, put off prospective students. Out of that concern came a new identity for RPI as the "Cobblestone Campus," a reference to the cobblestone alleys behind the school's buildings, which students still use as shortcuts today. The name also conveyed antiquity and quaintness, suggesting a location in the city but one not very urban.[3]

Neither MCV nor RPI had the resources to fulfill ambitions quickly and fully, but both schools independently experienced the tensions building in U.S. higher education in the 1950s and 1960s. Universities with research focus and selective admissions had long held high status, but after World War II, with expanded funding sources and a growing demand for access, other universities could seek higher status for themselves by prioritizing research and making admissions more selective. Simultaneously, the demand for higher education had democratized, first via the GI Bill, then through higher rates of graduation from high schools and, by the mid-1960s, the arrival of the postwar "baby boom" generation. Public universities and especially urban universities experienced tensions between aspirations for higher status and expectations that they would meet that student demand. Similarly, the evident problems of cities in an era of suburbanization highlighted expectations that urban universities and professional schools would apply research toward practical problem solving. Across the next half century, these tensions would resolve (and issues of status would matter less) as higher education generally democratized admissions and encouraged applied research and experiential learning, and as revitalizing cities became attractive places in which to live, especially to students brought up in the suburbs. But in Richmond, Virginia, in the early 1960s, it was state political processes, not strategic planning at MCV or RPI, that resulted in Virginia Commonwealth University.

LLOYD CAMPBELL Bird made an unlikely educational reformer. A native of Highland County in northwestern Virginia, he was seventy years old in 1964. He graduated from the Medical College of Virginia in 1917 with a degree in pharmacy and in 1925 partnered with Morris Phipps, his teacher at MCV, to create Phipps and Bird, a manufacturer of scientific apparatuses. Bird managed the successful business and entered public life as a state senator from Chesterfield County, a rural, albeit swiftly suburbanizing county located on Richmond's southern border. A Democrat and loyal foot soldier in U.S. Senator Harry Flood Byrd's "Organization," Bird followed along as a defender of Massive Resistance.[4]

Nonetheless, as a businessman and advocate of scientific progress—he served as president of the Virginia Academy of Science from 1952 to 1953—Bird saw clearly an impending crisis for Virginia higher education. As was the case across the nation, the so-called baby boom, a post-1945 demographic bulge reflecting a higher birth rate and larger families, brought the pressures of numbers first on elementary schools, then on secondary schools, and, by 1964, on the state's colleges and universities. Concerns of constituents for the education of their sons and daughters were enough to catch his attention, but Bird no doubt also felt the worry born of Cold War competition with the USSR—symbolized by the "race for space" and the Soviet satellite *Sputnik* in 1957—that the United States was falling behind in science. The numbers pressing on Virginia's insufficient higher education facilities worried him.

Governor Albertis Harrison shared Bird's outlook on education. Harrison won election as attorney general in 1957, just in time to implement the state's Massive Resistance policy of closing whites-only public schools rather than permit black children to attend them. Schools closed in Charlottesville, Norfolk, and Warren County in 1958, but the federal courts ruled against the state. Governor J. Lindsay Almond earned the lasting enmity of Senator Byrd for his obedience to the court's order to reopen schools, while Harrison not only remained in the senator's good graces but also persuaded Byrd that a new policy of "freedom of choice" would meet the letter of the law while holding meaningful desegregation to the minimum. Thus, in 1962, while Senator Byrd held up Almond's appointment to a federal judgeship, Albertis Harrison was inaugurated as governor of Virginia.[5]

Despite the upheaval of Massive Resistance, the state's political system, as historian Peter Wallenstein notes, had hardly changed since Harry Byrd's term as governor in the 1920s. The swift increase in population in urban Virginia after 1945, fueled by military spending and growth of the federal government, contrasted sharply with legislative representation that made rural counties, with large nonvoting African American populations, such as Harrison's native Brunswick County, the base of the Byrd organization's power. Many of the anti-Organization Democrats, especially the so-called Young Turks, a vocal minority, came instead from those growing regions—places where suburban families sought better schools and education for their children.[6]

The situation was not unique to Virginia, and in March 1962 the U.S. Supreme Court intervened in the case of *Baker v. Carr*, from Memphis, Tennessee, enunciating the doctrine of "one man, one vote," which required states to redistrict and often to reflect population changes, such as those that had been occurring in Virginia. Two years later, in *Davis v. Mann*, the court applied this principle specifically to Virginia in a case involving burgeoning Arlington County. Wallenstein notes that the decisions gave Virginia's urban areas "far more pull" than before, benefited the growing suburban districts most of all, and caused the legislature to begin "to operate in new ways, especially in matters of taxing and spending."[7]

At the same time, the poll tax—a measure designed to make voting difficult, not to raise revenue—came under legislative assault. In early 1962 Congress sent to the states the Twenty-fourth Amendment, prohibiting federal and state governments from requiring payment of poll taxes to vote in federal elections. Enough of the states had ratified the amendment for it to go into effect in January 1964, in time for that year's presidential election. Virginia was one of five states still to use the poll tax in state and local elections, but cases brought by black women in Northern Virginia and in Norfolk came before the Supreme Court in 1966, which outlawed the tax. Some eighty thousand additional African American voters registered to vote in

1964, and political leaders took note. Despite the preference of Senator Byrd for Republican candidate Barry Goldwater, both Governor Harrison and Lieutenant Governor Mills E. Godwin, also a one-time Organization stalwart, campaigned for the liberal Democrat, Lyndon Johnson, who carried Virginia.[8] The traditional foundations for conservative policies in Virginia had been undermined, and newly energized voters demanded more from state government.

The crush of new college-aged students in 1964, of course, came from the baby boom, but in Virginia the demographic jump also reflected significant in-migration as government spending on defense, especially in Hampton Roads and Northern Virginia, brought newcomers in unprecedented numbers to the state. These were educated and skilled people, and their expectations for adequate public schools for their children bumped against the long-standing frugality of the Byrd organization. Many among Virginia's white elite, especially businessmen with interests beyond the state's boundaries, realized that the once-dominant political philosophy— rigid frugality, restricted electorate, and resistance to change—could not manage the challenges that Virginians then faced. Hardly revolutionaries, for many of the leading figures in the state's educational push of the 1960s had been proponents of Massive Resistance a decade before, these men nonetheless steered the state's system of higher education toward the national mainstream and diverged from traditional political practices to do so.[9]

The long-term consequences of these trends could not be known then, of course, and leaders responded to the immediate problems. In the case of Virginia higher education in 1964, the problem was the inexorable press of prospective students against the limited number of institutions and even more limited classroom and residential spaces at the existing institutions. Virginia ranked low among even southern states in the portion of college-aged residents attending state schools. Few African Americans attended state-supported schools except for the historically black Virginia State College (later University; today's Norfolk State University was affiliated with it until 1969), and only the College of William and Mary was truly coeducational. Indeed, the University of Virginia and the Virginia Military Institute were fundamentally male-only institutions, and the normal schools, established in different regions to prepare women for teaching careers, were also single-sex institutions for all intents and purposes. Although most of the state schools—Radford, Madison, Longwood, Mary

Washington, Virginia Polytechnic Institute, and Virginia State—were less than a century old, and there were several new branch campuses of established universities in other regions of the state, Virginia's higher education system in 1964 was more reflective of conditions as they were before 1945. The Virginia State Council of Higher Education's biennial report to the governor and General Assembly in June 1964 urged the state to initiate a program of long-range planning, with the first phase to be completed by the 1966 meeting of the legislature.[10]

Thus, Virginia Commonwealth University had its immediate origins in the 1964 session of the Virginia General Assembly. Senate Joint Resolution No. 30 established a Virginia Commission on Higher Education to prepare a comprehensive, long-range study of Virginia's system of higher education. The only specific injunction to the commission was to plan for "a statewide system of comprehensive community colleges." The resolution was introduced on Friday, 7 February 1964. Two days later, on Sunday, the Beatles performed for the first time on the *Ed Sullivan Show*, and on Monday the U.S. House of Representatives passed the Civil Rights Act of 1964, sending that historic bill on to several months of debate in the Senate. At RPI, the student newspaper, the *Proscript*, greeted the Beatles with bemused notice of the foursome's long hair; at MCV, the *Medicovan* for February 1964 included an article that advised readers tempted by the welfare state—especially the prospect of government-sponsored health insurance—to resist by remembering the Bill of Rights.[11]

Virginia's system of higher education needed study. Not only did the state face unprecedented demand for access but its economy since World War II had shifted decisively from agriculture toward industry. Future economic development, especially in the state's urban corridor from the Northern Virginia suburbs of Washington, D.C., south to Richmond and then east to Hampton Roads, would require college graduates with specialized skills. Complicating the widespread pressure for access was the long effort of black Virginians to desegregate the traditionally white schools and, just emerging then, of women to enter traditionally all-male schools and professions.

Richmond Professional Institute embodied all these pressures and more. In early 1963, the state formally separated RPI from the College of William and Mary to operate under its own board of visitors. The separation looked ahead to the school becoming a full university, which the new board and others believed primarily required building up the liberal arts.

They soon realized that problems of an expanding student body needed solving, too. The *Proscript* opened the 1963–64 school year by expressing gratitude for the new Science Building (later replaced by the Shafer Court Dining Center) but noted that with record numbers of students registered, crowding continued. The school enrolled 5,600 students, making it the third-largest college in the state, yet the state hardly provided equivalent funding. A November *Proscript* editorial described the campus: "She is a maze of half-built buildings, makeshift living quarters, classrooms hidden in labyrinths and eating facilities stuffed into a basement. She is riddled with city streets." The complaints won a supportive editorial from the *Richmond News Leader*, which declared that the state should "recognize RPI's sturdy existence."[12]

As the legislature went into session in January 1964 (the same month that women residing in the dormitories won permission to wear slacks on campus during daylight on Saturday), RPI learned that the governor had slashed its requested funding from $4.4 million to less than $1 million. Some two hundred students prepared to march from RPI to the capitol building to protest the parsimony. President George Oliver convinced them that such action would only antagonize legislators. RPI's requests for funding had been ignored before, but this time the newspapers noticed. The *Richmond Times-Dispatch* condemned the state's "kicking RPI around."[13]

By contrast, the Medical College of Virginia seemed on an upward path. In fall 1963, the new medical education building opened, and the school celebrated its 125th anniversary with a banquet at a downtown hotel. A brief history, "The First 125 Years, 1838–1963," prepared for the event by Thelma Vain Hoke, the editor of the monthly *Medicovan*, was published in the school's *Bulletin*. The *Medicovan* noted that the history did not highlight the $10 million in construction since 1956, nor the increased state appropriations and $15 million in grants. Gifts and grants for the fiscal year 1963–64 totaled $4.2 million, $500,000 more than in the previous year.[14]

The grant funds reflected the emphasis on research at post-1945 medical schools generally, and specifically measured MCV's success at developing its own research specialties. In March 1964, the Richmond Academy of Medicine, the local physicians' association, invited Dr. David Milford Hume, chair of the Department of Surgery, to speak on his research into liver transplantations, promising work on the frontier of clinical medicine at that time. The speaking invitation reflected the respect that Hume's formidable abilities compelled, even from those who found his brusque indifference to traditional ways disturbing. Only two years before, the academy's new president, John P. Lynch, a part-time MCV faculty member, had used his inaugural address "to lambaste MCV's emphasis on research at the expense of education and service to the sick of Virginia." That followed a harsh editorial in December 1961 in the *Richmond News Leader*, memorably titled "Foggy Days at MCV," that repeated similar complaints from other local physicians.[15]

Subsequently, a committee of the academy and a survey team from the American Medical Association and the American Association of Medical Colleges studied the situation in Richmond. The latter group praised the progress in scientific research at MCV but joined the academy's committee in calling for better communication between the medical school and local physicians. Perhaps the invitation to Hume was a move to improve communications.[16]

The most important development occurred in April 1963, when Kinloch Nelson was named dean of medicine. Nelson came to MCV in 1929, and in 1948 President W. T. Sanger chose him to head the school's new Regional Education Program to bring continuing education to physicians in rural Virginia. He had since then successfully handled a plethora of other administrative positions. The alumni magazine responded to his appointment with praise for his "constructive thinking, tact, sympathetic understanding, and genius for inspiring friendships and loyalties." He needed all those qualities, for his predecessor William F. Maloney had just proposed a major reform of the medical curriculum that, as Nelson put it, sought "to tie the basic sciences and the patient together." Nelson not only declared his support but also ordered the curriculum to begin with the start of classes in September 1964.[17]

Thus, because of other issues on those campuses, few people at either RPI or MCV noted that the legislature's commission to study Virginia's higher education was preparing for work. Governor Harrison would appoint eleven members of the commission, who would serve with the nine current members of the State Council of Higher Education. Harrison's appointments to the commission went out in summer 1964, with one of them, T. Edward Temple, then city manager of Danville, Virginia, beginning a career shift that led him eventually to become the second president of Virginia Commonwealth University. Despite grumbling from the state's conference of the American Association of University Professors, most of the commission's members, like Temple, came from politics and government rather than from university faculties. The exceptions were Robert Prentiss Daniel, president of Virginia State College, Samuel R. Spencer Jr., president of private Mary Baldwin College, and Doris B. Yingling, dean of the School of Nursing at MCV. Meanwhile, on 2 August 1964, President Johnson signed into law the sweeping Civil Rights Act of 1964, which set an agenda for desegregation in Virginia.[18]

At the organizational meeting of the commission on 18 September 1964, Harrison conveyed a sense of "urgency," for, he said, the "college age population in Virginia is increasing rapidly," and existing schools lacked classroom and dormitory space "to accommodate the rising tide of applicants." Classes were underway at RPI, and the *Proscript* announced that fall enrollment topped 6,370, the largest ever. The new School of Education got underway in September 1964, too, and within a year claimed six hundred full-time students.[19]

The commission did not begin its work in full force until January 1965. The original resolution called for a report by 1 October 1965, a month prior to the next gubernatorial election, but Chairman Bird was not going to hurry the work. This would be no "superficial study," he explained to the president of the private Randolph-Macon Woman's College (later Randolph College), and the state's private schools would be part of the planning. "There is too much at stake," Bird declared. "The future of Virginia depends primarily on our colleges and universities." Bird himself believed that community colleges, although not yet popular in Virginia, were the best means by which to meet increased enrollments.[20]

The commission's charge went beyond solving the problem of looming demand for higher education. The Senate resolution stated that Virginia's economic development required more college graduates, and the professions, especially in medicine and the sciences, continued to demand more specialized skills. Since 1945, funding by the federal government for higher education had expanded, especially in those fields, but in 1964 a quantum leap was in the offing. It is telling that the administrative expenses of the commission came from the moneys appropriated in the federal Higher Education Facilities Act of 1963. Recognizing the sweeping authority that the commission claimed, the State Council of Higher Education in September 1964 declared a moratorium on establishment of new educational programs until the commission had reported.[21]

As the commission set to work, enrollments continued to rise at RPI. President Oliver joined other Virginia university presidents to warn

Governor Harrison in January 1965 that applications for admission to Virginia's schools were up by a third over the previous year. That spring saw the dramatic march for voting rights from Selma to Montgomery, Alabama, which the conservative *Proscript* grumbled cost that state much and accomplished little, and the subsequent passage of the federal Voting Rights Act of 1965. Of more immediate impact was the Higher Education Act of 1965, signed by the president in November 1965, which provided federal funds to universities and scholarships and low-cost loans to students.[22]

The *Proscript* welcomed the new school year in September 1965 with headlines reporting an all-time high in enrollments, and, in December, announced that RPI had a larger enrollment—7,800 students—than any other school in Virginia. Back in October, President Oliver predicted at the annual fall convocation that RPI would be a full university within five years. It already had characteristics of an urban university, he declared, without further elaboration. By 1980, he predicted, enrollment would reach twenty thousand.[23]

MCV's leaders also expected enrollments to rise. Estimates provided to the federal Department of Health, Education, and Welfare predicted an increase from the expected 1967 enrollment of 1,609 (1,143 from Virginia) to 2,057 (1,534 from Virginia) in 1975. Meanwhile, construction of a new clinical center (today the Nelson Clinic) began in August 1965, and that fall the hospitals received new names—the MCV Hospital became West Hospital, Memorial Hospital became South Hospital, St. Philip Hospital became East Hospital, and Williams Hospital became North Hospital— better fitting a modern medical complex.[24]

The commission's report finally went public on 26 December 1965, after the election of a new governor, Mills E. Godwin, who would put its proposals into action. The Bird Commission delivered on its charge. The report's major recommendation called for a comprehensive statewide community college system in Virginia to meet the expected doubling of the potential college enrollment in the state by 1975. It also proposed new four-year universities in urbanizing Northern Virginia and Hampton Roads, founded on the existing two-year George Mason and Christopher Newport Colleges, respectively.[25]

The report noted that the Richmond metropolitan area lacked a comprehensive university. The commission proposed that the Medical College of Virginia and the Richmond Professional Institute merge to form such a university. It went on to recommend that land outside Richmond's city limits be purchased for a site where the two schools could be united in a new university. The new school's location would prove more controversial, and the merger more daunting, than the commissioners could have imagined.[26]

Godwin's annual message to the legislature on 17 January 1966 endorsed an ambitious program of government action. In it he declared that Richmond had an opportunity "to form a new university" by merger. The proposal offered "advantages" to both MCV and RPI, and "great advantages" for the city. He proposed to form a commission to lay out a plan for the new university, offering the full cooperation of his office in the task. He wrote shortly after to President R. Blackwell Smith at MCV, and President George J. Oliver of RPI, asking them to respond with suggestions for "implementing" the merger.[27]

As the legislative session got underway, RPI sought nearly $17 million to build a classroom building on Harrison Street (later the Pollak Building) and a new library building. The *Proscript* noted, in a less prominent story, that the Bird Commission had proposed a merger of RPI and MCV into a new university on a new campus. During January 1966 also, RPI's administration rolled out the master site plan, which was to guide the school in its current location through 1980. The promise of the master plan, which had been in the works prior to the proposed merger, aroused the *Proscript*'s editors. A merger would not aid in developing a liberal arts program, RPI's greatest need, the editorial warned. "We had best concern ourselves with our own unique problems in the foreseeable future."[28]

No doubt other RPI students shared the editors' concerns, and President Oliver offered reassurances at the convocation in March. The "individuality" of RPI and MCV would persist, he said. The multi-acre campus outside Richmond was just "for further expansion." Although the master site plan preceded the proposed merger, it would continue to guide development of the Cobblestone Campus. Just a week later, the paper reported that the General Assembly had allocated $16 million to RPI, an increase of 240 percent. The news cheered all, and when the governor named the commission to study creation of the new university, the *Proscript* pointed out that the presidents of both schools had already created committees to explore areas of cooperation.[29]

To chair the group that would plan for the new university, Godwin selected Edward A. Wayne. A native of South Carolina, Wayne began his banking career there as a teenager after World War I. He came to Richmond in 1943 as vice president of the city's Federal Reserve Bank and was serving as its president when Godwin called on him. Wayne was civic-minded, with an interest in education, and had served on the Board of Visitors for Virginia State College.[30]

Godwin's chief advisor and secretary of administration, Carter O. Lowance, managed the selection process for what would become known as the Wayne Commission. Lowance was a former journalist whose service as press secretary and advisor to Virginia governors since the late 1940s gave him a deserved reputation as the "assistant governor." He may have felt a personal interest in the commission's task, for he had served as "assistant president" to R. Blackwell Smith at the Medical College of Virginia from 1958 until he returned to the executive branch under Governor Harrison in 1962. Lowance was politically astute and understood the constituencies of the new university. He ensured that the commission would include among its members a woman, Eleanor Sheppard, Richmond's first woman mayor, and an African American, J. Franklin Gayles, an administrator at Virginia Union University.[31]

As the Wayne Commission deliberated, President George Oliver determined to retire. The 1966–67 school year began with the announcement of a search committee to choose his successor. The chair, Henry Irving Willett, the long-time superintendent of Richmond public schools and a member of the Wayne Commission, agreed to serve to dispel rumors that he wanted the job. The *Proscript* noted that Oliver's dream had been university status for RPI, now in the offing.[32]

Meanwhile, at MCV, nearly every issue of the *Medicovan* reported new grants, including funding from the federal government to expand the dental school. Even more exciting was the work of the Department of Surgery. In 1965, David Hume brought to MCV a cardiovascular surgeon named Richard Lower, who had developed surgical techniques for heart transplantation with dogs, leaving the patient's immune response as the main obstacle to successful human heart transplants. During this period the South African surgeon Christiaan N. Barnard visited Richmond to observe Lower's work. Barnard subsequently won fame for performing the first human heart transplant operation at Cape Town on 3 December 1967.[33]

If coverage in the *Medicovan* is any indication, little discussion occurred at MCV about the plan to create a new university. The *Scarab*, on the other hand, informed alumni about the proposed "RPI-MCV Merger" in

February 1967 via a reprinted newspaper interview with Edward Wayne himself. Wayne acknowledged that creating the new university would be a long-term task—he estimated "1980 or even 1985"—but he hoped the legal and organizational foundation might be laid in 1968. The state should approve the budget requests of both RPI and MCV for 1968 to 1970, authorize employment of a president and administrative officers, select a site, and then allow a "framework" to jell in the first biennium. The highest priority was developing a strong undergraduate program in the humanities and sciences, he said, and the commission would retain consultants from Temple University, an urban university in Philadelphia that had "developed 'piecemeal, something like RPI.'" Another priority was strengthening graduate courses, including in health sciences and in education. A wing of the university would also conduct urban research "to solve city problems." Here, Wayne said, he had "in mind the 'urban university concept—an institution that is a living part of the city.'"

As seemed to be the consensus, Wayne foresaw the merger bringing the greatest changes to RPI. The new community colleges would relieve the school of its role in helping students get started in higher education and allow it "more concentration on quality." MCV, on the other hand, he declared, was "a 'highly respected institution' that 'provides already part of the advanced research we're talking about.'" Wayne expected MCV to keep its name—perhaps "the Medical College of Virginia division" of the yet-to-be-named university; "RPI's name would likely be dropped."[34]

Rejecting the proposed merger was never a serious option for MCV's leaders, and Dean of Medicine Kinloch Nelson and others crafted in February 1967 a memorandum making two arguments for MCV's benefiting from the merger. The memorandum was first presented to the Administrative Council of MCV, and then Nelson circulated it in April to all faculty in the School of Medicine. The first argument answered, at length, the key question of whether MCV should be part of a university. The answer began with the Flexner Report's half-century-old recommendations that medical schools affiliate with universities and finished with three recent reports on medical education. The recent reports emphasized that health care in the future would depend on collaborative research in social sciences, natural sciences, and basic sciences, which was possible only in a university environment. As important, Nelson's memorandum declared, "From bitter experience we know that the national foundations, such as The Commonwealth Fund, will not support the proposals of non-university affiliated medical schools." With this argument, MCV's leadership embraced the research-oriented agenda of ambitious faculty like David Hume. The memorandum answered its first question with the conclusion that "the Medical College of Virginia would benefit greatly by becoming part of a university of the first rank."[35]

The answer to the second question followed. Should MCV and RPI be part of a new university in Richmond? The memorandum quoted from the Bird Commission's report describing MCV as "the strongest available institution academically in the area" and therefore "the nucleus around which the new university could be organized." Yes, the memorandum concluded, "a university of the first rank should be developed in the Richmond area" with MCV and RPI as "the nuclei of such a university." Walter Griggs, a longtime faculty member at VCU and historian of the merger, speculates that the memorandum's call for a "university of the first rank" was not only to reassure skeptical medical faculty but also to put pressure on the Wayne Commission's deliberations about the future university.[36] It is safe to say that the phrase "university of the first rank" did not bring to readers' minds the traditional image of an urban university serving underprepared commuter students.

The *Medicovan's* first notice came in January 1968 with a story that MCV's board had endorsed the Wayne Commission's recommendations. It included assurances that MCV "would retain its name." That spring, when Governor Godwin signed the bill creating VCU, the *Medicovan* observed again that "under the legislation, MCV will retain its name as the health sciences division of VCU."[37]

While MCV sought to hold onto its name, RPI sought to retain its campus. Once the Wayne Commission began its deliberations, the *Proscript* endorsed the city of Richmond's proposal to build the new university on RPI's foundation. Students that fall noted that, with sites outside the city limits clamoring for the new university, Richmond seemed to gain a better appreciation for RPI. The *Proscript* had complained in April 1967 that too many Richmonders saw RPI only "as a place to gape at with horror as they drive by." That summer, the city council finally voted to close Shafer Street to traffic between Franklin and Park Streets (today's Shafer Court) after many years of students sharing this central gathering place with automobiles.[38]

That year was the fiftieth anniversary of RPI's founding as the Richmond School of Social Work. In September, new president Roland H.

Nelson, the former dean of the Department of Education at Duke University, quietly rescinded the ban on beards that Oliver had enforced by refusing admission to a trio of hirsute students in 1965 (they took their case to the U.S. Supreme Court, which refused to hear it). In September 1967 also, the school's first full-time African American faculty members began distinguished academic careers. Rizpah L. Welch would eventually serve as chair of the School of Education's Department of Special Education, and Regenia Perry, the nation's first African American PhD in art history, spent a quarter century in the Department of Art History. At the time, however, Perry discovered that white Richmond landlords would not rent to her. Had she known that Virginia lacked an open housing law, Perry said, she would not have come to Richmond. Today, scholarships in their names honor these pioneers. Joining them was Grace E. Harris, assistant professor of social work, who would become dean, provost, and acting president; of whom, more anon.[39]

The main alternative to a Richmond-based campus for the new school came from Henrico County's leaders. That county formed a geographical clamp around the city on the north from the rural east to the suburbanizing west. Just a few years before, the city had unsuccessfully attempted to consolidate with the county. The referendum brought together county residents and African Americans in Richmond, who saw the incorporation of largely white neighborhoods as an attempt to diminish their voting power, in successful opposition. Henrico's leaders and residents continued to eye the city warily.[40]

The site proposed to the Wayne Commission was in the eastern, rural end of the county, some two thousand acres known as the Elko Tract. Following World War II, the tract came to the state, and proposals to construct a new hospital there for African Americans resulted in political wrangling and then abandonment of the site despite its new roads and sewage treatment plant. The leader of the Henrico County campaign was William F. Parkerson, a highly regarded state senator.[41]

The primary justification for the Richmond site consequently became its urban location, which squared with a mission that RPI seemed ready to embrace. Much credit for that goes to President Roland Hill Nelson Jr. The announcement of his hiring from Duke University in February 1967 stated that he would be expected to take a "major administrative position" in the event of a merger. Nelson quickly began pushing for RPI, merger or not, to become an urban university. Such a university, he told the Richmond

Chamber of Commerce, must be a "battleground of ideas," and therefore, the university "must be a part of and yet remain apart from the city." Nelson officially became the second president (and third executive head) of RPI in July 1967, and he welcomed students to the 1967–68 school year by stating again that an urban university should be "truly concerned with the problems of an urban age." RPI must "train for work in this urban age" and "educate for life in this urban society," he declared. President Roland Nelson's advocacy for RPI's future as an urban university likely provided ammunition to the Wayne Commission as it reached a similar conclusion about the new university's location and mission.[42]

The campaign for an urban university caused State Senator Parkerson to revise arguments for the Elko Tract as the site. In October 1967, he contrasted the wide expanse in Henrico to the 165 acres offered by the city (Broad Street on the north, Belvidere Street on the east, and the James River to the south), which he noted would displace many residents and cost more. Finally, at the end of November, just before the Wayne Commission

RPI's three leaders—Henry H. Hibbs, Roland H. Nelson, and George J. Oliver—at the dedication of Rhoads Hall, 14 May 1968. (Virginia Commonwealth University Libraries)

report was released, he proposed "a tri-campus university," with the RPI site constituting the laboratory for urban studies and the Elko Tract as the site for the "major university" with the graduate programs that the General Assembly had called for in creating the Wayne Commission. No one had contemplated creating merely a "specialized urban college," he complained.[43]

Historians of urban universities have emphasized a traditional anti-urban prejudice, which presents campuses isolated from city temptations as preferred locations for higher education, but Parkerson's advocacy of the Elko Tract suggests another, contemporary, anti-urban prejudice to be overcome. From the 1950s, Cold War research funding had encouraged dispersal of sites from cities into developing suburban areas, with office parks and research universities growing there together. California's Silicon Valley, adjacent to Stanford University, became the model, although Parkerson never described such a lofty vision for eastern Henrico County. The point, though, is that for the Wayne Commission to give VCU its urban mission, its members had to overcome not only traditional anti-urban prejudices but also more modern expectations for a new university, too.[44]

The Wayne Commission's call for an urban university, building from RPI's present campus, "produced widely favorable reaction" at RPI. Wayne told the press that Virginia Commonwealth University's location proved the most difficult problem for the commission, but "the urban 'concept' of the proposed university demanded that it be located in an urban environment." The Proscript interviewed students at both schools and found much uncertainty and grumbling, especially at MCV. There seemed to be general agreement on "a distaste for the name."[45]

It is unclear just who deserves credit for the name of Virginia Commonwealth University, but so the Wayne Commission dubbed it. A constituent wrote in early 1968 to State Senator J. Sargeant Reynolds, a member of the commission, to complain. His response conceded that it was "hardly a name that sparkles," but no one had "an acceptable substitute." He then told a story. A man suggested naming the school "Byrd University." But, people said, there will be confusion whether the name honored William Byrd or Harry Byrd. The man replied, very well, they would call it "William and Harry."[46]

The proposal for the merger went before the legislature in February 1968, and both Senate and House of Delegates gave it unanimous support. The House added language to the bill requiring that MCV retain its name as part of Virginia Commonwealth University. The provision was probably valuable in calming concerns at MCV, but in the coming years it would complicate matters for the university. The *Proscript*'s editorial headline probably spoke for many: "Merger—Now What?"[47]

On 30 April 1968, the new Board of Visitors, meeting for a second time, chose Virginius Dabney, editor of the *Richmond Times-Dispatch*, to serve as VCU's first rector. Wayne became the vice rector, and lawyer Andrew J. Brent the secretary. After the vote, Governor Godwin joined the meeting to convey recommendations his office had received for the school's first president. At the meeting of 24 May 1968, the executive committee determined that all MCV and RPI employees would continue to hold their positions. The only exceptions were the two presidents of the soon-to-be-defunct schools, although the board had agreed that the new administrative structure would retain top administrators at both parts of the new school, under a university president. The first annual meeting took place three days later, and the full board not only confirmed the executive committee's plan but also adopted a resolution designating Smith and Nelson as the respective provosts of the Heath Sciences Division and the Academic Division. Smith conveyed to the board that due to illness he would not be a candidate for president of the new school.[48]

In the meantime, on 25 May 1968, surgeon Richard Lower led a team at the medical school in the first heart transplant operation there. It was ninth in the United States and the sixteenth in the world, but the MCV transplant gained importance because the family of the donor charged that the heart had been removed prior to the donor's death. Their lawyer, L. Douglas Wilder, later governor of Virginia and a VCU faculty member, sued, which resulted in an ultimate decision that brain death, the measure that the MCV surgeons employed, constituted legal death. The 1972 decision cleared the legal ambiguity about transplants, but the slow course of the law prohibited further heart transplants at the medical school for more than three years.[49]

The excitement about the transplant program still existed when the board convened for a special meeting on 10 June 1968. Wayne informed his colleagues that Roland Nelson was leaving to serve as president of Marshall University in West Virginia. Nelson could not accept the lesser office of provost; it was not a "professionally viable position," he told the *Times-Dispatch*. He submitted his resignation with deep regrets, he told the governor, for he had hoped to help develop "a model for urban universities in the United States here in Richmond." The Board of Visitors had the more modest goal of smoothing the merger without placing either Smith or Nelson above the other. Now, with Smith's illness and Nelson's imminent departure, creating an administrative structure became more complicated. Nonetheless, Nelson agreed to serve as provost until August. Meanwhile, the board had hired Francis J. Brooke as vice president for academic affairs, and Nelson proposed, and the board agreed, that Brooke be named acting provost on his departure.[50]

Nelson's decision, and Brooke's inexperience at RPI, forced the board's hand. On 24 June, they met to discuss appointment of Fred O. Wygal as temporary executive administrative assistant to the board. Wygal was present and joined the discussion about how to merge the two schools. Immediately afterward, the executive committee met to confirm Smith's agreement to serve as provost, Nelson's decision to leave, Brooke's hiring as vice president and acting provost, and Wygal's appointment as executive administrative head. Wygal appeared again before the board and agreed that he "would serve in a caretaker capacity and would explore, with the appropriate officials of the two divisions of the University, general policies looking to the unification of the two institutions."[51]

Fred Orr Wygal had wide experience in Virginia education, including work for the state Department of Education from 1942 until his retirement in 1964, with two stints as acting president of Longwood College (today Longwood University), the latest of which he had just completed. He was old enough not to seek VCU's first presidency and had enough relevant experience to win the board's confidence.[52]

Although Rector Virginius Dabney later thanked him for stepping "into the breach" when Nelson departed, Wygal did not replace Nelson. Rather, he served as executive administrator to the Board of Visitors, with the provosts on both campuses reporting to him. Moreover, the "Duties and Responsibilities" the board drew up when hiring him stated, "This is not the same thing as Acting President." Wygal was to attempt no "bold innovations."[53]

Nonetheless, even a caretaker executive could not avoid setting precedents in the new university's first year. As an example, after his first official meeting with the board, Wygal told Provost Smith that he needed an immediate letter giving the official name for the "Medical College of Virginia, Health Sciences Division of the Virginia Commonwealth University and how this should be arranged for official use on stationery and the like." Unfortunately, R. Blackwell Smith was in failing health, and he soon took a leave of absence and then resigned as provost before the end of 1968. John Heil was named acting provost. Although both Heil and Francis Brooke provided yeoman service to VCU in its infancy, the departures of Smith and Nelson reinforced the board's inclination to proceed cautiously.[54]

Before long, Wygal and his administrators had agreed on "Areas of Planning and Action." Planning primarily involved "setting forth the general and specific purposes of the university" in relation to the "total University" and "as it relates to each division." Action involved developing a "University Coordinating Committee," with three representatives each from "the two divisions," to clarify policies and procedures and to develop long-range planning for the school. Despite these initiatives, probably the most important precedent, though unintended, was the seeming organization of the former MCV and the former RPI as separately administered entities under provosts reporting directly to the executive. As the fall 1968 semester began, the *Proscript* might be forgiven for describing Francis Brooke's "dual roles" as provost and president, although in fact, he was provost and vice president of the General Academics Division of Virginia Commonwealth University, the name that appeared now on the paper's masthead.[55]

For his part, R. Blackwell Smith told the *Proscript* that he had long favored the idea of MCV being part of a university and declared that the merger "always seemed 'to make sense.'" As provost, Smith said, he had the same duties as before, only his Board of Visitors had changed. Asa B. Lee, student in dentistry and president of the MCV student government, agreed that not much had changed. He saw "no 'visible' changes since merger [*sic*]," which he now approved. It was "like a 'bloodless coup.'"[56]

2

Setting Out, 1968–1969

IF VCU SEEMED to have mastered the challenges of change (albeit by not changing very much), U.S. society emphatically had not in 1968. Inspired by the direct-action tactics of the civil rights movement, young people organized to protest the escalating U.S. war in Vietnam, and, perhaps even more disturbing to many of their elders, embraced the dress and behavior of the so-called counterculture. The first months of 1968 saw official optimism about the war undermined by the Tet Offensive in February, and then the presidential campaign thrown open by Lyndon Johnson's decision at the end of March not to seek reelection.

In that last week in March, protesting students took over Virginia State College, and a day later, Virginia Union University in Richmond. The campus atmosphere, described as "festive but defiant," changed dramatically on 4 April 1968 as news came that Martin Luther King Jr. had been assassinated in Tennessee. King's murder provoked riots in cities across the nation, including violence at scattered locations throughout Richmond, where police in force occupied downtown at night and where thousands gathered at the state capitol grounds for an outdoor memorial service on Sunday.[1]

Little noticed that painful first week in April were arguments before the U.S. Supreme Court about school segregation in rural New Kent County, east of Richmond. On 27 May 1968 the court declared in *Green v. New Kent County* that school boards had a positive duty to eradicate segregation in schools. The court rejected "freedom of choice" plans for desegregation, the method that Richmond City Schools had embraced, as inadequate. Meanwhile, Richmond officials continued secret negotiations with Chesterfield County to annex residential neighborhoods on the south side of the James River that would restore the city's white majority. Both the *Green* decision and the annexation would profoundly shape the city's course through the next decade. The traumatic and divisive events of 1968 and after would reinforce the separation of the MCV campus from the former RPI campus at the very beginning of the new university.[2]

ON 23 SEPTEMBER 1968, Dr. Francis John Brooke III, acting provost and academic vice president, welcomed students at the fall convocation at the Academic Campus. Not yet forty years old, Frank Brooke, a scholar of German language and literature, had arrived at VCU from Centre College in Kentucky to discover that he was not only the new academic vice president but also, with Roland Nelson's resignation, acting provost in charge of the former RPI campus. Speaking to an audience of four thousand at the Mosque (later Altria Theater), Brooke declared VCU, as an urban university, was "where the action is." His speech was more practical than inspirational, and he emphasized throughout that the students needed to help win support for the referendum on $81 million in bonds scheduled for the November election. Passage of the bond issue would mean three new classroom buildings for VCU, he declared.[3]

Any hopes for a quiet first year at VCU died quickly. The ruckus called the "Puppy Burn" brought VCU national publicity, nearly all of it undesired by the school's administration. The episode began in early 1968 with a group of RPI students who, like many students elsewhere, joined the national presidential campaign of Eugene McCarthy, U.S. senator from Minnesota. His candidacy for the Democratic presidential nomination was an antiwar protest against President Lyndon Johnson's Vietnam policies. The local group determined to take a role in the VCU Student Government Association (SGA). Because the SGA excluded purely political organizations, the McCarthyites took the name Students for a Liberal Government, and, as a recognized university organization, sent representatives to the SGA's House of Representatives. Leader Jeff Kelso said later that a conservative political group made the same move, but he could not recall which group inspired the other's tactic. At a time when the radical Students for a Democratic Society organized on many campuses, at generally conservative VCU, the SLG was the next best thing.[4]

In early October 1968, the *Proscript* called the Students for a Liberal Government misguided for asking the Student Government Association to enact a Student Bill of Rights. Better to work with the university's administration to develop a policy, it said, reflecting the student newspaper's generally pro-administration editorial policy that year. By then, the SLG had discussed in its own meetings protesting the ongoing violence in Vietnam by burning a puppy. As Kelso recalled, he raised the idea at a meeting of the organization largely to get laughs, but when the student newspaper reported that the SLG had, indeed, contemplated burning a puppy, Kelso and his colleagues decided to embrace the situation. The proposal was not original to them, for representatives of the National Student Association had been suggesting to groups at other schools the idea of threatening a puppy burn as an act of political theater. The idea was that when people predictably expressed outrage, the organizers could then make the point that violence in Vietnam—and burning called to mind images of napalm attacks—surely merited even greater outrage. The puppy burn was a notion best quickly dismissed, but the newspaper's condemnation of the SLG's "rash ideas" encouraged the group to go forward.[5]

The event was to occur on 29 October 1968, and once the news got out, letters and telegrams poured into the office of Acting Provost Brooke. Almost all came from people profoundly disturbed by the idea of cruelty to an animal, not from defenders of the war in Vietnam. Brooke assured them that he and VCU abhorred the proposal. As he put it a week prior to the threatened event: "The taking of life to illustrate the value of life is not in the tradition of logic which educated men respect. We are confident that VCU students are sufficiently mature so as not to be deceived by such sensationalism." According to Kelso, the SLG did its part to win national attention for the new Virginia Commonwealth University by informing the conservative radio broadcaster Paul Harvey about the puppy burn, and Harvey lent his stentorian voice to the national chorus of condemnation.[6]

An emergency meeting of the Student Government Association on 21 October withstood administration pressure and refused to ban the SLG. That only inspired the SLG members to attend the next day's regular student government meeting en masse to invite all present to attend the puppy burn. The administration moved then to bar the SLG from using Shafer Court, on campus, for the event. The SLG moved the rally to nearby Monroe Park and, Kelso recalled, stationed monitors all along its boundaries to ensure that no one brought a dog of any age to the event. Kelso explained the political point of the puppy burn to the crowd, and political speakers followed him. The event, which had left the war in Vietnam, its ostensible subject, far behind, passed off peacefully, but letters of complaint continued to arrive at VCU, the university where students burned puppies.[7]

The SGA appointed an ad hoc committee to determine, as Charles Renneisen, the dean of students, phrased it, whether the SLG "did or did not embarrass the university and the student body." The investigation fell apart as the SLG countered with calls for investigation of the *Proscript*'s sensationalized coverage of the event, and the committee itself charged Dean Renneisen with "'using' the SGA." Renneisen, who came to RPI in 1965, when students with beards were expelled, had overseen relaxation of behavioral regulations—greater personal responsibility, he said—but these events showed just how fractious relations on campus had become.[8]

In this period, before the Downtown Expressway had been built, commuters from Richmond's upper-middle-class neighborhoods in the west still passed along Franklin Street through the RPI and now VCU campus, identifying the school with the pedestrians they observed. "The beatniks of the 1950s had been replaced by the hippies of the 1960s, and derelicts and other degenerates continued to meander through the neighborhood and campus," Ann Laurens Williams wrote of this period. "Many Richmonders found a drive through the Richmond Professional Institute campus both a challenge and a source of humor."[9] To the dismay of administrators, the "puppy burn" reinforced the stereotypes.

The reality was that VCU students were rather more conservative than appearances might suggest to proper Richmond residents. The *Proscript* conducted a straw vote prior to the presidential election in November 1968; the majority of respondents favored Republican Richard Nixon and the campus runner-up was Alabama's famed segregationist, George Wallace, the American Independent Party's candidate. Regardless, VCU retained and built on RPI's bohemian reputation. Fortunately, the Virginia voters did not react negatively against student protests, and the bond referendum passed by a large margin at the November elections.[10]

Meanwhile, at the request of the Board of Visitors, Schechter and Luth, a marketing and industrial design firm from New York City, presented in mid-September 1968 a proposal for "Development of a Total Identification System for Virginia Commonwealth University." The old identities would not do, the proposal argued. Richmond Professional Institute's acronym had already been claimed by the better-known Rensselaer Polytechnic Institute. The name of the Medical College of Virginia was commonplace, but the proposal wisely stated that MCV would continue as an identifier. The important goal, the proposal observed, was to distinguish it from the University of Virginia's medical school.[11]

The consultants got underway with a series of interviews on both campuses in October and November 1968 to gauge student opinion. Attitudes at the medical campus were unanimously negative about what the informants still referred to as RPI: "nauseated by the appearance," "dirty," "hippies," "questionable character," "slobs." The merger was equally despised. It would "grossly degrade" MCV's standing. VCU is "so tainted that to be an alumnus will be an embarrassment." Presaging an issue that would soon emerge, a student, field unknown, declared, "I may cut the Virginia Commonwealth University symbol off my diploma."[12]

VCU in November 1968 joined the University of Richmond, Randolph-Macon College, and Virginia Union University in a consortium of local schools to encourage cooperative action and long-range planning. The University of Richmond (UR) had long been a popular undergraduate school for Richmond's future physicians (and attorneys, too), many of whom lived in the affluent western suburbs near that school. Vast changes were in the offing for UR, however, for the family of local businessman and philanthropist E. Claiborne Robins Sr. gave the school $50 million in June 1969, at that time the largest gift ever given to an American university. Heretofore, Richmond residents had comprised the largest portion of the school's student body, but now, with VCU emerging locally, the University of Richmond expanded its recruitment to students outside of Virginia. Rather than competing, the Robins gift to UR enabled the two schools to coexist and cooperate (albeit not on the athletic field). The once-Baptist school's alumni connections to Richmond's medical community would grow thinner, but at the time, many at MCV would probably have preferred that the merger had been with that school.[13]

Student resistance at the medical school came to a head in spring 1969. At the beginning of March, John Heil, acting provost for the Health Sciences Center, informed Joann Spitler, editor of publications at the medical school, that the diplomas for graduates for the next four years must bear the words "Medical College of Virginia" and resemble past diplomas, as graduating students had entered the school under its previous name. Spitler decided to assess student opinion for herself, and James Dunn, then assistant director of the university's Development Office, did the same at the Academic Campus. Spitler showed sample diplomas to faculty and students at MCV. The students were emphatic that MCV should be prominent: "Their feeling, obviously, was very strong." Dunn, however, reported that students and faculty at the Academic Campus wanted a single university diploma, and they did not agree with the sentiment expressed at MCV. The medical students' rebellion against graduating with diplomas from

Virginia Commonwealth University that first spring evidenced that making the merger real would be more difficult and take longer than many optimists hoped.[14]

While there was resistance to change from students at the medical school, at the Academic Campus, African American students pressed the university to make changes. RPI had admitted a few African American students to graduate study in social work in the early 1950s, but desegregation for undergraduate studies did not come until after 1960, with neither protest nor acknowledgment of the change. In fall 1967, a small, interracial group of approximately twenty students held a series of meetings at RPI, out of which came the determination to address race relations on campus and to promote establishment of a black studies program. They formed Students for an Afro-American Philosophy (SAAP) and successfully gained recognition as a constituent student organization in fall 1968 from the Student Government Association.[15]

Most black students at VCU kept a low profile, but the *Proscript* reported in December 1966 the election of Beatrice Wynn, a drama major from Crewe, as that year's Harvest Ball Queen. A transfer from Hampton University, Wynn was "the first Negro to be chosen Harvest Ball Queen." Voting had been open to all students, and the photographs of all the candidates for queen were on display, so the voters knew for whom they cast their votes. The ball itself was off-campus, at the Hotel John Marshall downtown, and an engineering student, Jeff Parker, also black, escorted Wynn. This event seemed not to cause any commotion on campus, although a student columnist noted it as another thing that the conservative Richmond community would hold against the school.[16]

The 1966–67 basketball team included three black players—Donald Gordon, John Collins, and Charles McLeod, recruited by longtime coach Ed Allen. McLeod played basketball again in 1967–68, and a preseason story noted that he "excels on defense." A year later, he was still in school but no longer on the basketball team, now coached by Bennie Dees. By November 1968, as the team prepared for the new season, McLeod was cochair and spokesman for the SAAP.[17]

The SAAP's recognition by the SGA, which included funds from the activities budget, made possible a campus Afro-American Week in February 1969, under the slogan: "Think Black!" The events included a speech by Floyd McKissick, the militant former leader of the Congress of Racial Equality (CORE); other speeches by Edgar A. Toppin, historian at Virginia

State University, and James Sheffield, a Richmond attorney and member of the VCU Board of Visitors; and a performance of *Dutchman*, a play by Leroi Jones, who, after changing his name to Amiri Baraka, later spoke at VCU in 1987. Tickets for all events cost $2.50, and SAAP members got in for free. The success of the week gave the organizers confidence and encouraged black students to consider VCU their place, too.[18]

Early in its deliberations, the SAAP had declared the goal of "getting courses on Afro-American Culture offered as part of VCU's curriculum." Although VCU could boast a larger number of African American students than any other historically nonblack school in Virginia, it had done little to offer a curriculum that acknowledged their presence. The *Richmond Afro-American* of 26 April 1969 reported on developments across the state. The University of Virginia, with only eighty blacks among thirteen thousand students, listed thirty-three courses relevant to race relations and African American history and culture. Virginia Tech, with about the same number of blacks in a student body of ten thousand, had not seen protests but voluntarily offered a course in African American history and one in African American literature. In Norfolk, Old Dominion College (now University) and Norfolk State College (now University) seemed to preserve a separate existence, although a white faculty member expressed a desire for more cooperation. The College of William and Mary, with few black students, offered some courses in the sociology of race relations, but a faculty spokesman conceded that it would be "a long time" before blacks attended in significant numbers. The Richmond institutions—VCU, the private, suburban University of Richmond, and historically black Virginia Union University—shared an educational television course, most likely the course developed by historian Toppin of Virginia State University (and later a VCU faculty member), but the University of Richmond had not admitted black students until 1967, and only then under threat of losing federal funds. Clearly, while ahead of its state peers in recruiting black students, VCU lagged them in providing a black-oriented curriculum. On 25 March 1969, SAAP leaders presented a petition "endorsing Afro studies for all interested students" to Brooke; the *Proscript*, for its part, reported that department chairs felt that both student interest and qualified faculty were lacking. The student paper also published a column written by a staff member declaring, "Afro Courses Not Needed."[19]

Two weeks later, at the end of April, SAAP members and supporters presented a set of fifteen demands to the university and surrounded the administration building to force a meeting with Brooke. The protest of the SAAP never denigrated the pioneering integrationist activities of earlier black students. Rather, it proposed that admission to, inclusion in, and election of black students solely within the traditional institutions of a white university would not lead to serious intellectual and social change. Their statement about the shape of the future at VCU corresponded with blacks' national rejection of mere tokenism—as in the case of the limited results of Richmond City School Board's policy of "freedom of choice" in school attendance—for full racial integration and the consequent requirement for white institutions, if not white people, to respect and respond to the presence of blacks. As historian Martha Biondi explains, protests by black college students, occurring nationally but generated independently, called on U.S. universities, and society, to value and encourage pluralism and diversity. Here, via the protest made by the SAAP, was that year's most lasting contribution by students to VCU's future development.[20]

Observers treated the SAAP's demands—especially those for a black studies curriculum, for more African American faculty and administrators, and for recruitment of black students—as the "usual demands," a reflection of similar petitions being presented on campuses across the nation. As historian Richard McCormick Sr. said of the protest at Rutgers University, however, through such demands black students sought "the construction of an environment within which they could feel emotionally and physically secure and where their cultural values would be respected and legitimized." The students at VCU would have agreed that they learned from other protests at other universities, but their demands also reflected careful consideration of what VCU, as an urban university, ought to become.[21]

Receiving most attention then was the SAAP's demand that Rector Virginius Dabney, as an opponent of black advancement, resign from the Board of Visitors. That demand not only got the most press but also seemed the least valid to whites at the time. Dabney, the longtime editor of the *Richmond Times-Dispatch* and a winner of the Pulitzer Prize, had been an important supporter of Governor Godwin's educational program that brought VCU into being. Dabney then accepted appointment as one of the newcomers to the initial Board of Visitors of VCU, and his election by the board as the school's first rector suggested that he played a unifying role. By 1969 he had retired from the newspaper, but the illness of Provost Smith at the medical school and the departure of Provost Nelson from the Academic Campus had obligated him to accept a larger than expected administrative role during VCU's first year. After Dabney's many services to VCU, it seemed to his defenders that he was being shabbily treated by insolent young people.[22]

Charles McLeod's recollection of why the SAAP targeted Dabney, however, shows that the demand for Dabney's resignation was central to the thinking of the SAAP and very much the students' own conclusion. They had read the Wayne Commission report and welcomed the promise of a new type of university, large enough to include them. They also knew that Dabney, as editor, had silently acquiesced in the Richmond newspapers' cheerleading for Massive Resistance to school desegregation, and his own editorials showed little sympathy for changes sought by the civil rights movement. "You're not going to fly into the twentieth, or twenty-first century, into this whole new era bringing along that kind of baggage," McLeod recalled. "I saw him as baggage for an urban university." They had no personal animosity toward Dabney, he continued, but the issue was a message of respect for those the university now sought to engage as students and future supporters. "They had gone on record saying this university was moving in a different direction, that there was going to be a different time." The SAAP would hold the university to its promise.[23]

The *Richmond Afro-American* also highlighted the SAAP's demand for "the boot for Dabney." The latter, in turn, stated that he had no intention of resigning. He also told the *Afro* that he understood the reasoning behind the demand for a program of black studies and believed that the entire board favored it. Provost Brooke, too, said the demands, "by and large," represented concerns he shared. The *Afro* endorsed the SAAP demand for recruitment of more black students and participation in the new Upward Bound program for disadvantaged young people to "make this urban university more responsible to the needs of this urban community," as the SAAP put it. Nonetheless, attention to the demand for Dabney's resignation obscured the connection between the SAAP's criticism of the editor and the larger context of the demands as a statement about the future of VCU as an urban university.[24]

What VCU, as an urban university, would become remained uncertain in 1969, but the administration, as well as the students, sought to give meaning to the concept. Coinciding with the SAAP's demands was the announcement that a new professorship of urban studies had been created, and Harlan Westermann, director of the Center for Urban and Regional Studies at Virginia Tech, would fill the position. Westermann would teach, but Brooke explained that his main role at VCU would be to work with deans and department chairmen "to develop courses and programs within the broad scope of urban studies."[25]

On that Monday, some thirty students called for Brooke to meet with them outside the administration building at 901 Franklin Street. Brooke refused, and more than a dozen of them entered his office to meet there with him, Raymond T. Holmes, the university's comptroller, and Arnold Fleshood, dean of the School of Education. Fleshood, who joined the RPI Department of Elementary Education in 1965, was, according to McLeod, one of the few administrators that the SAAP members trusted, and Brooke was astute in including him. Photographs show an intent group standing around the provost's table, eight students seated, and McLeod speaking for the group.[26]

Brooke responded after each demand was presented. He turned away several of the demands as beyond his control, including the status of Rector Dabney, dismissed a few, agreed about recruiting minority students and faculty, and then embraced the curricular and library proposals. "Everything is not okay," he acknowledged. Brooke also warned the students that there was "a considerable backlash in this entire nation against students," and radical protests risked needed legislative support for VCU. That consideration no doubt explains his later emphasis to the press that what happened was merely an unscheduled meeting, not a sit-in or occupation. Nonetheless, the students gave him only until Wednesday to respond to their demands, with a mass meeting of students scheduled for Thursday to discuss the administration's response.[27]

McLeod later groused that the wishful newspaper coverage presented the protesters as content to work within the system, but Brooke's willingness to hear the students out and to act did affect their response. He appointed a small committee, with Dean Fleshood as chair, to report back to the mass meeting on Thursday. Historian Alan Briceland, then an assistant professor in his third year at the school and a member of Fleshood's committee, recalled that having a dean chair the committee also conveyed the importance of the university's response to the SAAP petition. The mass meeting on Thursday, despite militant rhetoric, adopted a wait-and-see approach.[28]

The black students certainly did not see all their demands met, but the university expressed commitment to the recruitment of black students and faculty and expansion of courses on African American history and culture. Inevitably, at the May meeting of the Board of Visitors concerns arose about the possible consequent lowering of standards for admission, as though it was high standards at RPI alone that had discouraged blacks from attending. Brooke allayed those concerns, with Warren Brandt, just named president, there to back the provost and to endorse to the board VCU's future as an urban university. Brandt spoke with some authority, having already conferred with leaders of the SAAP, a meeting that board member James Sheffield had arranged.[29]

A faculty committee, headed by Alan Briceland, met through the summer to be able to offer courses in the fall semester. Recognizing that VCU lacked the funds to lure away established scholars, the committee also did an inventory of existing faculty expertise and potential courses. As the next school year began, the *Richmond Times-Dispatch* declared, perhaps hopefully, that VCU appeared to have met the black students' demands: there were "six new Negroes on the faculty," the curriculum had expanded, and Dabney had resigned as rector, although he remained on the Board of Visitors. Brooke said that two relevant courses had been added for the fall semester and two more would be offered in the spring. There were also new administrators, including an admissions counselor and a new assistant dean of students, Vincent Wright, a musician and educator from New York. Nonetheless, Brooke emphasized that recruiting black faculty continued to be "a difficult task."[30]

AT VCU's first commencement ceremony, on 8 June 1969 for graduates of the Academic Division, the first student to receive her diploma was none other than Elizabeth Scott Bocock, BA English. Mrs. Bocock, then aged sixty-eight, had for years rented to RPI and then VCU students part of the mansion on Franklin Street where she had grown up and still lived. Scott House, later purchased by VCU, was where she had convened the founding meeting of the Virginia Nature Conservancy. Ardent and irrepressible in all she took up, Bocock worked with her cousin, Mary Wingfield Scott, to establish historic preservation in Richmond and, in 1969, she was a leader of the opposition to the proposed Downtown Expressway. In her spare time, she successfully pursued a college education, course by course. Mrs. Bocock came from a very different generation, but when she stepped forward as the first to accept her VCU diploma, applause erupted from the student audience, despite the commencement program's prohibition on such expressions until the close of the ceremony. Mrs. Bocock's place at the head of the graduation parade, cheered by a disobedient audience, seemed entirely appropriate in a year of outspoken students.[31]

3

A University Emerges

FALL SEMESTER 1969 marked the beginning of VCU's second academic year and the first year of Warren Brandt's presidency. The registrar announced that enrollment at the Academic Campus totaled 11,650, about 1,000 more than in 1968, and another 1,600 students had registered at the Medical Center. There would be two new courses in Afro-American studies, and three to be offered in the spring semester. The Student Government Association began a constitutional convention, and the Academic Senate named members of its committees. An editorial in the second-ever issue of the *Commonwealth Times* (*CT*) complained about "the many wordy titles of VCU's two divisions"—and the word "division" itself, it said, "makes evident the disunity of this university. We want unity to be enhanced." The editorial promised, "From now on, you'll not see 'Medical College of Virginia' or 'Health Sciences Division' used in this student newspaper (except for in explanatory references to the university merger)."[1]

The August 1969 issue of the Medical College of Virginia Alumni Association's *Scarab* also welcomed the new academic year, reporting on faculty appointments and the nearly $4 million spent on renovations for West Hospital, the thirty-year-old main hospital at "the Medical College of Virginia." An advertisement appeared on page 26 for "Medical College of Virginia / Health Sciences Division / Virginia Commonwealth University / UNIVERSITY HOSPITALS." The larger part of that issue was given over to the alumni reunion in early June, where new President Brandt "made a splendid talk" at the banquet. The report continued, "Much concern was expressed over the identity of the Medical College of Virginia, and our Board of Trustees and our president, Dr. Fred Hines, have really been to bat for it and us."[2]

By the end of the 1960s, federal grant support for higher education was in decline, and, as Earl Cheit reported, universities began to feel the budgetary pinch. One response was to centralize and professionalize administration methods and to adopt new computer technologies, which John Thelin describes as a nothing less than a managerial revolution for higher education. At VCU in those first years, however, even basic efforts at cross-university coordination seemed to defenders of MCV's identity as threats to be staved off, resulting in conflict and frustration.[3]

IN 1968, as the Board of Visitors' search committee, chaired by Edward Wayne, screened candidates for president, the university began to fill other high administrative posts, although most of Roland Nelson's team at RPI carried over to the new university. At the end of October 1968, the Academic Division proposed for the board's approval the appointment of H. I. Willett as professor of education, effective 1 September 1969. Willett was to "assume leadership responsibility for an 'urban thrust' of the Academic Division." The Medical Center welcomed fourteen new faculty members, and the Academic Division reported in early December 1968 that new faculty there totaled 126, with more than ninety of them filling new positions at the school.[4]

Announcement of Warren William Brandt's hiring as VCU's first president came on 29 January 1969. As the executive vice president at Virginia Polytechnic Institute, since 1963 he had been the right hand of President T. Marshall Hahn in the dynamic development of VPI into a full university. Brandt was forty-five years old at his appointment, and a chemist

Warren Brandt, first president of VCU, in 1970. (Virginia Commonwealth University Libraries)

by training. He had been chair of the Chemistry Departments at Purdue and Kansas State Universities; in 1958–59 he was a Guggenheim Fellow at Oxford University in England. His black horn-rimmed glasses and short, brush-cut hair had conveyed youth and energy only a few years before, but styles had changed, seemingly overnight, and no doubt he looked a bit stuffy and conservative, which in 1969 might have appealed to some observers. Brandt told the *Proscript* that "the opportunity to work with the melding of the two institutions into one major university" excited him.[5]

Brandt recalled years later that VPI, under Marshall Hahn, was making progress "hand over fist," but the opportunity to be president of a university, especially in Virginia, where he already knew the people important for a university president to know, was hard to resist. Hahn entertained ambitions to become governor—he would have been a good one, Brandt declared—and that might also have caused Brandt to look to a future beyond VPI. Regardless, Hahn endorsed him as "one of the nation's most able young educational administrators."[6]

Asked in 2007 what had been his biggest challenge, Brandt declared immediately that it had been the effort to bring the medical school into line with the university as a whole. He told the medical school's retiring provost Blackwell Smith on 3 February 1969, just after his hiring was announced, "It can't help but cause emotional pangs to see the great name of the Medical College of Virginia, which you have developed so successfully, merged into a new university name." If Brandt considered that statement kind commiseration, others were prepared to read it as a threat to be blocked. The medical school would lift the university, Brandt went on, and in turn the university would increase the medical school's strength. Even after four months of weekly visits to Richmond, Brandt remained confident that nomenclature was a minor problem. He told a friend in the governor's office, "As Virginia Commonwealth University becomes a better-known name and achieves stature, the past practices will tend to disappear and people will want to be known as VCU." The process could not be hurried, but "it isn't worth rousing a great deal of ire about."[7]

The same issue of the *Proscript* that told of Brandt's selection also reported the adoption of "a new 'total identification system' consisting of symbol, colors and verbal identification" for VCU. The two campuses would receive new names—the Medical Center and the Academic Center—and the names Health Sciences Division and General Academics Division would no longer be used outside the university. The new university seal specified the year 1838, the date of MCV's opening, as the founding date for the university. It was customary when two institutions merged for the founding date of the elder to be the founding date for the new institution, but in the eyes of some associated with MCV, that seemed a grab at the older institution's prestige.[8]

The most controversial element was the design for the VCU seal. It was an abstraction, said a vice president from the industrial design firm, intended to call to mind variously a tree, symbolizing growth, and a fountain, symbolizing knowledge, while remaining entirely abstract, thus representing, as the VCU Office of Development put it, "the bold thrust of the university called for by the Wayne Commission." The consultants introduced the identification system at the "mid-year faculty dinner," and when they showed the new symbol and declared that it would "be in a class by itself," laughter broke out. The *Times-Dispatch* reported that the reaction was "less than enthusiastic" and "a small group at the Medical Center did not applaud last night after the presentation had been completed." Indeed, as an otherwise positive article in the Virginia State Chamber of Commerce's *Commonwealth Magazine* put it, critics would long "sneer at the queer looking symbol which the board of visitors bought off a high-priced Madison Ave. designer."[9]

The *Medicovan*'s report did not mention the laughter, but noted unhappily that MCV would be called the Medical Center and that neither RPI nor MCV would "be used as identifiers of the University." Rector Dabney declared that a "consensus of approval" backed the identification system, but he may have misread sentiment at the Medical Center. In fact, the generic blandness of the name "Medical Center" so bothered people previously employed at the Medical College of Virginia that they petitioned the Board of Visitors to change the name to "Health Sciences Center." The board received assurances that the change was acceptable in the identity plan, and the name was duly changed at the meeting of 27 March 1969.[10]

As the names changed, Brandt prepared his own plan for administering the university. He proposed to replace the dual provosts (acting provosts, to be exact) with a half-dozen vice presidents reporting directly to him. There would be vice presidents for health sciences and academic affairs, absorbing the provosts' functions, and vice presidents for finance, for planning and operations, for student affairs, and a vice president for university hospitals. President Brandt first brought his organizational plan—emphasizing the six new vice presidents, not the "lower echelons," which would be filled out later—to the Board of Visitors on 24 April 1969. The board had to revise the university's bylaws to accept the plan, which it did, and then elected Raymond T. Holmes as vice president for finance and Francis Brooke as vice president for academic affairs.[11]

Brandt also presented the board with the five-page memorandum on the reorganization that he distributed to the "Faculty of VCU" later that day. The memo expressed confidence that the "new organization will initiate the unification of many of the diverse and duplicated administrative units into an effective team." The memo also acknowledged the "strain" that this yet-to-be-determined plan would place on existing administrators and employees who might fear for their jobs.[12]

Almost immediately, there were questions from the faculty at the Health Sciences Division. The time was right for the reorganization, Brandt responded. Director of Hospitals William Morrison was retiring in June, and both Harry Lyons, dean of dentistry, and Kinloch Nelson, dean of medicine, desired to retire soon. Putting an organization into place prior to those departures was essential. As for the justified concern that organizing RPI and MCV into VCU would cost jobs, Brandt was reassuring: "It is doubtful that it will take fewer people to conduct the operations of the combined institutions."[13]

Early in June 1969, Governor Mills Godwin directed a letter to Brandt. He was blunt: "The Health Sciences Division of Virginia Commonwealth University, as I am sure you are aware, will close out the first year of operations in the current biennium with a deficit in excess of $1,000,000." Several days passed before Brandt replied, and it was, he apologized, "only a partial reply because we are not in a position to provide a sufficiently detailed explanation at this time." The deficit had complex causes, Brandt continued, but a large number of nonpaying patients combined with "antiquated furniture and equipment" and "dreary" rooms and halls to drive paying patients to newer hospitals. Renovations were underway, but the number of indigent patients continued to spiral upward. Most important, the hospital lacked "good management control" and "good statistical information," and it could take two to three years before new systems could be in place. Meanwhile, the hospital needed assistance from the state to be able to offer "the levels of compensation" that would attract outstanding personnel. Certainly, Brandt observed, the Medical Center offered "a tremendous challenge." He promised the governor "to correct this deficit situation as rapidly as possible."[14]

A few days later, Acting Provost Heil reminded Brandt of a memorandum drafted by David Hume and revised by medical school faculty in the spring, recommending that Heil appoint a committee to analyze hospital problems and propose solutions. He asked Brandt to meet with the committee, for the committee members believed that they should have direct access not merely to the acting provost but also to the president, the Board of Visitors, and the governor.[15] It is possible that Heil's perception of mismanagement at the hospital, compounded by the hospital's operating losses and Governor Godwin's dissatisfaction, reinforced Brandt's confidence in his decision to make the head of university hospitals a vice president reporting directly to him.

Three years later, David Hume and other physicians would carry out their threat to go directly to the governor, but in September 1969 Brandt's organizational plan failed to earn the full confidence of a survey team representing the Liaison Committee on Medical Education of the Council on Education of the American Medical Association and the Executive Council of the Association of American Medical Colleges. The two prior surveys by the liaison committee were in 1953 and 1962, and the 1953 survey enabled MCV finally to have removed the "conditional probationary status" it had received in 1935 and become fully accredited. The 1962 survey came at the request of the dean because of the controversy in the local newspapers in 1961 about the new medical curriculum and research orientation. That survey approved the school's direction with accreditation for another seven years.[16]

The committee's report stated that facilities badly needed improvement. The Medical Education Building, completed in 1963, had an addition being built for completion in early 1970, and further renovation of West Hospital was promised. An obstetric-pediatric hospital with five hundred beds had been proposed, with hope that construction would start in 1971. The survey approved the building program as "generally sound," but said that enrollments ought not to increase until completion of the new facilities. The committee then recommended that "the School of Medicine of the Virginia Commonwealth University continue to be fully accredited for a period of two years from date of this survey, September 8, 1969." Only two years, not the usual seven. The committee explained that concern about the proposed administrative structure and vacancies in key posts yet to be filled justified the shorter term. The newspaper reported that the "accrediting group" was concerned that under Brandt's organizational plan "the chief hospital officer would outrank the medical school dean." Certainly, that bothered medical school faculty.[17]

ON RECEIVING a communication from Brandt—probably the memorandum about reorganization sent to faculty—the Board of Trustees of the Medical College of Virginia Alumni Association convened a special meeting on 4 May 1969. The association's leaders objected to two aspects of the new structure: first, there was no mention of MCV by name "(as called for by law)," and, second, the search committees to select the vice presidents for the Health Services Division and the University Hospitals did not include alumni representatives. The meeting issued a protest about nomenclature "as set forth in the spirit and the letter of the law" and proceeded to nominate members to serve on the search committees.[18]

Then came August and the university's new stationery design, which ran "Virginia Commonwealth University" in large type at the top and, on the bottom, in smaller type, "Medical College of Virginia—Health Sciences Center—Richmond, Virginia 23219." In his letter of 22 August announcing the new letterhead to the university, Brandt described it as a means "effectively and appropriately [to] present Virginia Commonwealth University to its publics." That seemed to be exactly what the MCV Alumni Association feared, and the advertisement for the UNIVERSITY HOSPITALS in the August *Scarab* illustrating the new logo system proved it. The October *Scarab* reproduced the new letterhead, again with Virginia Commonwealth University in a larger font than Medical College of Virginia, stating that it illustrated the Board of Trustees' conclusion that the identity of the Medical College of Virginia was "in jeopardy." As further proof, the *Scarab* reproduced an article from the *Richmond Times-Dispatch*, published on 30 August and titled "Spotlight Dimming on the Name 'MCV.'" A press release from the university that referred only to the Health Sciences Center of VCU without mentioning MCV had prompted the story, but university officials denied that the omission represented a policy. Brandt, in fact, was quoted as pointing to the new stationery as proof that the MCV name would be retained. The *Scarab* asked alumni readers who wanted the identity of the medical school to be maintained to return an enclosed postcard.[19]

In mid-June 1969, after Brandt had presented his organizational plan, he summed up the university to a friend as "a very exciting place." In terms that he would continue to use, Brandt described the situation as he saw it:

"In many ways, it is like a shotgun wedding and in several ways it's like Noah's Ark." Many at MCV "resented the forced merger," and the alumni "are particularly disturbed." Thus, he went on, "I've got two of everything. Two alumni associations, two deans of students, two fiscal officers, two this and that up and down the line. It is going to be a very interesting situation to bring together."[20]

As the issue of nomenclature brewed behind the scenes, the campaign to end the Vietnam War erupted again in fall 1969. Proposals in spring for a nationwide strike if the war had not ended by October moderated into a day of protests scheduled for 15 October, with mass demonstrations to follow on 15 November in Washington. President Brandt emphasized that classes would be held as scheduled in October, but students opposed to the war planned a teach-in for Monroe Park in the morning with a march down Franklin Street to the capitol building to follow. Prior to the 15 November Moratorium Day, on 3 November, President Richard Nixon spoke on national television and asked the "great silent majority" of Americans to back his policy. The Richmond Academy of Medicine sent a supportive letter to the president. Two medical students, Martin Lazoritz and Brian Peck, then put an advertisement in the local newspapers supporting the moratorium and signed by "Richmond Doctors and Medical Students for Peace." The Academy of Medicine fired back with its own advertisement declaring that the antiwar advertisement "WAS NOT supported by the RICHMOND ACADEMY OF MEDICINE which represents 796 physicians in the Richmond Community." One could hardly avoid the suspicion that the academy was prepared to ensure that antiwar activism and a medical career in Richmond did not go together. The accreditation survey that September had concluded: "There is virtually no student activism at the Medical College of Virginia."[21]

At the Academic Center, William Blake also believed that the president's policy in Vietnam deserved support, and he enlisted a group of VCU faculty members, most of them from his own history department, to take out a full-page advertisement in the Richmond papers to show that contrary to stereotypes some college faculty were in agreement with the president. The moratorium, nonetheless, drew VCU students and other Richmonders to join a crowd estimated at five hundred thousand people in Washington on 15 November. President Nixon had already indicated that the protest would have no influence on his policy, and the implementation in early December of a draft lottery, ending the limited exemption for students and also the uncertainty about a young man's likelihood to be called to military service, seemed, for the moment, to quiet the antiwar movement.[22]

PRESIDENT BRANDT had set off an internal campus controversy with his announcement in September 1969 of the University Assembly, a unicameral body that would advise the president on university policy. It would be composed of fifteen faculty representatives, fifteen administrators, and six students. The announcement seemed to take people by surprise. Although a university-wide faculty organization did not yet exist, the Academic Senate expressed dismay that the faculty had no voice in creating the new organization. Brandt asked for time enough to observe the assembly in action and noted that the Academic Senate would name three members, giving that body "a significant input and liaison." The faculty response was mild compared to that of the students. In October, the Student Government Association angrily discussed the "tokenism" of their scant six representatives (three from each campus) on the assembly. At the assembly's inaugural meeting on 10 November 1969, the students asked for greater student representation, but the assembly voted against them. Brandt had earlier ordered the reporters from the *Commonwealth Times* out of the room, prompting a page-one letter of complaint from the paper's editors in the next issue. Leaders of student government on the Academic Campus organized a candlelight protest in Shafer Court on 13 November, which drew a thousand people, and proposed that all student government bodies dissolve themselves if proper representation were not forthcoming.[23]

In the midst of this, representatives of Oregon Hill, the neighborhood to VCU's south, which had been consigned to oblivion in the Wayne Commission's report that initiated the university, invaded the meeting of the student House of Representatives to demand student support for a petition that the Oregon Hill organization had presented to Brandt two weeks earlier. They wanted VCU to turn over to Oregon Hill land there that the city had cleared of residences in anticipation of the Downtown Expressway. Opponents of the expressway had wielded financial, historical, and environmental tools to delay construction, and, in the interim, VCU claimed the razed space for parking. The neighborhood representatives also wanted an additional promise that VCU would not expand further into the neighborhood, an issue that would trouble relations between the university and its neighborhood on the south for decades to come.[24]

The Academic Senate met on 13 November and voted to support expanded representation for the students. In early December the assembly met in special session to consider student representation and voted 19 to 16 to retain the original organization. The angry response of student leaders to their underrepresentation, and the failure to change the assembly's make-up, contributed to the decline and, for several years in the 1970s, actual demise of student government at the Academic Division.[25]

As the fall 1969 semester, Brandt's first, wound down, Governor-Elect Linwood Holton asked him for a copy of VCU's "operational manual." The university did not have one, Brandt said, but then explained his organization, with six vice presidents. Two of the vice presidents had academic responsibilities, with Francis Brooke heading affairs at the Academic Center, and a search committee now seeking the vice president for the Health Sciences Center. The new vice president for University Hospitals, John F. Imirie Jr., would begin his duties on 1 February 1970. The remaining three vice presidents had university-wide responsibilities, with Raymond T. Holmes Jr. since summer the vice president for finance; Richard I. Wilson, former director of special services for the Peace Corps, having begun his duties as vice president for student affairs on 1 December 1969; and, just two weeks earlier, Roger L. Smith, whom Brandt had known at Virginia Tech, having become vice president for planning and operations. Brandt expressed hope that the new governor would appreciate the organizational changes and stated his own belief that "VCU is serving the Commonwealth of Virginia in an exemplary manner."[26]

The results of the postcard survey of medical-school alumni appeared in the February 1970 *Scarab*, prefaced with a "memo" to Brandt and Rector Eppa Hunton from the Alumni Association. It stated that 4,377 members responded to the October inquiry, and 4,255 of them "were emphatic in their wish that the identity of the Medical College of Virginia be maintained." Several pages of excerpts from the responses followed. Running through all the comments was a general theme of dismay at unwelcome changes being forced on people, a reflection of the times as well as the nomenclature issue. The alumni writing from outside Virginia shared the distress of the Virginia residents, but their comments concerned VCU's lack of name recognition and prestige compared to MCV. Sprinkled throughout the comments from Virginians, in addition, were angry disparagements of RPI and VCU as tainted and inferior, with the merger a disgrace and degrading to MCV. "When I hear anything concerning VCU the first thing that comes to my mind is a group of long hair hippies and pot users," a typical comment read. The controversy over nomenclature reinforced this tendency to identify VCU with students at the Academic Center, while associating the medical school with medical professionals. The Alumni Association had rallied strong support for maintaining the name, but how that was to be done short of formal separation of the institutions remained temporarily unclear.[27]

In that same issue of the *Scarab*, following pages and pages of a national outpouring of angst and vitriol, Dr. Brandt's first "Report from the President" was an anticlimax. He described "impressive progress," including the opening of the "Dentistry Building II," federal funds to support state funds for the expansion of Sanger Hall and the medical library, the new nurse anesthetist training program, and expansions of the Schools of Nursing, Pharmacy, and Allied Health Professions. Where the Alumni Association saw a tragic loss of identity, Brandt presented "a rapidly developing University in which the Medical College of Virginia is playing a prominent role."[28]

Brandt's peace offering made no difference, as the Alumni Association turned to the legislature for protection. On 20 February 1970, House Joint Resolution No. 73, "Requesting the Board of Visitors of Virginia Commonwealth University to maintain the identity of the Medical College of Virginia as an individual college within the framework of the University," made its appearance. The resolution's sponsor, Beverly R. Middleton of Virginia Beach, introduced it without the Alumni Association asking him directly, but four graduates of MCV (three from the Pharmacy School and one from the Dental School) were among the resolution's other patrons. One of them, W. Roy Smith, Pharmacy 1947, was the brother of the late provost R. Blackwell Smith and chair of the powerful House Appropriations Committee. The Senate soon joined the House in endorsing the resolution unanimously.[29]

At the university, cooperative developments contrasted with the legislature's action. In fall 1969 Acting Provost Heil had appointed a twelve-member committee on university governance to create a faculty senate for the Health Sciences Division. That committee included members who also served on the constitution and bylaws committee of the Academic Senate, and both committees agreed to make their bylaws consistent. The Academic Senate originated at RPI in December 1967, after merger of the Faculty Central Committee and the Academic Administrative Committee, with chemistry professor Jerry Bass as its first president. In October 1968, that body dissolved itself, and the VCU Academic Senate took its place. In spring 1969 history professor William Blake was elected president to serve in the 1969–70 academic year. He had assumed office when the Health Sciences Division's committee determined that a university-wide senate would be best able to represent the faculty, and that committee began meeting with the constitution and bylaws committee of the Academic Senate to establish faculty governance procedures for the university. On 3 February 1970, B. W. Haynes Jr., chair of the Health Sciences Division's committee, and Elizabeth R. Reynolds, chair of the Academic Senate's committee, presented the Bylaws of the Faculty of VCU to the faculty for ratification. The vote was 505 in favor and 33 opposed, and Blake declared that the result reflected "the development of unity between the two campuses."[30]

On a related front, hopes for a new hospital received a boost with the decision to develop a full university master site plan. Brandt requested that all faculty and staff assist representatives of the two firms chosen to develop the plan, Llewelyn-Davies Associates, of New York, and Glave, Newman, Anderson, of Richmond, and reminded them that "this is a very significant study in the development of our University." The planners were told to assume growth of the student population to twenty-five thousand by the mid-1970s and possibly to forty thousand by the mid-1980s. The predictions reflected demographic expectations aroused by the baby boom, soon dashed by the so-called baby bust, bottoming out in 1973.[31]

The Board of Visitors adopted the plan as presented on 3 August 1970 to be incorporated into the city of Richmond's master plan. In late December 1970, Brandt submitted the plan—filling three volumes—to state review. From the Division of Engineering and Buildings, the plan went to the state's Art Commission, with meetings on campus in February. The commission rejected the plan's proposed location of student recreation areas on the roofs of buildings as impractically expensive and also unanimously condemned plans to save "the fronts of certain houses" while making modern additions behind the preserved facades. The protection of old buildings on both campuses was a concern of the committee, but it endorsed the plan in general.[32]

Planning for the physical layout of the former RPI campus coincided with restructuring of the academic organization there, too. The swift expansion of academic programs after RPI's separation from William and Mary in 1963 led in fall 1968 to the Academic Division engaging a consulting firm to analyze position papers from departments and to conduct interviews with faculty. With report in hand, the Board of Visitors agreed in July 1969 to a thorough restructuring. The new School of the Arts, under Dean Herbert J. Burgart, now combined the old School of Art with the former School of Music and the Department of Dramatic Art and Speech. The Departments of Journalism, Psychology, and Sociology departed the School of Social Science for the bulging School of Arts and Sciences, leaving the School of Social Sciences to combine with the School of Rehabilitation Counseling to become the new School of Community Services, with dean and mission yet to be determined. Retailing and advertising went to the School of Business, distributive education to the School of Education, and engineering technology would go to a local community college. Finally, the School of Occupational Therapy would move into the School of Allied Health Professions at the Health Sciences Division. Only the School of Social Work remained unchanged by the reorganization.[33]

ON 10 MARCH 1970, plaintiffs in Richmond's ongoing struggle to desegregate the public schools filed a motion for court action in view of the Supreme Court's 1968 decision in *Green v. County School Board of New Kent County* that school boards had the responsibility to develop workable plans for speedy desegregation. Moreover, previously all-white schools, especially in the city's north side, saw whites departing for the suburban counties when blacks moved into their neighborhoods, causing once-white schools to resegregate as black schools. Any possible solutions had to confront Richmond's historically developed pattern of intense neighborhood segregation, and the example from the north side of town suggested that the suburban counties would receive refugees from neighborhood change, for many white parents would not permit their children to remain in truly desegregated schools.[34]

Complicating the situation was the city's controversial annexation of twenty-three square miles of land from Chesterfield County to the south. The annexed territory added nearly fifty thousand new citizens, of which some forty-five thousand were whites. The city's population prior to the annexation was 202,359, a decline from a quarter million in 1950, thanks to suburbanization, with a slight black majority. The annexation became effective on 1 January 1970, restored a white majority for elections, and stirred immediate challenges as a violation of the Voting Rights Act of 1965.

The Virginia Supreme Court rejected an appeal from the neighborhood associations in the annexed territory, and city elections took place on 10 June 1970 as scheduled. Although the African American political organization, the Richmond Crusade for Voters, won places on city council for three candidates despite citywide at-large voting, the white "Richmond power structure," previously organized as Richmond Forward but now operating under the name Teams of Progress, took six seats, retaining political control as planned. Seven years, and much litigation, would pass before Richmond citizens next voted for city council members.[35]

At VCU, the spring 1970 semester proceeded smoothly. After a run-off election, Jim Elam, a sociology major from Richmond, was elected president of the Student Government Association, the first African American student to hold that post. On 22 April 1970, VCU joined in the first Earth Day with a rally at Monroe Park (a pile of earth delivered to Shafer Court was portioned out to participants to carry to the park's flower beds).[36]

The master plan for MCV also was announced on Earth Day, although apparently without any intention to make a connection. Two weeks earlier, on 9 April 1970, university officials presented the master plan for the Academic Campus to a meeting of the Fan District Association, representing the residential neighborhood to the west of that campus. Naturally, the association members objected that the plan failed to get students and their cars out of the neighborhood. On the night of that meeting, students living in the 1100 block of Grove Avenue, on the edge of the Fan District closest to the university, closed their block for a party with loud music, which brought out the police—over and over. Even more people came there to party on the next night, again bringing out the police. The episode inspired the creation of the Grove Avenue Republic, with a flag immortalized on the cover of the May 1970 issue of *The Richmond Chronicle*, and a manifesto in free verse on an inside page: "THE GROVE AVENUE REPUBLIC! / To find the way / How can we . . . / Sit on our front porch / NUDE / Listen to Rock in the street / At 3:00 a.m. / Live . . . SAFELY /?"[37]

At the Health Sciences Center, the city's plans for widening Leigh Street, including a bridge across the Shockoe Valley to replace the Marshall Street Viaduct, enabled the master plan for the Medical Campus to envision Marshall Street, with traffic restricted, as a rough dividing line between a medical education zone to the south and a hospital complex to the north. The plan was ambitious, not least because the existing East, South, and

West Hospitals sat in the education zone. Nonetheless, future development of the MCV Campus largely respected that dividing line.[38]

On the day that the crisis began, 30 April 1970, the Black Panthers were to recruit students at the new residence building, Rhoads Hall, but a conflict involving the Baltimore chapter had required the attendance there of the Washington Panthers, so the meeting proceeded without actual Black Panthers. Despite some preliminary talk of poor whites allying along class lines with the militant organization, voices called for a black-only meeting, and whites, including journalists, left for nearby Monroe Park, where the blacks from the meeting eventually joined them. Kenny Rogers and the First Edition were announced as the musical attraction for May Jubilee Week; tickets would go on sale next Tuesday. That evening, President Richard M. Nixon informed the nation that, contrary to expectations that his policy of "Vietnamization" would shrink the military intervention in Southeast Asia, American forces had invaded the neutral nation of Cambodia.[39]

The Cambodian incursion provoked antiwar demonstrations on campuses across the country. The governor of Ohio called out the National Guard to keep order in that state, and on Monday, 4 May, soldiers fired on students at Kent State University, wounding nine and killing four. The National Student Association immediately called for a student strike, but students across the country had already reacted. More than one hundred students were arrested at Virginia Polytechnic Institute, and days of conflict at the University of Virginia outraged newspaper editors and legislators, although classes remained in session throughout.[40]

As news of the killings flashed to Richmond, a group of students and nonstudents met at Hibbs Hall on Monday night. They called for a protest strike, and another meeting of 150 to 200 persons followed at midnight at a residence on Grove Avenue. That group petitioned SGA president Jim Elam to call an emergency meeting of the student legislature, which met Tuesday morning. After much debate, the SGA decided by a vote of 13 to 11 not to endorse a strike at VCU. A special meeting of the Faculty Senate also took up the students' request for a strike, with President Blake successfully arguing that the university must maintain a position of "institutional neutrality." Unknown parties called bomb threats to the administration building, and the people working there evacuated until early afternoon. Despite the votes, a rally with speakers calling for a strike gathered on Shafer Court near Founders Hall. Elam explained there that he favored a boycott of classes, but by individuals, and nearly all the other speakers shared that call. The only administrator or faculty member to speak was Vincent Wright, now assistant dean to the dean of students. His comparison of the murders at Kent State to the Boston Massacre prior to the American Revolution brought cheers. People of all opinions noticed that the flags on campus had been lowered to half-mast at Dr. Brandt's orders, in mourning for the four dead in Ohio, but Brandt had no further comment.[41]

That night, several students entered the President's House—now used as offices, not as a residence—on Franklin Street. They proposed to stay in order to press their demand that the university close for the rest of the week, but with promises that Brandt would meet with them the next day, they left. Others camped outside Ginter House, across the street, until Brandt arrived. The president met privately with the students and then with the press, repeating to both that the university would not close. He issued a formal statement, too, which commended the Faculty Senate's vote to continue classes and noted that the invaluable functions of universities required that they remain open. Bennett Nelson and Bill Oliver, student leaders of the Grove Avenue Republic, appeared with Brandt, and Nelson dismissed fears of violence but promised to continue seeking support for a strike. A memorial service for the dead Kent State students that day drew "hundreds of VCU students," and a rally that followed featured speakers such as Blake from the Faculty Senate arguing for keeping the university open.[42]

By the end of the week, all parties had expressed themselves at rallies and in the *Commonwealth Times*. Brandt canceled his scheduled appointments to continue meeting with small groups of students in his office. The Pi Sigma Epsilon car show had to be postponed as the contending parties filled Shafer Court. Brandt informed the Board of Visitors that weekend that the boycotting students would return to classes on Monday. He said that "the administrative group" deserved "tremendous credit" for the university continuing to function normally. "Though we do not like everything that was done," he continued, "I think each of us appreciates that if we had not had some fairly stable leadership among the radicals, we might be sitting in quite a different boat this week-end."[43]

On Monday, 11 May, two opposed student delegations went to the capitol to meet with the governor. Holton had travel plans, so his commissioner of administration, T. Edward Temple, met with the group calling for

Brandt's dismissal and with the group calling for VCU to remain open but with a variety of reforms to add student voices to university administration. He politely promised to brief the governor about their petitions. The president of the Virginia Farm Bureau Federation called for the governor to withhold funding from state schools where disorders occurred and to freeze faculty salaries as a warning against supporting student protests. On 12 May the governor referred to the Farm Bureau's statement to tell dissident students to return to their classes. By the end of that week at VCU, classes continued as scheduled, and the *Commonwealth Times* turned to other topics, such as election of the May Queen to be presented at the Kenny Rogers and First Edition concert.[44]

It would be a mistake, though, to underestimate the anger and despair at the war's expansion and the murders of student protestors. That week the Academic Campus saw many public gatherings that featured strong rhetoric and angry emotions, yet no riots occurred nor did the police have excuse to sweep the campus to make arrests (and the run-ins with the Grove Avenue Republic's loud parties had demonstrated the police force's willingness to take on students). The university—faculty, students, and administrators—stated opinions and debated them. Classes continued, unlike at nearly nine hundred other colleges and universities, where some four million students stayed out of classes. The *Richmond News Leader* characterized conditions at the Academic Center as "physical order in the midst of strong philosophical discussion."[45]

The May 1970 issue of the *Scarab* posted the text of House Resolution No. 73 triumphantly on page 1, but its pages also reported the appointments of Lauren Albert Woods, a nationally known pharmacologist, as vice president "of the Medical College of Virginia," to use the *Scarab*'s identification. The article also quoted Brandt's expression of his enthusiasm at Woods's appointment as chief academic officer at "the Health Sciences Division." Announcement of the appointment of John F. Imirie Jr. as vice president for the "Medical College of Virginia hospitals" (*Scarab*) or "for University Hospitals" (Brandt) appeared on the same page. Regardless of nomenclature, both new vice presidents had hard work ahead of them.[46]

The Board of Visitors met on 4 June, just prior to the first postannexation city election, and discussed House Joint Resolution No. 73 for nearly two hours. The only specific order to the board in the resolution was "to confer diplomas that are in keeping with those heretofore conferred by the Medical College of Virginia," which aroused exasperation, given that diplomas properly should give some prominence to the degree-granting institution and already had the name Medical College of Virginia "centered in heavy type." At Brandt's suggestion, the board agreed to reassure the Alumni Association of its concern to maintain the name. At its annual meeting on 6 June 1970, the Alumni Association's president noted proudly that the name of the hospitals had been changed to "Medical College of Virginia Hospitals." One member then asked if the association had ever approved the merger of MCV and RPI. To the undoubted disappointment of some, the secretary reported that yes, a resolution of approval had been passed in 1967. The Board of Visitors, at its 23 July 1970 meeting, called for acknowledgement to be sent to the clerk of the House and to the resolution's sponsors that the board had been and would continue maintaining MCV's identity. Given the prominence of MCV graduates in the legislature, it would have been foolhardy to challenge the resolution.[47]

On 26 June 1970, District Court Judge Robert Merhige Jr. informed the city school board that patterns of residential segregation guaranteed that the board's proposed desegregation plan would not meet the Supreme Court's order for plans that "promise[d] realistically to work now." Merhige rejected a second board desegregation plan in July and gave ninety days to devise a better one. Schools opened with the second, interim, plan in place, which included limited busing of students in the higher grades to schools outside their neighborhoods.[48]

On 31 August 1970, Governor Linwood Holton personally escorted his daughter to predominantly black John Marshall High School, and Mrs. Holton took their two younger children to all-black Mosby Middle School. Their action was heartfelt and courageous, for, technically, the children lived at the Governor's Mansion, state property, and that exempted them from the city desegregation plan. A photo of the governor and his daughter made the front page of the New York Times, as they presented a counterimage to that of the South's governors as fanatics for resistance to desegregation. The governor's example notwithstanding, school officials quickly realized that some five thousand of the projected number of white students were missing. As historian Robert A. Pratt notes, given the court's rejection of the interim plan as inadequate, the school board's next plan would have to provide for even more busing, and "the white exodus from Richmond's public schools would only intensify."[49] VCU was an urban university in a time when that adjective was becoming associated, in some minds, with African Americans, with crime, and with poverty.

As the fall 1970 semester got underway at VCU, the new James Branch Cabell Library opened (faculty of the School of the Arts convinced the university to reopen the former library building as the Anderson Gallery), and plans for an addition to Tompkins-McCaw Library at the Medical Campus were underway.[50] With the library open, his reorganization of the university complete, his management team in place, the University Assembly operational, and the Alumni Association confident of protection from the legislature, Brandt could look forward to his inauguration as VCU's first president, scheduled for Tuesday, 10 November 1970.

Then, on 11 October, poet Allen Ginsberg performed at the gymnasium. In the midst of his singing, reciting, and chanting, someone passed him a note, which he read from the stage: all were invited that night to a block party on Grove Avenue, with free beer. His audience knew that block, the first one west of the Harrison Street edge of campus, as the Grove Avenue Republic. After the contentious block parties there in April, supporters— "Grove Avenue Republicans," the *Commonwealth Times* called them—sold bumper stickers with a red peace sign to raise funds to pay the unusually high bails required of those arrested. This party drew an even larger crowd than the poet's standing-room-only audience at the gym, as the amplified sounds of the band playing on a second-floor balcony echoed through the neighborhood. The police were summoned, and a riot ensued. Ginsberg generously arrived from his lodgings to try to draw the party away to Monroe Park, where some three hundred people joined him in chanting, but an angry crowd remained, and police and their dogs swept them into apartments or down the street. Brandt and other university officials hurried to the scene, but the police were in no mood to defer to them. A rough peace finally settled on the neighborhood, but at least one policeman was injured, and seventeen persons were arrested. Governor Holton warned again that campus unrest threatened to convince taxpayers to stop supporting higher education, and Brandt waited to determine how many, if any, students had been arrested.[51] The parties, and the riots, made the Grove Avenue Republic legendary.

Despite the riot, and persistent jurisdictional problems with the Richmond Police Department, President Brandt's inauguration went on as scheduled on Tuesday, 10 November 1970. The MCV Alumni Association convened a general alumni homecoming the weekend prior, with sessions on Sunday afternoon devoted to the relationship between VCU and the Medical College of Virginia. That forum for the MCV alumni was just one of several events marking the inauguration. Under the general theme "Why an Urban University?," the activities highlighted the history of the university and the mission given to it by the Wayne Commission. Harlan Westermann, dean of the School of Community Services, helped organize a weeklong symposium on the idea of an urban university. Both Wester-mann and H. I. Willett, consultant in urban affairs, defined the urban university as an institution that engaged with its community but also val-ued the view from the ivory tower as a practical means to fulfill the Wayne Commission's call for VCU to be a catalyst for community efforts to solve problems.[52]

Brandt's inaugural address ranged widely but also emphasized VCU as an urban university, with "the betterment of human life as a goal" and the education of students from a variety of backgrounds as the means. The crowd gave him a standing ovation. Outside the theater a small group of students passed out flyers attacking Brandt for, among other misdeeds, giving students only token representation on the University Assembly and not condemning the police's use of dogs in quelling the disturbance on Grove Avenue in October.[53]

By then, VCU had moved, somewhat haltingly, toward a standardized administrative organization and formalized rules and procedures. That shift, away from the less-structured, freewheeling earliest days of the uni-versity, helps to explain the most public controversy of 1971. Vincent F. Wright had come to VCU in fall 1969, hired in that period of forward think-ing and crisis management that followed the SAAP demands in May, and his mandate was no less than to aid in developing the urban university. He had been a teacher of orchestral music in New York City and was a skilled saxophonist, but Wright, an African American, was hired to give partic-ular attention to aiding African American students and strengthening connections between the university and the community. On 4 May 1970, Wright met with Vice President for Student Affairs Richard Wilson, who had been hired after Wright, to discuss his job performance. Wright and Wilson agreed to a contract for one year, to 30 April 1971, and Wright signed it on 18 May 1970.[54]

Conflicts arose quickly, particularly with budgets for Wright's Oppor-tunity Scholars Program that summer. Wilson met with Wright in Novem-ber to discuss Wright's inadequate reporting on his work and assigned him to closer supervision in the Office of Student Life, under Dean Alfred Matthews. They met again in early February to talk about continuing failures to adhere to procedures, and Matthews followed with a memorandum dated 17 February 1971 about his own communication problems with Wright. Matthews sent Wilson another memo about Wright in March, and Wright's decision then to take a day off, missing a scheduled meeting, caused Matthews to complain to him that "I still do not know what you are doing." On 8 April all three men met to review Wright's performance, and Wilson informed him that his employment would not be renewed, although it would be continued to 8 October 1971.[55]

During these same months, the city of Richmond's school desegregation plans took a radical turn. The limited busing employed in the 1970–71 school year, which had caused numbers of whites to flee to the adjoining counties, did not affect elementary schools. Judge Robert Merhige in January had warned that the racial differences manifest in the elementary schools appeared to him to continue segregation. Thus, on 5 April 1971, Merhige ordered into effect a new desegregation plan that would ensure that the ratio of blacks and whites at each school would approximate the ratio for the school district as a whole. To make that plan work, Merhige extended busing to all grades. The U.S. Supreme Court's decision on 20 April endorsing the busing plan in Charlotte, North Carolina, indicated that, if challenged, Merhige's plan for Richmond would receive court approval. John V. Moeser arrived in 1970 as a faculty member in VCU's new program in urban studies. "The combination of annexation and cross-town busing was explosive," he recalled. "Richmond at that time was an ugly place politically and socially."[56]

The final issue of the *CT* for the spring 1971 semester reported that Vincent Wright's termination would go to an appeals board. Neither Wright nor Wilson offered comment. The paper also reported that Wright had been named outstanding faculty member in 1970 by the SGA, had been involved in numerous service projects, taught courses in African American history and the sociology of racism, and had been named to the Richmond Human Relations Commission by the city council. An editorial elaborated on those achievements, declaring that Wright had "done more probably in his position than any other school official to help build the image of VCU as an urban university." He was "an asset that the university cannot afford to lose." The Black Educators' Association, comprised of VCU faculty and administrators, made a similar protest in a private letter to Brandt. The letter invoked the Wayne Commission to charge that "what happened to

Mr. Wright is indicative of this school's failure to have an urban commitment to upgrade the plight of Black people in our state and inner city."[57]

The university's hearing on 24 May 1971 lasted for several hours. The review panel consisted of three blacks (one a student) and two whites, a fact that administrators would later emphasize to critics. Also present were Brandt, Wright, his attorney, and others. One of the witnesses, Charles McLeod, leader of the SAAP's protests in spring 1969 and now a recruiter for the university, charged that the university hired Wright primarily to show that a black administrator had been hired, and left him with latitude to choose his own activities. Wilson's effort after the fact to plug Wright into the bureaucracy, he said, was "like trying to fit a square peg into a round hole." As a handwritten comment on a page now in a folder in the archives put it: "Summary not something he did—but, what he didn't do." On the hearing's conclusion, Brandt upheld the termination for "inadequate performance of assigned duties."[58]

That summer saw preparations for desegregated public schools in Richmond, as the school board purchased buses and parents decided what was best for their children's education. Governor Holton remained true to his bold registration of his children in desegregated schools, determined that the public schools remain open and able to solve the issues before them. The Richmond daily newspapers continued to squawk against the busing plan as evidence of federal government interference with local matters. And white migration to the suburban counties accelerated, with real estate brokers arousing whites' fears of depreciating property values in the city and then happily selling vacated properties to African American families.[59]

In mid-September 1971 Vincent Wright filed a suit in federal court for $125,000 in damages caused by the university's "arbitrary and capricious" action, not long before his official termination date of 8 October 1971. His lawyer was Cabell Venable, who had made himself known as the attorney for black activist Curtis Holt's suit to overturn the city's annexation of white neighborhoods in 1969, then making its way through the judicial system. Students, led by SAAP but including three former SGA presidents, rallied twice for Wright at Shafer Court, with speakers commending Wright for his humanizing influence on the administration. A flyer appeared, with a portrait of Wright and an accusatory headline: "V.C.U. hired Vincent Wright to do a specific job. And fired him when he did it too well."[60]

Then, about midnight on 6 October, someone soaked with gasoline and set afire the office of Richard Wilson, who had terminated Vincent Wright. The blaze in the President's House required ten units from the city fire department to quell, and just as they began to depart, another fire, also set by an arsonist, broke out behind the Hibbs Building in a storage shed for the bookstore. The fire at the President's House destroyed fine wallpaper, paintings, and letters of commendation for Wilson's work with the Peace Corps signed by Sargent Shriver and John F. Kennedy. Administrative records of the dispute over Vincent Wright's termination housed in his office survived, but scorch marks on every page remind the researcher in the archive today of the arson attack. The perpetrator or perpetrators were never identified.[61]

After the controversy over Vincent Wright's case and the distress of the firebombing of the President's House, there was happiness on 14 November 1971 on the dedication of the Theresa Pollak Building, the new home for the School of the Arts on Harrison Street just south of Franklin Street. Pollak pioneered art education at Richmond Professional Institute and might fairly be credited with developing the School of the Arts during her forty-one years at the school (retiring from VCU in 1969). The Pollak Building, with its low profile ("residential scale," said architect Louis W. Ballou) and open courtyard on the first floor, reflects the 1966 RPI master site plan by Ballou and Justice, Architects and Engineers. Almost immediately, the popular School of Arts began seeking additional spaces for instruction and studios.[62]

Also in fall 1971, the university began a self-study as part of the accreditation process for the Southern Association of Colleges and Schools (SACS). An administrative retreat produced agreement to add two areas to the twelve SACS-recommended self-study standards: the computer center and the university hospitals. The addendum was well chosen, for those areas would be high on the university's agenda for the remainder of President Brandt's tenure.

Events in 1972, during the drafting of the self-study, shaped the study's discussions of the hospital, but those events had earlier origins. In May 1970, Brandt prepared for Governor Holton a report on financial conditions at the hospitals, and he must have hoped that the governor knew nothing of Governor Godwin's letter a year earlier insisting on reduction of operating losses. The deficit for fiscal 1970 was nearly twice that of the previous fiscal year. He had an explanation. State support for the hospitals had been reduced, both Medicare and Medicaid pushed down charges and limited hospital stays, and renovations to West Hospital reduced available beds.[63]

The problems went deeper than management. The hospitals were also plagued by "nursing shortages, poor facilities, and changing patterns of the type of patient served." Brandt put it bluntly: "Malicious comments about the percentage of Black patients appears [sic] to be cutting into our paying patient business." Brandt assured the governor that, despite budget reductions, the hospitals operated "at a near break-even level for the paying patients." Services to indigents—patients who lacked insurance or the means otherwise to pay for care—produced the largest part of the annual losses.[64]

In early June 1970 David Hume, the dedicated and impetuous chair of the Department of Surgery, had enough. He sent Brandt a single-spaced, six-page letter detailing everything that the department needed and lacked. Morale was "at its lowest ebb in history," he warned, and the surgical program was "in danger of further immediate disintegration." His main complaints had to do with the inadequate operating rooms in West Hospital. Hume, confident of his persuasiveness, asked not only to talk directly to Brandt but also for the latter's permission for Hume to meet with the Board of Visitors and the governor as well as to seek funds from private donors. Brandt waited a couple of weeks to reply, and his letter gently dashed Hume's hopes for immediate action. Surely it was better to hold off on renovations until full funding was available than to have to halt work before finishing, he wrote. Hume should defer to the judgments of Vice President Woods and Dean Nelson.[65]

Following the Board of Visitors' approval of the university's master site plan, Brandt's administration did seek funds for planning a new hospital and renovations of West and North Hospitals. On 17 June 1971, H. I. Willett suggested to Brandt that he write letters of appreciation to Delegate Roy Smith and Senator Edward Willey, chairs of the House Appropriations Committee and Senate Finance Committee and pharmacy graduates of MCV, and a few others "in connection with . . . the release to the Governor of planning funds . . . to begin planning the new hospital facility at the Health Sciences Division." Willett continued: questions raised in the Senate Finance Committee indicated that VCU needed to gather information about costs and financing revenue bonds, as well as "how much direct appropriation will be necessary from the State."[66]

MCV transplant team, 1966. David M. Hume, on the right, and H. M. Lee, center, gave their names to the present Hume-Lee Transplant Center. (Virginia Commonwealth University Libraries)

Nearly a year later, at the Board of Visitors' meeting on 23 March 1972, President Brandt reported, "We asked for funds for the Pharmacy, Nursing and Allied Health Building and for planning money for the hospital. We will get $500,000 for the planning of the hospital provided that we prove its financial feasibility." The university had been working with the national consulting firm Booz Allen Hamilton to establish the feasibility. Once the funds were released, planning to eliminate South and East Hospitals and to make the new hospital a hub connecting the North and West Hospitals and the new clinical center would follow.[67]

The long delay and deteriorating conditions at the hospitals finally convinced David Hume that, President Brandt notwithstanding, he could wait no longer. He recruited his colleagues Richard Lower and Taliaferro Thompson, and, with John Imirie, head of the hospitals, in tow, they hand-delivered a petition to the governor on 31 March 1972. They told him that a crisis existed at the hospitals that affected medical students, "desperately ill people" in Virginia, and "the futures of many of the clinical faculty of the Medical College of Virginia." There was low morale among the nurses and the faculty, and the state must accept that "frontline duty under fire requires combat pay." This last line, for better or worse, reinforced the growing perception that VCU's hospitals—referred to as the MCV hospitals throughout this episode—stood isolated in a decaying city and filled with impoverished and minority patients. In fact, other Richmond hospitals had largely joined the flight from the city for the suburbs, and the later report to the governor that the petition inspired stated that "poor, non-white residents of Richmond are the heaviest users of the hospital services."[68]

Governor Holton assigned his commissioner of administration, T. Edward Temple, to investigate the petition's charges. His task force reported on 16 June 1972. A main problem, it found, was the lack of a clear mission for the MCV Hospital. Both the administrators and the legislature needed a defined mission in order to plan and to appropriate. Priorities, as a consequence, "change from day to day."[69]

The process that Hume set in motion continued in October 1972 with a meeting of all parties with the governor, after which the Temple Committee's report was made public. The press played up the problems identified in that report, but also noted that the Board of Visitors had already responded to the Temple Committee's report, including crafting a mission statement for the hospitals: they were to be a teaching laboratory, a site for clinical research, and a community-oriented part of an urban university, "with particular reference to the care of the indigent population of Virginia." All agreed that some problems, including the hospitals' inability to offer competitive salaries for nurses and other professional staff, did require state action. Holton spoke to reporters afterward and expressed his confidence that problems would be solved.[70]

At the end of November 1972, the *Times-Dispatch* reported that university officials presented the "extensive renovation" planned for "the Medical College of Virginia" to Governor Holton and to Delegate Smith and Senator Willey, MCV alumni who also headed the respective appropriations committees in the legislature. This plan went beyond earlier proposals, with renovations of West and North Hospitals to be part of an interconnected hospital complex anchored by the new hospital, which would have a central emergency room, central operating rooms, and a diagnostic x-ray center. If approved, site work for the new hospital would begin in late 1973, with construction completed in mid-1978, and then renovation of the existing hospitals would follow, to be done by 1981. The positive financial feasibility report from the consulting firm accompanied the plans.[71]

Nonetheless, the discussions of problems at the Medical Campus convinced some parties that it was an opportune time to seek the secession of the Medical College of Virginia from the university. Rumors circulated widely enough that the *Richmond Times-Dispatch* reported them on 29 November 1972. David Hume proceeded to nip the secession in the bud. On 30 November he wrote to Richard A. Michaux, former board member and president of the Richmond Academy of Medicine, that he had learned that Michaux and other MCV alumni planned a meeting to discuss secession. Hume declared that neither he nor the other members of the Department of Surgery desired "whatsoever to secede from VCU." Most of the medical school's problems were the responsibility of the state government, and other matters, such as the administrative structure for the hospitals, "can be, and I think will be corrected within the framework of VCU without any need to consider secession or any such radical move." If the alumni really wanted to aid their alma mater, Hume declared, they would drop the idea of secession and "exert every ounce of effort they could to induce the legislators to vote favorably on the bond issue for the new hospital construction." David M. Hume could be impatient and impetuous, but he consistently championed the university as the right solution for the Medical College of Virginia's future.[72]

The *Virginia Commonwealth University Self-Study* appeared in late 1972, and its comments on the hospitals emphasized the need for change. There was "a dire need to renovate all areas of the hospital, in-patient care facilities, outpatient care facilities, faculty areas, and classroom areas." Poor pay and working conditions led to low morale and heavy turnover, with resultant shabby maintenance. "In summary," the *Self-Study* declared, "there is general agreement that the University Hospital in 1972 is in serious trouble."[73]

The January 1973 VCU presentation to the General Assembly emphasized the dire need for a new hospital. The Medical Center was down to two hundred births per year (compared to two thousand births a year just a decade ago), and the hospital also was losing physicians. But years of planning ensured success: "Key to our proposal is our ability to finance the cost of capital construction by improved operating efficiency," Vice President for Hospitals John Imirie wrote. That is, rather than running deficits, the new university hospitals would pay for themselves. The package for the legislature also included letters from professional societies, including the Medical Society of Virginia and the Richmond Academy of Medicine.[74]

The proposed bond issue won unanimous approval from both houses of the legislature in February 1973. The revenue bonds, in the amount of $78.8 million, would finance the construction of a new 558-bed hospital and renovations at West and North Hospitals and the A. D. Williams Memorial Clinic. Governor Holton signed the bill for the bond issue on 12 March 1973, and present for the occasion were pharmacy graduates Delegate W. Roy Smith, Delegate Carl E. Bain, and Senator Edward E. Willey.[75]

The day after the ceremonial signing of the bill for the hospital, Brandt sent a memorandum to "VCU Faculty and Staff" informing them that M. Pinson Neal, assistant vice president for health services, had been named provost, with responsibility for coordinating the activities of Vice President for Health Sciences Lauren Wood and Vice President for Hospitals John Imirie. The medical school's complaint that Brandt's organization by vice presidents reduced the physicians' say about hospitals had been heard. Brandt's explanation for the change pointed to the increased activity at the MCV Campus that would follow the legislative success, and the fact that he could no longer neglect the rest of the university. The provost position would enable him "to provide a more balanced effort to the needs of the total university."[76]

Regardless of its virtues, the appointment of a provost had a specific origin. Senator Willey had cracked the whip in a letter to Brandt in late February. "It was the understanding of Roy Smith and myself that the Board of Directors would take immediate action to restore the identity of the Medical College of Virginia and would have appointed one key man to oversee a complete operation of the medical school and its facilities." He continued, "We further understood that this would be done immediately and on this agreement we proceeded to introduce and have passed the legislation calling for the construction and reconstruction of the facilities at MCV."[77]

Willey went on. He conceded that "all medical schools in order to receive accreditation must be part of a university." Nonetheless, he had a warning: "Believe it or not, there is still a strong feeling among the majority of members of the General Assembly that the consolidation of the two schools was a mistake and there is still some discussion that the former status of the two schools should be restored." He closed with a request that Brandt "please let Roy and me know what progress is being made in this regard."[78]

Brandt passed Willey's letter along to Rector Wyndham B. Blanton Jr. in early March. He would soon announce Neal's appointment, he told Blanton. As for the identity issue, "the law requires MCV as designation of schools on the East Campus." The Board of Visitors would have to decide how to placate Willey and his fellows, and the university would do whatever the board decided. Brandt, in the end, could not hold back a comment about the senator: "Nice guy!"[79]

That occurred behind the scenes, however, and for most observers the long struggle to improve facilities at the Medical College of Virginia Campus had resulted in a great victory. Then, on 19 May 1973, came the news that David Hume's airplane—he was an enthusiastic pilot—had crashed into a mountain in California. The brilliant chair of the Department of Surgery, a pioneer in transplant surgery and an advocate for the university, was dead at the age of fifty-five. His untimely passing left a void. "His unbound, youthful enthusiasm was infectious and readily transmitted to people around him," wrote his colleague, Dr. H. M. Lee. "To him, there was nothing impossible."[80]

The board took almost a year before acting on Senator Willey's demand regarding nomenclature. At the 21 February 1974 meeting, after much discussion, and with two members opposed, the board resolved "that the designated name, Medical College of Virginia, shall be used in all publications, communications, and other printed matter issued by the Medical College of Virginia, Virginia Commonwealth University. In all such publications, communications, and other printed matter, the name, the Medical College of Virginia, shall appear first, followed by Virginia Commonwealth University, in not more dominant type."[81]

At this meeting, President Brandt also sought the board's backing in a dispute with the faculty over tenure policy. As at other universities, faculty members with tenure could not be removed without cause, and Brandt feared that tenured-in departments took away administrators' ability, at a time of declining enrollments, to plan for new programs and to phase out older ones. He wanted quotas on tenured positions. The faculty, viewing this as interference with faculty governance, opposed them. The board put off the issue until the March meeting and then tabled Brandt's quota proposal indefinitely.[82] Faculty members later said that it was typical of Brandt that he brought with him to the board meeting several faculty members who made the case against his proposal. That the board's failure to back him disturbed and angered him also did not surprise.

His accumulating exasperation bleeds through the lines in his letter authorizing Provost Neal to institute the board's nomenclature changes at the Medical Campus. Among other things, Brandt said, the diplomas for

1974 needed to be changed, and if it was too late, "you may just wish to go back to the old MCV diploma." Rather than the "absurdity of coercing The Medical College of Virginia students to come to a VCU commencement to get Medical College of Virginia diplomas," Brandt said, it was better to have a "separate ceremony." The nomenclature change, he averred, must be comprehensive: "The parking permit stickers will need to be changed, for example."[83]

Matters of organization and nomenclature aside, the hospital legislation made imperative the managing of the Medical Center efficiently and without financial losses. It is telling that Barbara Keyser, headmistress of the Madeira School in Greenway, Virginia, and a member of the Board of Visitors, resigned in mid-1974, complaining to Governor Mills Godwin that the board "is basically concerned with the business of running and building hospitals and not with the creation of a university." As a consequence of that focus by the board, and with consultants from Booz Allen Hamilton watching closely, the university's long struggle to create and manage a computer network became another source of conflict between the university and the Medical Campus.[84]

The 27 August 1975 issue of the *Richmond Mercury*, which proved to be that publication's last issue, carried a front-page story, "Millions Lost on MCV Computers." The tabloid newspaper charged that between $3.5 million and $7.3 million had been lost through mismanagement. For the *Mercury*, the main charge was that the "computer failures" had been among the "financial mistakes" that caused Warren Brandt's resignation as president one year earlier. Brandt, it went on, had been "the chief proponent for centralizing all computer resources at VCU's west campus" and he "made several key decisions regarding MCV's computers."[85]

One theme that runs through the archival materials on university computing then is Brandt's desire for a centralized system. In fact, when the *Self-Study* was released in November 1973, Brandt informed faculty and staff that a consultant's report on computing at both campuses called for consolidation under one director reporting to the president. Thus, Richard E. Grove, former chair of the Department of Physics at nearby Randolph-Macon College, would become director of university computing activities.[86] Regardless of the virtues of centralization of computing and administration of computing, one cannot resist speculating that centralization might appeal to Brandt, and decentralization might appeal to his critics at the Medical Campus, for reasons beyond devotion to efficient computing.

On the day in August 1974 when Brandt announced his resignation as president, someone at VCU contacted the news media to complain about computers. A local television station broke the news that according to an unnamed source, a still-secret report by Booz Allen Hamilton warned that the hospital billing system had no backup system and, in the event of a breakdown, the hospital might find itself unable to collect money owed by patients. Contacted by the television station, Brandt acknowledged that the consultant's report was critical of elements of the operation at VCU but he pointed out that the computer was operating without any problems at present.[87]

The Board of Visitors' executive committee had met at the end of May with administrators and a representative from Booz Allen Hamilton. All parties promised to work together to develop recommendations for accounting, admitting, and financial management at the hospitals. The executive committee met again on 25 July; this time without Brandt, whose absence went unmentioned. The committee endorsed the goals of the consultants' plan for revising systems at the hospitals, with the acknowledgement that the committee members lacked "the background to adequately comment on the details."[88] It is irresistible to speculate that Brandt resented the board's direct intervention in the management of the computer systems, which might have contributed to his decision to resign. Regardless, there was no public acknowledgement of a disagreement.

Whatever the conflict between Brandt and the consultants, by the end of September 1974, Booz Allen Hamilton had concluded that "net accrued revenue to be generated by the Hospitals will be adequate to meet the debt service payments of the two bond issues . . . that will be used to meet 82% of required capital outlays." This would require "improved financial management systems," as set forth in the consultants' full report, but the project was "financially feasible." Construction of the new hospital could move forward.[89]

By then, Warren W. Brandt was no longer president of Virginia Commonwealth University. It had been a difficult year for him. In late spring he suffered an attack of Guillain-Barre Syndrome, an autoimmune illness that potentially leads to paralysis and death. Brandt, a healthy man before the illness, recovered quickly but walked with a limp for some time after. No one blamed his illness for the resignation, and his decision came as a surprise to many. Brandt simply said that he decided to look for opportunities elsewhere and felt that honor required him to inform the board that he could not continue as president. The board accepted the resignation as of 1 October 1974, when Brandt would become a consultant to the board.[90]

Before that arrangement could take effect, the announcement came that Brandt had accepted the presidency of Southern Illinois University. The *Carbondale Southern Illinoisan* sent a reporter to Richmond to learn more about Brandt's tenure at VCU. He found that faculty and others spoke highly of Brandt. Although many agreed that pushing VCU's identity was his "most controversial decision," faculty speculation had it that his inability to get backing from the Board of Visitors for the quota system for tenure earlier in 1974 most likely led to his resignation. Several persons said that Brandt had magnified disagreement with the Board of Visitors into conviction of "a full-scale lack of support," and that, they felt, explained his resignation. Yet, all agreed that the resignation was voluntary, and, the reporter concluded, "Brandt apparently has no skeletons in his closet."[91]

The 29 August 1974 issue of *VCU Today* summed up Warren Brandt's tenure as VCU's first president. Not only had the university grown but the strength of the faculty lifted VCU into the top 100 universities, as measured by grant support. The requirements for tenure, promotion, and hiring, all developed under his aegis, had professionalized the faculty, while a structure for faculty governance—the Faculty Senate as well as the University Assembly—was now in place. The university added thirty-two degree programs and two new schools, the School of Allied Health Professions and the School of Community Studies. More than $20 million in construction had been completed or started, including the School of Business building (later Harris Hall), the Pollak Building, Cabell Library, an addition to the gymnasium, the Lyons Dental Building, an addition to Sanger Hall, an addition to Tompkins-McCaw Library, the Multiphasic Health Testing Center, the MCV parking deck, and the Science-Education Building; not to mention the hard-fought effort to build and renovate hospitals.[92]

That fall, a historian at Southern Illinois University named Eugene P. Trani spent his spare time working on the successful congressional campaign of Paul M. Simon, the only political campaign Trani ever gave himself over to. One evening, as he drove into Carbondale from campaign stops, he saw on the marquee of a local bank: "Welcome President Warren W. Brandt."[93]

4

T. Edward Temple and the Comprehensive University

VCU's FIRST rector, Virginius Dabney, published a history of Richmond in 1976; he concluded the book with a portrait of the city in the mid-1970s. There were plans for economic development of the dilapidated blocks in the "Main-to-the-James" section of downtown, and the "local business community" still viewed the Downtown Expressway as essential for that development. The expressway opened in 1976, after nearly a decade of delays by opponents who saw it as a barrier between the city and the river, separating Main from the James. The trench for the western part of the expressway had been gouged through Oregon Hill and other neighborhoods south of VCU several years earlier.

In the mid-1970s, the legal challenge to the city's annexation of twenty-three square miles of Chesterfield County—largely residential neighborhoods with white voters—remained in the courts. Because of the legal battle, no elections for city government had occurred since 1970. Meanwhile, in 1971, the legislature had imposed a temporary moratorium on annexations that also remained in effect.[1]

The annexation ban dismayed Dabney, as he strongly believed that merger of the city with the surrounding suburban counties was "the city's greatest single need." He wrote that perhaps the opposition in the counties to consolidation was because of Richmond's reputation for snobbery. Assuredly, he knew better. He complained in his book about "compulsory busing" for school desegregation even though "nearly all whites and many blacks" opposed it. In addition, "because of busing," thousands of white children had departed city schools for the whiter neighborhood schools of the suburbs.[2]

In fact, Dabney mentioned only in passing earlier in the book that in 1971 federal judge Robert H. Merhige had ordered the consolidation of the public schools of Chesterfield and Henrico Counties with the Richmond city system. The Richmond City School Board, having implemented busing within the city, now proposed cross-district busing as a means of preventing the deepening racial segregation of city schools because of white flight to the suburbs. Both Chesterfield and Henrico Counties fought against any connection with the city. The struggles over school desegregation and annexation created a toxic environment for Governor Linwood Holton's efforts to encourage economy in government through regional cooperation. Holton's commissioner of administration, T. Edward Temple, a former city manager, favored a voluntary merger of the three localities but admitted in early 1971 that it was unlikely to happen.[3]

Merhige's 1971 cross-district busing decision was appealed, of course, and on 10 January 1972, in the case of *Bradley v. Richmond*, the U.S. District Court approved Merhige's decision. People prepared, some very unhappily, for a consolidated school district. The conservative Fourth District Court of Appeals then ruled on 10 June 1972 that Merhige's decision exceeded his power by proposing to restructure local governments. Thus, busing continued in the city, and the counties remained refuges for white flight.[4]

The possibility of a new busing order for Richmond remained until the U.S. Supreme Court ruled against a Michigan plan to consolidate city and county schools. The decision in that case, *Millikin v. Bradley*, was announced on 25 July 1974, not long after the twentieth anniversary of the *Brown* decision declaring racial segregation in the schools unconstitutional, and a month prior to Warren Brandt's resignation at VCU.[5]

Dabney closed his history of Richmond with optimism, thanks to the city's institutions of higher learning. He made special mention of construction at VCU, both at the Medical Campus and the new School of Business building and the expansion of Cabell Library at the Academic Campus. Yet, Dabney separately noted the preeminence of the Medical College of Virginia and the "physicians of wide repute" that it employed and produced. That combination—an ambitious program of construction for a modern university set in motion and the persistence of a separate identity of the Medical College of Virginia—might well sum up VCU's first years.[6]

Two VCU professors of education, Howard Ozmon and Sam Craver, published in 1972 a pamphlet, *Busing: A Moral Issue*, in which they reported on a survey conducted by a local biracial organization, Citizens for Excellent Public Schools. CEPS took no stand on busing but "found that most Richmond residents responding to the survey favored school consolidation and 73 percent felt that the racial mix resulting from consolidation would have 'a beneficial or neutral effect on a child's education.'" Desegregation, Ozmon and Craver explained, was more popular than busing.[7]

Their work exemplified the scholarly engagement with the community expected of the urban university, and that commitment was widespread at VCU then, hurried into existence by the conflicts and problems that Dabney described. Yet, the city's problems also impacted VCU's image, and before the university's first decade had passed, administrators preferred the label of comprehensive university.

FOR A variety of reasons, the divisive issues of the late 1960s and early 1970s seemed by 1974 to have calmed. Observers of college students had already begun to lament their apathy and to recall with nostalgia the days of student engagement. At VCU, on the evening of 4 March 1974, six naked male students sprinted down Park Avenue from Harrison Street to the corner by the library building, where they leaped into a waiting automobile and departed, to the cheers of the expectant crowd that had encouraged them with chants of "Streak, streak, streak." The national fad of streaking— dashing about in the nude in public—had come to VCU. On being told of rumors that streakers were expected at Capitol Square, Governor Mills Godwin called for arrests and proclaimed, ambiguously, that "nudity is offensive to the great majority of our people and it invites far more serious consequences from those with latent tendencies in that direction."[8]

Spring break at VCU may have delayed copycat streakers for a week, but on 19 March the sights, or the prospect of them, attracted a large crowd to Franklin Street, where they saw a few streakers and, almost as quickly, the Richmond police force. Seventeen people were arrested, only four of them for indecent exposure (out of a total that night of some forty naked sprinters), and according to witnesses, the police enthusiastically employed excessive force on the arrested (most for disorderly conduct). President Brandt and other administrators quickly arrived at the scene, and there was a report that they had confronted nonstudents at the scene who were intent on blocking the street to protest the police.[9]

By 1974, although Richmond's outpost of the counterculture still centered north of VCU on Grace Street, it had overflowed southward onto the Academic Campus. As novelist Lee Zacharias recalled of volunteering in a Big Brother/Big Sister program then: "Our recruits might be among VCU's straightest students, but by then mainstream youth had so assimilated hippie style that it was not always apparent at a glance who were the

Marxist girls and who the Young Republicans."[10] If Richmonders had grown accustomed by then to men and women in hippie clothes and long hair, the police seemed to view such dress and hair as predictions of law breaking. Streaking was the least of it, from their perspective. The Richmond police could not distinguish between students and nonstudents, and, in fact, neither could the public. The serious students and hardworking faculty belied the image of VCU as the countercultural school, yet, in truth, it was the least conventional of the state's universities. Thus, both reality and image widened the separation in the eyes of the public between VCU, the hippie school at the Academic Campus, and MCV, the white-jacketed medical school.

This normalization of the counterculture also reflected a shift away from the political radicalism of the late 1960s, which had challenged fundamental premises of the society and the university. Following the example and embracing the rhetoric of the civil rights movement and, at VCU, of the Students for an Afro-American Philosophy, other groups, most notably women and gays and lesbians, demanded a more equal, and public, place at VCU. Directives from the federal government for affirmative action to increase the numbers of blacks and women among students and faculty arrived—suddenly, it seemed—in the mid-1970s. Not only that, but also the economic events of the decade—energy crisis, recession, and inflation—changed the terms of debate for higher education, too.[11]

These new issues arose in a period when the basic governance of the university seemed settled. Creation of university governance policies, including the first-ever tenure system, were among numerous achievements mentioned after Warren Brandt announced his resignation in August. Until his successor could be chosen, the Board of Visitors appointed a committee to run the school. T. Edward Temple, the former chief administrator for Governors Godwin and Holton and since September 1973 vice president for development and university relations, would chair the Interim Administrative Committee, the remainder of which consisted of the two provosts, Pinson Neal and Frank Brooke, and, as consultant, H. I. Willett. The same group, with Willett as committee chair, would join representatives from the Board of Visitors, the administration, the faculty, and the student body on a presidential search committee. The *Commonwealth Times* invited students to use its columns to weigh in on the qualities needed in the next president.[12]

One oft-mentioned candidate for the presidency, naturally, was T. Edward Temple, who, as chair of the triumvirate in charge, was, as the *Times-Dispatch* put it, "in effect VCU's acting president." Temple was known as a "crack administrator," but "state sources" also noted that his health—a heart attack in November 1972—and lack of a doctoral degree were disadvantages. The College of William and Mary announced in early 1975 that it would award him an honorary doctorate, and that degree seemed to dissolve objections to Temple as VCU's second president. Despite a formal search for a new president, most observers had considered Temple the leading candidate from the time that he became chair of the Interim Administrative Committee.[13]

Theodore Edward Temple, born on 15 November 1915, was a native of Prince George County, Virginia, a rural enclave southeast of Petersburg. He attended the College of William and Mary, graduating in 1937. He then taught school at Hopewell, near where he grew up, before being named the town's manager. Following World War II, Temple served as a city manager in Greenville, South Carolina, and then city manager for Danville, Virginia, another textile mill town. While in Danville, his service as a Methodist layman brought connections that led to an appointment to the Board of Visitors for his college alma mater. There he played an important supporting role in the decision in 1962 to give full independence to the Richmond Professional Institute.[14]

By then, Temple was deeply implicated in the City of Danville's hard-line resistance to desegregation. When blacks sought access to the public library in 1960, Temple tried a compromise—removing all tables and chairs and banning browsing—that hardly satisfied anyone. Matters turned violent in response to protest demonstrations in the summer of 1963, and by means of police violence and judicial repression the city's segregationist leadership postponed desegregation in Danville. Temple lagged behind rather than led the segregationists, but he went along. The experience, for all, was stressful, and Temple referred to health problems when he resigned as city manager in December 1966. A few days later, he joined the administration of Governor Mills Godwin as director of the new state Division of Planning and Community Affairs. Although his tenure at Danville might suggest otherwise, many persons testified that he had, in the words of Governor Linwood Holton, "an uncanny ability to pour oil on troubled waters." Holton named him in January 1970 to serve as commissioner of administration, essentially the governor's chief of staff. Holton recalled that Temple had the respect of agency heads, and thus his appointment would soothe the uncertainty that many state workers had with the advent of Virginia's first Republican executive since Reconstruction. Following the successful implementation of Holton's reorganization of the executive branch in 1972, Temple took the formal cabinet position of director of administration. Typical of the roles he played for Holton were his meetings with David Hume and other VCU physicians protesting conditions at the Medical Campus and with student leaders after the killings at Kent State.[15]

While serving in Governor Godwin's first term, he commuted to Williamsburg to earn a graduate degree in education. After VCU got underway, he taught in the evening college for the Department of Urban Studies. "There were a number of 'militant' students in my class at that time, and simply having worked with them, having taught them was the most challenging and rewarding experience I've ever had," Temple recalled in 1975.[16]

His familiarity with the university and its students must have been an attraction when the opportunity arose in fall 1973 to become vice president for development and university relations. The campaign for governor in 1973 had marked another milestone in the development of the Republican Party in Virginia, as conservatives convinced former Governor Mills Godwin to run against populist Democrat Henry Howell, and Republicans convinced Godwin to do so as a Republican. There might have been a place for Temple in a second Godwin administration, but he had suffered a mild heart attack while part of the Holton cabinet in 1972, and the university post no doubt looked to be less demanding than the upper echelons of state government. Reportedly, he also had an offer of a professorship at the University of Virginia, but, in his own account, he agreed to serve for a time as vice president at VCU but told Warren Brandt that he really looked forward to teaching, not administrating.[17]

THE BOARD of Visitors met on 12 September 1974. Provost Neal reported that consultants Booz Allen Hamilton were evaluating the hospitals' end-of-year accounts to show that hospital revenues could pay for the construction bonds approved in 1973. The "proposed 'friendly suit,'" he went on, would then be filed by 5 October 1974, with a hearing in November and a ruling in January 1975. The minutes give no further description of this "friendly suit," but its purpose was to test whether the type of state-issued bonds designated to back the construction of the new hospital could in fact be used for that purpose under Virginia law. The executive committee of the board then constituted itself as the Presidential Search Committee, the rest of the board became the Presidential Selection Committee, and with the members of the university-wide Presidential Search Assistance Committee, they would determine qualifications for the next president. The board also created the University Interim Administration Committee at that meeting.[18]

The Faculty Senate met not long after, and its president, historian Alan Briceland, then sent a letter to the members of the Interim Committee conveying support from the senate but also expressing concern that the two provosts might act separately and further divide the university. The senate, he declared, had been a force for unity within the university and thus desired that the university "grow as one diverse but integrated body." Brooke, Neal, and Temple responded with strong assurances that individually and together they were committed, as Neal put it, "to the integrity and growth of the University." They would do so under conditions of fiscal stringency. The governor's office informed all state agencies on 2 December 1974 that budgets had to be cut by 3 percent and all positions vacant for a year were abolished.[19]

The issue of nomenclature (and behind it, issues of centralized administration and of the nature of the university) persisted. If only through exhaustion, the university's leaders seemed to have settled on a policy of autonomy for the campuses in nomenclature while professing commitment to the university's unity in action, as Temple and the provosts had done in their replies to the Faculty Senate. Evidence of this outlook appeared in a feature story about VCU by veteran journalist Shelley Rolfe in a series he did on local universities in the *Richmond Times-Dispatch* in October 1974. Rolfe noted that "many believe" that Temple would be named president. He also repeated anonymous "suggestions" that Warren Brandt had offended "MCV sensibilities" and he highlighted the opinion of a man not connected to VCU but aware of the situation who averred that Brandt had paid insufficient attention to the legislative mandate that "called for each of the campuses to have a high degree of autonomy."

The evidence of the article, however, also showed a commitment from top administrators to the urban university. Both Dean of Medicine Warren Pearce and Dean of Dentistry John DiBiaggio professed that the merger had given the whole school vitality. They pointed to increased numbers of black and female students as a source of that vitality. In addition to the MCV Hospitals becoming the "city hospital by default," stronger connections to the city came through the family practitioner program, started in 1973, and a new community health program directed by Jean H. Harris,

MCV's first African American graduate in 1955. Rolfe noted that the Academic Campus was known in Richmond "as a rather raffish place," but student activism had declined, and students had even voted to abolish student government. Quoting Temple's opinion that VCU had "just scratched the surface," Rolfe declared that VCU's mission remained open but full of possibilities.[20]

Six months later the presidential search neared an end. On 19 April 1975, the *Richmond Times-Dispatch* reported that the Presidential Search Committee would consider Temple and Rector Blanton among the short list of candidates for the job. The Board of Visitors must have discussed the presidential search at its meeting on 17 April, but the minutes do not record it. As it happened, that meeting was interrupted by the sad news of the death of William T. Sanger, the president of the Medical College of Virginia (1925–56) and strong supporter of the university.[21]

The semester's final issue of the *Commonwealth Times*, on 2 May, reported that the new science and education building (later Oliver Hall) was on schedule for completion in July. The university had also closed 909 West Franklin Street (Scott House) as a women's dormitory, disappointing the dozen students who wanted to continue quiet living without the distraction of male visitation. The house, then still owned by Mrs. Elizabeth Scott Bocock, who also lived there and set the visitation policies, cost the university more in upkeep than the students paid. By moving offices into the house instead, the university could use state funds for maintenance and repairs.[22]

The spring semester ended with VCU graduating its largest class to date. Temple officiated and then prepared to go to Williamsburg on 1 June to receive an honorary doctorate from the College of William and Mary. Students and faculty departed for the summer, and the campus quieted.[23]

The Board of Visitors thus found parking spaces available when it met on Wednesday, 28 May. Vice Rector Buford Scott presided and presented to the board the qualifications of three candidates for president, two of them from outside Virginia. After discussion, Scott told the board that the committee had recommended the internal candidate, T. Edward Temple. The board agreed. Scott addressed the press after the meeting. Temple was "a top-flight administrator who knows his way around the General Assembly," he said. He also declared that in his short tenure in charge, Temple had "done more to draw old Richmond Professional Institute (RPI) and the Medical College of Virginia (MCV) together than Dr. Brandt did in five

T. Edward Temple, second
president of VCU, delivers his
inaugural address, 4 December
1975. Note the first VCU logo on
the podium. (Virginia Commonwealth University Libraries)

years as president." Temple said that the meeting and the announcement
were surprises to him.[24]

The announcement made Temple's scheduled remarks to the reunion of
the MCV Alumni Association his official first event as president of VCU.
He described his role in overseeing RPI as part of the William and Mary
system, his study of the Medical College of Virginia hospitals for Governor Holton in 1972, and his membership on the Study Commission on
Higher Education, which had proposed the merger. He told the alumni
that the commission saw a never-again "opportunity in Virginia to bring
together two schools, each unique in its own way, that could contribute to a
great urban university." He promised that they would hear him say many
times "that this emerging urban university will indeed become one of the
great urban institutions in America." When he referred to "MCV/VCU," it
was unclear whether he meant the Medical Campus alone, but his enthusiasm for the university and the medical school was evident.[25]

In April 1975 the *Commonwealth Times* had published a photo of the
Broad Street facade of the Sanger Building at the Medical Campus, with

its enlarged letters "MCV-VCU" at the top of the building. The caption asked, "Remember when the university used to be called simply VCU?" No one does, it went on, and, "according to the 'official' story," MCV-VCU was now the proper name for the Health Sciences Division. "Know anybody who goes to RPI-VCU?," it asked.[26]

The sarcasm was perhaps merited, but Temple confirmed that the Medical Campus was now called MCV/VCU in his first interview with the *Commonwealth Times*. The student journalists suggested that if that were the case, why not declare the merger a failure and leave VCU to the history books? Temple demonstrated his diplomatic skills here, too. Not only had the faculty, via the Faculty Senate, developed strong cross-campus relationships, but the absence of a president for a year was "a blessing in disguise." The two provosts served with him on the Interim Administrative Committee, and "it afforded us an opportunity to see each other's problems on a first-hand basis. . . . It was a grand experience and we built a lot of bridges."[27]

Temple's immediate agenda had a clear focus. The university needed a budget for submission to the legislature in January, and the planning depended on moving targets. A decline in the expected numbers of students justified delay in construction of a student commons, but the steady pressure of inflation had also raised the cost of construction such that the university could not afford it, regardless. Allied to fiscal management of the university was Temple's promise to reform the administrative structure by undoing the separation of functions that Brandt had overseen after the 1973 dictation from the legislature for greater autonomy at the medical school. He planned to install "one administrator who will be responsible for business, budget and management details on both the academic and health sciences campuses."[28]

Above all, he intended to improve VCU's image in city, state, and nation. Dismay about VCU's poor image had existed from the time of the merger, but it became an institutional concern following the accreditation self-study in 1972–73. An "Ad-hoc Committee on University Image," including faculty engaged with marketing and communication, grew out of the self-study, and the Interim Administrative Committee had called on it to develop a report on the university's image. The committee members all came from the Academic Campus, which explained the focus there, but the preliminary report, in March 1975, declared that VCU was "seldom perceived as being a first class" institution, and safety and security issues hurt, too. The report was blunt: parking was difficult, lighting was poor, and the campus was generally filthy.[29]

On 19 June 1975, Temple made his first report to the Board of Visitors as president and spoke about the university's image. "It is important that the image improvement program begin with the students," he declared, but he promised further discussion, inside and outside the university. By then, he had received the Image Committee's reports from surveys of Richmond residents and of guidance counselors. The latter group thought well of VCU but noted that "the old R. P. I. art school image" persisted. The main image problem, according to the guidance counselors, was "that of being an inner city university" and unsafe. Richmond residents agreed that location was a problem for VCU. Only a scant majority of city residents considered the school a safe location at night. Suburbanization, desegregation, and crime had taken a toll. Indeed, at the end of that year the city's iconic downtown department stores, Thalhimers and Miller & Rhoads, announced that neither would remain open in the evenings. Spokesmen for both stores attributed the closing to competition from suburban shopping centers, but the closings left the city's one-time retail center even darker at night.[30]

The VCU image report skirted the problem of persistent racial prejudices ("current visuals may tend to highlight minority appearances") and proposed emphasizing instead "that VCU is at the hub of the Fan district, is well lighted and patrolled, etc." No one seemed to notice that VCU had become the name associated with the Academic Campus, and MCV was a different place.[31]

As Temple's image-improvement campaign began, the university could take pride in the upgrading of library facilities at both campuses. The new addition to Tompkins-McCaw Library opened at the Medical Campus on October 11, 1974. Built at a cost of $2.2 million, it nearly tripled the size of the existing facility. Then, during exam week in the spring 1975 semester, the three-story addition to James Branch Cabell Library on the Academic Campus opened for students to use (although the 140,000 volumes to be shelved there did not move in until June). Gerald McCabe, director of university libraries since 1970, proudly declared that the libraries now were fully up to the building standards expected of a research university.[32]

PRESIDENT TEMPLE'S immediate problem was that the friendly suit regarding the hospital bonds, which Provost Neal mentioned to the Board of

Visitors in September 1974, had resulted in April 1975 in an unfriendly decision from the state supreme court. The court ruled that "it is illegal to use the interest from the sale of public bonds to construct the hospital when there is no sure way of guaranteeing the amount of income the hospital will bring in during a year." Even though the consultants from Booz Allen Hamilton had attested to the hard-earned conclusion that the hospitals could run a profit, the state constitution blocked construction financed by such bonds, a major setback to a project that had been planned since 1966. But all hope was not lost, for the court had merely prohibited the state from backing construction with 9-C bonds (some $78 million of the total projected cost of $89 million). Revenue (9-D) bonds might do the trick, if the legislature approved. Provost Neal sent a message to faculty and staff that planning would continue, and university officials warned all that patient safety and accreditation were at risk without action.[33]

At the Board of Visitors' meeting on 18 September, President Temple announced that brokers in New York City had declared bonds for the hospital "very marketable." At a time when inflation steadily undermined cost estimates, pushed by the unprecedented surge in energy costs following the oil embargo of October 1973 to March 1974, the months of delay meant the cost of the project would grow substantially. In October, Temple estimated that the construction would require $130.9 million over the next ten years, an increase of nearly $50 million over the expectations in 1973.[34]

None of these issues mattered when the university paused on 4 December 1975 for the inauguration of its second president. The procession stretched from the Franklin Street Gymnasium, where the delegates and faculty participants donned their robes, south down Laurel Street to the Mosque (later Altria Theater), where a sizeable audience waited. Reflecting Temple's years in government, three former governors joined Governor Mills Godwin and Lieutenant Governor John Dalton among the officials present. Dr. Wyndham Blanton, the rector, served as master of ceremonies and introduced dozens of guests who brought official greetings from students, alumni, governments, other universities, and learned societies.

Then T. Edward Temple came to the podium, waited for the applauding audience to sit again, and began his address. It was confident but sober. "We are now in an era marked not only by scarce resources, but also some public skepticism of all institutions," he said. He spoke of a "malaise of spirit that permeates our society" and of "our social disorientation." Rather than asserting the promise of an urban university to solve social problems, which had been the theme of Warren Brandt's inauguration, Temple declared that American universities "can become lighthouses of hope to dispel the clouds of doubt and frustration," and he dedicated VCU "to being one of these lighthouses of hope to help build a better world." Old friends then gathered to congratulate him at a luncheon, followed that evening by a reception at "the Larrick Student Center on the MCV campus."[35]

With funding for the hospital going before the legislature again, and with a higher price tag than in 1973, the MCV Hospitals had to generate profits enough to repay the bonds. Confident testimony to that effect from Booz Allen Hamilton was essential. On 12 December 1975, Temple announced that Gennaro J. Vasile, a trained hospital administrator and a former consultant for that firm, had been chosen to be assistant provost for MCV. The Board of Visitors had created the position in accord with recommendations in the "MCVH Management Enhancement Recommendation," presented at the board's September meeting. Vasile would also be able to speak authoritatively about finances. Less than a week later, at the board's December meeting, Temple reported that the fire marshall found 133 violations at MCV Hospitals, some of which would require significant funds to resolve. The bonds would pay for needed renovations as well as for the new hospital.[36]

Governor Godwin gave a recommendation to the hospital project in his annual budget message to the legislature on 19 January 1976. VCU's administrators geared up to lobby for the proposal, for without the project there "was very real danger of loss of licensure and accreditation." Hunter H. McGuire Jr., the acting dean of the medical school, asked the alumni for support and reminded them that the hospitals were old and had been "designed for racial and economic segregation." The new consolidated hospital would be far more efficient.[37]

Meanwhile, a major dustup at the School of Dentistry occurred amid the campaign for the new hospital bonds. In the November 1974 issue of the MCV Alumni Association's *Scarab*, John DiBiaggio, dean of the dental school, announced proudly that the school had received "a grant for $100,000 for this year, $300,000 next year, and probably $300,000 the following year to train dental students in the management of dental teams." He judged that the school probably had received "the largest grant of this kind in the country at this time."[38]

Training in Expanded Auxiliary Management (TEAM) was a national program, sponsored by the Department of Health, Education, and Welfare, to prepare dental students and students training as dental assistants and hygienists for teamwork arrangements in dental practice. From the perspective of public health, the program promised expanded dental care for Americans, which Dean DiBiaggio had long endorsed, but the program also aroused concern among practicing dentists that nonprofessional auxiliaries would be trained to do work properly reserved for dentists.[39]

In August 1975, the State Board of Dentistry announced that it stood by its previous rulings that the treatment roles for dental assistants, "such as placement of fillings and temporary plastic restorations," proposed in the TEAM program, actually "require professional judgment" and could not be performed by assistants. The board implicitly criticized the School of Dentistry by condemning the Department of Health, Education, and Welfare (HEW) for coercing state dental schools, via grants, into advocating changes in the laws of dental practice. VCU's TEAM leaders apparently then appealed to the Virginia Dental Association (VDA), and its executive committee "voted 13-to-3 in favor of public hearings on the issue." HEW agreed to extend the grant until the board responded to the hearings, scheduled for 1 November 1975.

Before that could happen, though, Dr. Robert R. Waller, the head of the TEAM program at VCU, called a news conference to declare that the state board had interfered, illegally, with his right to teach. Joining him at the news conference was a representative of consumer advocate Ralph Nader who denounced the "dental cartel" for blocking lower-cost treatments by paraprofessionals. VCU's Board of Visitors met the next day, and Temple explained the TEAM program and noted the future public hearing. The board unanimously resolved support for the freedom of the university to determine its own teaching programs, "with full respect for the laws of the Commonwealth."[40]

The hearing changed nothing. At the next Board of Visitors meeting on 20 November, DiBiaggio reviewed the TEAM grant and the issues with the VDA and the state board. After discussion, the board resolved, unanimously, to seek a change in the present laws that made the TEAM program unlawful. Meanwhile, the dental association's executive board so resented the October press conference (especially the consumer advocate's comments) that it first asked the ethics committee of the Richmond Dental Society to investigate the propriety of the news conference and then it recommended that the VDA itself censure Dr. Waller and Jonathan D. Nash, clinical director at the School of Dentistry.

At the board meeting on 18 December, Dean DiBiaggio presented "a proposed modified program in the management of dental auxiliaries," which the board approved in a divided vote. Opposition to the TEAM program grew stronger, and, frankly, VCU needed the support of the VDA in obtaining the new bonds to construct the hospital. At the meeting on 15 January, the board agreed that the November resolution about changing the state law regarding dental practice was "permissive . . . and not mandatory." President Temple then reported on the meeting he and Rector Blanton had with the executive committee of the VDA, which ended with the VCU leaders asking for the VDA's backing for "the Hospital Bond issue." The executive board of the VDA met on 25 January 1976 and recommended that the VDA "support the capital outlay providing for a revenue bond issue for the construction of a new hospital in connection with the Medical College of Virginia and renovation of existing facilities."[41]

As crucial as the hospital construction and renovations were, VCU had other budgetary requests, even after abandoning immediate plans for the student commons building. Governor Godwin did express support in his budget address for the proposed music and theater building but said nothing about the proposed health sciences building. VCU requested a regular budget of $86 million, but the governor recommended just $70 million. The MCV Hospitals fared a bit better with a recommendation of $102 million, but it was still several million dollars less than requested. As William O. Edwards, director of university relations, explained to the MCV Alumni Association, "MCV and the total university will be in a period of austerity during the next biennium (1976–1978)."[42]

On 19 February 1976, Temple told the Board of Visitors that Robert C. Kidd II had been hired as executive director of MCV Hospitals, succeeding John Imirie. Just days before, Temple had sent an impassioned letter—three full single-spaced pages—protesting the meager funding allotted to VCU compared to that allocated to the other state schools, to Delegate Edward E. Lane of Richmond, chair of the House Appropriations Committee. Lane assured Temple that the bond issue for the hospital would pass and suggested that VCU keep a low profile in the session.[43]

The board met again in March 1976, after the legislature adjourned. Temple presented his administration plan, eliminating the "fragmentation of responsibilities" at VCU's campuses that caused inefficiencies. The plan called for three new positions—"a provost for administration, a director of operations, and a director of administration information management."

The new provost, Temple assured the board, would be equal in responsibilities to the other two provosts, with each reporting directly to Temple, as would the recently hired university attorney. Temple also planned to leave vacant both the vice presidency he once held and a new vice presidency for planning and operations to save funds enough to move forward at least with hiring the provost for administration. The Board of Visitors approved his plan.[44]

The legislature had, as promised, approved the hospital bond issue, but, important as that was, from the university's perspective the new hospital was a matter decided in 1973. There were new requests now for construction, but they went nowhere. Funding for the planned health sciences building, which was to be an extension of the already crowded Sanger Hall, had been cut by 25 percent, and the "Music and Drama Classroom facility" received nothing at all. Temple emphasized to the board that the reorganization would free him for long-range strategic planning and for interactions with outside organizations. After the legislative session, he did not have to say out loud that VCU needed more friends in high places.[45]

On 9 April 1976, the University of Connecticut named John A. DiBiaggio, the dean of the School of Dentistry since 1970, its new vice president for health affairs. DiBiaggio declared it was a "unique opportunity." The leaders of the TEAM program also departed. Dr. Nash left VCU for the University of Pennsylvania that summer, and Dr. Waller moved to public health service in Chicago and later worked at the Centers for Disease Control. Temple did not mention the departures in his address to the annual meeting of the MCV Alumni Association. He did state that the demise of the TEAM grant program in the dental school was "a disappointment," "a controversy," and "confrontation that we would have preferred not to have experienced."[46]

Despite the success with the hospital bonds, Temple judged the 1976 legislative session a great disappointment. As he explained to a distressed student in July, the state expected now that students' tuition must cover 30 percent of the cost of their education. With the miserly appropriation VCU received, doing that would require tuition to increase by as much as 12 percent. That was too much, and Temple had informed the faculty on 9 April that VCU would hold the tuition increase at the Academic Campus to 6 percent and, instead, defer hiring of additional faculty and staff.[47]

He told the MCV Alumni Association at the end of May that VCU "should have fared better." All that he asked was that the legislators "treat us in the same manner as they treated other comparable institutions." That is to say, "the General Assembly was not aware that we ranked with the University of Virginia and Virginia Polytechnic Institute and State University." His administration had prepared documentation that showed "beyond a shadow of a doubt that this institution does stand as a *comprehensive* university." That decision on how best to present the university to the legislature marked a move away from VCU's original identity as an urban university. If the change in terminology to "comprehensive university" had little effect with the legislature, it appealed to VCU administrators. Not only did "comprehensive university" have a specific meaning that associated VCU with the state's two largest universities, it also aided efforts to change VCU's image, an image of shabbiness, mediocrity, minorities, and general unconventionality that the words "urban university" tended to conjure up.[48]

The indifference of the legislature to VCU's legitimate needs required action. The school put together the case for VCU's role as one of Virginia's three comprehensive universities, and Temple would take it to the governor, his cabinet, to the Richmond legislative delegation, and to the state of Virginia. "We are equals in the diversity and quality of programs, in our research effort, in our health care services, and in our community services," he declared. That VCU was a comprehensive university was hardly hyperbole, for the American Association of University Professors rated it one of Virginia's three comprehensive universities (of 150 nationwide) and the National Science Foundation included VCU in its list of the top 100 universities measured by research effort. Clearly, reputation lagged reality. "This will be both an image building effort, as well as an effort to assure adequate funding from future sessions of the Legislature," Temple promised. "We will take the message across the Commonwealth."[49]

VCU would need the support. As the rate of college enrollment dropped across the nation, the school revised downward the projection of 30,000 students by the 1980s to just 20,000 students, with 17,500 of them at the Academic Campus. The revision did not change the university's construction needs—an additional 500,000 square feet of classroom space and the same of dormitory space, plus a parking deck, on top of the unmet requests of the past legislative session—but fewer students meant less in state funds based on enrollments. Improving VCU's standing in the state had to be top priority for Temple and, as he told the MCV Alumni Association, he was "counting heavily" on the administration, the alumni, and "every friend of the institution to give us the support we so badly need in the days ahead."[50]

As THE smoke of the legislative session finally cleared, and Temple's first year as president ended, the administration could take time to assess legal controversies of national import involving the university. The case of *Cramer v. Virginia Commonwealth University* began when the Sociology and Anthropology Department hired James A. Cramer as an instructor just prior to the start of the 1973 fall semester. Cramer indicated his preference to seek future employment in the Washington area by setting up residence in Rockville, Maryland, and commuting to Richmond for his classes. He did apply, somewhat half-heartedly, for the two permanent positions that the department advertised that year, but accepted employment with the University of Maryland and withdrew his application at VCU. Two women were hired at VCU, and Cramer learned that the department had separated out applications from women for special consideration. He eventually filed suit in June 1975 against the university, with Cabell Venable—the attorney for Curtis Holt's suit against the city of Richmond's 1969 annexation and for Vincent Wright's suit against Brandt and VCU—as his lawyer. In one of Warren Brandt's last meetings with the Board of Visitors, he warned: "We have been told that Mr. Cabell Venable is trying to work up a reverse discrimination case involving VCU. Last year, VCU had a white male teaching sociology on a one-year appointment, and he is being replaced by a white female. We do not think he has a good case."[51]

Cramer had by now accepted a position at Georgetown University, but he sought employment and back pay from VCU and an injunction against sex-based discrimination in hiring, based on the prohibition of such discrimination in the Civil Rights Act of 1964. In early 1976, his lawyers met with the university's lawyers and agreed on a stipulation of the facts in the case. Cramer dropped his demand for payment and employment. Thus, with the facts before him, on 28 May 1976, Judge Dortch Warriner found for Cramer. Warriner's opinion, released on 1 June 1976, complained that VCU's affirmative action plan, and plans like VCU's, perpetuated past discriminations—"there will never be sex or racial peace until the idea of sex and racial discrimination is dead and buried"—and must be ended. Poor Cramer, Warriner declared, had been "flattened by the civil rights steamroller." To be sure, he acknowledged that the two women hired were qualified, but they should not have been selected over Cramer solely because they were women.[52]

Temple informed the university community that with the court having found VCU's affirmative action plan unconstitutional, new or vacant positions must be filled "without taking into account the applicant's sex." He promised that the board and administration would determine shortly whether to appeal the decision. The filing deadline loomed when the executive committee of the Board of Visitors authorized an appeal on 23 June 1976. According to the committee, Judge Warriner's decision presented VCU with such problems for "the administration of employment practices" that the issues "should be resolved by a court of appeals." President Temple emphasized that the executive committee had taken no position on Warriner's reasoning, but, he explained, "to use a layman's phrase, we're caught between a rock and a hard place." On the one hand, Temple continued, the federal Department of Health, Education, and Welfare pressed the school "to employ minorities, both blacks and women," but the judge declared implementation of that policy unconstitutional. VCU had "nothing to lose and everything to gain," he concluded.[53]

Historian Dennis Deslippe argues that in the fifteen years prior to *Regents of the University of California v. Bakke* in 1978, when the Supreme Court approved "preference programs" to create a diverse campus without using quotas, cases like Cramer's challenging affirmative action hiring came from a variety of positions, including liberals defending a color-blind policy. Only later did opposition to affirmative action become largely associated with conservative political views. He notes, too, that many cases then arose in higher education, where the ideal of meritocracy in admissions and employment was strong, with far fewer legal challenges arising from either the military or private enterprise.[54] VCU's appeal did not change the court's original decision, although another three years passed before the case finally ended with a dismissal in March 1980.[55]

The other consequential case involved the Gay Alliance of Students, which began its two-year struggle for official recognition as a student organization in September 1974. The *Commonwealth Times* reported that month on "Homosexuality: A Normal Life Style," a headline that reflected the American Psychiatric Association's then-controversial 1973 decision to no longer define homosexuality as a mental disorder. The article noted that many remained closeted but there was a group called "gays." "These men," it said, "openly participate in the public world of gay bars and organizations such as the Mattachine Society and the Gay Awareness Group here on campus."[56]

That group, officially called the Gay Alliance of Students (GAS), petitioned for recognition as a student organization on 9 September and again on 2 October. Richard I. Wilson, vice president for student affairs, and other administrators seemed sympathetic but felt it safer that the decision be made by the Board of Visitors. Thus, Wilson and James Mathis, chair of the Psychiatry Department, appeared at the board's October meeting to report on the GAS. Much discussion followed before the board adopted the following resolution: "With deep regard for the severe human problem involved, it is expressed as the sense of the Board that the Gay Alliance of Students not be registered."[57]

Rector Blanton's statement afterward that registering the GAS might, at least potentially, have bad effect on perceptions of VCU, might hamper fundraising, and might reduce state funding did not impress the *Commonwealth Times*. Editor Paul Woody noted on 1 November that the GAS had been told of the decision but had not yet responded. The GAS might go "to the actual courts," he predicted. Another reporter spoke with unnamed gay students who considered the decision blatant discrimination, and an editorial declared that the Board of Visitors had taken "a step backward." In January 1975, four student organization leaders sent a petition to leaders of more than one hundred VCU student organizations asking them to join in requesting that the board reconsider its decision, "which was discriminatory, pure and simple."[58]

Historian John D'Emilio suggests that advocates of gay and lesbian rights began shifting strategies in the mid-1970s from the initial liberating, even revolutionary, act of "coming out" to more reformist strategies of changing discriminatory laws and policies and creating organizations and institutions to make a visible community. The Gay Alliance of Students fits that pattern, and in April 1975 the group took the Board of Visitors and VCU to court. The GAS contended that it had requested VCU's recognition because the members wanted to offer a telephone "hotline" and thus needed to use school facilities, which required official status. The civil suit pointed out that of the 145 student groups requesting university recognition since 1968, only one, the GAS, had been denied. For its part, VCU's leaders seemed to welcome the suit. As an unidentified member of the Board of Visitors told a reporter, the board considered the issue a hot potato and wanted "to make the courts force us."[59]

Led by Walter A. Foery, its president, the GAS obtained assistance from the Virginia branch of the American Civil Liberties Union and from the National Gay Task Force and the Lambda Legal Defense and Education Fund, and Richmond attorney John McCarthy took the case. The case went before conservative Judge Dortch Warriner, who had ruled against the university in the case of *Cramer v. VCU*. His decision was a curious compromise, ruling that VCU could not be compelled to recognize the organization but it did have to extend to it several privileges granted to recognized student groups. In fact, Assistant Dean of Students Stephen Lenton had served as the group's advisor throughout, and what Warriner proposed as a solution was close to the status quo.[60]

The Gay Alliance of Students had argued that VCU's refusal to recognize it violated constitutional rights, and thus it appealed the decision. VCU appealed, too. After another year, on 28 October 1976, the Fourth U.S. Circuit Court of Appeals upheld the group's argument that the university could not withhold privileges just because it disagreed with the group's ideas. There was no evidence that the GAS was breaking any of the state's antihomosexual laws, and, "the opinion pointed out, homosexuality itself is permissible and protected by the U.S. Constitution." More important, the university had rejected the GAS because of the nature of the issues that the organization would highlight. Such a limitation on the exercise of First Amendment rights must demonstrably "serve a substantial government interest," and, because it did not, VCU had also violated the group's rights under the Fourteenth Amendment. The court ordered VCU to register GAS with all privileges offered to other student organizations.[61]

When the board next met, on 18 November, Walter Ryland, assistant attorney general and lawyer for the university in the case, "reported that, in essence, the court gave the group everything that it had asked for." He advised against an appeal, and the board unanimously agreed to let the decision stand. Walter Foery, president of the GAS at the beginning of the story, and Steve Pierce, acting spokesman for the group, were gracious in victory, promising that the group would be of service to VCU. Pierce rightly suggested that Judge Howard T. Markey's concurrent opinion expressed well the principle involved: "It is of no moment, in First Amendment jurisprudence, that ideas advocated by an association may to some or most of us be abhorrent, even sickening. The stifling of advocacy is even more abhorrent, even more sickening. It rings the death knell of a free society."[62]

Two years later, the University of Richmond's student paper reported on the constricted environment there for gay students. A university official said that the school's gay students "probably" associated with the Gay Alliance of Students at VCU: "The VCU community is more open and accepting of homosexuals." The student newspaper at the College of William and Mary also reported on the Gay Alliance of Students' battle, and Assistant Dean Lenton told its reporters that a recent dance at VCU had seen students from W&M present.[63]

Meanwhile, the university's faculty, many recruited into fledgling departments just a few years before, came into its own. Salaries, as always, were a source of complaint, and Temple lobbied the state for salary equity for VCU faculty. The problem was that the State Council of Higher Education had a benchmark system for faculty salary budgets based on an expected distribution of academic ranks. VCU's profile reflected its youth; the more recent hiring of faculty resulted in more of them at the lower ranks. A year later, Frank Brooke reported to Temple that some 85 percent of the faculty had joined VCU since 1968, and only 31 percent of the faculty held tenured ranks of associate and full professor. Temporary faculty, called adjuncts, however, handled only 14 percent of instruction.[64]

Salaries might be a problem, but a faculty largely at the lower ranks exhibited energy and made for fewer potential obstacles for new ideas to be tried. For instance, three faculty members in the School of Education, Howard C. Garner, Jack D. Glover, and Howard Ozmon (coauthor of the 1972 pamphlet on busing), formed a band called the East Virginia Toadsuckers, playing old-time string music, often for laughs. They performed regularly at the university and even made an appearance on the popular country music television program *Hee Haw*.[65]

Academic accomplishments, of which a few examples must represent the remarkable whole, also testified to the creative energy on both VCU campuses. In 1974, the university established a cancer center on the MCV Campus with a planning grant from the National Cancer Institute (NCI). A year later, under the direction of Walter Lawrence Jr., a former president of the American Cancer Society, the center received a Cancer Center Support Grant from the NCI, making it one of the few among the nation's cancer research centers to receive the NCI's designation as a leader in the field. The School of Nursing introduced a Family Nurse Practitioner Certificate Program in 1973, admitted the first class in 1974, and in 1975 became the first such program in the state to prepare family nurse practitioners at the master's degree level. The School of Business moved into its own building in 1972, which then was connected via overhead walkway across Main Street to the new home for math, chemistry, and physics and the School of Education, named Oliver Hall in honor of RPI's second leader on 9 October 1976. On the MCV Campus Frederick Spencer initiated an innovative program in preventive medicine, and the Department of Physiology doubled in size between 1971 and 1977, becoming the Department of Physiology and Biophysics. Meanwhile, following the resignation of Warren Pearce as dean of the School of Medicine, Jesse L. Steinfeld, the distinguished former surgeon general of the United States, became the dean in 1976. In fall 1974, the program in urban studies, spearheaded by Harlan W. Westermann, became the Department of Urban Studies and Planning, and the new Department of Political Science, under Nelson Wikstrom and with seventy-five majors, separated from the Department of History. Meanwhile, several historians joined with colleagues in other departments to establish the Richmond Oral History Association, published two volumes of the *Journal of the Richmond Oral History Association* (1976–79), and laid the groundwork for Cabell Library's strong oral history collection. Cabell Library's opening in 1970 made possible the reinstitution of fine art exhibitions at the former library building, behind the Lewis Ginter House, known as the Anderson Gallery, which quickly became "the visual front for VCU's School of the Arts." Frances Wessells established VCU's program in dance in 1975, and the VCU Dance Company performed its first formal concert in April 1976. The Virginia Museum of Fine Arts sponsored a Virginia Designers Show in 1975 that included work by four VCU students and three faculty members. One of the latter, Philip B. Meggs, the chair of the Department of Communication Arts and Design, won a prize for his design of the first official *Virginia Commonwealth University Faculty Handbook*.[66]

Ann M. Woodlief arrived in Richmond in 1971, when her husband became a resident in radiology at the MCV Hospitals, and she joined the English Department a year later. She remembers that teachers felt free to develop ideas for new courses and new ways of teaching. By 1976, she had convinced her department chair to add the department's first course on women writers, which she taught. In developing a course on nature writing, her own writing subject became the James River, long fouled by pollution and official indifference. In 1975, a decade of dumping the nonbiodegradable insecticide Kepone into the James River south of Richmond at Hopewell came to light when contaminated workers were brought for treatment at the MCV Hospitals. Governor Godwin closed the now-poisoned river to fishing from Richmond east to the Chesapeake Bay, a ban that lasted into the 1980s, and all these developments received national news coverage. Citizen activists in Richmond, with Newton Ancarrow and Louise Burke prominent among them, fought not only to clean the James River but also to transform its course through Richmond into a public park. Among the river's defenders associated with VCU were political scientist Ralph Hambrick and Reuben B. Young, a pediatric endocrinologist. Woodlief told the story of the activists as part of a larger story of the river from its origins to a potentially healthier future in her 1985 book, *In River Time: The Way of the James*. "I don't know what it's like teaching at VCU now," Woodlief said in 2010. "But I tell you it was great then."[67]

NOTWITHSTANDING PRESIDENT Temple's plan to herald VCU as a comprehensive university known for its range of academic programs and the level of research funding, VCU's evening school defined the university for many Richmonders in traditional terms of urban universities as service centers for working students. VCU had the second-largest overall enrollment of Virginia schools, behind only VPI, as 1976 began, but according to John A. Mapp, the dean of the VCU "evening college and summer sessions," VCU was second in the nation only to the University of Cincinnati "in night school enrollment."

The evening school program had its origins in the earliest days of RPI, when a class offering that might attract too few students during the day to pay—and Dean Henry Hibbs expected classes to pay for themselves—would, if scheduled in the evening after work hours, bring in enough working students to make a go of it. The program got underway in 1920 with 174 students. Rozanne Epps, the assistant dean, said that the old practice continued with departments often scheduling less-popular courses in late afternoon or evening to catch working students.

The numbers caused crowding. The enrollments had jumped in the mid-1960s, and "we've never caught up since then," Mapp said. Classrooms were in use at VCU from morning until late at night, while adjunct faculty typified the teaching force, comprising nearly half of the total faculty in the evening school—260 of 560 teachers. The evening school benefited VCU, of course, but the students also benefited. Many other universities separated their evening programs by treating them as "extensions or continuing education programs," but VCU offered sixty-four degrees through the evening school. Mapp was justifiably proud of his still-growing program and predicted that "the day will come when VCU has more part-time later afternoon, evening and weekend students than full-time students."[68]

If Mapp had not been such a modest and collegial person, people might have seen him as an empire builder. He managed the summer school—some 7,500 students in 1977, with nearly a third of them from other universities—and initiated the Christmas intersession, the first in the nation, in 1973. As important, he persuaded the local newspapers to circulate a catalog for the evening college and summer sessions with regular editions of the newspapers. Everyone in the Richmond region could consider attending the evening school.

VCU's Evening College in 1977 became the largest in the United States. In the spring 1977 semester, the Evening College offered about 900 courses. The formal enrollment in the Evening College was more than 5,900 students, but some 16,600 VCU students took at least one course in the evening, far ahead of the next largest evening school.[69] As the evening school's flourishing suggests, the idea that VCU was a comprehensive research university for the state of Virginia, as Temple was preparing to propose, would take some explaining, at least in Richmond.

Suddenly, a major problem with the basketball program arose. From the early years of Warren Brandt's presidency, basketball had been the centerpiece not only of the sports program but also of efforts to build community support. As Brandt explained to Governor Holton in 1970, basketball "could become a strong rallying point for a unified thinking with regard to Virginia Commonwealth University." The consequence, of course, was that problems with the program would receive public attention, too.[70]

On Tuesday, 26 October 1976, with practice for the coming season getting underway, President Temple announced that basketball coach and athletic director Chuck Noe had resigned. Lewis Mills, assistant athletic director, would become athletic director, Temple said.

Coach Noe held a press conference at the Holiday Inn–Downtown that Tuesday afternoon. He was uncomfortable, a contrast to his usual affable persona. He said that his resignation came from a mistake he had made the previous Friday in the firing of a new assistant coach, Harley "Skeeter" Swift. According to Noe, Swift came to his office on Thursday, 21 October, and stated that he was resigning. Mills later confirmed that Noe informed him that night about Swift's resignation. The next morning Swift came to

Noe again and tried to withdraw his resignation. Noe refused and, when Swift demanded his job back, fired him.

Members of the basketball team later described friction between the coaches in practice sessions. On learning of Swift's dismissal on Friday, the team discussed the situation and voted to meet with President Temple. Most of the team seemed to side with Swift, although all worried about what might happen to their scholarships if they refused to practice.

Temple informed the players through Swift that he wanted to meet with them, and he took the situation seriously. There would be no practice on Sunday, he told them, but he asked them to return for him and for the school. The players practiced on Monday under the direction of Charley Moses, a pharmacist and former assistant coach, who told the players that Temple wanted to meet with them at 4:30 p.m. A player asked that Temple speak privately with each player. He agreed, asking each whether he would still play for Noe. On Tuesday, Noe submitted his resignation, and Temple asked Mills to become athletic director. Noe and Temple each denied that he had been forced to resign.

On Friday, 5 November, less than a month before the season's first game, Dana Kirk was announced as the new basketball coach. Kirk had experience as a head coach at the University of Tampa, but more recently and more importantly, he had been an assistant coach under Denny Crum, coach at the University of Louisville, also an urban university and boasting a basketball program among the nation's very best. Athletic Director Mills said that Kirk was authorized to hire an assistant coach, too.[71] Led by Gerald Henderson and Lorenza Watson, the Rams posted a 13–13 record in the 1976–77 season. Such results, under the circumstances, left fans looking forward to the next season.[72]

In the midst of the controversy, on 20 November 1976, President Temple suffered the loss of his wife, Polly D. Temple, a teacher herself, after months of ill health (she had been too ill to attend his inauguration a year before). He threw himself into his work, setting out with a cluster of administrators on his promised statewide effort to make Virginians aware of VCU as a comprehensive university. Temple's presentation argued that comprehensive universities had previously emerged in three ways: older universities grew out from an arts and sciences core, state universities developed from an agricultural and mechanical emphasis via the Morrill Act (1862), and a third set of universities began as normal schools training teachers. VCU was different from all in origin but had "a mega-university structure more complex than any of the traditional universities in Virginia." In effect, he sidestepped the identification of VCU as an urban university, and his argument enabled a rhetorical remerger of RPI and MCV. Temple declared that it was out of the merger of "two fully developed and comprehensive professional institutions that the Commonwealth's third truly comprehensive university serving statewide and national needs was formed." By 1977, VCU offered 136 degrees in 91 separate fields of concentration and "terminal-practitioner degrees in 28 separate fields." About 18 of these 136 programs were unique in Virginia.[73]

That the commitment to presenting VCU as a comprehensive university had not fully erased the urban university showed clearly in a mission statement adopted on 18 February 1977 by the Institutional Planning Task Force. VCU was "a comprehensive, urban, public university," the statement began, and "its thrust" was education of citizens to deal with "society's increasingly urban-influenced problems, wherever these problems may exist." The university's mission included provision of education, scholarship, the arts and humanities, health care services, and, finally, "establishment of the University as a planning and resource center which, drawing upon the unique resources of a major urban area, is devoted to the solution of problems confronting Virginia's communities." Rather than VCU's reason for being, however, the city had devolved to an accident of location, of which the university would make the best.[74]

In two weekly issues in February 1977, the *Commonwealth Times* published feature articles on the histories of the Medical College of Virginia and the Richmond Professional Institute, respectively. A third, and final, article, published in the issue of 1 March, recounted the history since the merger of those institutions into VCU. The article told about the Bird Commission on Higher Education and the Wayne Commission and declared, correctly, that "the RPI-MCV merger was welcomed by some people and despised by others," although the only critics mentioned were "many MCV faculty members and alumni." VCU had continued "the unique contributions made by its parents," it had become one of the state's three comprehensive universities, and it had maintained an "urban emphasis." To be sure, budget cuts and enrollment slides had delayed some of the school's bigger plans, and "it may be some time before MCV students admit that they also attend VCU," but the school was only nine years old. VCU was "blessed with time ahead."[75]

Just two days after the final basketball game of the 1976–77 season, on Sunday, 6 March 1977, Theodore Edward Temple, VCU's second president, died at the MCV Hospitals, after suffering a heart attack on Friday. As the *Richmond Times-Dispatch* put it, he became president in May 1975 "with the task of ending the internal conflicts that had plagued the merger." He had "revamped the administrative structure," built up the university's reputation, and brought about "a new MCV hospital." Governor Godwin ordered flags at the state capitol lowered to half-staff until after Temple's funeral and he himself served as one of his friend's pallbearers.[76]

The *VCU Magazine* expressed well the effect of the news: "Never in its history has the university community received so great a shock as at the sudden death of President T. Edward Temple." Grief was universal. He was that rare leader who seemed without enemies.[77] The Board of Visitors convened on 17 March 1977 and, among other business, adopted a new mission statement that declared VCU "a comprehensive, urban, public university." The addition of that first adjective to the statement was the lasting achievement of Temple's too-short presidency. At the meeting the board also adopted a resolution of sorrow at his passing. "No man could have given more of himself to move our university closer to its goals," the resolution stated. "Indeed, he gave his life."[78]

ON 1 MARCH 1977, less than a week before President Temple died, Richmonders cast votes for a new city council under rules established by federal judges. The legal challenge to the annexation of white residential neighborhoods in Chesterfield, which had prevented city elections since 1970, finally came before the U.S. Supreme Court in 1975. The court, with Justice Lewis Powell, of Richmond, recusing himself, found that the annexation was racially motivated, but it was divided on the remedy. The case returned to the Washington district court, which in August 1976 by way of remedy affirmed the annexation and called for councilmanic elections in nine single-member districts. Under the old system of at-large, citywide elections, whites might have kept control of city hall, but the 1977 election brought a black majority to the city council. White leaders reacted to the results with surprise and foreboding. The *Richmond Times-Dispatch* and the evening *Richmond News Leader*, both under the same ownership and, as the *Washington Post* put it, "often voices of racial stridency in the past," offered polite congratulations and cautious hope for unity. Even white incumbent Councilman Henry L. Valentine II, known as a relatively progressive official, expressed uncertainty. "It's a whole new ball game," he said.

President Temple's sudden passing caused the executive committee of the Board of Visitors to meet on 10 March. The consensus at the meeting was that H. I. Willett, former superintendent of Richmond Public Schools and consultant to VCU's presidents since the university's founding, should either chair a governing committee or be acting president on his own. One member recalled that Temple had chafed at the committee structure after Brandt's resignation, but Willett, who was present, explained that Temple's problems arose from the fact that he was also a candidate for the presidency and a member of the Presidential Search Committee. Willett must have known that his own age, seventy-one, was against him as a candidate for the presidency. The main issue for the board committee was to make the presidential search as expeditious as possible. Again, Willett stepped in to remind the board that the last search had set a precedent for involving the university community in the process. A new president would need acceptance from all elements of the university, he said, and a proper search would ensure that. No decision emerged from the meeting, and the committee adjourned until the board meeting scheduled for 17 March.[79]

On 17 March, Henry Irving Willett Sr. accepted the board's request that he serve as interim president of VCU. A native of Gloucester County, Willett graduated from the College of William and Mary, began his career as teaching principal of a school in Smythe County, and came to Richmond as superintendent of public schools in 1946. He held that position for twenty-three years, through Massive Resistance and early desegregation, before resigning in 1969. At VCU, he handled public relations, lobbying, and other duties assigned to him by the presidents. Willett held three honorary doctorates—from his alma mater, Washington and Lee College, and the University of Richmond—but he did not use the title. Willett's appointment also meant that he joined his son, H. I. Willett Jr., the president of Longwood College (later University), in the state's "first father-son team of college presidents."[80]

A couple of weeks later, the *Commonwealth Times* introduced President Willett to the university via a feature article. Willett saw himself very much as caretaker for the university between presidents, and his plans reflected Temple's priorities. The administrative team—vice presidents, assistant vice presidents, and the provosts from both campuses—continued meeting weekly, and Ronald Beller, the new provost for administration, who had been at VCU less than a week before Temple's death, proved very helpful, Willett said. Construction projects—the new hospital and new dormitory—were underway, and if voters backed the bond referendum in November, the cancer center and the performing arts center would begin construction, too.[81]

The Board of Visitors disseminated announcements of its search for a new president also in early April. The search committee of seventeen was heavy with administrators but also included a student from each campus. Interviews, the board hoped, might begin in June.[82]

News of the search committee appeared on the same page of the *Commonwealth Times* with a story suggesting that Temple's unexpected passing also marked the beginning of a new era for VCU. Henry H. Hibbs, the founder of Richmond Professional Institute and its provost until 1959, had also died, at age eighty-nine. No doubt many students in 1977 knew Hibbs only as the name of a central classroom building on the Academic Campus, but his legacy was their education. Now, except for the unstoppable Theresa Pollak, all the founders of RPI and MCV who were present at the merger had passed from the scene. The search for the next president promised to bring new direction to the university.[83]

5

Edmund Ackell and the Comprehensive Research University

THE BOARD of Visitors' meeting on 23 March 1983 marked the fifth anniversary of Edmund Ackell's tenure as the third president of Virginia Commonwealth University. The meeting occurred in the midst of budget cuts mandated by the governor, but, nonetheless, it measured the advances at the university under Ackell's leadership. The board took first steps toward developing a plan for fundraising for the university, took out a loan for construction of the Student Commons building, issued bonds for construction of the second phase of dormitories on Main Street (later Gladding Residence Center), and approved resolutions for construction of a parking deck off Main at Laurel Street and for renovation of the gymnasium at the Medical Campus. The chair of the Hospital Committee reported that a year after the new main hospital opened, employee morale there was very good.

Then President Ackell reported to the board. The city of Richmond, he said, had honored the faculty of the School of the Arts for planning interior design projects in the city schools, and the second Richmond Revitalization project, for the Shockoe Bottom neighborhood, was underway with the city and the School of Community and Public Affairs partnering again as they had two years before in Jackson Ward. Meanwhile, the Prague String Quartet had performed at the new performing arts center and praised it as one of the finest venues in the world. The cancer center had been dedicated just four days before, a new Army Reserve officer training program was approved, and the basketball team, after winning the regular season Sun Belt Conference championship, lost by just two points to the University of Georgia in the NCAA tournament. And, not least, the university was engaged confidently in the self-study required for reaccreditation by the Southern Association of Colleges and Schools.[1]

Edmund Ackell's initial five years (of a dozen) at VCU, climaxed by the university's successful reaccreditation process, saw him put his stamp on the school by reorganizing financial and governance systems. In Virginia, as in the nation then, urban problems awoke faculty and students to the original mission of the urban university, at the same time that limited resources and anti-urban prejudices made problem solving difficult. President Ackell thus continued the trend initiated in President Temple's years to identify VCU more as a comprehensive research university than as an urban university. Yet, SCHEV envisioned only a limited role for Virginia's urban universities as commuter schools, without the doctoral programs that measured research university status. For cities and their universities, there was no easy way forward.[2]

The city of Richmond during those years saw the long-delayed arrival of the African American majority in city politics, with bitter power struggles along racial lines ensuing. The state government prohibited future annexations, leaving the city surrounded by white-majority suburban counties where legacies of white flight bolstered reluctance to engage with urban problems. Meanwhile, in national politics, inflation and then recession, reinforced by the election of the conservative Ronald Reagan as president in 1980, reduced federal funding of new programs for cities to the disappearing point.

VCU faculty in African American studies, political science, sociology, and urban affairs, among others, took up the city's travails as their research subject. Urban affairs professor Morton Gulak's planning for Richmond Revitalization provided a hopeful direction for the city in an era of limited resources and of preferences for individual, private solutions to urban problems. Books by faculty authors analyzed the city's annexation struggles, conflicts between black political leaders and white economic elites, and the compromises that brought relative peace to city government after 1982. Those books recount Richmond's history vividly but with remarkably little to say about any part that VCU might have played in it.[3]

VCU's relationship with Richmond changed as the university changed. The *Self-Study* noted that the 1977 mission statement, adopted just after President Temple's death, shifted the "dominant concept" from urban university to comprehensive university. Institutional priority statements in 1981 and again in 1983 still emphasized "comprehensive," but "the scope of the constituency has broadened" to the state and the nation. Edmund Ackell's first five years pushed VCU a long way toward conceiving itself to be a comprehensive research university.[4]

BACK IN 1977, on 20 June, Acting President Willett and the board happily gathered, after more than a decade of planning and politicking, at the groundbreaking for the new hospital building. His short tenure had begun with a petition to the Board of Visitors signed by six current student leaders and contending that Vice President for Student Affairs Richard I. Wilson and other employees of the Office of Student Life dominated student government, thereby usurping student rights, and operated the Office of Student Life as their own fiefdom.[5]

The petition reflected long-simmering problems regarding student governance. The death knell began with President Brandt's University Assembly, with representation for students and a subassembly, the Council for Undergraduate Student Affairs (CUSA), with nine students among its fifteen members. The Student Government Association saw the CUSA as a rival, and a rival with an official function that the SGA lacked. A referendum in 1971 then produced a majority for disbanding the SGA—it "died by student hands," said Dean Jane Bell Gladding. Without an elected student government on the Academic Campus, the CUSA handled important issues, such as rescinding the ban on fraternities and sororities, and created a media board, under its jurisdiction, to provide some oversight for the *Commonwealth Times* and other student outlets. Efforts in 1973 to revive the SGA failed, though, and the absence of an independent student government seemed to support the continued charges of student apathy justifying the status quo.[6]

In fact, VCU's student culture had never fit the image of "college life," to use Helen Lefkowitz Horowitz's terminology, of extracurricular activities founded on fraternities and sororities at a residential campus. In fact, Horowitz argues, that image had ever fit only a minority of college students, with the larger portion being "outsiders" there to gain career advantages from higher education. Certainly, the Richmond Professional Institute, which banned Greek organizations, had always positioned itself as serving such students, and as ever-higher tuition and ever-larger student loans became facts of life at all institutions, students with an occupational orientation—the "New Outsiders," Horowitz dubs them—came to characterize college life generally.[7]

Even so, from a student-centric perspective, faculty and administrators at VCU had a rather large role in student affairs. The defeated 1973 student government proposal caused the CUSA to create an appointments board to choose students for service on governing boards, including the appropriations, media, and program boards, along with the CUSA and the University Assembly. In 1976, the *CT* pointed out that the vice president for student affairs chaired the CUSA and faculty and administrators served on the student boards. The May 1977 petition to the Board of Visitors reflected long-standing concerns as well as its specific charges.

The board asked Willett and the Student Affairs Committee to investigate, and at the 18 August meeting it received and approved the "Report of the Committee on Student Affairs of the Board of Visitors and the Administration Committee of VCU." The board agreed that the complaints merited efforts to make student government, largely run out of Wilson's office since the SGA's demise in 1971, more a student-run operation. In the meantime, as at other schools, student activists—the "rebels," as Horowitz dubbed this student group—tended to migrate to the staffs of student newspapers, as VCU's new president would discover.[8]

THE BOARD of Visitors met at the President's House on Franklin Street at 9 a.m. on 17 November 1977. After a short discussion in executive session, the board named Edmund Ackell as the third president of VCU (Willett's interim service apparently did not count in the official succession). The experience with Temple's health no doubt explained why the board conditioned Ackell's appointment "on his receiving a comprehensive medical examination." Ackell himself was present and then joined the meeting to accept the board's offer of the position.[9]

Edmund Ferris Ackell, born in Connecticut in 1925 to Lebanese immigrant parents, came to VCU from the University of Southern California, where he was vice president for health affairs and served the USC president as special assistant for governmental affairs. A team from the search committee had journeyed to Los Angeles to conduct interviews there with Ackell's coworkers, a demonstration that he was a true outsider as president (Brandt came from Virginia Tech, and Temple came from state government). He also brought an impressive resume of accomplishments. Ackell received his dental degree from Tufts University in 1953 and earned an MD at Case Western Reserve University in 1962. In 1966 he became dean of the University of Florida's School of Dentistry, then provost of that university's medical center, and its vice president for health affairs in 1971. In 1974, he moved to USC as vice president for health affairs.[10]

At the press conference after the board named him president, Ackell said that he looked forward to a long tenure at VCU and, as evidence, would begin with long-range plans. Rector Blanton said that he was "extremely pleased" with the selection of a president with a background in health sciences. "It

Edmund Ackell, third president of VCU, in 1986. (Virginia Commonwealth University Libraries)

is hoped that with this appointment, that the new president will be able to handle, and perhaps quell the increased internal conflicts which have erupted over the years between the VCU health and academic campuses."[11]

Ackell did not report for fulltime duty until February 1978 in the middle of the legislative session. As it happened, Virginia voters in November had approved five bond issues, including one for $86.5 million to higher education, of which $5.7 million would come to VCU for construction of the music and performing arts building, one of President Temple's priorities. The burgeoning cancer center at the MCV Campus would receive another $1.5 million. Three months before, in November 1977, MCV Hospitals successfully sold bonds totaling $64.4 million at a "very good rate" of interest, enabling construction of the new hospital to go forward.[12]

Thus, although VCU had several important issues before the General Assembly in 1978, the session, for the first time since the university's creation, did not involve do-or-die requests for funding. The session went well enough, with a budget increase of 39 percent, for which Ackell credited the "Temple missionary work" of the previous year. The basketball team also won attention, finishing with a 24–5 record, the best to date, and participation in the National Invitational Tournament, with coach Dana Kirk and players Ren Watson and Gerald Henderson winning state honors.[13]

Ackell finally sat down to discuss his presidency with the *Times-Dispatch* in late March. His comments then squared with his recollections a quarter century later of his first impressions of VCU. Those who expected (or feared) that he would be partial to the Medical Center might have been surprised. He arrived expecting to head a comprehensive research university, as he had been told VCU was. Yet, the university, he found, was not yet there. Thus, the fine reputations of the medical and dental schools meant that Ackell was confident that he could safely turn away from them to concentrate on the "'duplications and gaps' in the university's organizational machinery." He also planned to expand VCU's fundraising capabilities, which put him on a collision course with the separate, independent MCV alumni society. Ackell was forthright that he wanted "to work for a rebirth of liberal arts," a goal that would mean less emphasis on the Evening School and other nontraditional programs. The *Times-Dispatch*'s headline said that Ackell wanted to "soothe growing pains" at VCU, but his agenda was better suited for shaking up complacency. Most important, it was an agenda to which he adhered.[14]

Not long after Ackell arrived, the university prepared a "Fifth-Year Report" for the Southern Association of Colleges and Schools (SACS), the agency that accredited the school. The report detailed changes— improvements, of course—since the 1973 self-study, and the introduction gave the administrative history of the school and Ackell's plans for its future. The report began with President Brandt's structure of a president and six vice presidents. In 1973, partly on the recommendation of SACS and partly on "recommendations from some State sources," as the report put it, VCU introduced a setup with provosts for each campus. The functions of the vice president for planning and operations then devolved to the separate campuses, under the provosts.

President Temple had announced a new administrative structure in early 1976, which he called "the Transitional Organization." Now there were three provosts, the new one being the provost for administration, who would have directors of seven administrative functions for the campus reporting to him and a direct line to the vice president for finance. Ronald Beller arrived in March 1977 to become provost for administration, just before Temple's untimely death.

The fifth-year report stated that President Ackell had not yet determined "what the future structure of the university will be, however, the direction of his thinking is reasonably apparent." He wanted "a movement toward a more centralized administration in terms of service and auxiliary enterprise areas." He felt that the provost system of administration had served the university poorly, having "brought greater isolation of each campus." Ackell's plan was for a "series of vice presidents" as university leaders. Sounding rather like Warren Brandt in 1969, Ackell believed such an administration was necessary "if we are to develop a university with shared goals and objectives and if we are to operate on the basis of shared resources." Ackell's "direction" could not but disturb those satisfied with the status quo at VCU, and it must have dismayed his provosts.[15]

One of the first indications of change was the announcement in late June 1978 that Dr. Gennaro J. Vasile, interim executive director of MCV Hospitals, had asked President Ackell "to relieve him of his post because he thinks he lacks the president's confidence and support." Vasile had been there only since March but now asked to return to his former position as assistant provost. In April, he said, he had received Ackell's okay for reassigning three hospital administrators and eliminating another, and the MCV provost sent the proposal on to the state's Department of Planning and Budget. Ackell directed that the paperwork be retrieved and canceled Vasile's plan. According to Ackell, Vasile's proposal would have changed twelve positions, not just three, and he did not want to interfere with a future permanent director's freedom of action, but it seems likely that the procedure, which sent Vasile's proposal through the medical school's provost directly to the state, bypassing the university president, must have rankled, too. Ackell told the *Times-Dispatch*, "I am looking at the administrative structure of the whole university," including "directors, staff and philosophy."[16]

The rumor mill began in earnest with the announcement soon after that Provost M. Pinson Neal would step down to become an associate dean for continuing education in the medical school and to return to his professorship of radiology, effective at the end of August. According to the *Times-Dispatch*, a "source who has frequently been reliable" told the newspaper, "The VCU tree is shaking and other big apples will fall soon"; Ackell was "launching a top-to-bottom reorganization of both the academic campus and MCV."[17]

A few weeks later, in mid-July 1978, Lauren A. Woods, associate provost, was named acting vice president for health sciences to replace Provost

Neal. A search for a permanent vice president would soon get underway. The current administrative structure included two assistant provost positions, also to be filled in the future.[18]

The first, and perhaps most fundamental, of the reorganizations effected under President Ackell was the new plan for managing the university's accounting functions. It was hardly the most romantic of topics, yet the inability of the university to generate accurate and timely financial reports impaired its operations in an environment of ever-more complicated requirements for such reporting. The process began in July 1977 for "development and implementation" of a new VCU financial accounting system, which Beller, the new provost for administration, set in motion. Ackell recalled later being appalled by the inability of the university to provide him with financial reports needed for planning. Consequently, he strongly endorsed the reorganization. So, too, did the Board of Visitors, on 15 March 1978.[19]

In addition, the reorganization coincided with the state's development of the new Commonwealth Accounting and Reporting System (CARS). Although the new financial accounting system had origins in earlier administrations, it signaled President Ackell's intention to bring procedural order to what he saw as the dangerously ad hoc style of governance and administration at VCU. The changes took hold, as Ackell told student journalists in 1980: "You know when I got here there wasn't even an inventory for the campus? I've never heard of an organization not having an inventory. Now we're developing an inventory."[20]

THE FEBRUARY 1978 issue of the MCV Alumni Association's *Scarab* carried a portrait of Edmund Ackell on its cover as the association welcomed him to the university. Herbert Boyd Jr., the president of the association, declared that he was impressed by Ackell's "grasp of the situation here." For many alumni, no doubt the headline to the story was enough: "Physician-Dentist to Be VCU Head."[21]

Warm feelings soon dissipated, and the May 1978 issue included a letter from Boyd with a dire warning. The association was "under great pressure from some circles to become a part of the Virginia Commonwealth University Alumni Association," he wrote. "We have been asked to give up our autonomy" and come under the administrative umbrella of VCU. He asked for members to send their comments and promised a special issue of the *Scarab* dedicated to the question of cooperation or autonomy.[22]

The November 1978 issue of the *Scarab* was not the promised special issue, but it did publish responses from alumni to Boyd's request in the May issue. All argued for keeping the MCV Alumni Association. One old grad conceded that time would resolve the issue as more recent graduates would consider themselves graduates of VCU. No one else agreed; they wanted nothing to do with VCU.[23]

That unanimity was misleading, for the association's board continued to negotiate with Ackell about the Alumni Association's future. At the end of November, Ackell gave an ultimatum: he would tell the deans to go forward with plans for separate alumni associations or, if the board requested, he would arrange for one more meeting on the association's future. The board requested the meeting, and in December proposed a new committee be formed to start negotiations again. Then, at the June 1979 Alumni Association meeting, Robert O. Hudgens, the new president, announced that an agreement had been reached: "More than a dozen years of conflict between the organized alumni and the University (its deans, its administrators, and its faculty) now has a strong likelihood of coming to an end."[24]

Money must have also been a problem, for the association published only three issues of the quarterly *Scarab* in 1979. The November 1979 issue gave members the news. The association would remain independent, but its name would become the Medical College of Virginia Alumni Association of Virginia Commonwealth University. That change would have been anathema just a decade before, but time and inflation had done their work. The most important changes were administrative: the address systems for alumni at both campuses would be merged, and the MCV Alumni Association would henceforth request from VCU funding for its annual budget. Now VCU could centralize fundraising and begin planning for the university's first capital campaign. As Virginius Dabney, longtime board member and historian of the university, put it: "Truly there had been a drastic turnaround in the university's alumni affairs."[25]

IN MID-MARCH 1978, early in President Ackell's tenure, press conferences in Washington and Richmond featuring, respectively, officials of the U.S. Department of Health, Education, and Welfare and Governor John Dalton, announced that Virginia and HEW had reached agreement on a plan to desegregate Virginia higher education. As historian Peter Wallenstein explains, Virginia's "previously nonblack institutions" by the 1970s had enrolled black students and hired black faculty and administrators, but those schools "that started out all-white," like the University of Virginia and Virginia Tech, remained predominantly white, and historically black schools, like Norfolk State College and Virginia State College (both became universities in 1979), remained predominantly black. VCU enrolled more black students than any of the state's nonblack institutions, about 17 percent of the student body in 1978, but lagged as badly as the rest in hiring black faculty and administrators.[26]

In 1977, the U.S. District Court for the District of Columbia found HEW's efforts to desegregate higher education in six states, one of them Virginia, to be inadequate (and under Title VI of the Civil Rights Act of 1964, HEW had the power to deny federal funds to noncompliant states).[27] Unlike Governor Mills Godwin, who had refused to negotiate with HEW, Governor Dalton changed course to protect the estimated $75 million in federal funds coming to Virginia institutions. The plan announced in 1978 proposed to encourage white students to enroll at Norfolk State and Virginia State, to give those schools priority when planning new degree programs, and to increase black enrollments at white schools by 150 percent. Dalton emphasized that these were goals, not "quotas," which Godwin had strenuously denounced, and Joseph Califano, head of HEW, praised Dalton for his cooperation.[28]

Two months later, on 28 June 1978, the Supreme Court issued its awaited decision in the case of *Regents of the University of California v. Bakke*. The plaintiff, a white man, contended that he had been denied admission to the medical school at the University of California at Davis because of a "set-aside" of places in the entering class for racial minorities. The court found for Bakke, although in a 5–4 split and with continued permission for universities to value racial diversity in admission decisions. Virginia authorities and HEW officials alike insisted that the decision changed nothing in the state's plan for desegregating higher education, but, at least as symbolism, the *Bakke* decision drained the energy from affirmative action efforts even before the conservative Reagan administration took office.[29]

Earlier, during the spring semester 1978, the League of Black Journalists and the Black Student Alliance sponsored a new periodical, *Reflections in Ink*, to express "the ideas of Black students at Virginia Commonwealth University." *Reflections in Ink* would win financial support as a student activity and continue to publish regularly for more than a decade. The inaugural issue bore a cover photograph of Richmond's first black mayor, Henry Marsh, and included a story on a talk he delivered to a black fraternity social at VCU. Marsh continued the conciliatory theme struck after his election as mayor the year before by the new black majority on city council, installed by voters in the city's first elections since the annexation year of 1970. VCU had connections to two members of the council's majority: Henry W. "Chuck" Richardson was taking graduate courses in urban studies, and Claudette Black McDaniel was and would remain a staff member in occupational therapy at the Medical Campus.[30]

Marsh claimed that despite the controversy aroused among whites by his election, the city council had accomplishments including reversing the ban on outdoor rock concerts imposed by City Manager William Leidinger. More important, the city council had backed the so-called Project One, a plan favored by the city's white economic leaders for a hotel, office building, and convention center in the Broad Street retail district, midway between VCU's two campuses. The May 1978 elections, with racial issues central, returned the black majority to office and continued Marsh's term as mayor.[31]

The council majority had campaigned on a promise to shift the city's resources to the neglected neighborhoods, a change from what they called excessive devotion to downtown commercial development. Inevitably, conflict began to simmer with City Manager William J. Leidinger, who had held his position since 1972. The city's white business leaders viewed city government as serving their interests, and the city manager necessarily saw the economic elite as a most important constituency. Indeed, in 1981, journalist Shelley Rolfe recalled "a half-decade ago, a former Richmond city manager spoke to a college seminar and said, yes, Richmond had an establishment and that he, for one, speaking as a government administrator, was glad that it did because it made his task easier." At the beginning of August 1978, Mayor Marsh informed Leidinger that the majority wanted him gone. Leidinger fought his dismissal and contacted allies in the business elite. In a dramatic episode, white economic leaders privately demanded that the black members of city council reconsider or see development stall and businesses depart for the suburban counties. One of the black council members observed, "They're not used to dealing with black people on their level."[32]

Leidinger's firing won approval from *Reflections in Ink* and the black press, but the white Richmond newspapers condemned the black majority's supposed arrogance and mismanagement. As the *Times-Dispatch* put it on 22 August, "This antibusiness attitude, if it prevails, could be the ruin of Richmond." VCU sociologist Rutledge Dennis and urban affairs scholar John Moeser analyzed these events and concluded that racism, however one defined it, was not the root of the conflict. Rather, political power in Richmond had shifted to the black majority while economic power remained in the hands of whites. Without cooperation, neither group could succeed, but in 1978 the divisions seemed unbridgeable.[33]

That summer, as VCU prepared budget requests for 1979–80, President Ackell faced another decision. The health sciences building, long planned, was to house allied health sciences, nursing, and pharmacy/pharmacology at a site along Broad Street, adjacent to the Sanger Building. The proposed building, however, would require destruction of the old First Baptist Church, constructed in 1841 and named to the Virginia Landmarks Register in 1969. In 1938 MCV purchased the church, which its congregation had abandoned a decade earlier for larger modern quarters on Monument Avenue. Preservationists fought to save the church from destruction, and VCU's complaint that any alternative plan would require construction of separate facilities for each school carried no weight with them.[34]

Governor Dalton heard the preservationists, although it was the fact that federal funds could not be used for construction on a site where a building on the National Register had been demolished that no doubt got his attention. In May 1978, his office asked VCU for a record of all the alternative sites considered for the health sciences building and the reasons for choosing the proposed site at the First Baptist Church on Broad Street. Roger L. Smith, director of institutional research and planning, compiled the report for President Ackell in mid-June. No alternative site would do, Smith told Ackell, and delays and inflation had already forced the architects to scale back the building. As important, he concluded, was that "the University's experience with other 'old buildings'" showed that if the church were saved, making it a "functional building for University use" might be very expensive.[35]

Nonetheless, President Ackell could see the writing on the wall. On 9 August 1978, he informed the governor that the delays caused by the fight over the church site had raised costs of construction too far above the original estimates. The School of Pharmacy had to take priority, as without a new building it might lose accreditation; VCU would seek state funding for a building for that school first.[36]

It took more than a year to ready the request for the legislature, and the university asked for $10 million of the estimated $12 million cost for the pharmacy/pharmacology building. According to Ralph Ware, the university's lobbyist, the breakthrough came courtesy of powerful state senator Edward E. Willey, a pharmacy graduate himself. As Ware recalled, Willey one day told him to be at his office the next day at 10 a.m., with President Ackell. They arrived to find there as well representatives of Virginia Tech's proposed veterinary school and the state's secretary of finance. Willey bid the latter to speak; he told them that the budget would include $10 million for each project. Willey then asked if that would be enough. Delighted, Ware declared that it would be, and the school did raise the remainder of the funds, with the generous aid of Lora M. Robins and E. Claiborne Robins, another pharmacy alumnus. Meanwhile, after several transitions, the old Baptist church building became Hunton Hall in 1989 and the Hunton Student Center in 2005.[37]

All this activity, from his first months as president, reinforced President Ackell's agenda for VCU. That led him to the Faculty Senate and, in almost no time at all, bitter conflict with the faculty about university governance and tenure policy. From the senate's perspective, Temple's presidency had been a golden age of faculty participation, with the senate responding to the president's sympathies by drawing up a set of recommendations, completed after Ackell became president, for an enhanced faculty role in governance.[38] That the new president saw things differently became clear quickly.

One of President Ackell's first opportunities to communicate directly with a university constituency came on 18 April 1978 when he reported to the Faculty Senate on "his observations and activities since his arrival in February." He was brisk and forthright. VCU had lacked administrative continuity in its first decade, he said, and now it was time for a ten-year plan. To that purpose, he was recruiting a vice president for planning and budget. VCU's organizational structure was top-heavy, and he intended to clarify responsibilities and end duplication of effort. He described the university as a "depressing" environment and committed to renovations to "meet minimum civilized standards for very basic facilities." The university needed more space, but it was also too decentralized. Budget woes limited his action, but the governor had included funds in the budget for land purchases "between Main Street and the new highway," in the Oregon Hill neighborhood.

Faculty senators then asked about tenure, and the alarm bells went off. Ackell was confident that tenuring could continue, albeit with planning to account for the expected declines in enrollment, as VCU's tenure rate was not yet a problem. Old timers must have heard echoes of Warren Brandt's 1974 suggestion of tenure quotas as part of VCU's planning. Moreover, Ackell gave his opinion that the current practice of deans granting tenure was probably illegal, as the Board of Visitors was the proper final authority for such decisions. The president spoke about other matters, too, but senators might be forgiven for leaving the meeting thinking only that the new president doubted whether anyone at VCU was legally tenured.[39]

The Faculty Senate's report on university governance was dated 30 June 1978, although revisions continued into the fall. The recommendations, predictably, called for the faculty to have greater power, including a veto for the Faculty Senate over the University Assembly on matters of faculty concern, "such as curriculum, tenure and promotion." The first of the ten recommendations called for the university president to endorse "in principle" the faculty's role in university governance.[40]

Ackell's response to the Faculty Senate's report seemed generally favorable, although he disputed the senate veto over decisions of the University Assembly in matters of faculty responsibility. William Stepka, from the School of Pharmacy and the senate's vice president (and president of the VCU chapter of the American Association of University Professors), replied that he looked forward to discussing these matters at the president's regular meeting with the executive committee of the senate. The monthly meeting between the president and the executive committee was a legacy of the Temple years, and its days were numbered. Ackell then created his own Task Force on Governance in December 1978, with Charles P. Ruch, the dean of the School of Education, in charge, and it first met in March 1979.[41]

The full senate approved the faculty report on governance and called, once again, for the university president to endorse "in principle" the faculty's role in university governance. The senate also suggested seventeen faculty members for his new Task Force on Governance. Ackell rejected all but one of them. In response, the Faculty Senate approved, by a vote of 30–6, a motion expressing "extreme disappointment" that Ackell's process "virtually ignored" the senate and thus showed "a lack of faith" in it.[42]

Those last months in 1978 also found VCU's administration surprised by opposition to plans for new recreational facilities just south of Main Street in the Oregon Hill neighborhood. The 1976 master plan officially abandoned the Wayne Commission's idea of VCU expanding south to the James River, which residents of the Oregon Hill neighborhood had fought since 1968, but the plan left open the possibility of acquiring property on the north side of the Downtown Expressway, which bisected that neighborhood. The long fight against the expressway, a block-wide trench scraped through Oregon Hill, had united residents on both sides of the expressway in a strong neighborhood identity. The leader of the opposition to VCU's plan to take three blocks on the southern edge of campus for athletic fields was Earl Jenkins, who had resided on Cherry Street in the threatened area since 1945 ("We think we have tenure in this instance," he said). Residents would soon organize to oppose VCU, but Jenkins set things in motion by erecting a sign questioning VCU's plans in front of his house.[43]

The first meeting between VCU planners and the new Save Our Homes organization, representing the Oregon Hill residents subject to relocation, convened on 15 December 1978. It went badly. Donald Bruegman, vice president for planning and budget, promised that VCU would ease any hardships for residents, but Earl Jenkins called it just "pie in the sky" and accused VCU of "institutional imperialism." The VCU representatives agreed to carry the committee's request for a meeting to the Board of Visitors.[44]

President Ackell published an essay in 28 December 1978 issue of the *Richmond Times-Dispatch* on VCU as an "urban university in change." The essay described how VCU's commitment to teaching, research, and service, with emphasis on the "university hospitals," benefited the metropolitan region. The essay closed with his account of his administrative changes after he arrived to find the school "over-administered and under-managed." Now, he had a system in place for "improved financial management and accountability." He summed up his first year at VCU with the statement that VCU's "full potential" awaited, making it "an exciting and challenging university." Nowhere did he mention Oregon Hill.[45]

When the Board of Visitors met again on 18 January 1979, protesters from Oregon Hill marched outside the President's House with banners and chants of "Save our homes" and "Shame on you." A meeting between the neighborhood activists and President Ackell was set for 2 February. A few days before, a "teach-in" on campus featuring Earl Jenkins, of Oregon Hill, and university planner Louis Saksen drew nearly one hundred students, who reserved their applause for Jenkins alone. Saksen warned that the university was sure to obtain the land, even if it had to rely on eminent domain—the expropriation of property, with compensation, for public use. Sponsors of the event included Social Workers for Social Action, and the School of Social Work had sent students into the neighborhood to conduct studies for several years previous.[46]

Protests targeted meetings of the Board of Visitors. At the January 1979 meeting, some students joined residents of Oregon Hill to pace the sidewalk outside, and in March the frigid temperature and wind made conditions miserable at Monroe Park for a rally that drew about ninety people. Jenkins promised to keep up the fight.[47]

The Richmond Planning Commission had endorsed in February 1979 a plan for the city to give to VCU two lots, used for parking, situated across Main Street south from the Mosque (later the Altria Theater). What made the arrangement feasible was that the plan to construct a parking deck on one of the lots (where the West Main Street parking deck is today) included use of the deck by patrons of performances at the city's Mosque. Heretofore, planners had warned that parking was so plentiful in the area around the university that no parking deck could charge enough to pay for its construction. Commuter students circling blocks in their cars in hope of a space coming open might disagree, but this had long been the university's argument to adjoining neighborhood associations for not building dedicated parking areas on campus. The newspaper story expressed hope that the deck would improve relations with the Fan neighborhood to the west. For Oregon Hill residents, the deck just confirmed VCU's plans to expand southward.[48]

As WINTER turned to spring, President Ackell sat down with the editors of the *Commonwealth Times* for what soon became notorious as "the Ackell interview." Ackell declared again that his first year brought valuable changes, such as streamlined organization and governance, the new financial accounting system, and greater unity of the campuses. His goal in all the organizational improvements was to ensure that VCU was one university with two different locations, not two separate universities, which, he said, was the case when he arrived.

Then he began tossing bombs. The role of students in governance was a problem "because we have not had an organized student body." The Academic Campus had so many "externally directed," part-time students that student government there might never be workable (unlike at the Medical Campus). His Task Force on Governance would take up that issue, but its main purpose, he said, was to determine the roles of the Faculty Senate and the University Assembly (and whether both bodies were needed).

The student journalists brought up the faculty's disagreement with Ackell about the composition of his Task Force on Governance. He replied, "My complaint was that they had given me some names of people who are always on everything, a clique." It was not *who* they named, he went on, but that those chosen should reflect the whole faculty.

What then, they asked, about his promise to name a faculty member to chair the promotion and tenure committee? He had selected Walter Nance, chair of the Department of Human Genetics. "In my opinion, and as long as I'm president, department chairmen are faculty," Ackell replied. The interviewers were well prepared, and they cited the faculty handbook. "I know," he said, "but the faculty handbook, as you may know also, is going to be changed." Ackell insisted, "Administrators are defined by the president, not by the faculty."

On Oregon Hill, Ackell said that VCU only wanted part of the area north of the expressway: "We're looking at that little two block area." Expansion west into the Fan was no good because of the younger people living there and the number of people who would be uprooted. Moving north to Broad Street would be prohibitively expensive and, he seemed to say, too visible. "I'm trying to get away from the thoroughfare, because I think a lot of people come through here and they see a few students who might be wearing jeans instead of a tie—like they think they should be wearing someplace else—or have long hair, or have their arms around their girl, or see a black and a white walking together, and then they get the wrong impressions about the institution." He wanted to keep students away from "the thoroughfare, and away from Franklin Street."

On VCU's future, he foresaw problems as the population aged seventeen to twenty-one declined. That's why, he said, "I think the recreational facilities and the new dormitory are important. That's part of what makes somebody want to go to school—not only the academic program, but the environment." An urban university was not for everyone, but "those who want to go to an urban institution can go to many urban institutions. We will have something to offer that will make them want to come here."[49]

The interview supplied plenty of fuel for outrage, but Ackell's comments about students being too visible on the streets for conservative Richmonders produced the biggest flames. The first postinterview issue of the *Commonwealth Times* carried a letter from a student angry enough that he suggested recalling all copies of the interview for the good of the university. Meanwhile, the editors criticized the unknown persons who had doctored the interview issue's cover portrait to depict Ackell as a Nazi, then distributed it on campus. It was, therefore, easy to miss the short letter from political scientist Nelson Wikstrom, the president of the Faculty Senate, asserting that the senate's relationship with the president had "been in the main marked by mutual respect, honesty, and significant cooperation." The executive committee of the Faculty Senate took a similar tack in its next meeting with President Ackell, assuring him that even though he seemed "bellicose and authoritarian" in the *Commonwealth Times*, the committee had "not found him so." Finally, in the 3 April issue of the *CT*, Ackell apologized publicly to any offended by his mistaken remarks about the appearances of VCU students.[50]

A week before that, Save Our Homes took Oregon Hill's fight with VCU to the governor, presenting petitions to the secretary of education and at the offices of the State Council on the Environment. Residents of Oregon Hill also joined in the chorus of condemnation of President Ackell's remarks in his interview with the *Commonwealth Times*. They saw his comments as a weak and offensive justification for VCU's encroachment on its southern neighbor.[51]

Negative reactions to his interview took the shine off the simultaneous announcement that VCU had been invited to become the eighth member of the Sun Belt Conference, a collegiate athletic conference organized in 1976 and comprised of other young southern urban universities. The basketball team under Dana Kirk had enjoyed consecutive twenty-win seasons in the Eastern College Athletic Conference, but in the past season that hard-earned respectability did not translate into an invitation to the NCAA basketball tournament nor even the less prestigious National Invitational Tournament. The Sun Belt Conference placed two of its teams in the NCAA tournament that year, and in announcing the conference affiliation President Ackell declared that to be a major attraction for VCU. Ackell said that he sought a conference with respect for academics and offering more recognition for VCU and its athletes. "The Sun Belt, with its all-urban institution makeup and no football—'We won't have to buck that,' said Ackell—was the answer."[52]

On the same day that VCU joined the Sun Belt Conference, and just a day after he discussed plans for the next season on his Richmond television show, Dana Kirk signed a four-year contract to coach the basketball team at Memphis State University. Athletic Director Lewis Mills regretted that the resignation cast a shadow on the good news of VCU's new conference affiliation, but he thought that the affiliation made VCU more attractive for an ambitious young coach.[53]

At the end of April, VCU named a new coach, J. D. Barnett (named Joseph Donald for his grandfathers, he was known from birth as J. D.). Stints as an assistant coach (Roanoke, Richmond, and West Texas State) and as head coach (Lenoir Rhyne, High Point, and most recently Louisiana Tech) prepared him for VCU and the school's inaugural season in the Sun Belt Conference. He would face high expectations despite the change to a tougher conference, for Dana Kirk's teams had managed a record of 44–10 in the previous two seasons.[54]

ACKELL'S CAMPAIGN to improve administration at the MCV Hospitals had a success with the March 1979 announcement that Miles P. Lash, director of the hospital at Ohio State University, had been hired to direct the MCV Hospitals. Dr. Reuben B. Young, director of medical staff services, served as interim hospitals director after Gennaro Vasile had stepped down in 1978, and his term probably stretched a bit longer than he expected. The new hospital was on schedule for a 1981 opening, and then renovations would begin at the other hospitals. In "a typical day" in 1979, ninety patients entered, forty operations were performed, and ten babies were born; the emergency room handled 150 visits, and the A. D. Williams Memorial Clinic saw 480 visits.[55]

A condition of Lash's hiring was creation of two new administrative posts—a chief financial officer and a general day-to-day administrator. The hospitals needed to operate "as a private enterprise" to create the revenues to pay for the bonds for the new hospital, and Lash had that kind of experience. Ackell was typically blunt: the hospitals had been "highly recognized for their quality of care but they have always been in trouble managementwise."[56]

Lash proved to be an effective administrator, coordinating final construction of the new hospital and then the new operations of MCV Hospitals when it finally opened, after construction delays, in 1982. Ackell later credited him with making the hospitals businesslike, and he commended Lauren Woods, who soon had the word "acting" removed from his vice presidency, for maintaining a good relationship with the medical school, which aided Ackell's work at the university.[57] By summer 1979, the university knew that, for better or worse, Ed Ackell spoke bluntly and acted aggressively.

That year, the State Council of Higher Education released another edition of *The Virginia Plan for Higher Education*, a report issued at intervals since 1967. The 1979 *Plan* noted that Virginia's urban universities—George Mason, in Northern Virginia; Old Dominion University, serving Hampton Roads; and VCU, in Richmond—had flourishing graduate programs, a development that earlier reports had not anticipated. Indeed, the *Plan* noted, the 1972 Carnegie Commission report on the urban university in America also had neglected the potential for advanced graduate and professional training as a component of urban higher education in the United States. The trick for these universities, including VCU, would be to maintain an urban orientation while the institution's development replicated that of comprehensive universities of longer existence and different environments. The currents in higher education at that time ran in the latter direction, with cities in decline and with status-seeking universities looking to research and graduate programs more than to urban service. In fact, in 1977, the Association of Urban Universities, wracked by these forces "and reflecting the resistance of its members to the term 'urban university,'" voted to go out of existence.[58]

Nonetheless, said SCHEV in 1979, the urban universities were to provide undergraduate education for urbanites, which meant not only the state's swiftly growing metropolitan areas but also specifically minority students, a group increasingly identified with the euphemism of "urban." The universities also were to provide service, especially via specialized research, to the state's "densely populated areas." And, finally, they were to offer graduate and professional education largely to a part-time student population drawn from the cities' working adults. This mission had fewer consequences for George Mason and Old Dominion, for they did not have academic medical centers. For VCU, committed to its academic medical center maintaining a national reputation, not just to educating practitioners for the Richmond region, SCHEV's 1979 recommendations supported the university specializing in health research. The report also recommended that doctoral programs be limited largely to UVA and Virginia Tech, which conflicted with the ambitions of VCU's faculty and president.[59]

VCU had already claimed that it stood with the two larger and older universities as the state's three comprehensive universities, a legacy of President Temple's planned campaign for 1977. Ackell had questioned whether

VCU had achieved comprehensive university status, but he accepted that as his goal as president. Now, regardless of "some institutional aspirations," SCHEV declared, "circumscribed" growth was the responsible plan. Thus, in contrast to Ackell's commitment to developing a comprehensive university, SCHEV's view of VCU in 1979 was a little bit expansive—a research institution for health services and a strong program in the arts—and a lot restrictive—a school dedicated to the needs of its local service area.[60]

Ackell could only wonder at SCHEV's reasoning, for SCHEV had also in 1979 recommended that the governor designate VCU as the state's third class 1-A institution, alongside UVA and Virginia Tech. Such status required turning out fifty or more new doctorates per year and attracting $10 million or more in grants annually. Whether he agreed with SCHEV's statement or not, President Ackell nonetheless realized that VCU's resources would continue to be strained. He reported to the Board of Visitors that state funding for 1980–81 would be lower than funding for 1979–80. "These definitely are the times that try men's souls," he concluded.[61]

By then, the city of Richmond's government had collapsed into bitter racial conflict. Policy differences explain the previous year's firing of the city manager, but in Richmond many people viewed the motive as racial— he was white, and the majority on council was black. To say that the firing distressed whites "is to understate the emotional level of Richmond politics." The local newspapers—a dual monopoly under publisher J. Stewart Bryan—lambasted Marsh and his partners with comparisons to a "band of black Bibos," a minstrel show, and monkeys. The intemperate editorials reinforced convictions among black Richmonders of the bigotry behind white criticism of the city council.[62]

In turn, whites viewed the council majority's actions, such as blowing up a plan for a hotel development in the Main Street business district to protect hotel development on Broad Street in the shopping district, as incompetence, if not sheer perversity. The controversy over the Broad Street development—Project One, it was called—provoked lawsuits that delayed the city issuing $32.2 million in bonds in 1978, and another lawsuit filed in January 1979 halted the bond issue again. Rather than coming from the white business elite, this challenge came from the Richmond Independent Taxpayers Association. Organized by a realtor, the Independent Taxpayers Association charged that real estate and other taxes had increased so much that taxpayers and businesses were responding by moving to the less-oppressive suburban counties. Richmond, like other Virginia cities, did depend on property taxes for revenue, but because Richmond was the state capitol, many properties, such as VCU's, were tax exempt, ratcheting up the taxes on privately owned properties.[63]

The tax protest also came at a time when the state of Virginia took actions that left cities even more dependent on their own resources. After much study and debate, the General Assembly passed a three-bill package of legislation in 1979. One bill granted immunity from annexation to counties requesting it, and Chesterfield and Henrico Counties jumped at the opportunity. To placate the cities, a second piece of legislation provided state funds for road construction and repair in cities and a third act offered funding to supplement urban police budgets, a proposal that also reflected suburban fears of migrating city crime. The idea was "to increase state aid to localities to ease the need for annexation," but by summer 1979, the city of Richmond, hemmed in by the counties, divided by race, and facing a taxpayer rebellion, was in a bad situation with no clear direction out.[64]

A sign of Richmond's desperate straits was Mayor Marsh's appeal to the White House to block construction of the long-planned beltway (now Interstate 295) through the counties and bypassing the city of Richmond. Marsh argued that the beltway would take traffic, and potential consumers, away from the city, which meant that the counties or the state ought to provide revenues to cover the damages. Officials of the Carter administration agreed that the roadway project, as the *Washington Post* put it, "violated the president's urban policy of avoiding projects that could do economic damage to cities." The Virginia State Highway Commission, angered by the federal interference, approved the beltway project anyway.[65]

On 20 September 1979 the Board of Visitors met and, without noting it in the minutes, approved plans for buying seventy-two parcels of land between Cary Street and the Downtown Expressway to the south and between Harrison Street and Cherry Street to the east. The land, on the northern edge of the Oregon Hill neighborhood, was to become a set of athletic fields and tennis courts around the renovated City Auditorium on Cary Street, which would itself become a gymnasium.[66]

The Oregon Hill activists, under the Save Our Homes umbrella, turned to the state and city political leaders for protection. An audience of singing and chanting neighborhood residents at the William Byrd Community House on 21 October 1979 received assurances that Governor John Dalton would block any use of state funding should VCU attempt to take property through the power of eminent domain. Delegate James S.

Christian Jr. condemned destruction of homes for tennis courts. "I don't like tennis anyhow," he declared to cheers. State Senator Edward E. Willey echoed Christian: "They haven't even got a football team," he jeered. Other members of the Richmond legislative delegation offered similar complaints about VCU, and representatives from other neighborhood associations promised solidarity with Oregon Hill.[67] No matter, Ackell was determined not to back down.[68]

IN 1977 the Board of Visitors had investigated student charges against the Office of Student Life and concluded that efforts be made to restart student government. Finally, in mid-November 1979, the first Academic Campus Student Association elections took place on the West Campus, with 20 percent of the student body voting, more than enough to meet constitutional requirements. By an overwhelming margin they approved the new constitution and elected twenty-nine senators. The new student government assumed office in January 1980.[69]

Meanwhile, the Faculty Senate's disagreement with the president grew wider. Ackell met with the executive committee of the Faculty Senate on 10 September 1979, and there historian Alan Briceland, the editor of the *Faculty Handbook*, challenged, with statistics, what he and others considered to be the president's insulting suggestion that VCU's original tenure plan, with a grandfather clause to grant tenure automatically to faculty with sufficient years of experience at RPI or MCV, had tenured in "a lot of dead wood." Ackell, as Briceland recalled it, angrily swept the report aside without a glance at its contents. From the Faculty Senate's perspective, it seemed that Ackell wanted to undermine the principle of tenure itself.[70]

The University Task Forces on Governance and on Tenure and Promotion, respectively, continued their work in 1979–80. The latter group held a hearing on the West Campus on 19 October 1979, and the Faculty Senate sent Briceland, fellow historian William Blake, and Lawrence Laban, from the Department of English, to present the senate's official opposition to four proposals—against extending the probationary period for tenure, against establishing tenure quotas, against identifying an optimum proportion of tenured and nontenured faculty for the university, and against developing non–tenure-track positions—all of which the senate believed the task force had under consideration. The senate's alarm was not mistaken, for, as numerous contemporary scholars have pointed out, the long-term trend in faculty employment since the 1970s has been away from tenure to more contingent teaching faculty at American universities. President Ackell still seemed indifferent to the anger and dismay that his plan to rethink faculty tenure policies had created.[71]

In fact, his report to the Board of Visitors about the Faculty Senate's retreat on 15 September, which he and other administrators attended, mentioned faculty concerns only about internal communication. As a solution to that problem, he declared the biweekly *VCU Today*, publishing since 1972, the official organ for the administration. That also signaled his lack of confidence in the *Commonwealth Times* as a news vehicle for VCU. As it happened, the *CT* marked its tenth anniversary at about the same time. Editor Bill Pahnelas celebrated the paper's career as "the largest student organization on campus," but acknowledged that some readers "were unprepared for our multi-faceted approach—the holistic view of our environment which the variegated community calls for." In December, the *VCU Magazine* informed alumni that the *CT* had been chosen "the #1 ranked college newspaper in Virginia" for the third year in a row.[72]

The report of the University Task Force on Governance appeared as scheduled in *VCU Today* after a year of labor. Clearly, the task force had followed Ackell's charge to assess the usefulness of the University Assembly and the Faculty Senate, both created in VCU's founding years, for it proposed to fold both into a new "unicameral, multi-constituent forum" to be called the University Senate. There would be twenty-four faculty members (two per school), and only ten administrators and eight students, with four standing committees: an executive committee and councils on faculty affairs, student affairs, and academic affairs. The Faculty Senate would disappear. The Faculty Senate responded: faculty elected to the University Senate, as proposed, would represent their own schools, and thus only "faculty elected from the Faculty Senate, continuing under its present Bylaws, will speak as the voice of the faculty as a whole."[73]

By then, faculty and administrators alike knew that budget projections showed significant shortfalls in 1980–81 and 1981–82. *VCU Today* summarized the consequences: "Reallocation and retrenchment will have to be the primary means of program enhancement throughout the next decade." Ackell told the board in March that hiring had been frozen at the number of positions now filled and tuition would have to go up. The board also learned that the cost of renovating the old City Auditorium for use as a student gymnasium had doubled, thanks to roof repairs, inflation, and delays. Outside the meeting, a contingent of about thirty people from Save Our Homes protested VCU's encroachment on the Oregon Hill neighborhood.[74]

Ackell then sat down with four student journalists for the second annual installment of what the *CT* now called "The Ackell Interview." Unlike the previous year's interview, this one did not provoke much controversy. He spoke of accomplishments—pushing for "the one university concept," making *VCU Today* the "university organ," and developing a new student government. He kept alive his dispute with the Faculty Senate, saying that the senate should stick to areas "that concern faculty," and remained adamant that VCU needed the recreational spaces on the edge of Oregon Hill. He gave himself a grade of *B* for the year.[75]

ELECTIONS FOR city council came again in May 1980, and the elected city council would redraw the city's ward lines based on the 1980 U.S. census, then underway. The *Times-Dispatch* told voters to choose a majority "that would be dedicated to the interests of the city as a whole." The editorial then endorsed five white candidates, its preferred majority. Candidates from the Richmond Independent Taxpayers Association provided a little competition in a few largely white districts, but Marsh and two other black incumbents were unopposed. The fired city manager, William Leidinger, was one of the white council candidates expected to win election.[76]

"The widening chasm between the races here is evident in this year's endorsements," the *Washington Post* observed the day before the election. "While the city's dominant white and black political groups have traditionally endorsed at least one candidate from the opposite race in the past, this time neither has done so." By then, at least three candidates had requested police protection after receiving threats. The elections passed off as expected, with the 5–4 black majority still in charge. Councilwoman Claudette Black McDaniel, a VCU graduate and longtime university employee, had been targeted for defeat by white political forces but survived by fewer than three hundred votes. But racial division persisted, abetted, according to many observers, by reckless editorials in the *News Leader*.[77]

That summer's two special issues of the *CT* foreshadowed conflict with the president. A new group of editors and designers took command at the paper, infusing it fully with the cheeky, faster-faster-harder-harder spirit of the so-called punk movement. For example, accompanying one article was a candid photo of Ackell inelegantly pulling up his trousers with the caption: "President Ackell: Caught with His Pants Down?" The report on the Board of Visitors' election of Anne P. Satterfield as VCU's first woman rector got the headline: "Spirited Mrs. Elected by Board of Visitors." Similarly, the report on the departure of former provost Francis J. Brooke to the presidency of Columbus College, in Georgia, and the imminent departure of Ronald E. Beller, executive vice president, to the presidency of East Tennessee State University, was headlined, "University Changes Socks." Worse, the article ended by quoting Ackell's cold response to the possibility of Beller leaving: "I hadn't even thought about it."[78]

During the summer a petition circulated among the faculty and then was presented to Ackell, signed by nearly a thousand persons, calling for the Faculty Senate to be a part of any future university governance scheme. Historian William E. Blake, the founding president of the Faculty Senate, was elected to a second term as president, and he vowed that the senate must help shape a policy on tenure and promotion "acceptable to the faculty."[79] At the meeting of the University Assembly on 18 September 1980, President Ackell summarized the most important changes recommended by the Task Force on Tenure and Promotion. The president, with approval from the Board of Visitors, would grant tenure, rather than having the deans make tenure decisions, and a university-wide committee would oversee tenure and promotion. Blake then rose to present a resolution adopted by the senate two days earlier, expressing reservations that the new Statement on Tenure might be revised in the future by the Promotion and Tenure Committee without oversight or advice. Blake then expanded on those concerns, including that the task force's report again used insulting terms like "over-tenured," "hazardous tenure burden," and the like without providing any evidence of "the derogatory effects on a university, resulting from a high percentage of tenured faculty." When Blake asked if the Council on Faculty Affairs of the University Assembly would be asked to review the document, Ackell dismissed his question. Any group in the university could review the document, he replied, but "officially" he was asking the deans to make recommendations to him.[80]

Meanwhile, a senate committee was meeting with the Task Force on Governance to "negotiate differences," and another committee was engaged with the Task Force on Promotion and Tenure. Both negotiations proceeded amicably, and in February 1981, the senate newsletter reported that Ackell had not only decided to appoint a drafting committee to prepare a promotion and tenure policy document reflecting the comments that the original document had elicited, but also asked the senate to nominate faculty members of the committee. In a similar fashion, the Faculty Senate's representatives and the Task Force on Governance "hammered out" a document that proposed an "upper level body to be called 'The University Council,'" with two representatives from the Faculty Senate and one from the University Libraries added to the originally proposed council of eight students, ten administrators, and twenty-four faculty representatives from the various schools. As the newsletter happily put it, "Other changes of importance to faculty were also included in the agreement."[81] Nonetheless, faculty involved in these negotiations would long recall their worried conviction that the president sought to eliminate the Faculty Senate and to seize control over the promotion and tenure system.

The *CT*'s first issue of the fall semester 1980 was the last straw for President Ackell. In addition to a snarky cover image of a man displaying a "Nobody for President '80" poster, headlines like "A Kick in the Grass," about a defeat for the soccer team, and the editor's accurate promise "to inform and entertain you *and* piss you off," there was Bill Pahnelas's banal but profanity-filled interview with Dickie Disgusting, lead singer of the Degenerate Blind Boys ("We were punk before people heard of Sex Pistols and all this"). The paper's next issue included an assessment that judged the band as "punk by rote," but an editorial also vaguely noted much discussion on campus about the interview.[82]

That discussion came to the pages of the newspaper's next issue on 7 October. President Ackell sent an angry letter stating his "disappointment and displeasure" at the article. It was a disservice to the university and caused him to question "the appropriateness of the *Times* as it is presently identified with this university." Writer Peter Blake penned a defiant response, signed by twenty other staff members. He argued that Ackell spoke "for a hearty bunch of big money holders" who despised VCU's diversity and wanted "to change our 'diversity' into 'university.'" There was some truth to the charge, in that Ackell saw little of value in VCU's countercultural image and desired instead that the image be that of a research university. Blake contended that, in fact, the *CT*'s staff was representative of the university and the pages of the *CT*, consequently, represented "the crux of VCU."[83]

Regardless, the letters to the editor were pretty much unanimous: the article was offensive and inappropriate. The article was remembered, too. In 1985, reporters from the *CT* interviewed Virginius Dabney, the first rector, who was then at work on a history of VCU. "Were you on the

Commonwealth Times when they published the filthy interview with that punk-rock individual?" Dabney asked them. "It was a most inexcusable performance."[84]

Ackell informed the Board of Visitors that the *CT* had "provoked a few people, including me," and he intended to "appoint a group to look at all the student media to make recommendations to me on possible changes." He was true to his word, and before the semester's end he had a Task Force on Student Media at work. The *CT* viewed it with disdain—using the headline "Today's Chuckle" to announce the task force in November.[85]

The local press coverage noted that everyone knew that the Dickie Disgusting interview had prompted Ackell's action. The *CT* acknowledged there were good reasons for a task force, such as the university's possible legal liability "for the actions of the media" and the potential for censorship by a student government controlling finances, but Ackell had told the Board of Visitors that he created the task force because of his displeasure with the *CT*. That statement, the *CT* declared, rivaled Ackell's "1979 statement that black and white students who associate in public create a bad community image for VCU." The task force, chaired by George Crutchfield, of the Department of Mass Communications, began its work in February 1981.[86]

Meanwhile, in the same October 1980 issue of the *CT* that contained Ackell's condemnatory letter and the staff's defiant response, Sue Dayton, who developed the paper's design—"early Punk," she said later—in 1979, presented a suite of photographs of the elderly residents of the Jefferson Hotel. Located on Franklin Street east of Monroe Park in a decaying neighborhood of houses built by the city's antebellum elite, the hotel had been the city's finest when it opened in 1895 but had fallen on hard times. Dayton worked at the hotel and gained the trust of those she photographed, but her presentation in the *CT* was a eulogy of sorts, for the Jefferson had closed at the end of August. The shuttered hotel provided symbolic support for the widespread conviction that Richmond's central business district, adjacent to both VCU campuses, was in a decline that might not be reversible.[87]

The hotel's closing eliminated one of the nearby hostelries where VCU had housed students who could not yet be accommodated on campus. The housing demand pointed toward VCU's future as a residential campus, but it remained a commuter campus. The *Richmond Times-Dispatch* reported as classes began in 1978 that nearly six hundred VCU students lived in area hotels because the university lacked housing for them. The practice was as old as the university, but the numbers had jumped, in part because buildings previously used for dormitories along Franklin Street were being turned into offices. By fall 1980, the number of students living in hotels was about the same, primarily because Johnson Hall was being renovated. The "New Residence Center" opened successfully in 1979, and, with plans stripped to the basics because of "skyrocketing construction costs," phase 2 of the new residence center would soon be underway. The residence center would be named in honor of Jane Bell Gladding, former associate dean of students.[88]

ON 3 SEPTEMBER 1981, the University Assembly convened for its first meeting of the new academic year. President Ackell welcomed new members and stated that the assembly would review the governance and the promotion and tenure policies, which he noted had already been reviewed and revised at other levels of the university. The assembly then voted to become a committee of the whole, and Grace Harris, chair of the Promotion and Tenure Drafting Committee, outlined the document, which now included, as was the case at other universities, possible financial exigency as a legal basis for abrogating tenure. As Ackell pointed out, the document was left vague and he would convene a university-wide task force "to establish an exigency plan for the university." Discussion continued, and the assembly agreed to reconvene on 15 September. Reporters for the CT were present that time, and the group agreed that they could use recorders. With changes proposed and agreed to, the meeting closed. Ackell said that he would present the document to the Board of Visitors at its next meeting. On 24 September 1981, the Board of Visitors adopted "the Promotion and Tenure Policies and Procedures of Virginia Commonwealth University." The acrimony and distrust that the process had generated with the faculty only grew worse as hard times and reallocations of resources gave validity to fears that financial exigency might be declared to undermine tenure.[89]

Peace talks came to Richmond then, too. The conflicts in Richmond city government nearly tipped over into violence in 1980, according to many estimates, and leading citizens began organizing to help lead the city away from that precipice. That year's furious electoral campaign convinced the Richmond Commission on Human Relations, which included VCU faculty members John V. Moeser (urban studies) and Edward H. Peeples (sociology and preventive medicine), that the community needed to address mounting racial tensions. It proposed to call black and white leaders together for "free and casual discussion" and, more realistically, "to vent their feelings." Better communication could aid in reducing tensions. The "vast majority" of participants in the four discussion groups agreed that racial tensions existed and were worsening. Many also criticized the local newspapers for editorials "fanning the city's racial division." Yet, all participants agreed that biracial action was the best way forward for Richmond.[90]

As the commission's group discussions got underway, *Ebony* magazine ran a cover story on Richmond politics with the provocative subtitle "The Confederate Capital Finally Falls to Blacks." The tone of the story, however, was sunny, with little mention of conflict. Rather, it emphasized that unlike the ascension to power of blacks in northern cities, Richmond's black leaders "did not inherit a dying city." Readers of the local white newspapers might not have known that, but *Ebony* made a good case. Richmond was financially stable, with state government furnishing some thirty thousand jobs, and cigarette manufacturer Philip Morris, the largest private employer, expanding. There were problems, to be sure, with public schools 90 percent black and white flight continuing, but Richmond might yet be a model for sharing of power.[91]

Meanwhile, another entity committed to biracial progress for the city, the Richmond Urban Institute, created in 1979 with full urban representation but with its roots in the churches, especially St. Paul's Episcopal Church, where it was housed, took up a similar study of racial polarization in summer 1980. Things were tense enough that it prefaced the report with the warning that its purpose was reconciliation, not to fuel hatred.

Participants here also saw conflict, with whites blaming city council, and blacks blaming the Richmond newspapers and the white economic elite. Yet, the report averred, there were signs of hope, too: "a deep loyalty to Richmond," and a willingness to speak candidly. But it concluded that Richmond was two groups, racial and separate, with their own histories and goals, and "each feels that it has to win on its own terms in order to preserve its own integrity." The report called for toning down the rhetoric, especially at the newspapers, and cooperation in economic development of the city. Richmond's survival was at stake, and cooperation was to mutual benefit.[92]

In fall 1980, while at VCU the Faculty Senate wrestled with the Task Forces on Tenure and Promotion and on University Governance and

President Ackell skirmished with the *CT*, the Richmond Chamber of Commerce took up the Urban Institute's report. The chamber's Committee on Community Relations by November had met three times to discuss the polarization. Quietly, the chamber proposed to work with the Commission on Human Relations as that body prepared its report on the city. In January 1981, white banker William V. Daniel, a former member of city council and a leader in the chamber's efforts at interracial communication, and black optometrist John L. Howlette, head of the chamber's Committee on Community Relations, convened and moderated four mixed groups of white and black Richmonders to discuss conditions in the city.[93]

President Ackell was a member of Group One. His fight with the *CT* remained fresh, for he told his group that VCU's student body was 18 percent black, but those students lacked a voice, and consequently racial polarization was a problem on campus. Making things worse, he continued, was a "one-sided" student newspaper. Ackell's comment ignored the existence of *Reflections in Ink*, now nearly three years old, but his comments had some validity. The *CT* did not provide much coverage of black students' activities, and a misguided opinion piece in that paper in fall 1980 had suggested, with an undertone of arrogance, that the poor production quality of *Ink* called for it to be folded into the *CT*. Letters to the editor made clear that the two publications needed to remain separate, but the controversy might still have been on Ackell's mind when he met with the committee in January.[94]

Leaders of these behind-the-scenes deliberations hoped that shared interest in economic development of the city of Richmond might be a way out of the racial impasse in Richmond governance. Despite the complaints of the Richmond Taxpayers Association, the committees had little to say about continued white flight from the city and the necessity, with annexations prohibited, to depend largely on real estate taxes for city revenues. In addition, neither the report of the Commission on Human Relations nor that of the Chamber of Commerce pushed the council majority's original emphasis on benefits for the neighborhoods as well as the business districts.[95]

Just then, from VCU's Center for Public Affairs came a proposal for the Richmond Revitalization Project. Morton B. Gulak, early in his nearly forty years as a professor of urban studies and planning at VCU, led presentations to a group of bankers, realtors, architects, and community leaders on how city planners and VCU faculty and students could work together "to restore the vigor of residential and commercial neighborhoods through preservation, adaptive use, and conservation planning." Countering the destruction of urban renewal, the Richmond Revitalization Program would engage property owners and investors in saving neighborhoods and making them attractive to new homeowners. A gift from an anonymous donor kick-started the project, with the city and the university promising support into the future.[96]

The first study project was dubbed the Brook Crossing Commercial Center Revitalization Plan, focusing on the area between Broad Street and Marshall Street in the Jackson Ward neighborhood, historically associated with black Richmond. The project was part of a larger trend in U.S. cities to make older parts of cities attractive for developers and businesses, as well as for old and new residents. It reflected a shift in American governance in urban affairs away from government-sponsored programs to efforts to encourage private investment. The trend also coincided with a rise in support for historic preservation, as was the case in Richmond.[97]

Almost immediately, though, the cry arose that revitalization, by raising property values, had the bad effect of driving original neighborhood residents from their homes. In 1983, two scholars, with aid in Richmond from Peter Roggeman, then of VCU's Urban Studies Department, assessed the impact of this process—called "gentrification." They concluded that, on balance, neighborhood reinvestment would not solve the "'urban crisis,'" but it did provide "substantial benefits for the city and its residents."[98]

Among the urban neighborhoods assessed for the study were two from Richmond: Jackson Ward and Oregon Hill. The study observed that Jackson Ward's revitalization depended on historic preservationists. As for Oregon Hill, the authors described it as a possible refuge for homebuyers priced out of the Fan District to the west of VCU's campus, but they found little evidence of newcomers entering the neighborhood. People in Oregon Hill, they wrote, "are worried that Virginia Commonwealth University may expand and displace neighborhood residents."[99]

In summer 1981, VCU began destruction of homes in the disputed territory of Oregon Hill, with the rubble to be replaced by tennis courts in early 1982. Thanks to the Save Our Homes organization's enlistment of Governor Dalton to block VCU's use of eminent domain for acquiring land there, the current project would lead to only three tennis courts, not the dozen envisioned in the 1976 update of the master plan. VCU also proceeded with renovation of the old City Auditorium on Cary Street to provide, by summer 1982, handball and basketball courts.[100]

VCU's move on Oregon Hill was hardly noticed because of continued fireworks in city politics. One of the reasons for Richmond Revitalization to begin with the Brook Crossing Commercial Center was its proximity to "Project One, a convention, hotel, and office complex." Project One had been in the works for years prior to the election of the council's black majority, for its purpose was to rejuvenate the city's declining retail shopping district on Broad Street, and many saw Project One as something that all groups could support for the city's benefit. Then, in late July 1981, the Virginia National Bank announced plans for a new, 350-room Hilton hotel, located at Kanawha Plaza, in the Richmond financial district and several blocks south of Project One, where construction was already underway on the office building. After analysis suggested that only one hotel of that size might thrive in downtown, seeming to doom Project One, black leaders were certain that if white elites had still controlled city hall the Hilton hotel project would never have emerged. Council passed an ordinance that blocked the Hilton project, and white businessmen angrily charged that Richmond's economic reputation had been permanently stained.[101]

If the council majority's action to block the Hilton hotel reinforced critics' conviction that the black council members were antibusiness, another development in summer 1981 seemed to show that white leaders in Richmond remained dedicated to blocking African Americans from political power. On 29 June, the city council, by a 5–4 vote, adopted the redistricting plan devised by the majority and condemned by the minority for ensuring a continued African American majority. On 19 August, the four white council members, along with a phalanx of other white civic and business leaders, met with officials of the U.S. Department of Justice to petition for the redistricting plan to be overturned as a violation of the Voting Rights Act of 1965. Officials at Justice reported that this was the first-ever complaint by whites under the act. The response was quick: on 31 August 1981, the Justice Department stated that it accepted the majority's plan. It was a victory for Mayor Marsh, but the challenge seemed proof that Richmond white elite still sought to limit black political power.[102]

The city went forward with Project One, announcing in early 1982 that a Marriott hotel would be constructed there. The Associated Press story declared that the announcement "was the culmination of almost twenty years of effort to breathe new life into the city's deteriorating downtown core and the area north of East Broad Street." The Hilton interests then turned to the courts, where the city lost, resulting in large costs for legal fees and an out-of-court settlement that cost Richmond even more.[103]

The university played no role in these conflicts, although Project One's success would seem closer to its interests than the Hilton hotel, which was, critics claimed, a return to the "Main-to-the James" development strategy that had been a justification for the controversial Downtown Expressway. Project One fell about midway between the Academic Campus and the Medical Campus, and a lively retail district benefited both students and employees. Certainly, the Richmond Revitalization Program was in keeping with VCU's origins as an urban university in service to its city.

At the MCV campus, it had been a busy year. The work on the new 536-bed main hospital continued, with its completion predicted for the end of the year. Then patients would be moved out of the old East and South Hospitals permanently, and North Hospital would be vacated for renovations that included a new wing connected to the new cancer center. Finally, when that renovation finished, West Hospital, where David Hume and his colleagues began their march to the governor's office a decade earlier to demand better facilities, would be converted for academic and health science work. The Egyptian Building, another landmark structure, finally converted the laboratory spaces—with poor ventilation and out of compliance with safety rules—to administrative offices. Work on the new pharmacy building began on 2 April 1981, and the Board of Visitors agreed to name the building in honor of Robert Blackwell Smith, a pharmacy graduate and president of the Medical College of Virginia in the years leading to the merger with RPI.[104]

On the West Campus, construction of athletic fields and renovation of the City Auditorium as a gymnasium had begun. The former parking lot east of the business school (later Harris Hall) was ready to become the site of the long-awaited student commons building, with construction to begin in fall 1981, and the parking lot at Laurel and Main would close to become the site of phase 2 of the new residence center (later Gladding Residence Center). Meanwhile, construction of the new performing arts center (later the Singleton Center) continued at the site of the old Scottish Rite Masonic Temple, with the grand opening scheduled for November 1981.[105]

In June 1981, the Task Force on Student Media, which had been meeting since February, made its report. It proposed the goal of student media becoming independent of the university as soon as possible. The trend nationally was toward independent student media, and the task force also noted that the First Amendment prohibited universities from "controlling the content 'of the very media it created and supports.'"[106]

The report was not what the president wanted. In late July Ackell responded to George Crutchfield, the chair of the media task force, with a complaint that the report "seemed to be written from the point of view of those students directly involved in the student media." A "more help-ful report" would have reflected the interests of "'non-media' students," he declared. The report's focus on "academic freedom," which he would never permit to be compromised at VCU, impressed him as written with "professional media people in mind," not the university, but, as Ackell had appointed the task force, he "must take responsibility." He closed by stat-ing that he accepted the report "as an informational document, which will receive consideration in the future."[107]

Thus, it may have surprised all involved that, first, the president sat down with reporters from the *CT* in August for an interview, and, second, the resulting story was something of a lovefest. Ackell had just come from a meeting with student government leaders, and he was pleased with his communication with them. Asked about the perception that VCU's cam-puses seemed separate entities, he calmly pointed to his administrative reorganization to build one institution in action and planning. The story carried a headline that Ackell had called VCU a "street university," but his comment came in a larger discussion of his efforts to expand recreational and meeting spaces for students. The interview then turned to the Task Force on Student Media. Ackell explained that the task force, and its report, was too oriented toward the media perspective; he wanted an analysis from the perspective of everyday students who needed a source for university news. None of the current student publications—*Reflections in Ink*, the *CT*, or *ThroTTle*—served those students. The interviewers pointed out that *ThroTTle* was not a university publication. In fact, it was the brainchild of the *CT*'s most recent band of editors, with the first issue published in January 1981, and it carried away with it the iconoclastic stance and distinct design sensibility that had most offended in the *CT*. Rather than bristling when corrected, Ackell merely pointed out that people associated that pub-lication with VCU. Finally, as in previous years, the interviewers asked him to grade his performance. "I think I'm nearing an *A*," he replied. "I've gotten most of the things I went after accomplished."[108]

The university entered 1982 with deep worries about the budget. When the University Assembly met on 4 February, President Ackell plunged immediately into discussion of the situation. Governor Dalton's final budget did not include moneys for the move into the new hospital, which would, for a time, require maintenance of two facilities. The biggest worry was the proposal to change the 70/30 tuition plan to a 65/35 plan, which would cause "enormous tuition increases" because of VCU's higher proportion of in-state students. If the change went through, Ackell warned, tuition would increase by 25 percent each of the next two years. The news was so dire and immediate that the group remembered to approve the minutes from the 3 December meeting only just before adjourning. The shoe dropped for students at the Board of Visitors' meeting in May with its approval of increases in tuition and fees ranging from 14.9 percent for undergraduates to 60 percent for out-of-state graduate students.[109]

The emerging financial stringency provided an unhappy backdrop to what was otherwise a grand moment of success after long struggle: the new main hospital opened to patients in summer 1982, the culmination of efforts by many people since the mid-1960s, before VCU existed. A survey of conditions at the medical school two years before described progress and stability under Dean Jesse L. Steinfeld. A former surgeon general of the United States whose warnings about the health consequences of tobacco consumption, especially the effects of "second-hand smoke," had led to his ouster by the Nixon administration, Steinfeld arrived at VCU to protests from some associated with Richmond's cigarette manufacturers. As dean, he did not crusade against tobacco, but his administration saw a greater emphasis on preventive medicine and training of physicians for general practices. First-year students now took a course in emergency medicine and, after passing the examination, became licensed emergency medical technicians. Despite a national decline in applicants to medical schools, the numbers of applicants far exceeded the numbers admitted, and their "scholastic abilities" continued to improve. Accreditation no longer troubled the school either, for the Liaison Committee on Medical Education had reaccredited the school in late 1976 without reservation and for the full term of seven years.[110]

The cover of the May 1982 issue of the MCV Alumni Association's *Scarab* showed the new hospital building looming over the Egyptian Building, suggesting the distance the institution had traveled since its founding. The

The Egyptian Building (1844) with Main Hospital looming behind, 1984. The opening of the new hospital in 1982 culminated an effort that began even before the merger that created VCU in 1968. (Virginia Commonwealth University Libraries)

"14-story, 536-bed, 600,000 square foot" building cost $56 million, at that time "the largest expenditure ever made by the state of Virginia on a single building." The new hospital consolidated services scattered about the Medical Center. One of the most important of these was the new emergency facility, "one of the largest in the country." In November 1981, the state Department of Health identified the hospitals' emergency rooms, staffed in part by student emergency medical technicians, as a Level 1 trauma center, the first in the state, based on standards set by the American College of Surgeons. Enclosed walkways above the streets connected the new building with other Medical Center facilities, at last eliminating the old practice of hustling patients from place to place via the old steam tunnels.[111]

The university boasted a robust construction program in 1982, with the Massey Cancer Center to open in early 1983, the pharmacy/pharmacology building underway at the Medical Campus, and the parking deck, dormitory, performing arts center, and student commons underway at the

Academic Campus. Louis Saksen, then assistant vice president for facilities management, reminded a journalist in 1983 that the legislature had denied VCU any construction funds whatsoever in the 1976–78 budget. By demonstrating that it was a comprehensive research institution, the university, in President Ackell's first five years, had managed to make significant progress.[112]

Richmond's city government battles entered a new phase in early 1982 when Mayor Henry Marsh and T. Justin Moore, the chief executive officer of Virginia Power and a respected figure in the business community, announced the formation of a joint private-public venture in economic development called Richmond Renaissance. As noted earlier, various groups in Richmond, including the Chamber of Commerce, had sought to reduce racial conflict in city government, but the key to Richmond Renaissance was that the black majority on the council had always favored economic development downtown. The conflict over the Hilton hotel stemmed from concern to make Project One successful, not populist-style antibusiness sentiment. Richmond Renaissance, headed by widely respected black businessman Clarence Townes and with half its initial $2.4 million provided by the city from federal block grants for community development, even won the endorsement of the *Richmond News Leader*, heretofore an implacable critic of the black majority on the council.[113]

Then, in the May elections, Roy West, an African American and administrator in the public schools, defeated Councilwoman Willie Dell. A VCU faculty member in social work when first appointed to council in 1973, Dell, an African American, voted with the black majority. A dramatic moment ensued when the new council first met in July 1982. The four white councilmen voted for West, resulting in a 4–4 tie with incumbent mayor Marsh, and then West cast his first council vote, for himself, and became Richmond's second black mayor, bringing relief to Marsh's many white critics. West was no figurehead, though, and in 1983 the black majority pushed through Richmond's Minority Business Utilization Plan, which held that companies contracting with the city must subcontract at least 30 percent of the dollar value of the contract to minority businesses. The city would also seek to spend 20 percent of expenditures for goods and services with minority firms. By this means, economic development projects might go forward and, in the process, "benefit directly the African American community." Through these means, white business elites and black political leaders found a way to live together, albeit warily.[114]

VCU's many constituencies and interests seemed to have found a moment of calm as well, although one no more likely to last than the calm in city politics after the new mayor's election. As the fall 1982 semester got underway, the university convened its first-ever honors convocation at the new performing arts center on the Academic Campus. Four faculty members were the first recipients of annual honors: Marion Martinez-Carrion, chair of the Department of Biochemistry, received the University Award of Excellence; Alexandre Fabiato, professor of physiology, received the research award; Pratip N. Raychowdhury, professor of mathematical sciences, received the service award; and Thomas P. Reinders, associate professor of pharmacy and pharmaceuticals, received the teaching award. The event not only heralded VCU's advance as a research university and as a teaching university (VCU then offered sixty bachelor's degrees, sixty-three master's degrees, twenty doctoral degrees, and three first professional degrees), it also testified to the stronger sense of a unified, two-campus university. That year also, Jane H. Crawley, of the School of Social Work, was the first official recipient of the Doris Douglas Budd Award, an annual recognition of an office administrator in honor of Doris Budd, whose thirty-plus years of service long predated the university and who was named Secretary of the Year in 1981.[115]

There would be, however, no celebration of Edmund Ackell's fifth anniversary at VCU. In fact, he had already informed faculty and students that times had changed for higher education, and financial constraints—economic recession, declining enrollments, and reductions in state and federal funding—made his forecasts for the future decidedly gloomy.[116] These problems would shape the coming years, for Richmond as well as for VCU.

6

Hard Times, Hard Feelings, and Conflicts with the Neighbors, 1980s

THE 1980s at VCU, as for American higher education in general, were years of budget reductions, at both state and federal levels, and contests over allocations of what remained. American medical schools, thanks to continued generosity from the National Institutes of Health and other granting agencies, perhaps suffered less financial pain, but at VCU disagreements about the direction and independence of the Medical Campus came to a showdown between President Ackell and the vice president for health services, which was settled in Ackell's favor by the Board of Visitors but left many unhappy. Qualities that had served Ackell well in the beginning—a gruff honesty and persistent effort toward his goals—became liabilities, and his misfortunes as a communicator contributed to his isolation as a leader.

In the last years of Ackell's presidency also a new campus master plan enflamed the smoldering conflict between VCU and the Oregon Hill neighborhood, and the neighborhood's leaders secured near unanimous opposition to VCU from neighborhood associations, city council, and the local legislative delegation. Since the 1950s, urban universities had used a variety of methods, subsumed under the label of "urban renewal," to ameliorate, as they saw it, blighted conditions in adjoining neighborhoods, almost always arousing opposition from the neighbors themselves.[1] VCU's conflict with Oregon Hill came late in that history, and by the 1980s beleaguered neighborhoods had defensive weapons, such as historic preservation regulations and political protests, at the ready. VCU's master plan hardly fit the full destructive model of "urban renewal," but it did look inward rather than, in the mode of an urban university, toward engagement with the school's neighbors, and the fight with Oregon Hill produced plenty of hard feelings.

IT ALL started innocently enough. David Ross, the university's general counsel, suggested in June 1981 to Grace Harris, then a faculty member in

141

social work and chair of the committee on the university's tenure policy, that the policy's statement that tenured faculty might be terminated only in case of "financial exigency" needed a fuller explanation. Harris brought the suggestion to the attention of Wayne C. Hall, the vice president for academic affairs, who, in turn, suggested to President Ackell that the term, which he noted was "standard 'boiler plate'" in tenure documents, needed clarification. Indeed, VCU had no plan for financial exigency, and it made sense to develop one. Ackell agreed, suggesting that a subcommittee of the university's planning committee might handle it.[2]

That year's gubernatorial election pitted Democrat lieutenant governor Charles Robb against Republican attorney general Marshall Coleman. Coleman campaigned on a promise to veto any tax increases, a vow at which Democrats scoffed after outgoing Republican governor John Dalton's prediction that Virginia might face a $500 million shortfall in revenues as a consequence of federal budget cutting. Robb's election as governor in November 1981 coincided with the American economy's fall into a sharp (and longer than predicted in Virginia) recession, and, from the perspective of Virginia universities, the theme of his administration would be budget cutting.[3]

The bad fiscal situation added urgency at VCU to faculty worries about the administration's plans for defining fiscal exigency. The draft policy was titled, "Procedures for Reduction, Reorganization and/or Termination of Programs and Consequent Termination of Faculty Members Due to Financial Emergency," which Barbara Fuhrman, of the School of Education and president of the Faculty Senate, accurately described as "ominous sounding." Speaking to the Faculty Senate as the 1982–83 academic year got underway, Fuhrman referred specifically to President Ackell's dismissive comment, reported in the news media, that he did not care about faculty worries because faculty members always worried. If the administration had provided a larger role for faculty in policy making, she said, there'd be less worrying. Declining state tax revenues led to a 5 percent budget reduction in early 1983 and another 1.8 percent taken back in September 1983, and the governor's proposed budget for 1984–86 offered no restoration of any of those funds. VCU and other schools began raising tuitions, reallocating funds, and seeking efficiencies.[4]

Meanwhile, some positive developments countered the gloom. President Ackell hosted a reception on 16 September 1983 for the seventy-five students enrolled in the new honors program at VCU. The program, developed by Thomas O. Hall, the founding chair of the Department of Philosophy and Religious Studies, had been a decade in the making. Hall, a Baptist minister and theologian, first came to Richmond Professional Institute as an adjunct professor. Both the State Council of Higher Education and VCU honored him with teaching and service awards, and Hall so loved his work that his wish was to be buried in his academic robe and VCU tie. That the Honors Program reflected special appreciation for scholarly excellence, the *CT* observed, some saw as a change from the egalitarian 1960s. To be sure, VCU's embrace of an identity as a comprehensive research university in the 1970s had included a commitment to academic excellence, and the Honors Program was another way to attract students with such commitments, too.[5]

The MCV/VCU Cancer Center, as it was called then, was dedicated in March 1983 after long effort, and renamed the Massey Cancer Center in May in recognition of William E. Massey's and his family's support. By year's end, its radiation facilities saw as many as two hundred patients a day, far more than expected, and a full array of research projects were underway. Walter Lawrence, the founding director of the center, recalled that, thanks to generosity from large and small donors, the center raised nearly four times the amount the board of visitors thought could be achieved. This success boded well for the university's upcoming first-ever capital campaign. As a new university without a deep alumni base, VCU's fundraising had to depend on nonalumni who believed in the cause.[6]

After ten years of stops and starts, the new Student Commons building finally opened on 17 January 1984 at the Academic Campus with a week of entertainment and other activities. Richard I. Wilson, vice president of student affairs, warned that the facility was already smaller than what the campus now needed, but he mustered plenty of enthusiasm for the building, where, as he saw it, commuter students seeking a refuge from bad weather or a bite to eat might find community.[7]

On the other hand, university oversight of student media remained contentious, as Ackell's brusque dismissal of his Task Force on Student Media in 1982 left matters up in the air. In spring 1983, the Academic Campus Student Association requested that the Media Committee be removed from its oversight. Vice President Wilson had favored that move for several years, and a subcommittee began studying a new setup for the *CT*, *Reflections in Ink*, WVCW radio, *Richmond Arts* magazine, and MCV's annual *X-Ray*. Its report at the end of October 1983 called for a Commission on

Media, with students, faculty, and administrators serving together. The new Commission on Media should also establish a code of ethics for student media, it said. To the *CT*'s editors, this prospect looked like another attempt by the administration to control policy and the means of communication. The Committee on Student Affairs rejected the proposed Commission on Media and in November created a new committee to draft a new proposal for governance of student media.[8]

The Commission on Media resurfaced in revised form and received approval from the University Council early in 1984. Formally designated as a "lay commission," it would include only one media member, chosen from the Mass Communications Department, and it would protect First Amendment freedoms, choose "media heads," adopt "journalistic ethics," and allocate funds. Members had yet to be named, but the commission would be underway in the next school year.[9]

Worry about the fiscal future and the Ackell administration's preference for reticence produced distress among the faculty. The *CT* obtained a document written by Elske v. P. Smith, dean of the College of Humanities and Sciences, stating that the budget cuts had forced the administration to develop an "Academic Plan" that would consolidate the Political Science and Sociology Departments with the School of Community and Public Affairs and the School of Social Work into a new combined School of Applied Social Sciences. Faculty objected, seeing the proposal as part of "the so-called 'doomsday documents'" that, as rumor had it, the administration had been developing in secret. By late January 1984, opposition to the consolidation—condemned by some as "a significant first step toward the gutting of liberal arts at VCU"—grew so unanimous that Provost Hall informed the college's Faculty Council Executive Committee that he would not present the proposal to President Ackell.[10]

The Faculty Senate then called a special meeting, with Ackell attending, to discuss "matters of mutual interest." Ackell was blunt: more budget cuts were expected; areas of overlap, such as political science and urban studies, would be consolidated; and VCU's focus on "career and professional programs" meant that the liberal arts would lose resources. The meeting turned hostile. Under fire, Ackell complained that faculty always blamed the administration for problems, though department chairs made most decisions. The statement "was greeted with spontaneous laughter." Undaunted, Ackell scoffed at fears that mandatory reviews of faculty threatened tenure, declaring, "If you only knew how many times each week

I have to defend tenure." The *CT*'s report declared in its final sentence: "As more than one person noted, Ackell may be permanently estranged from the faculty."[11] Estrangement may have overstated the case, but the president and the faculty leadership were hardly hitched for tandem work.

PRESIDENT ACKELL began the 1984–85 academic year, as had become his custom, with separate addresses to the faculty at each campus. He called for the liberal arts to be "an on-going and constant component of every student's curriculum," but he also called for "jettisoning" the old model of two years of general education followed by two years of courses in a student's major. As he put it, an accounting major could acquire a liberal arts education while also gaining competence in accounting and, potentially, become "'liberally educated without ever taking an upper division course in philosophy or English.'" The State Council of Higher Education had recently issued warnings to university presidents to promote the liberal arts, or else declining enrollments in those majors would require "'unproductive'" programs to be abandoned. After the dismay in the spring about the leaked proposal to consolidate programs, Ackell's comments hardly improved faculty morale.[12]

The 1984–85 academic year also saw Ackell scheduling his first-ever news conference with VCU student media. Despite rigid restrictions—only one representative from each entity, with only one question and one follow-up each, and no photographers—the *CT*, to whom he had refused to speak for the past two and half years, saw this as a "marked improvement." The highlight, also according to the *CT*, was the president's denial that he was inaccessible.[13]

The next week's paper featured a discussion of Ackell's inaccessibility, starting with a joke supposedly circulating that the president needed directions to find Shafer Court, at the center of the Academic Campus (and the implication of the joke was not that he spent all his time at the Medical Campus). Many department chairs contacted by the *CT* had never met the president, and the story compared him unfavorably to presidents at other Virginia schools who set aside time each week for open-door meetings.[14]

Someone, or something, got to the president and to the *CT*, for all changed in the new year. The *CT* requested an interview, and after surveying administrators and faculty, President Ackell agreed. Editor Ronnie Greene talked with him for an hour, and it went well. Ackell again stated his goal of making VCU financially sound and of service to Richmond ("part of the renovation that's going on throughout the city"). He wanted faculty and staff to join him in "making VCU and MCV one unified university" (the institutional names were Greene's, but they reflected common usage). Greene did not bring up Ackell's inaccessibility, and the president, in turn, was mellow about the university's news media, although he said that communication could be improved. The interview closed with a question about Ackell's future. He said that he planned to stay through the university's first fundraising campaign, and then, in three to five years, he would step down. The interview marked a new, more peaceful era for media relations.[15]

President Ackell, too, considered 1985 a turning point after nearly a decade of financial difficulties. Indeed, he told the faculty in August— again, in separate convocations for the Academic and the Medical College of Virginia Campuses—that VCU was positioned well for progress. VCU had advanced from eighty-eighth to seventy-first in rankings of American research institutions receiving federal support; VCU had moved into the top fifty institutions for medical research in America; and new doctoral programs had been initiated in urban services, business, public administration, and basic sciences, along with master's degree programs in "almost every school and college." The consequence for the faculty, he said, was higher expectations for scholarly research in "attaining the senior rank in most departments." VCU, he said, had come through "the most difficult four years in the history of our institution."[16]

The second semester began in January 1986 with a new governor, Gerald Baliles, but also with Governor Robb's final budget. Robb recommended faculty salary improvements and aid for the hospital's care of indigent patients, but also cut the university's overall budget. Ackell told the Higher Education Subcommittee of the House that enrollments had declined slightly by three hundred students but that hardly justified budget cuts of nearly $5 million and reductions of more than one hundred staff positions.[17]

The university had barely adjusted to the new budget plans when observers got a reminder that VCU sports, and especially the basketball program, mattered for many in the community. On 17 April 1986, President Ackell confirmed that Lewis Mills would be let go as athletic director at the end of June. Bill Millsaps, sports editor of the *Times-Dispatch*, claimed that the relationship broke a year before when basketball coach J. D. Barnett got cold feet after accepting the job at the University of Tulsa and asked to return to VCU. Ackell said yes; Mills said no, and held firm, with Ackell acquiescing but remembering.[18]

Basketball fans had lamented the forced finality of Coach Barnett's departure in 1985, but nationwide attention to the poor academic records of student athletes, including at VCU, aroused calls for reform. Under the then-proposed Proposition 48, a mandate from the NCAA for minimum high school grades and standardized test scores, VCU would not have been able to enroll twelve of the twenty scholarship basketball players from 1980 through 1984. That the other Virginia schools competing in Division One intercollegiate sports had comparable records was little solace.[19]

The university had already acted to strengthen the academic advising for athletes. The advising, which dated only from 1982, was under the direction of a former bookstore manager and had a member of the radio team in charge of basketball players' academics. VCU officials signaled the need for a change in summer 1985 by hiring Charles McLeod, a former VCU basketball player himself and the leader of the Students for an Afro-American Philosophy at VCU in 1969. After working as a counselor/recruiter for minority students at VCU, McLeod had earned a doctorate in education from the University of Virginia. Backing McLeod was a new intercollegiate athletics council composed of faculty, administrators, and alumni. The situation also engaged leaders in Richmond's black community, who disliked the appearance of a university exploiting, without educating, young black men. Clarence Townes, a businessman and leader in Richmond Renaissance, traced his involvement with VCU, including service on the Board of Visitors, to that issue.[20]

The new coach, Mike Pollio, saw the direction of events and stepped up his own academic expectations for basketball players. Pollio came to VCU after five successful seasons at Kentucky Wesleyan College. Victories did not come often enough, for the team's record from 1984–85's 26–6, the best in school history, fell to 12–16, the first losing season since VCU's founding in 1968.[21]

Pollio remained, but after the past year of lackluster performances and academic embarrassment, Athletic Director Lewis Mills paid the price when President Ackell allowed his contract to end in July 1986. "I'm looking for a lot of improvement in the overall structure, image and development of our athletic program," Ackell explained. Mills had been at VCU since 1974, and his accomplishments as athletic director included joining the Sun Belt Conference and gaining the Diamond, Richmond's then-new

baseball stadium, as the home park for VCU's baseball team. His supporters took out a full-page advertisement in the *Richmond Times-Dispatch* on
his behalf, and two major donors to the athletic program announced they
would withdraw their funds, but Ackell would not renew Mills's contract.[22]

In early July, VCU announced that Dr. Richard Sander, of Memphis
State University, would become the athletic director. President Ackell noted
Sander's strong record as a fundraiser, and he fit Ackell's preference for a
director with primarily administrative, rather than coaching, experience.
Sander agreed with Ackell's concern about the financial health of the program. "There's only one way to administer an athletic program today," he
told reporters. "You have to run it the same way you'd run a $2 1/2 million
business."[23]

Sander also addressed the issue of basketball players failing to graduate, by enrolling VCU in a consortium of universities that offered tuition
waivers to all former players who wanted to take classes toward a degree.
The student athletes would, in return, serve as role models in the community. Among the first players to take advantage of the opportunity were
Calvin Duncan and Edmund Sherod, two of the best to play at VCU.[24]

FUNDRAISING WAS a priority for the university as well as for the Athletics
Department. After the Board of Visitors' meeting in August 1986, the president announced that the first university-wide campaign to raise funds
from private donors would start in the fall. The campaign would continue
for four years, with an overall goal of raising $52 million. The board named
Richmond businessman Charles G. Thalhimer to chair the campaign. He
was a strong supporter of VCU, and his wife, Rhoda Thalhimer, had recently
retired after many years of service on the Board of Visitors. Ackell explained
that the state provided only about a third of the university's operating budget. Private financial support was essential for VCU to achieve distinction.
Just three months later, on 19 November, Ackell announced at a campaign
reception that VCU had already raised $20 million. The Thalhimers gave
funds for an endowed chair in art history, and the family of Samuel S.
Wurtzel, founder of what became Circuit City, endowed in his memory a
professorship in social work.[25]

The November issue of the *Scarab* discussed the capital campaign at the
Medical Campus, explaining that the campaign goal was divided evenly
between the two campuses and that donations to the planned moving of
the MCV Alumni House would count for the campaign. The university

sought the house's site, north of the Nelson Clinic, for creation of today's Ambulatory Care Center. On 5 March 1985 city officials had condemned the building (electrical and plumbing problems, termite damage, and a leaking roof), and the Alumni Association set out to raise funds to save the building by moving it.[26]

The enrollment figures for fall 1986 showed another decline, from 19,730 in 1985 to 19,373 in 1986. President Ackell told the Board of Visitors that the numbers masked progress, for freshmen applications were up by 20 percent and there was, for the first time, a waiting list. The board also confirmed new appointments, including two of lasting significance: Francis L. Macrina as director of the Center for Innovative Technology's Institute of Biotechnology, located at VCU, and Dr. Sheldon Retchin as chair of the Division of Geriatric Medicine.[27]

Ackell happily reported to the board in November 1986 that a recent FBI report on crimes at colleges and universities showed a 26 percent decline in reported crimes at VCU from 1982 to 1986. The reduction was a very positive development. "We're right in the middle of the city," Ackell noted. "Crime is a reality of urban life." Yet, budget constraints had left the school without an increase "in the number of sworn officers" on the VCU police force since 1978. Ackell was correct about crime in cities, as the homicide rate—often taken as representing all crime and violence—began rising steeply in cities after 1980.[28] Richmond was no exception, and crime was both a symptom of persistent poverty in the city and proof to suburbanites of urban disorder and danger.

Evidence of the latter had come the previous fall with the celebratory opening of the new Sixth Street Festival Marketplace on 18 September 1985. Spanning Broad Street to make a symbolic bridge connecting black and white Richmond, the marketplace had theaters and other venues for live entertainment, more than fifty retail tenants, and the Miller & Rhoads and Thalhimers department stores as its anchors. It was intended to revitalize the city's retail center by bringing suburban shoppers back to the city and thus creating jobs for city residents. When Mayor West and the white members of city council arranged for Richmond police officers to be assigned to the marketplace as "ambassadors" to welcome visitors, critics disparaged the move as yielding to stereotyped fears of the (black) city while also depriving city residents of needed police protection.[29]

The controversy in the midst of celebration symbolized what could be called political drift in Richmond. The goal of African American political mobilization had been to confront racism, to reduce poverty, and to expand opportunity. The actions of Mayor Henry Marsh's successor, Roy West, to ally with the white members of city council seemed politics as usual, with business interests trumping neighborhood interests. Racial divisions persisted in Richmond, but the single-district representation that brought the first black majority to city council also encouraged competing interests to emerge within black-majority districts, contrasting with the previous era of seeming solidarity. Dispirited electorates and a tax-strapped city government made for fewer political fireworks but also stymied ambitious improvement. Leaders at VCU could feel encouraged to focus on the university. The favored adjective to describe VCU was no longer "urban" or "comprehensive" but "research." The rising rate of violent crime, which finally peaked in the mid-1990s, only reinforced that inward turning.[30]

The sociopolitical situation in Richmond was the context for development of the VCU master plan after 1985. That year, VCU sought approval from the city to close streets on both campuses. The street closing on the Academic Campus had been first requested the previous November and then again in January, and the city had responded with conditions, including that the university cover the costs of the closings and provide parking enough to replace lost spaces. The closings also would make the campus "appear more safe," university planner Louis Saksen said. "Within the fact that we accept that we're an urban university within the city, we want to make the campus as safe and nice as possible." Students in the night school, he said, would especially appreciate the changes.[31]

The night school, with eleven thousand students, was changing, too. For one thing, in 1986 Rozanne Epps resigned after eight years as director of VCU's evening, summer, and off-campus studies. Her supervisor, Howard Sparks, complimented her for her commitment to adult students and to matching student demand with courses offered. The evening school dated to the days of RPI, but since then, community colleges, higher tuition, and day classes (part-time students now could take day classes) had reduced the numbers at night. The night school retained its spirit of inclusion and experimentation, but night classes now also functioned to serve full-time students unable to fit all their classes into their days.[32]

If the night school evidenced changes at VCU, the seemingly perpetual nomenclature issue resurfaced in 1987, with university administrators and the MCV Alumni Association again in contention. In April 1987, the VCU Academic Planning Committee proposed that "all free-standing schools" be called colleges of VCU, with the medical school thus becoming "the Medical College of Virginia Commonwealth University." Worse, a guide-book for using university names in publications stated the policy that "MCV" should be employed only "in historic references before 1968." The schools would be identified as, for instance, the "VCU School of Medicine," and only the hospitals would be known as the "Medical College of Virginia Hospitals." MCV alumni complained, and, as before, President Ackell responded that the 1968 founding legislation still prevailed. MCV would continue to be designated as the "Medical College of Virginia, Health Sciences Division of Virginia Commonwealth University."[33]

The problem remained: organizational efficiency demanded policies of centralization, yet the cultures at both campuses two decades after the merger assumed separation. The local media reflected and perpetuated that perspective, often with a pejorative tone. For example, a *Times-Dispatch* article in 1988 declared that VCU "was born after a shotgun wedding uniting, by arrangement of the General Assembly, the venerable Medical College of Virginia and an unusual collection of students and programs at Richmond Professional Institute."[34]

The organizational problem had practical consequences, too. In July 1987, VCU's purchasing procedures received a poor grade from an investigator from the state's Division of Purchases and Supply, and the division's director threatened to limit the university's independence in making contracts. The report noted that the Academic Campus and the Medical Campus used "a differing 'mishmash of documents and manuals,'" with "no single source to which the uninitiated requisitioner may refer." The report found no illegalities, and Ackell's administration made strong efforts to eliminate the "mishmash" and to provide "single source" procedures for staff at both campuses to follow. This work was not only uncelebrated but also potentially in conflict with the different work cultures at the campuses.[35]

An organizational problem did boil over into the newspapers in early June 1988. A letter sent to the governor, signed by two hundred employees in the Facilities Management Division, charged that the university oversaw them with "threats, intimidation and rule by fear." University spokesman Thomas Poe promised a full investigation. One sign of poor morale was a sick-out in April by some sixty employees to protest a change in their working schedules. The change brought them into line with the usual 8 a.m. to 4:30 p.m. schedule for other workers at VCU, but it seemed to the strikers unnecessary and arbitrary. The supervisor of the Housekeeping

Division told the *CT* that had his workers known about the action, at least two hundred others would have fallen ill on that day.

The university had a grievance procedure, Poe told the press, but the employees' letter to the governor charged that the personnel office instead immediately informed a complainant's supervisor of the grievance, leading to retaliation. At this distance, one can read the complaints as responses to determined efforts to impose administrative control over the division, which employees charged took the forms of denying supervisors' decision-making authority, imposing strict accounting of lunch hours and break times, and mandating inflexible work schedules. The defense of traditional workers' control of labor conditions seemed largely to come from the Medical Campus—at least, all the quoted examples of support for the old work rules referred to work at that campus and in the hospitals. Efficiency was the university's top priority, Poe responded.[36]

Amid this bad publicity, the *Times-Dispatch* published a feature story about Ackell, the result of a long interview at the "richly paneled President's House." To the inevitable charge of remoteness, Ackell declared that his job required him to act on a state and national stage—"We make progress by being there, not on campus." He defended the changes to work rules in facilities management as improvements that only a small number of workers opposed. Once his panel investigation finished, he warned, "some of these people are going to be embarrassed."[37]

The investigatory panel began its work in August with a questionnaire. Some workers feared the completed questionnaires might be traced back to them, but others looked forward to "airing their grievances to the panel." Although strikes by state employees were illegal, a "loosely organized employee alliance" contemplated another sick-out, promising that this time four hundred workers would participate.[38]

Then, in what even the university acknowledged as "inappropriate timing," the Facilities Management Division abolished the walls and windows department and laid off the unit's seven employees, all of whom had participated in the April sick-out. Within a week, the university rescinded the action, while denying charges that the department's abolition was retaliation for the workers' actions. Thomas Poe insisted that the only concern was cutting costs, and the workers might find other jobs at VCU.[39]

The panel's report went to the governor, and a summary of it went to employees on 11 November 1988. Better training for supervisors and clearer performance standards for workers seem obvious recommendations, but those recommendations also suggest some truth to workers' allegations that management had previously depended on threats and retaliation. No heads rolled, yet, but the report called for an outside consultant to study the organizational structure of the division for improvements.[40] Problems no doubt remained, but they departed from the news.

DURING THE conflict with the facilities workers, another, more profound controversy broke out at the Medical Campus. Alumni readers of the *Scarab* would hardly have noticed. In February 1988, the *Scarab* began the school's anniversary year with a series of feature articles about "the schools on the MCV Campus." Dean Stephen Ayres, of the School of Medicine, noted with pride in the first article that graduates continued to score in "the top third of graduates" on "part II of the National Board of Medicine examinations." Ayres could praise the quality of care at the Main Hospital from experience, for he had received an artificial hip replacement there in summer 1987. Yet, the problem of indigent care persisted, for one-third of the patients "treated at MCV" lacked insurance and could not pay for their treatment.[41]

The August issue of the *Scarab*, mailed to subscribers during the controversy over facilities management at the medical college, calmly reported on the School of Basic Health Sciences, which Dean S. Gaylen Bradley proudly described as the smallest of the schools on the Medical Campus but the largest in terms of federal research funding. An article about the School of Dentistry followed in the October 1988 issue, which highlighted the school's revision of the dental curriculum. As the state's only dental school, VCU also had to coordinate the BS program in dental hygiene with the education of dentists. The article suggested by its silence on the subject that the rift between Virginia dentists and the school had healed. Just a few pages farther into that issue there was a news story, amid the usual reports on appointments and grants, telling in a few understated paragraphs, "Dr. Connell's Contract Not Renewed; Dr. Andrako Named Acting V.-P."[42] In fact, all may have been well in the schools, but all hell had broken out at the top.

The bland report in the *Scarab* of Vice President Connell's replacement belied the controversy that his dismissal aroused. Four years earlier, the Board of Visitors had appointed Alastair McCrae Connell to be vice president for health services, following the retirement of Lauren Woods, as of 1 October 1984. Before coming to VCU, Connell, a native of Scotland with his MD degree from the University of Glasgow, had been dean of the School of Medicine and College of Allied Health at the University of Nebraska. President Ackell was pleased, too. With Connell in charge, and the hiring of Ayres as dean of the School of Medicine and Lindsay M. Hunt Jr. as dean of the School of Dentistry, both in July 1985, Ackell had fulfilled his promise to the medical faculty in fall 1984 that "the administrative structure of this campus will be in place and we will be ready to develop realistic plans for the future."[43]

Compared to Ackell's fall 1984 address to medical faculty, which mulled declining enrollments and budget cuts for teaching hospitals, Connell's first formal address to the medical faculty was optimistic. When hired, he, too, had acknowledged the problem of budget reductions but emphasized, in what became a theme of his tenure, that teaching was the Medical Center's primary mission. His address to faculty in November 1985, which the *Richmond Times-Dispatch* liked well enough to publish, concerned the whole university and, in truth, might have sounded just as swell coming from the university president. Connell had flair as a speaker, and no doubt his Scots burr made his speeches even more interesting for his listeners. Beverly Orndorff, longtime science reporter for the *Times-Dispatch*, still recalled a year later how Connell described the Medical Center to his faculty: "'It is all here,' he said. 'Discovery, achievement, advance, hubris, courage, confidence, anxiety, success and failure. All life made more piquant and poignant by the hovering pervasiveness of death.'"[44]

In 1986, the medical school celebrated the 125th anniversary of what had become MCV Hospitals with the completion of the renovation of North Hospital (opened in 1956 as Ennion Williams Hospital). All inpatient services now took place on the north side of Marshall Street, as planned in the early years of Warren Brandt's presidency. Vice President Connell noted that West Hospital, onetime hub of patient services, had been slated for eventual demolition, but that fate waited further review.[45]

Suddenly, in early July 1988, the press reported widespread rumors that Ackell wanted Connell gone. Not only was the vice president's contract unlikely to be renewed, but, rumor had it, Ackell had sought to replace Connell almost immediately after the latter's arrival in Richmond. Board members had asked Ackell to give the relationship a try, but now he was adamant. As the *Times-Dispatch* noted, the board elected university vice presidents on the president's recommendation. According to the bylaws, Connell served at the board's pleasure. Connell's supporters at the Medical Campus—both faculty and administrators—questioned the timing.

VCU was conducting its first capital campaign, when projecting stability mattered, and Ackell had promised to retire in three years. Who would take the post of vice president knowing that a new president might shortly choose to bring in another administrator?[46]

The Board of Visitors met on 21 July, went into a lengthy executive session (wherein personnel and property matters might be discussed privately, and legally), and then returned for Rector James B. Farinholt Jr. to report the session's actions, including its decision that Alastair Connell would be relieved of the vice presidency as of 30 September 1988. Connell was present, and the press said that "disbelief swept [his] face." He declared that he was being penalized "for the offense of having flashed the spotlight of candor, scholarship and accountability into the dank corridors of uneasy power." That was about the fullest explanation available. Ackell declared it "one of the most difficult personnel matters" of his presidency but did not elaborate. University spokesman Thomas Poe smothered curiosity in the cradle: "In personnel matters, in the corporate or the academic world, there are things we don't know and probably never will know."[47]

The drama had another act, for Connell remained in office to deliver "his annual state-of-the-college speech" to the faculty as classes began again in August. It was, of course, a farewell address, and he spoke for nearly forty-five minutes to an unusually large audience that included President Ackell seated in the fifth row. The larger portion of the address heralded accomplishments at the medical school and hospitals, but Connell discussed rumors at the Medical Campus of a proposed merger of the School of Basic Health Sciences with the School of Medicine, declaring that he shared the medical deans' unanimous opposition to it. Warming to his subject, he then charged that the prescription for "a simple and flexible administrative structure" made at the time of the merger in 1968 had been superseded by the dangerous physic of centralized planning, resulting in "pervasive cynicism among faculty toward university administration." He concluded: "The eerie calm of the graveyard or the sullen, silent servitude of the gulag are not the atmosphere of scholarship." The university needed "a large dose of candor." His conclusion received a standing ovation of more than thirty seconds, with Ackell joining those standing (he told a reporter it was "a good speech"), and then faculty members left the auditorium.[48]

Despite his presence at the speech, President Ackell could not let the vice president have the last word, and his office issued a statement two days later.

It declared that Connell's complaint about the lack of candor was "absolute folly." There could no victory in making such a statement, but Ackell was out of town, and a spokesman said there would be no further elaboration.[49]

The *Times-Dispatch* then tied recent events into a package. Publishing excerpts from Connell's address and Ackell's response, it editorialized that Connell was "rather vague" in his criticisms and that Ackell in reply was "rather more vague." Referring also to the complaints from the facilities workers, the editorial concluded, "And the public knows from both Dr. Connell and maintenance personnel that all doesn't go hummingly at VCU."[50]

The final act occurred on 15 September 1988, when the Board of Visitors revised the university's bylaws to state that vice presidents would now serve "at the pleasure of the president." The decision not to renew the contract of Alastair Connell ostensibly did not figure in the board's discussion, but Ackell's decision to let him go did have "unanimous approval from the board." A week later, John Andrako, who had been the associate vice president for health sciences, was named acting vice president. Andrako, who originally joined the pharmacy faculty in 1956, served ably in the post until John Jones was hired in 1991, after Ackell's retirement. In the long run, the board's clarification of presidential administrative authority is the reason that this episode matters in VCU's history. In the short run, that summer's bad publicity provided the discordant fanfare to the university's celebration of its 150th anniversary.[51]

Planning for the birthday celebration began in September 1987 with the hiring of Richmond event organizer Phyllis J. DeMaurizi. She had a small staff and a two-year budget of $250,000. Meanwhile, the university contracted with Virginius Dabney, founding rector, retired editor of the *Richmond Times-Dispatch*, and, since his retirement, quasi-official historian of Virginia and Richmond, to produce a full history of the university from its founding as the medical department of Hampden-Sydney College in 1838. Published in November 1987 and replete with names (and bolstered in the later chapters by Dabney's own insider's knowledge of Richmond and Virginia), the book constructed two narratives—one about MCV and the other, shorter, about RPI—but did not merge them after the 1968 creation of VCU, instead covering the two different campuses. The final two chapters did assess the university in 1987 and Ackell's presidency, which included Dabney's explanation that Ackell's "management technique" precluded open access to him for students and faculty. Dabney concluded that VCU was headed in a direction that "seems right for the school, the commonwealth and the world of education."[52]

The celebration would continue into spring 1989, and, said one organizer, "The university has united to help produce a first-class project, both MCV and VCU." Despite that phrasing, the birthday celebration was intended not only to raise VCU's image but also to enhance relationships between the Medical and Academic Campuses. Thus, the festivities took place on 4 November 1988 midway between the campuses, with the main distinction a musical generation gap—Peter Duchin's orchestra played at the Richmond Centre (the tuxedoed VCU Ram mascot, not yet dubbed "Rodney," helped conduct) and "the Coasters and the Teenagers" performed next door at the Marriott hotel. Assuredly, no one thought to invite Dickie Disgusting and the Degenerate Blind Boys. Enthusiastic partygoers included old grads and current students, and they traveled back and forth between venues.[53]

No one enjoyed the night more than Edmund Ackell. "It's jam packed over there," he told a reporter. "Jam packed." He promised that the anniversary celebration would become a tradition. At month's close, the local telephone company revealed that the next year's directories, being sent to some three hundred thousand businesses and homes, featured a cover showcasing VCU's diverse buildings that was designed by Camden Whitehead, a member of the VCU Arts faculty.[54]

The emphasis on VCU was bound to produce some qualms among the stalwart defenders of the long tradition of MCV, and the next issue of the *Scarab* featured MCV Alumni Association President Michael O. McMunn's complaint that the program for the convocation marking the 150th anniversary used VCU, not MCV, to identify such speakers as Dean Stephen Ayres, from the School of Medicine. Was it deliberate, he asked? Yes, it was. But, he conceded, VCU was the university, and the MCV Campus was part of the whole. What he preferred was "the marriage of the six letters MCV/VCU."[55]

The Alumni Association marked its centennial in 1989, and the future of the Alumni House became another point of contention. The master plan for the Medical Campus, first developed in 1979–80 and revised in 1987, called for construction of a new ambulatory care center, recognizing that many common medical procedures no longer required inpatient hospital stays. The likeliest location was adjacent to the Nelson Clinic, at the southeast corner of Eleventh and Clay Streets, where the Maupin-Maury House, purchased by the MCV Alumni Association in 1947, had stood since 1846.[56]

The solution was a trade, with the ambulatory care center to take the site of the MCV Alumni House and the house to be moved to the northwest corner across the street. The association vacated the house for offices on the sixteenth floor of West Hospital, itself then being converted to medical offices. At the association's centennial meeting in May 1989, the house stood empty, so deteriorated from neglect that it had been condemned.[57]

THE PROBLEM with the MCV Alumni House was nothing compared to the uproar caused by the new master site plan for the Academic Campus, which once again set the Oregon Hill neighborhood at war with VCU. The longer aftermath of the Board of Visitors' meeting on 16 March 1989 largely concerned controversy over the master plan, but the immediate news from the meeting was the formal announcement that President Ackell would retire, effective 1 July 1990, years earlier than expected. Already there was talk that Gordon Davies, the highly regarded director of the State Council of Higher Education, and Governor Gerald Baliles, whose term would end in January 1990, would be candidates to lead VCU. The newspaper repeated what had become the standard charges that Dr. Ackell "has been characterized as a distant and often-absent administrator" and that he had "a management style regarded as removed and authoritarian." The article did note that VCU's budget had nearly quadrupled during his tenure, that eight new buildings went up, that the honors program got underway (and SAT scores for incoming students were sixty-one points higher than in 1977), and that the Campaign for VCU neared its goal for the school's first fundraising campaign. And, in fact, Ackell got the last word, declaring that "the university has found itself. I am satisfied that we are an emerging great university."[58]

Seven months later, on 25 October 1989, Charles Thalhimer, chairman of the Campaign for VCU, announced that the school had passed its goal of $52 million in its first university-wide fundraising campaign, and with eight months to go, too. About two-thirds of the gifts to the campaign were designated for "the MCV Campus," the press release said. The campaign would end on 30 June 1990, the date when President Ackell would retire.[59]

Controversy over the master plan obscured the capital campaign's success. Indeed, the plan had hardly been introduced before opposition appeared.

The plan's guiding idea, presented to the press on 22 March 1989, was to provide VCU's Academic Campus "with more of a campus atmosphere." Floyd and Grove Avenues would be closed, as would Linden Street; Grace Street's disreputable shops and bars would be replaced by new commercial development; and the new western boundary of the campus would be at Morris Street, just west of Harrison Street. The plan called for acquiring twenty-eight acres of city land, including nearly 150 residences and commercial buildings.[60]

The nationally known planning firm Dober and Associates had much experience with academic campus plans, and the plan for VCU's Academic Campus reflected that experience in that it proposed an inward focus, centered on a core "lying between the Student Commons and Cabell Library," as the CT phrased it, "to unify the campus physically." That also meant that with residence halls and parking areas designated to surround the campus perimeter, the plan separated the campus from its neighbors. In a way, that vision reflected the development of VCU as a research university under Edmund Ackell. Rather than emphasizing VCU as a unique urban experiment in Richmond, as had been the case with Brandt's administration, or as the less celebrated insouciant countercultural campus of the Temple years, the master plan saw VCU as a research university with its peers located elsewhere. VCU's Academic Campus would stand on its own, largely independent of Richmond's future.[61]

That it would be phased in across fifteen years calmed none of the critics. The Fan District Neighborhood Association, traditionally willing to cooperate with VCU, found the move west to Morris Street an ominous precedent, and residents of Oregon Hill joined businessmen from Grace Street in dissatisfaction. "It's just a plan," reassured Patrick J. Lawlor, assistant vice president for Facilities Management, "not an accomplished fact." The justification for the plan was VCU's lack of space, even though state forecasts had enrollments static and growth of the faculty and staff limited, but the plan had at least as much to do with improving the image of the university. Richard P. Dober, the plan's creator, was frank: "An 'appropriate campus' could be achieved by creating more 'green areas' and walkways, eliminating pockets of poverty along West Broad Street and cleaning up portions of Grace Street where there are 'some of the more unsavory aspects of urban life.'"[62]

Lawlor and other university officials in mid-April came to a joint meeting of the Fan District Association, the Lower Fan Civic Association, and the West Avenue Improvement Association. The meeting in March with Oregon Hill's representatives had dissolved in anger, and officers of the Save Oregon Hill Organization, successor to the Save Our Homes organization, came to this meeting. Joining them were two city councilmen, William J. Leidinger and Chuck Richardson, and a legislator, E. Hatcher Crenshaw Jr., all of whom supported the residents' opposition to the plan.[63]

During the contention about the master plan, a feature story appeared in the *Times-Dispatch* once again heralding VCU as an urban university. The article began with assurances from university leaders that VCU students included buttoned-down "preppies" as well as bohemian students, but President Ackell sounded very much like Warren Brandt twenty years before. "To be an urban institution, we must involve ourselves in all of the urban environment," he declared. "We must be involved in solving its social, political and economic problems." That program included development of the master plan, and the article quoted City Manager Robert C. Bobb in favor of making the city's budding relationship with VCU "blossom," including through joint creation of "an incubator that would encourage health-related industries to locate near the Medical College of Virginia campus." If the university's mission seemed the same, the student body was changing. The article noted that VCU still enrolled a larger proportion (about 16 percent) of minority students than the state's other historically white universities. The average age of students overall was up, the numbers from metropolitan Richmond were down, but the numbers of applicants, especially from northern Virginia, had increased greatly, along with the test scores of those applicants.[64]

Yet, the master plan marched on. Representatives from the Fan District and Oregon Hill neighborhoods attended the board's meeting on 19 May 1989. Unlike the protests a decade earlier, when VCU first floated the idea of constructing athletic fields in Oregon Hill, all parties behaved with cordiality, although the neighborhood associations remained adamant that VCU ought to expand to the north, toward Broad Street. Rector James B. Farinholt Jr. assured VCU's neighbors that the master plan, which the board did have to approve, would come up for a vote "in near months." Richard Dober, the plan's consultant, was there, too, and unlike in March, he now spoke of revisions to the draft plan that could "accommodate the university . . . and still be sensitive" to the neighborhoods.[65]

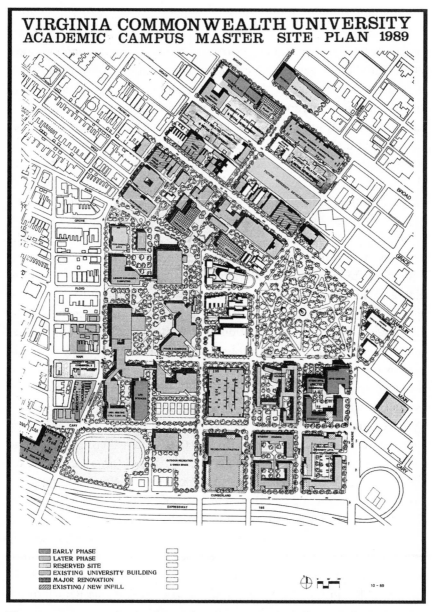

The 1989 master site plan for the Academic Campus provoked strong opposition from VCU's neighbors and the Richmond community, leading to its abandonment in 1990. (Virginia Commonwealth University Libraries)

An editorial in the *News Leader* four days later expressed opposition to the master plan. Rather than destroy "cohesive and coherent" (a phrase purposely borrowed from Dober's description of his plan) neighborhoods, VCU should consider limiting enrollments or consider building in Fulton Bottom (perhaps an ironic suggestion, for Fulton was a onetime cohesive and coherent neighborhood at the east end of Richmond that urban renewal had leveled). VCU might also become a senior college, offering only the last two years of undergraduate work, the editorial suggested. Or, VCU might move north of Broad. The *Times-Dispatch*'s editor agreed. Richmond's citizens had a better argument than VCU's "Massachusetts-based planning consultant." The editorial offered its own solution for VCU's future growth—upward, by way of "high-rise academic buildings."[66]

Negotiations with the neighborhood associations continued into the summer. In June the faculty in the Department of Urban Affairs sent a letter, respectful but signed by all, to the president, objecting to the master plan and the secretive process of its development. Though they made no specific recommendations, the letter did suggest expansion north to Grace and Broad Streets and construction of high-rise buildings as alternatives to consider. The administration held to the plan—moving north would destroy the master plan's intent that the campus center on the library, and those blocks on Broad were already slated for maintenance facilities.[67]

Elections for statewide offices took place in November, and both Marshall Coleman, Republican candidate for governor, and L. Douglas Wilder, the Democrat and the victor in the election, stated their opposition to VCU's move into the neighborhoods. So, too, did all three candidates for the district's seat in the legislature. At its meeting in November 1989, the Board of Visitors welcomed representatives of the neighborhood associations, Councilman Richardson, and others to comment on the amended VCU master plan. The board then went into executive session, returning after four hours to the open meeting to report approval of the revised master plan. The new plan excluded from VCU expansion two half blocks in Oregon Hill and proposed that VCU incorporate Monroe Park into the campus but keep it open to the public.[68]

The editor of the *Times-Dispatch* liked the compromise and told Oregon Hill residents before the board meeting that change would come to their neighborhood. Better that it come via a master plan than through haphazard development. The *News Leader*'s editor seemed to agree. And the *TD* editorialized again, after the board meeting, that the city ought to present Monroe Park to VCU as part of the plan. VCU "returns far more to the community than it takes."[69]

IF 1989–90 was a year of conflict with the community, it also saw the beginning of an official academic program in women's studies, the culmination of profound changes in the roles of women in society and in higher education as well as steady pressure from women at VCU. The takeoff, most obvious in the enrollments of women, occurred earlier, in the 1970s, with women's participation in higher education rising and barriers to their participation falling. Women had been significantly present at RPI from its founding, and they took places at MCV well before the University of Virginia admitted women on an equal basis, but even as women became the majority of college students—in the nation as well as at VCU— representation of women as faculty members lagged.[70]

That is not to suggest that women at VCU had been inactive and indifferent since the 1970s. Changes occurred at both campuses, with the percentage of women in the graduating medical class jumping from less than 6 percent in 1970 to 30 percent in 1980. By 1987, women made up nearly 60 percent of VCU students, the highest proportion among the state's PhD-granting schools. Together and individually, faculty and staff women, and women students, had advocated for changes that would reflect their presence and break down barriers to their progress. For instance, as head of the Evening School, Rozanne Epps not only supported recruitment of more women administrators but also developed a new course, "Focus on Choice," for women investigating career changes and self-development.

In 1985, Elske v. P. Smith, the dean of the College of Humanities and Sciences, convened a task force to plan for a program in women's studies at VCU. Almost coinciding with VCU's founding in 1968, a new field of study about women in society, literature, and history had emerged with and out of the so-called second wave of feminism, and the field's intellectual energy drew others to analyze and theorize issues relating to gender and to women's situations. Several women associated with local universities, including VCU's Diana Scully and Betsy Brinson, organized the first Virginia Women's Studies Conference in 1981 at Randolph-Macon College. The association met annually, including at VCU on 2 November 1985, to present scholarly papers and to discuss and debate. Dean Smith sent her task force's report to department chairs in the College of Humanities and

Sciences on 3 November 1986, telling them that she thought it "indeed high time that VCU did offer a minor in Women's Studies."[71]

Unlike the introduction of courses in African American history and culture, which came about through actions by students in 1969, women's studies emerged at VCU as a faculty initiative. By 1987, African American studies at VCU offered a minor field, and the then-program director, Avon Drake, a political scientist, said that it attracted a steady number of students. One effect of the growth of scholarship about African Americans, Drake pointed out, was that that material was also incorporated into traditional offerings in other disciplines. Nancy Bazin Topping, the founder of the women's studies program at Old Dominion University in 1978, the state's first, in fact did describe her work as "affirmative action," encouraging new courses representing women's and gender issues, akin to the earlier efforts for African American–related courses at VCU.[72]

By the late 1980s a core of VCU scholars teaching and researching women's issues had gained standing enough for academic legitimacy. The case of Susan Estabrook Kennedy is exemplary. Kennedy published the first book produced by a member of the VCU History Department, was the first woman to be promoted to professor, and was the first to chair the department. She also was VCU's first recipient of a Guggenheim Fellowship. Her first book, published in 1973, *The Banking Crisis of 1933*, was in the standard mode of politico-economic history; her second book, *If All We Did Was to Weep at Home: A History of White Working-Class Women in America*, published in 1979, showed both her intellectual direction and the vigor of the field of women's history. Two years later, she published a book-length historical bibliography on *America's White Working-Class Women* and celebrated the rich scholarship yet to be done: "Every new dissertation hints at the dozens of others which should be written." Before her untimely passing in 2003, Kennedy proved equally adept as an administrator, serving as administrative associate to the president, associate and interim dean of the college, and as acting vice provost for academic affairs.[73]

Kennedy joined Brinson and Scully on the Women's Studies Task Force, along with Leslie Slavin, psychology, and Lynn Z. Bloom, English (and author of, among other books, *The Assertive Woman*). Bloom's name came first of the authors of the task force's report, but one assumes that was an alphabetical convention, and the members all contributed. The report called for a women's studies program to be established as soon as possible, with an "interdisciplinary and unifying" pedagogical mission.[74]

Following the task force's work, in summer 1987 Diana Scully guided the drafting of a plan for a women's studies program. Dean Smith created a reaction document, submitting it to Bloom, Kennedy, Scully, and Dorothy Scura, the chair of the English Department, in late September, with the intention of sending the proposal to the university's curriculum committees and then to the State Council for Higher Education in Virginia (SCHEV). As the proposal made its way successfully upward, Smith appointed Scully coordinator of women's studies, and Scully crafted a proposal for a minor in women's studies that got underway in September 1989. It was hardly a robust child—the coordinator held a joint appointment, the office was a converted bathroom, and the program then had no permanent budget—but nonetheless, women's studies was finally born. Many women at VCU had aided in the birth of the women's studies program, but Diana Scully, as founder and nurturer, was the foremost of its midwives.[75]

Scully declared that the program would begin whether the funds materialized or not. The courses, she continued, would emphasize "multicultural diversity among women." The records of such programs elsewhere, she said, showed that female students of women's studies "have increased self-esteem and leadership skills." A student advisory group soon began meeting at the Commons and emerged as the VCU Women's Caucus. Alexis Ruffin, its founder and then a graduate student in sociology, recalled that the group sponsored an exhibition of visual representations of women—from fine art to advertisements—and in spring 1990, visiting speakers such as outspoken congresswoman Bella Abzug.[76]

Women's studies as well as African American studies had developed by the end of the 1980s into vital interdisciplinary fields of study, and yet VCU—like other universities nationally—still organized scholarship by discipline. Their indeterminate status left both programs, and others like them, limited in resources and vulnerable to critics, as the 1990s would show.

The creation of the women's studies program was important, but it hardly generated the public attention given to developments on the basketball court. The second annual homecoming Winterfest in 1987 was a success, but the basketball team was not, making a record of 17–14. That marked an improvement over the previous year but not enough to please

fans, and grumbling about Coach Pollio spread. Next year's team had better improve, for the Sun Belt Conference Tournament would be held in
Richmond in 1988, a scheduling success for university and city officials,
especially the new city manager, Robert Bobb, who pushed hard to get the
tournament. If VCU had a good team, more local fans would come out and
help pay for the tournament.[77]

Problems in the Athletics Department at Virginia Tech aroused Governor Gerald Baliles in summer 1987 to declare that Virginia's schools
must never subordinate academics to athletics. The governor's statement,
Ackell declared, was "what all of us believe in." That summer Alvin
Schexnider, hired as associate provost for academic affairs, was told that
the graduation rates for athletes should be his priority. A report prepared
that fall for the Board of Visitors showed that student athletes overall
graduated at a higher rate than other VCU students, but the basketball
players continued to lag badly behind. That season went well, with the
Rams finishing the season with a 23–12 record, good enough for second
place in the Sun Belt Conference and an invitation to the National Invitational Tournament.[78]

Despite that success, Pollio's contract would run out after the 1988–89
season, and how the season went would determine his future. Then trag-
edy struck. On 2 January 1989, during a routine midday practice session,
senior forward Michael Brown collapsed. Despite swift attention, he was
pronounced dead on arrival at the Medical College of Virginia Hospitals.
His death staggered the campus and the team. With losses mounting, in
early February Pollio announced that he would resign at the end of the season to become an assistant athletic director. The team played well enough,
considering, but finished with a losing record.[79]

Despite public assurances that academics trumped athletics, at VCU
winning basketball was very important, and the coach was at least as
prominent as the president in the school's public image. Even before the
season's close, Athletic Director Sander had opened negotiations with
Charles H. "Sonny" Smith, the longtime coach at Auburn University,
whose 1988–89 team also had a losing record. Smith brought name recognition and the promise of recruiting pull, but his salary demands
required hurry-up fundraising in Richmond. On arrival, he declared
his intent for this to be his final coaching job, and he embraced a challenge that he had not faced at Auburn, where football was dominant.

"There is going to be more pressure on me at VCU than there ever was at Auburn," Smith said.[80]

DURING THIS same period, Governor Baliles announced the Commission on the University of the Twenty-First Century, to plan for how Virginia would meet the expected increased demand for higher education in the next century. The commission conducted public hearings around the state, and VCU hosted one in January 1989. Most speakers advocated solutions that served their own institutions, and President Ackell was no exception, calling for the state to support universities' roles in economic development, including "education in evening and off-campus career programs." The governor's commission released its report on 15 November 1989, declaring on page 1, "We were asked for a vision, not a plan," yet the report nonetheless received criticism for "vagueness" and for offering "few specifics." Virginia had the eleventh largest system of higher education but only the twentieth greatest research volume. The commission called for enhanced international instruction as well as STEM (science, technology, engineering, and mathematics) competencies. The story in the *Times-Dispatch* noted that the commission said nothing about VCU's master plan and the neighborhoods' reactions to it.[81]

The city, too, seemed neglected. In early 1989 the Virginia Inter-Government Institute presented a report on the future of the Richmond region, a planning document sponsored by VCU and local businesses. Predictions were dire: tax rates would skyrocket, crime would spread to the counties, and squabbles between jurisdictions would fill the courts. Only regional cooperation could avoid that fate, while also saving millions of dollars. Ackell presented the report and agreed to serve in a Capital Area Assembly to encourage that cooperation. Comments from the audience indicated that bad blood from the era of annexation fights and white flight remained, and the study's call for city-county revenue sharing had little support, regardless of the crime rate in Richmond.[82]

In November 1989 news came that Richmond had dropped from fourth to fifth among major cities in murder rates. Unfortunately, the drop in the standings came from the rise in homicides in New Orleans, the new number four, and deaths in Richmond continued as before. The factors behind the violence were many, with poverty and the drug trade at the top of most analysts' lists, but, measured by the murder rate, violence kept increasing in Richmond. Because the victims of violence usually came to the MCV Hospitals for treatment, media coverage invariably linked the hospitals, and the university, with crime.[83]

Commencement that year honored the leaders of the capital campaign and Dr. Ackell, who was named president emeritus. An interview in June 1990 captured the gruff persona he conveyed to too many. "All the noise Oregon Hill makes is meaningless," he told a reporter. "Those people are going to sell those homes, and 10 years from now Oregon Hill is not going to be Oregon Hill." Yet, no one could say that he had not given his best efforts, as he saw them, to the university. Numbers can measure his presidency: the budget increased from $135 million to more than $500 million, and the university endowment "jumped" from $12.2 million to $47 million. Research grants made a comparable rise, from $11.2 million to $51 million. Eight new buildings opened, and master plans, for better or worse, were in place for both campuses. Since he took office in 1978, VCU had added nine undergraduate degree programs, thirteen master's degree programs, and six doctoral programs, and established eight off-campus degree programs. He departed from an institution in conflict with its neighbors, but it was a different, and better, institution.[84]

7

Playing through the Rain, 1990–1992

ROBERT C. BOBB, Richmond's city manager, in 1988 proposed that the city council develop a strategic plan for the city (and for regional cooperation). The project got underway in March 1989, with expectations that the full process might take up to two years. A ten-member steering committee, headed by Hays T. Watkins, chairman and chief executive officer of the CSX Corporation, then headquartered in Richmond, would guide the process. After years of discord in city council, the injunction to seek consensus made sense, but the environment for planning was hardly rosy. In addition to the city's own problems, the committee also understood that Richmond could expect little help from the federal and state governments.[1]

The state's and the nation's economies had revived in the mid-1980s, and Governor Gerald Baliles's administration in 1986 and 1987 successfully pushed for state investments in road building and education. Bobb became Richmond's city manager in mid-1986, coming from a similar post in Santa Ana, California, and he, too, brought energy to government, with a plan to fight crime and a reorganization of city government that won praise in early 1987 from the *Richmond Times-Dispatch*. Richmond continued to face the budgetary constraint of a limited and impoverished tax base, and would have operated at a loss in 1987 if not for accounting adjustments. Bobb nonetheless sought to address problems directly and immediately. Among those problems was the Sixth Street Marketplace, which was struggling along with other retailers in the Broad Street commercial center as customers stuck to suburban shopping centers.[2] There was a role here for an urban university; VCU had yet to accept it.

AT VCU, the 1989 fall semester began with a record twenty-one thousand students on campus (two-thirds of them full-time, the *Commonwealth Times* added). The university would convene an enrollment forum in October about future growth. Virginia, unlike most states, expected significant expansion in the number of prospective students in the 1990s, and Governor Baliles had charged his Commission on the University of the

City Manager Robert C. Bobb speaks on the pedestrian walkway of the Sixth Street Marketplace, November 1989. The Miller & Rhoads department store fronts Broad Street on the left. (Courtesy of *Richmond Times-Dispatch* and The Valentine)

Twenty-First Century to report on how to manage that expansion. Adding to the uncertainty about the future at VCU was the "gridlock" still enveloping the master plan. The university did have a newly revised mission statement, however. Under Warren Brandt, VCU had defined itself as an urban university, and, led by T. Edward Temple, VCU had redefined itself as a comprehensive urban university. Now, as Edmund Ackell's presidency entered its final academic year, VCU declared itself "a public, urban, research university." The revised mission statement—and VCU had been using the term "research university" for some time now—seemed cautious when contrasted with ambitious plans at other Virginia universities for new initiatives to be paid for by the expected state financial support to follow the soon-to-be-issued report of Governor Baliles's Commission on the University of the Twenty-First Century.[3]

The search for VCU's new president was underway, too, with the Chicago-based consulting firm Heidrick and Struggles retained to assist in the search. Echoing the new mission statement, one of the principal qualifications was that the new president understand "a public, urban, teaching, and research university with a comprehensive academic health center." In addition to the "special Committee on the Nomination of a President," headed by former rector James B. Farinholt Jr., there were four "steering committees," with representatives respectively from the faculty, students, staff, and administrators.[4]

On 2 November, the University Council approved the revised mission statement, and then heard a presentation on the revised master plan. President Ackell explained that the city had denied permission to build a pedestrian bridge across Belvidere Street, without which expansion to the east was impossible. The same problem of getting students safely across a busy street precluded development to the north across Broad Street, he continued. That left only moving south, deeper into the Oregon Hill neighborhood. Residents there promised to be present to protest when the plan went before the Board of Visitors on 16 November.[5]

The next evening, on 3 November, the second annual Founders Day Gala took place at the Omni Richmond Hotel on Main Street in the downtown financial center. The high-rise hotel was one of "a series of chrome, glass, and granite skyscrapers inhabited by law firms, insurance companies, banks and financial services [that] composed a new skyline between Capitol Square and the James River." The construction boom of the mid-1980s seemed to fulfill the predictions of the boosters of the Downtown Expressway but also warranted the warnings of Mayor Henry Marsh and others in the 1970s that development on Main Street would make it harder to revitalize the commercial district on Broad Street. Already, competition from the Omni and other new hotels had contributed to the closing in 1988 of the John Marshall Hotel, whose towers and brightly lit sign had been landmarks in downtown Richmond.[6]

The planners of the Founders Day Gala no doubt appreciated the convenience of the new Omni Hotel, but during the 1980s the Jefferson Hotel, on Franklin Street between the two campuses, arose from decrepit conditions to return to glory as a luxury hotel. Two films, the highly regarded *My Dinner with Andre* (1981) and the less highly regarded *Rock 'n' Roll Hotel* (1983), had used the abandoned hotel as a set. A newspaper columnist then called the hotel "an eyesore on the city's skyline," but new owners in 1983 began restoration, and, on 5 May 1986, the Jefferson reopened. The hotel made a splendid venue, indeed, for meals and lodging of visitors to VCU, and, as important, stabilized that area east of the Academic Campus. But, as historian Tricia Pearsall said of the nearby Ellen Glasgow House, for now it was "an island in a lake of asphalt parking lots."[7]

Less than a week after the gala, on 8 November 1989, Virginia voters went to the polls and, in a very narrow decision, made Democrat L. Douglas Wilder the nation's first elected African American state governor. Neither Wilder nor his Republican opponent, Marshall Coleman, would endorse VCU's master plan, but issues related to higher education played little part in the campaign.[8]

The Board of Visitors' meeting on 16 November got off to a rocky start when an electrical outage forced everyone to march over to the Franklin Street Gym. Despite dark murmurings among the protestors from Oregon Hill that the outage had been planned, they may have enjoyed the opportunity to sit in the gym's bleachers, holding their signs, while the board members sat in folding chairs on the gym's floor below. During the setup, board members, university officials, and protestors mingled over coffee and sweet rolls. The meeting began with approval of the new mission statement. Positive reports from the Medical Campus followed: architects had been chosen for the next parking deck, revenues at the hospital in the first quarter exceeded operating expenses, and new software for managing patients and for managing finances (a theme in board minutes from the earliest days of VCU) was soon to be operational. The board approved project plans for the Ambulatory Care Center and for renovations of classrooms and, appropriately, the Franklin Street Gym.[9]

Then, President Ackell introduced the university's planner, Patrick Lawlor, who explained the revised master plan. The main changes involved backing away from intrusion west into the Fan neighborhood, locating maintenance facilities on Broad Street, and expanding into Oregon Hill. Public comment followed, with Richmond City Councilman Chuck Richardson again objecting to the plan's incursions into neighborhoods. He and Councilman William Leidinger, who was not present, proposed to turn Monroe Park, on the eastern edge of the Academic Campus, over to VCU, contingent on the promise that future expansion would be east and north. The board then went into executive session. Four hours later, the board returned to regular session and immediately went into recess so that Ackell and Acting Rector James Farinholt could meet with the press at the President's House. The master plan as approved by the board now incorporated Monroe Park, halted at Harrison Street to the west, and proposed to acquire in Oregon Hill the scant half blocks between Green Alley on the north and

Cumberland Street on the south, between Cherry Street on the west, and Pine Street on the east. That reduced intrusion still drew continued fire from leaders of the Save Oregon Hill coalition. The battle, they said, would continue.[10]

Governor Baliles's Commission on the University of the Twenty-First Century issued its report at the same time. Those who had expected ambitious proposals were disappointed; the report called for cautious planning. The commission's caution was propitious, for shortly after the report appeared, the state's financial officers announced that revenues were down from the previous year. The state's shortfall grew worse, and in December the governor ordered state agencies, including VCU, to cut spending in the remainder of the fiscal year. The executive committee of the Board of Visitors met on 15 December, and President Ackell reported that VCU was to reduce its spending by 1 percent. Within less than a week, the governor increased the necessary reduction to 2 percent.[11]

When VCU's presidential search began, local observers considered Governor Baliles a likely candidate, with his demonstrated interest in higher education. The governor made clear soon after the elections in November that he sought his next position in the private sector. The other local candidate was Gordon Davies, the highly regarded veteran head of the State Council of Higher Education and author of the report of the Commission on the University of the Twenty-First Century. The *Times-Dispatch* commended him to VCU in an editorial, but his candidacy never caught fire with the search committee. Another "known" candidate, John Casteen, former state secretary of education and then president of the University of Connecticut, withdrew from consideration and accepted the presidency of the University of Virginia.[12]

The inauguration of L. Douglas Wilder as governor took place on 13 January 1990, a frigid but sunny day. The good feelings of the event—with the history-making governor proudly declaring himself "a son of Virginia"—had hardly faded away before hard economic realities set in. As VCU faculty member and administrator Alvin Schexnider later put it, Wilder's administration "began under a cloud of fiscal uncertainty more ominous than any in Virginia since the end of World War II." The Board of Visitors met on 18 January to bad news. In addition to the 2 percent cut in the present fiscal year, the school was to cut another 5 percent in each of the next two years. In practical terms, that meant that the Medical Sciences Building and renovations to West Hospital would wait for another two years, and classroom renovations faced delays, too. Two key projects in the master plan—obtaining the 1000 block of Broad Street vacated in January 1989 by Universal Ford (another Richmond business removing to the suburbs) and renovation of the fortress-like storage building at Belvidere and Main for the School of Arts (today the site of the Engineering School)—went unfunded in the governor's budget.[13]

The state's situation was gloomy enough, but simultaneously the venerable downtown department store, Miller & Rhoads, closed its doors. The Sixth Street Marketplace had not been a sufficient boost to meet the exaggerated returns required to sustain the leveraged acquisitions of the financier, Robert Campeau, whose empire, including the department store, was collapsing. The store closed its doors on 6 January, but liquidation of merchandise and furnishings continued for another three months, and the "lengthy death throes" prolonged the pain.[14]

The new skyline rising in the financial district and the body blow to the shopping district with Miller & Rhoads' demise effectively demonstrated that the politics of business versus the neighborhoods, compounded by race, that just a decade before divided the city had now sputtered to a conclusion. Those issues, of course, remained unsettled, but Richmond arrived at the 1990s seemingly without a consensus or a direction. City Manager Robert Bobb's energy gave confidence, and his strategic planning committee gave promise for the future, but the city seemed without the resources to made visions realities. Worst of all, the hyperviolence associated with the trade in crack cocaine, a national plague, made Richmond even less attractive. Residents of Church Hill at a community meeting voiced major concerns of "street-corner drug dealing, gunfire in front of their homes, assaults, robberies, and murders."[15]

The 16 February issue of the VCU Voice, successor to VCU Today as the administration's news outlet, announced that because of budget cuts it would now appear monthly rather than biweekly. On 20 February, Ackell said farewell by pointing with pride to VCU's emergence as a "truly urban university."[16] Three days later the Board of Visitors announced that three finalists for the presidency would be visiting for interviews. The Commonwealth Times' report provided details about the first two candidates—the provost of Vanderbilt University and the chancellor of the University of Illinois at Chicago—but the paper said nothing about the third candidate except for his name and position: Dr. Eugene P. Trani, vice president for academic affairs of the University of Wisconsin System.[17]

Trani was Brooklyn-born. His father, Frank Trani, was born in Sicily and brought to this country as an infant, spent part of his childhood in Sicily, and then returned to the United States. He was an engineer, educated at Cornell University. The family moved to Philadelphia, and Gene Trani grew up with that city's fabled college basketball competition. Trani made his high school's junior varsity team despite not having the height advantage needed for hoops success, and he remained a knowledgeable basketball fan. In fact, his first published writing was as a high schooler in a September 1956 letter to *Sport* magazine, chastising that national publication for failing to select LaSalle University's star forward, Tom Gola, as the magazine's college basketball player of the decade.[18]

Trani had in mind to follow his father to Cornell and engineering study, but the message then in Philadelphia's Catholic schools was that college-bound students were to choose Catholic colleges and universities. Consequently, he headed to northwestern Indiana and the University of Notre Dame. After flirting with engineering, he took a major in history as preparation for law school. Fate intervened, in the form of a course in American diplomatic history taught by a visiting professor named Robert H. Ferrell. Trani was so taken with Ferrell and the subject that after graduation in 1961 he followed Ferrell back to his home campus of Indiana University to study for a PhD in diplomatic history.[19]

Meanwhile, on a visit home to Philadelphia, Trani attended a dance where he met Lois Elizabeth Quigley, from across the river in Collingswood, New Jersey. As he tells the story, she and four friends, all students in nursing school, came to the dance together without transportation home. They agreed that if any one of them were offered a ride home by a suitable young man, all five would go. Fortunately, Gene Trani had a car that night. After delivering the friends, he arranged to see Lois Quigley again. They were married in 1962, and two children, Anne and Frank, followed before Trani completed graduate school.[20]

He worked as an instructor at the Ohio State University from 1965 to 1967, where he met another young historian, Melvin I. Urofsky, a later chair of the VCU History Department. The job enabled him to get access to the papers of President Warren Harding, finally opened for research. He completed the dissertation and received the PhD degree in 1966.[21]

After another year, the Trani family moved to Southern Illinois University (SIU) at Carbondale. There he encountered an institution created in large part by a visionary president. Delyte Wesley Morris built SIU from a small teacher's college in 1948 into a large research university with more than thirty-five thousand students, with an engineering school and a second major campus at Edwardsville, Illinois.[22]

Trani proved an effective teacher, published his first book, *The Treaty of Portsmouth*, and was awarded promotion and tenure at SIU in 1971. By then, Morris's reign at SIU had come apart. During the aftermath of the killings of student protesters at Kent State University in May 1970, students and others at SIU rampaged and forced the university to shut down. Morris announced his retirement shortly after. Trani was in those dramatic days an editorial fellow at the Woodrow Wilson Papers project at Princeton University, where he observed how President Robert Goheen and the faculty kept the peace. Trani felt that SIU never really recovered from the forced capitulation to the rioters.[23]

He took a research grant to Great Britain in summer 1972 and then went to Washington, D.C., in 1972–73 as a fellow at the Woodrow Wilson International Center for Scholars. Trani spent the next two years teaching at SIU with family responsibilities, while Lois Trani commuted to Springfield to earn credentials in the field of nurse anesthesia (she would become a proud supporter of the highly respected Nurse Anesthesia Program at VCU).

Trani was honest with himself. As the likelihood of moving to a broader field of action as a historian grew slimmer, the prospect of subsiding into the routines of faculty life at SIU until retirement did not appeal. In 1974, he became a campaign worker for Paul Simon, the independent Illinois Democrat who won election to Congress that year, but the political life never beckoned. He then conferred with his graduate school mentor, Robert Ferrell, about moving into university administration. Ferrell suggested that Trani first complete a second book and secure promotion to professor, as a proof of his academic bona fides in any future administrative post. With a colleague, David L. Wilson, he obtained a contract to publish a monograph on the presidency of Warren G. Harding (leading to his later course in the VCU Honors College on presidential leadership) and received promotion to professor in 1975.[24]

In 1976, then, Eugene Trani made his leap. He had obtained a leave of absence for 1975–76 from SIU to serve as an administrative intern at the University of Nebraska. There he worked for Vice President Steven B. Sample, an electrical engineer by training, who had just the year before come to Nebraska. Sample went on to the presidency of the University of Buffalo, in New York, and then to a nineteen-year tenure as president of the

University of Southern California. Students in Trani's later honors courses on leadership at VCU would read Sample's book, *The Contrarian's Guide to Leadership.*[25]

Trani considers Sample a mentor, but in fact they were about the same age and shared ambitions in higher education. After his year at Nebraska, Trani was a finalist for an administrative post at SIU, but when another candidate got the job, SIU released him, at his request, from his contract. He went back to Lincoln, officially, as assistant vice president for academic affairs and now fully committed to a career in administration.[26]

From Nebraska, Trani moved to the University of Missouri–Kansas City (UMKC) in July 1980 to be vice chancellor for academic affairs. When he sat down to negotiate terms of his contract, he declared himself open to compromise, even on salary, but his unconditional requirement was that he be permitted to take up a Fulbright Teaching Fellowship at Moscow State University in 1981. His application for the Fulbright reflected his continued scholarly interest in international affairs, but it also derived from his perception that international connections would be increasingly important in higher education. Trani found the four-months experience in the Soviet Union profoundly interesting and stimulating, and he would make a practice of regular foreign travel, sometimes as formal sabbaticals from his executive duties, to deepen his knowledge and rejuvenate his thinking.[27]

Kansas City's urban boosters established what became UMKC in the 1930s, and it joined the University of Missouri System in 1963. In 1971, the medical school began offering a unique six-year combined undergraduate/MD program. The founder of the medical school was E. Grey Dimond, a distinguished cardiologist and skilled administrator, who modeled the medical program after his own accelerated training during World War II. Trani credits Dimond with teaching him about the logic of a medical center at an urban university. Dimond had served in China during the war, and he nurtured Trani's own interest in that nation.[28]

For all that Trani learned from his mentors, Lois Trani remained his closest personal advisor. He talked with her about his goal of becoming a university president and his growing conviction that being vice chancellor at the University of Missouri–Kansas City did not provide the springboard to the kind of presidency he wanted. Then, the opportunity came. Kenneth A. "Buzz" Shaw was named president of the University of Wisconsin System in 1985, and he needed a vice president for academic affairs. Trani was his first major appointment, arriving in September 1986.

At Wisconsin, Ferrell's advice about that second book proved sound, for Trani was admitted with tenure to the distinguished University of Wisconsin–Madison History Department. He made a point of teaching as often as his schedule permitted, and he used his own vacation time for another foreign sabbatical, this one to the University of London in 1987, but he and President Shaw were officers of the statewide system, not just the flagship university at Madison. The system included thirteen universities and thirteen two-year centers, and the constituency for whom the top administrators worked was the governor, the legislature, and the board of regents. The size of the system made communication crucial, and Trani began there his practice of a constant flow of informational memos—soon known as "Trani-grams"—to administrators, faculty, students, and staff. Madison was his third state capitol, after Columbus (Ohio State University) and Lincoln (University of Nebraska), and he understood the circumstances of universities located at the seats of government, especially the need for coordinated planning involving the university, city, and the state.[29]

Soon he began looking for an opportunity to head his own university. He and Lois Trani talked about the ideal situation for them. Winters were long and cold in Wisconsin, and both wanted to be farther south. He wanted an urban university, with a medical center and a commitment to research. He also wanted a place not so burdened with traditions that change would be impossible. VCU met his criteria.

The search committee flew candidates to Washington to conduct screening interviews in January. Trani arrived with a raging head cold—"one of the worst colds I can ever recall anyone having and still being vertical," recalled Roger Gregory, a member of the committee. Trani had not been a leading candidate previously; his performance, though, convinced the committee that he had studied the university. "It wasn't canned kind of stuff," said Gregory. "People could understand and buy into his vision."[30]

The three finalists each visited the university. The third, Trani, was offered and accepted the presidency of Virginia Commonwealth University. "I knew coming to Richmond," he recalls, "there was a possibility of having a significant impact on VCU and the city of Richmond, and that's what interested me about this job." Yet, he came without a stated agenda other than a promise to work very hard for VCU. It was better, he thought, to inherit university administrators and see how things went than to make wholesale changes at the start.[31]

VCU's expanded mission statement, adopted just a few months earlier, emphasized the essential role of "faculty actively engaged in research, scholarship, and creative expression." It also closed with reference to VCU's "unique role as Virginia's major urban university." Trani may not have asserted an agenda, but he had convinced the search committee that he was comfortable operating within the framework created in the new mission statement.[32]

The Board of Visitors on 15 March 1990 unanimously affirmed the presidential search committee's recommendation that Trani be hired as VCU's fourth president, prompting a standing ovation. After a break for a press conference, the board returned to work. President Ackell, who had been given the title of president emeritus that day, reported that enrollments at VCU were now expected to remain flat through the remainder of the 1990s. A report from the Hospital Committee showed a small positive balance from the past year's operations, but the cost of indigent care remained a problem, as it had since Warren Brandt's presidency.[33]

The board tried, but this day was not for business as usual. Trani recalls that the university meeting center was filled with spectators when Rector French Moore announced the appointment and that the applause was genuine. The first questions, though, concerned the university's master plan and the future of Oregon Hill. Trani responded diplomatically that he did not yet know enough to comment but was confident in the judgment of the Board of Visitors. That did not please the placard-carrying protestors who filled the back of the room. His early agenda as president was already taking shape.[34]

Trani exemplified his self-description as a hard worker in his first days as the new president. He taught at Wisconsin on Wednesday before traveling to Richmond for his introduction as president on Thursday, and he then flew back to Wisconsin to participate in a "marathon budget session." He got back to Richmond on Friday, in time for that evening's tournament basketball game between Virginia and Notre Dame at the Richmond Coliseum (his alma mater lost). Trani had also walked the Academic Campus, in what the *Times-Dispatch* called "a departure in style" from President Ackell. Trani may have sensed that the story would include that contrast, for in his interview he credited his predecessor with "a heck of a good job integrating the campuses." He continued, "You can't do that walking the campus." Asked again about the master plan and Oregon Hill, he said that the board had made a studied decision, and he was "not going to relive" it. He went on, though: "I've learned that no matter how good your ideas are, if people believe the process is flawed, they're never going to focus on the idea or the issue."[35]

He would not be president officially until 2 July 1990, but he knew about the Board of Visitors' meeting on 20 April, when President Ackell presented VCU's budget for 1990–92. With state funds cut, tuition would jump by more than 5 percent. That was sufficient to replace only half of VCU's reductions, and the board accepted a plan to eliminate 175 jobs. The hospitals budgeted separately, but the situation there was dire, too, as the projected bottom line was a scant 1 percent profit, too small for confidence about the future. The board and the administrators agreed that new ventures at VCU would be few.[36]

On 31 May students and neighbors met to comment on VCU's proposal to take over maintenance of Monroe Park on the Academic Campus. Despite university representatives' assurances, an overwhelming majority of those present so distrusted the university that they insisted on written guarantees for the park's protection. Two members of the city council came to the meeting, and both condemned the proposal. Public officials and the public agreed, VCU could not be trusted.[37]

The hard work of university planners, led by Donald C. Bruegman, vice president of administration, to consult with the neighborhood associations and to adjust the master plan accordingly, although overshadowed by Oregon Hill's public intransigence, provided just enough good will to escape a similar condemnation from the entire city council. The western neighborhood associations and VCU made a letter of understanding on 7 June 1990 that protected the Harrison Street corridor, on the boundary between the Academic Campus and the Fan District, from inappropriate development, such as dormitories or high-rise buildings. The agreement also specified the Fan District Association's support for VCU's taking over Monroe Park, with explicit understanding that VCU's future development would be directed to the north and east, not to the south or the west. That agreement made a difference. On 11 June 1990, by a 5–4 vote, city council approved the plan for Monroe Park and then defeated a resolution urging no further encroachment into Oregon Hill. That result gave the new president some time to consider the school's future course, but an urban university, in service to its community, could hardly flourish by a vote of 5–4.[38]

Meanwhile, in May 1990 City Manager Bobb's strategic planning project resurfaced, now named Richmond Tomorrow, with a call for citizens to join brainstorming sessions scheduled at city schools. The committee proposed that the city's "five top problems are crime, drug abuse, teen-age pregnancy, homelessness, and lack of affordable medical care," but also asked to hear about residents' hopes for education, services, transportation, recreation, and "regional cooperation." The goal was a plan for Richmond's "long-term financial health." Absent from Richmond Tomorrow's prospectus was any mention of Virginia Commonwealth University.[39]

The *Richmond Times-Dispatch* welcomed the process with a supportive editorial suggesting an array of topics for discussion, among them "the expansion and role of VCU," seeming to relegate the university to the problem side of the city's balance sheet. The community discussions brought out some 350 Richmonders altogether, and the topics ranged widely. VCU apparently did not come up. Chairman Hays Watkins then convened a breakfast meeting in early July at the elite Commonwealth Club to solicit the views of corporate leaders. This group echoed the community meetings by focusing on the need for improved public schools, which both groups connected with the city's economic development, and the problem of crime.[40]

THE FORMAL start to Trani's presidency, on 1 July 1990, coincided with the conclusion to the university's first capital campaign and the end of Edmund Ackell's presidency. Ackell praised the community support evidenced in the campaign, and Trani declared that the successful campaign was one of the reasons he came to VCU. Only about 12 percent of the alumni contributed, however, compared with a national average of 18 percent. In fact, the campaign's leadership and the largest gifts came from Richmond business leaders who were not alumni. Trani noted that commitment, calling the leadership of such local backers remarkable for "a young, urban public university."[41]

Back in February, the MCV Alumni Association's magazine headlined its story about the fundraising campaign for VCU: "University Surpasses Campaign Goal; Most Gifts Are for MCV Campus." The gulf between the two campuses had widened during the last years of Ackell's presidency. That issue of the *Scarab* also gave the schedule of the alumni meeting in April; no one from the Academic Campus was named to appear.[42]

Alumni learned in the June issue of the *Scarab* about the new president of VCU. The article included Trani's self-characterization as "a workhorse not a show horse," his enthusiasm for VCU as a model for "urban universities," and his experience, with emphasis on international relations. The *Scarab* promised an "indepth [sic] interview" with the new president in the September issue.[43]

There was good news for the MCV Alumni Association that summer. On 9 August 1990, VCU and the Alumni Association agreed to trade "exact footprint land parcels," with the location of the Alumni House going to the university as the construction site for the ambulatory care center and the Alumni Association taking from the university a parcel on Eleventh Street across from the old site. John M. Kudless, vice president for development, had crafted a plan for fundraising for "the relocation/rebuilding of Alumni House." Photos accompanying the article showed the deteriorated entrance to the building and a happy group of alumni and President Trani.[44]

Less visible but perhaps of even greater long-term importance was Trani's decision shortly after he arrived in Richmond to reopen the search for the vice president for health sciences. This position, held by John Andrako on an interim basis since President Ackell's controversial removal of Alistair Connell in 1988, would have responsibility for coordinating all "programs on the Health Sciences Campus." Andrako agreed to serve as chair of the search committee, which in 1991 selected John E. Jones, then vice president for health services at West Virginia University.[45]

The *Scarab*'s interview with the new president occurred about the time of that search's announcement, but it appeared in the September 1990 issue of the *Scarab*. Trani declared to the medical alumni that he did not want the two campuses to become "clones of one another." In fact, the diversity of the campuses and their schools and the diversity of ages and ethnicities of the people at VCU was something Trani wanted "to caringly foster." He wanted diversity, accessibility, and, with them, "continued excellence." His message was confidence in the direction set for the university's future, yet he understood and valued its traditions. "The MCV name is part of our history and is going to stay that way," he declared.[46]

The state's revenue woes had worsened, and, at the end of August, just as classes began for the fall 1990 semester, the governor called for additional budget reductions totaling nearly $7 million annually for 1990–92. The Board of Visitors approved a 2 percent across-the-board permanent reduction, added a tuition surcharge, and used contingency funds and other temporary reductions to fulfill the state's directives. The issue of greatest urgency was the directive to reduce the MCV Hospitals' expenditures by nearly $7 million. That state money mainly went to finance care for indigent patients, essentially a fixed cost for VCU. Acting Vice President Andrako said that, if necessary, the hospitals would postpone nonemergency treatments for indigents and direct them elsewhere for care. The board members, meeting by teleconference, declared that strategy unacceptable and voted to petition the governor to rethink that reduction. Trani warned the board that if the governor rejected the tuition surcharge VCU might have to close whole programs.[47]

Budget cuts, and the prospect of more to come, provoked a student protest on campus, followed by a march of some 250 people to the state capitol. Their chants of "Where's Doug?" won a meeting for a smaller number of students with Governor Wilder. Afterward, the students promised to join with students from other Virginia campuses to lobby the legislature for relief. Compounding the situation was that VCU had enrolled 3,335 new students in fall 1990, with more than half of them, for the first time, being transfer students. The new freshmen totaled 1,615, the lowest number in a decade; nonetheless, VCU's student body—a record total of 21,986 students—threatened to overwhelm the campus, Trani warned the Board of Visitors.[48]

Despite all, Trani sounded upbeat in a conversation recorded in the 7 September issue of *VCU Voice*. "The more I get to know about VCU," he said, "the more impressed I am." He made no reference to the conflicts with neighbors but spoke of the public service expected of urban universities and how community collaborations might aid in moving forward despite the budget cuts. Trani had expressed similar confidence in the mission of the urban university to a reporter for the *CT* a month before. Despite the constraints of the budget, Trani said he hoped to provide faculty "with releases to do specific community projects."[49]

Clearly, he had something in mind. On his arrival in Richmond, Trani created a President's Council made up of the provost and vice presidents to meet weekly with him. There are no minutes to the meetings, but the agendas show that budget cuts and the West Campus master plan were main subjects from the group's very first meeting in July. By the middle of that first month, agenda items included a Community Assistance Program and Community Service Fellows.[50]

The public learned what the council had been discussing when the Board of Visitors met in mid-September. As usual, sign-carrying protesters from Oregon Hill and other community advocates crowded the meeting room, but the main item of business was approval of six new community initiatives presented by President Trani. These included community advisory boards for both campuses, incentives for property rehabilitation in the surrounding neighborhoods, a program to encourage faculty and staff to work on projects with the community, and a recreation program for the community in university facilities. The final two initiatives—restoring Monroe Park and cleaning up Grace Street near the university—had already been announced, but they fit well with the other initiatives.[51]

Representatives from the Save Oregon Hill Organization scoffed at the proposals—just a "public relations ploy"—and called for the master plan to be abandoned. Trani still defended the plan but emphasized that he intended his proposals to counter the ill will that the process, not the plan, had generated. "I don't want to ever have this situation again where our neighbors don't know or understand what we are doing." Leaders of other neighborhood associations present liked the proposals, as did Mayor Walter T. Kenney, who had cast his council vote in June against VCU. Even Councilman Richardson, who still opposed the master plan, said that the proposals "appear to be healthy and consistent with a cooperative attitude."[52]

The *News Leader* commended the initiatives as likely "to improve communications—hence relations—between the community and the university." The editorial noted that VCU in Richmond was "as valuable as it is influential" and "a major participant in the inner city." That latter term reflected well how many white Richmond suburbanites had come to view the once vibrant downtown section.[53]

Just after President Trani revealed VCU's community-relations initiatives, the leaders of Richmond Tomorrow announced creation of the citizen task forces that would study five problem areas identified through the summer's public meetings. Although crime had been a prominent topic, Chairman Hays Watkins explained that the study areas—city finances and revenue, economic development, education, social and human needs, and regional cooperation—provided positive ways to bring down the crime rate. Vice Provost Grace Harris was named vice chair of the Committee on Social and Human Needs, and several other VCU employees served on committees.[54]

Late one day as summer turned into fall, two of Richmond's most prominent white business and civic leaders, Henry Valentine and T. Justin Moore, made an unscheduled visit to the President's House. Valentine was a former city councilman, Moore was an attorney and former head of Virginia Power, and both were leaders of Richmond Renaissance. They came to talk with Trani about developing a biotechnology research center in downtown Richmond, or, as the *Richmond News Leader* now had it, the "inner city."[55]

Their mission had a back story. The visitors explained that Richmond Renaissance for several years had been interested in development of a center for biotechnology in Richmond to generate economic growth. They wanted to know what Trani thought of the idea. Certainly, he was aware of biotechnology, having observed the University of Wisconsin–Madison's Biotechnology Center and its work in the 1980s to encourage transfer of academic research results to businesses.[56]

They explained to him where Richmond stood with biotechnology. The Baliles administration had sought to energize the state's Center for Innovative Technology (CIT), created by Governor Robb in 1984 and headquartered in Northern Virginia, by appointing Ronald Carrier, the president of James Madison University, as its new director in April 1986. Carrier came forward in June with a presentation to the state's university presidents (approved by Governor Baliles, he said) that included a proposal for more than a dozen technology/scientific centers at state universities, including a biotechnology center at VCU's Medical College of Virginia. That Carrier also sought to reduce the expected cost of the unbuilt CIT headquarters in Herndon, Virginia, suggested that ambitions outstripped resources. Nonetheless, the presidents were enthusiastic about Carrier's plan because, as the *Times-Dispatch* put it, "each college and university would get a chunk of the high-technological center's pie."[57]

In September 1986 the Board of Visitors appointed Francis L. Macrina as director of the CIT's Institute of Biotechnology at the medical school. Macrina, well-known as a researcher of oral bacterial pathogens and resistance to antibiotics, had been chairman of the Department of Microbiology and Immunology for several years and held an affiliate position in the School of Dentistry. The CIT continued to face skepticism about its future, but Carrier's year at its head clarified that its mission was to facilitate economic development in Virginia, with biotechnology as a promising direction to take.[58]

The promise that new and innovative technologies could jumpstart economic development brought other entities into existence. In Richmond that year among the many local requests for funding from federal block grants was one put forward by a group of businessmen. The Metro Rich-mond Technology and Enterprise Center would enable experienced entre-preneurs and managers to aid "first-time minority business people" to incubate new companies. The center would locate in the renovating Tobacco Row section of former tobacco factories in Shockoe Bottom, housing ulti-mately fifteen to twenty businesses. With city approval of $50,000 in block grant funds, the businessmen expected to raise an additional $250,000 from various sources, including the CIT.[59]

When the center finally got underway in 1987, VCU had become a part-ner in what backers described as more than an incubator, which mainly featured inexpensive space for rent. The center would also offer advice from faculty at both VCU campuses and assist with identifying sources of oper-ating capital. Although business people still were prominent members of the board, the center had now corralled James McGovern, assistant vice president for health services, for its board, and Thomas C. Little, manager of special projects at VCU, as the center's first director. Not only had VCU taken a larger role, both with funding and with personnel, but the center now declared a special interest in attracting companies "in biotechnology and related fields."[60]

All those beginnings led Valentine and Moore to the President's House on Franklin Street with a proposal for VCU to spearhead Richmond's bio-technology development. Trani responded to them first with the reminder that he had to consider VCU's "eleven underfunded schools," but, he went on, VCU would hire a consultant to "talk to people in the community, talk to people in the university, talk to people in the Richmond Renaissance, talk to the political leadership, and see what was possible." His visitors departed happy with the meeting's results.[61]

Trani was eager to learn for himself about the city. Thus, when Cathe-rine Howard, an assistant professor of psychology and co-leader of an after-school program to encourage middle-school students to avoid the pitfalls of drugs and violence, invited him to visit the program at Gilpin Court, a low-income housing project, he readily agreed. Howard recalls that some in the Office of the President checked with her to be sure that he would be safe there. With that in mind, she grew a little nervous that day when the president disappeared. They found him in the next room, which had been fitted out with a few computers for the program participants, happily learn-ing from the kids. Howard's career at VCU coincided with Trani's com-mitment to building community engagement at VCU, and eventually she held the position of vice provost and head of the Division of Community Engagement, but that would come later.[62]

At the Board of Visitors' final meeting for 1990, on 2 November, Trani announced that the first meetings in October of community advisory boards, one for each campus, saw representatives from sixteen entities at the MCV Campus and twenty at the Academic Campus. He also presented the prospectus for the Biotechnology Research Park, noting that action still waited on the consultant's report. In addition to measuring the local business support for the project, the consultants would have to evaluate whether Richmond in 1991 was attractive enough to prospective companies.[63]

That week, the chair of the state's Art and Architectural Review Board declared his opposition to the master plan, which combined with the previous month's condemnations of the plan from the Department of Historic Resources and the Council on the Environment to make three strikes against VCU, as the *News Leader* pointed out on 6 November. "Virginia Commonwealth University is lucky that it isn't playing baseball."[64]

By then, Trani had made up his mind. He began informing members of the Board of Visitors that he would recommend that VCU withdraw the campus master plan. The announcement came on 15 November 1990. The decision was clearly his own, and the news stories quoted him, not university spokespeople. He declared that the damage done to the university by the controversy over expansion was too great to continue. "Emotionalism, rhetoric and politics have overshadowed the major issue that the campus needs to grow," he said, but he would wait at least six months for tensions to cool down before returning to the master site plan. The fight had left an impression among VCU's neighbors in Richmond, and more widely in Virginia, that VCU was a bully "bashing its neighbors." The impression was wrong. VCU had "a heart, a soul and a vision," Trani insisted, "but they have been obscured by the battle over the expansion plan."[65]

It took nearly a month to elicit a formal response from the Save Oregon Hill Organization. Officers Sue Staples and Kelley Lane began by noting that on 11 December the state's Department of Historic Resources recommended that the Oregon Hill Historic District be placed on the National Register of Historic Places. That, combined with Trani's withdrawal of the master plan, they believed, should put an end to VCU's threat to the neighborhood. More important, they declared that the controversy had benefited VCU. "By recognizing the significance of their adjacent historic neighbors, VCU will ultimately enhance the university's unique 'sense of place.'" No matter the professions of good intent, they said, that result awaited proof in action.[66]

Meanwhile, VCU announced formal planning for a possible biotechnology research park in downtown Richmond. Few outside VCU circles knew anything about the project until press releases went out in mid-December 1990. In addition to hiring the consultant, Trani announced "a committee of business and university leaders to foster plans for a research park." The main attraction for businesses would be proximity to "Virginia Commonwealth's Medical College of Virginia," as the Associated Press story put it. William L. Dewey, associate provost for research and an advocate for a biotechnology park, noted that university graduates represented a pool of potential employees and that biotech employees might continue their educations at the university. Already, three companies had been identified as potential tenants at the research park, even though Trani said he would not present a recommendation to the Board of Visitors until the next summer. Years later, Henry Valentine would declare with a laugh that Trani had grabbed the idea and run away with it. Certainly, the AP story gave all the credit to VCU for the proposal.[67]

Even so, the sense of hard times was widespread by the end of 1990. "The bad news was palpable," said the *Richmond News Leader*'s year-end summary of the city's economy, "and it hit home." The national collapse of the savings and loan industry saw four Richmond thrifts seized by the government, and the ill effects on Broad Street from the closing of Miller & Rhoads continued to spread. The May Department Stores, a St. Louis corporation, had purchased the Thalhimers department stores from the bankrupt Carter Hawley Hales Stores, which had purchased Thalhimers in 1978, and William B. Thalhimer, the last of his family in the stores' top management, retired as chairman of the company, a post that he had held since 1948. One bright spot, the newspaper noted, was that six of the region's dozen hospitals had major expansion projects underway. That trend, a continuation of the suburban migration of hospitals from Richmond, however, left the MCV Hospitals isolated in a declining downtown, with the long-standing financial problem of indigent care unsolved. Violence continued at a record rate, too.[68]

THE 1990–91 basketball season, Coach Sonny Smith's second at VCU, ended with another losing record, but by season's end it appeared that the Sun Belt Conference itself would be history.[69] The conference began coming apart a year before when Old Dominion University announced that it would join the Colonial Athletic Association, then Alabama at Birmingham departed, with rumors that two other conference schools were headed to the Metro Conference, itself seeking replacements for four departing schools. With only four schools, the Sun Belt would lose its automatic berth in the NCAA basketball tournament. Bill Millsaps explained in the *Richmond Times-Dispatch* what that meant: "In modern college basketball, no tournament bid essentially means no league. No league means scheduling and, ultimately, budgetary nightmares in all sports, not just in basketball." The conference commissioner proposed a merger with another conference, but those schools were located even farther away from Virginia. VCU had to make a move.[70]

Then, the National Collegiate Athletic Association ruled that the Metro Conference could replace its departing schools and retain automatic inclusion in the annual basketball tournament. Among the remaining schools was Virginia Tech, as well as the University of Louisville, a perennial member of the nation's basketball elite. With the University of North Carolina at Charlotte and South Florida leaving the Sun Belt for the Metro, it made sense for VCU to follow. By March 1991, VCU actively sought membership in the Metro Conference.[71]

Millsaps wrote that the time to pay attention to conference reorganizing was when the university presidents got involved. President Trani in March convinced President James D. McComas of Virginia Tech that VCU joining the conference would also be good for Tech's fans in central Virginia. Trani then traveled to Tulane and to Southern Mississippi to push VCU's candidacy, and he stayed in close telephone contact with McComas and President Donald Swain of Louisville. On 3 April 1991, the Metro welcomed VCU and two other former Sun Belt schools as members starting on 1 June 1991. The good result, sports writer John Markon declared, was "thanks in large part to a university president who didn't mind doubling as a traveling salesman."[72]

There might have been people at VCU indifferent to the drama of athletic conference affiliations, but they would have known that Eugene Trani's formal inauguration as the fourth president of VCU loomed. A full-page invitation from Rector French Moore to "the VCU family" appeared in the 2 April 1991 issue of the *Commonwealth Times*. The ceremony would take place at the Mosque (later Altria Theater), with a reception to follow at the Franklin Street Gym.[73]

Because of the budget cuts, the ceremony was simpler and smaller than originally planned, but Governor Wilder would be there to deliver an address, and the ceremony would feature the premiere performance of "The Peace Cantata," composed by Alan Blank of the Department of Music. That morning, the editorial page of the *Richmond Times-Dispatch* declared that Trani had "seemingly packed about nine years of activity into his first nine months," and especially praised him for withdrawing the master plan for further study.[74]

The inaugural address—titled "The Future of the Academy and the Community: Virginia Commonwealth University and the Urban Mission"—echoed a theme Trani had sounded from his arrival in Richmond, the role of the urban university in American higher education. At the annual convocation in February, Trani identified integration of scholarship, teaching, and public service as distinguishing VCU as an urban university. All three realms ultimately benefited the community, as exemplified, he said, by the Massey Cancer Center or the School of Education. The urban university, he declared then, was "urban by deliberate choice," using "resources of the academy" to "interact with the community." VCU's leaders had from its beginnings accepted the identity of "urban university," but, here, in the throes of conflicts with neighbors and in the depths of Richmond's "urban crisis," a president declared VCU "of" the community, not just "in" it.[75]

The inaugural address moved from financial constraints and limits to confidence that VCU "can become a role model of the urban university." Trani emphasized that VCU stood on foundations established by the Medical College of Virginia and the Richmond Professional Institute, but he also praised again the university's integration of research, teaching, and public service. That led outward, he declared, to partnerships for economic development, for better public schools, and for empowering local government for greater effectiveness. He closed the address by accepting the responsibility of the university's presidency: "Frankly, Mr. Rector, I would rather be nowhere else."[76]

Despite the local examples, Trani's vision of VCU as an urban university in his formal addresses remained rather abstract, as though he needed to win agreement to the concept before getting to the specifics. Nonetheless, after a year in Richmond, Trani could speak of VCU as an urban university without provoking scoffing from the community. Yet, VCU remained an urban university seeking a relationship with its city.[77]

Just a few months later, Richmond Tomorrow, the citizens' strategic planning process, issued its report, after two years of work involving more than two thousand citizens. The report called for a variety of actions—among them, recruiting and retaining businesses, improving public schools, developing the downtown center, building more affordable housing—that had been on the city's agenda for years. The report emphasized that the main need was for regional cooperation, with a proposal that the city regain power to annex territory from the surrounding counties, taken away in 1979, to encourage greater cooperation. The conservative *News Leader* dismissed the likelihood of annexation and scoffed at the report: "It lacks punch. It's oatmeal." Nowhere in Richmond Tomorrow's report, nor in the newspapers' commentary about it, could one find the words "Virginia Commonwealth University." Considering what followed in Richmond, that absence is striking. In summer 1991, however, neither VCU nor Richmond yet perceived their entwined future.[78]

TRANI WAS an avid golfer, and, to use images from that sport, the university had extracted itself from the "rough" in 1990, but the rain continued to fall in Richmond. The bad news was not just about budgets. In early September 1991, Media General, Inc., the parent company of the Richmond newspapers, announced that the *Richmond News Leader*, the afternoon paper, would close in June 1992 and its staff, heretofore competitors, would merge with that of the *Times-Dispatch*. The announcement blamed changing reading habits and pointed to afternoon newspapers closing in other cities, but the *News Leader*'s demise counted as a loss to the city's civic culture, even to those who disliked the paper's hyperconservative editorial policy.[79]

Two months later, the St. Louis company that had purchased the Thalhimers department stores announced the closing of the flagship department store in downtown Richmond, across from the now defunct Miller & Rhoads department store. The demise of the city's retail section in downtown, despite such efforts as the Sixth Street Marketplace, inspired worried reflection. The city faced the loss of tax revenues and the dilemma of creating enough activity—specifically, people living downtown and shopping there—to attract new businesses. As the soon-to-be-gone *News Leader* put it, "Engineering a population shift from the suburbs back downtown, if not impossible, promises to be a multiyear project." VCU's two campuses faced each other across a downtown in need of creative help, and the situation made the plans for a biotechnology research center even more important. Trani and VCU had no choice but to play through the rain.[80]

The university convocation in mid-February 1992 saw the president addressing the universal worry about hard times—the "protracted economic crisis for our university," as he put it. The stressful situation made taking stock of the good things at VCU essential, both for morale and for moving forward. The convocation, for the first time, honored an artist, sculptor Elizabeth King, with the Distinguished Scholar Award. As she explained to the gathering, "The really nice thing about someone from the arts receiving this award is that it finally suggests that there is a real discipline involved in 'making art.'" Trani declared that the faculty and staff were "the reason we will emerge on the other side of our current crisis stronger than when we started." Realists might have wondered at Trani's optimism, for the news continued bad: funding for the new fine arts center and the medical sciences building remained in budgetary limbo, and the possibility of raises for the first time in four years seemed to be fading, too.[81]

The economic situation spurred two related strategies. Trani and other university leaders strove to educate the public that investments in higher education were investments in the state's future. The legislature had okayed a package of general-obligation bonds to pay for construction projects, including projects at VCU and the new Biotechnology Research Park, which would face the voters on election day in November. In March in the *Times-Dispatch*, Trani pointed to the "international context" of business and government, with work now done in "a new technological milieu," to argue for reinvigorating "the role of higher education in our communities . . . for an era of interdependence."[82]

In addition to making that larger argument, Trani and VCU educated students, faculty, staff, and Richmond residents about the university's value to the local community. Notes from an informal talk at the Parents' Weekend Brunch in February 1992 show Trani emphasizing the diversity of VCU's student body as well as the fact that the majority of graduates stayed in Virginia. VCU's more than thirteen thousand employees and more than twenty-one thousand students, he explained, had a positive impact on the local economy. Trani and Donald Gehring, in charge of government relations for the university, made a similar argument to members of the General Assembly and community leaders.[83]

That spring Trani welcomed alumni of the Richmond Professional Institute and, meeting separately, alumni of the Medical College of Virginia as pioneer creators of VCU's present-day urban orientation. The historical approach came comfortably to him, but strategically his embrace of "this unique legacy, this urban heritage—a vision ahead of its time," handed down by Henry Hibbs and William T. Sanger, invited alumni to see their own connections to the university in the present. Trani had stated not long before that the financial support of local businessmen to VCU impressed him, but the backing of alumni, most of whom resided in Virginia, was now especially important in the campaign to pass the higher education bonds. Fortunately, the multitude of speaking invitations that come to a university president gave Trani many opportunities to present VCU's message and to encourage voters to help.[84]

The legislature completed its work, and then the university put together its budget for 1992–94. There was a bit more money for the libraries and for student aid, but tuition rates would rise by 17 percent (after rising by 17.6 percent the year before, and by 67.3 percent since 1986–87). In an open letter to students, Trani assured that VCU's tuition remained competitive with Virginia institutions. The university fee paid by students would increase by $60, of which $50 would go for recreational facilities. Trani remained convinced that VCU needed better facilities for recruiting and retaining students. In an era of state budget reductions, expanding the student body aided the university, and declining numbers of students presaged hard times.[85]

That summer, VCU made national news when novelist Paule Marshall, a member of the English faculty, received a prestigious MacArthur Fellowship, the so-called Genius Grant. Unfortunately, longtime faculty member Daryl Cumber Dance, professor of English and widely known as an African American folklorist, who first brought Marshall's novels to VCU's classrooms and then brought Marshall herself, departed after twenty years at VCU to the University of Richmond. Also moving was the legendary Village Cafe, which closed on 29 June after thirty-five years at 939 West Grace Street and reopened on 13 July across Harrison Street, where it continued to serve students, faculty, and everyone else.[86]

That summer also, VCU almost accepted an offer from the May Company, the owner of the recently closed Thalhimers department store on Broad Street, to give the building to VCU. The offer had first been made in December 1991, when the store went under, but revelations of complications in the title to the property caused VCU to turn it down. The building had appealed as an opportunity to consolidate offices scattered about the city in a location roughly midway between the two campuses, but after the failure, VCU cast eyes on the former Universal Ford property on Broad Street north of the Academic Campus.[87]

The Board of Visitors that summer elected Roger L. Gregory, lawyer and later federal judge, to the position of rector. Gregory was the first African American to serve in that position at a major research university in Virginia. The Greater Richmond Retail Merchants Association the day before had announced its largest contribution ever—$100,000—to the budding Virginia Biotechnology Research Park. The corporation to develop the park—involving university, business, city, and state representatives—organized in May, with all plans contingent on the general obligation bonds to be voted on in November. A privately funded research building was also planned, but the bond-funded facility would be the park's central building. The association's gift to the park matched Director Robert E. Olson's confidence about its future.[88]

The consultant's report—enthusiastic—also set guidelines for the research park's development. "Number one," as Trani recalled it, "the research park had to be in the area of research strength of the University, and that meant Life Sciences, BioTechnology." Second, the report emphasized that it could not be the university's research park alone. The project needed to engage the city, the business community and the state, and even the surrounding counties. Third, it had to be located immediately adjacent to the Medical Center, where there were plenty of parking lots. All three of those characteristics appealed to Trani as well as to the Board of Visitors.[89]

If the voters rejected the bond issue, there was no "plan B" for VCU. A memorandum—a Trani-gram—to "Dear Colleagues" in July explained that the decision to prioritize academic-related construction had won the Faculty Senate's backing for the bonds, and the president asked for suggestions of any civic groups to which VCU advocates might speak. A follow-up memorandum in August announced that the Governmental Relations Office had prepared a brochure about VCU and the bonds with suggestions for framing public remarks or written communications. The call was for all hands on deck. As Trani explained in his inaugural "President's Column" in the VCU Voice in September, his own "immediate priority [would] be to continue to keep constituencies informed of the merits of the 1992 General Obligation Bond bill for higher education and the $43 million in that bill for VCU's campus." Addressing audiences in the state and region, he emphasized VCU's economic impact and its partnerships with other entities. In addition to the Faculty Senate's endorsement, the new Classi-fied Staff Advisory Committee, which developed out of meetings with Trani in 1991, also took up the oars for the bond issue. The students did their part by registering voters and lobbying family members for the university.[90]

At the beginning of September also, VCU released its first-ever economic impact report. It was the region's largest employer, excluding state govern-ment as a whole; students and employees spent more than $320 million annually; and the university spent almost $75 million annually with local businesses and contractors. Of nearly 140 degree programs, 41 were unique in Virginia then, and the Medical Center was the state's largest.[91]

In late October 1992, the *Chronicle of Higher Education* reported that Virginia's spending on higher education since 1990 had dropped by 13 percent, leading the nation. The charge stung in the Old Dominion, but the more ominous fact reported by the *Chronicle* was that state appropria-tions for higher education across the nation declined by 1 percent, the first such national decline since the annual reports began in 1958 and, the *Chron-icle* speculated, probably the first in U.S. history. Tuition had consequently risen swiftly, and, as Trani warned, that threatened "to price Virginia's stu-dents out of Virginia's public institutions." Gordon Davies, director of SCHEV, predicted a dismal immediate future, with state schools "scratch-ing for every nickel."[92]

A small controversy ensued, as the *Chronicle*'s report stated that VCU's budget had fallen by 31 percent, the largest decline in the state. Trani imme-diately informed the Board of Visitors, and thus the press, that the per-centage mistakenly included state reductions in indigent care that Governor Wilder had permitted to be covered instead by way of federal Medicaid funds. The actual reduction for VCU was 10.5 percent, bad enough in itself. Trani's correction not only set the record straight but it also acknowledged the governor's aid in managing what otherwise would have been a finan-cially disastrous situation.[93]

Just in time, the election came. Incumbent president George H. W. Bush carried Virginia, though he lost the national vote to Bill Clinton, but the state's voters also voted overwhelmingly in favor of the bond issues on the ballot, with 73 percent of them favoring the higher education bond pack-age. During the preceding weeks, faculty, students, staff, and alumni mobi-lized on behalf of the university. All could see that the projects that the bonds made possible were essential to the school's future. They included the medical sciences building, a fine arts center, renovations to classrooms and laboratories, an addition to Tompkins-McCaw Library, renovations for the A. D. Williams Building and West Hospital, and, above all, funding for the first facility at the Biotechnology Research Park. "'This is the most important thing that has happened to VCU in years," Trani declared happily.[94]

The city's leaders also had endorsed the higher education bond issue for its promise of economic development in Richmond. In the last months of 1992, it did seem that prospects for the city had turned for the better. Apartments were going up on Tobacco Row, the cluster of abandoned cigarette factories near the river; Ethyl Corporation planned a research park on the site of the former state penitentiary on Belvidere southeast of VCU; new state office buildings, including for the Library of Virginia, the State Corporation Commission, and the Department of Social Services, were underway; and, with the bond issue, construction of the Virginia Biotechnology Research Park would start. As 1992 closed, a growing optimism seemed to counter the pessimism with which the year had begun for Richmond.[95]

If the city now seemed to have a wind at its back, Virginia's higher education system still faced into stiff headwinds. That was certainly the conclusion to draw from a report to the legislature from SCHEV, released to the public at the beginning of December after the *Richmond Times-Dispatch* obtained a copy. The report called for the state schools to enroll more than seven thousand additional students, almost immediately, and without any additional funds from the state. The report noted that there would be sixty-five thousand more Virginians seeking college admission in the next decade, but, happily, it said, this gave schools time to restructure, by, for instance, requiring faculty to teach more and do less research and service. The report's release prompted university presidents to hold lengthy private conversations and make short public statements, such as Trani's observation then that the report was just a draft.[96]

SCHEV backed down a bit from its original call for faculty to drop all but grant-financed research, but rebellion came from the older, larger universities, especially the University of Virginia, with faculty and students protesting the watering down that they foresaw as the result of SCHEV's plan. The problem for the educators was that the legislature, which requested the SCHEV report, favored college admissions for Virginians but not tax increases. The compromise, worked through in early 1993, maintained the report's recommendations but also permitted significant tuition increases in the 1993 and 1994 budgets. Virginia's solution fit a national pattern of diminished state funding for higher education replaced by higher charges for the students. The hostility of the University of Virginia and Virginia Tech to significant expansion of their student bodies also opened opportunity for VCU to welcome those new students, in hope that the school's faculty, staff, and physical plant could grow to meet their expectations.[97]

TRANI LATER recalled his reasoning in the first years of his presidency:

> So, what I determined was that we were going to use the budget cuts to redefine the University. There's a golfing expression—can we play through the rain. We were going to play through the rain. A lot of the universities became paralyzed in those budget cuts. But it's at that point that we began to look at an Engineering School. We began to look at supporting the Biotech Research Park, and eventually, VCU Life Sciences. . . . We really used the Wilder cuts to implement the first strategic plan and play through the rain and show that we could do things by ourselves, off of tuition, off of public—off of private funding. We were not going to be paralyzed.[98]

8

Planning One University, 1993–1994

VCU FACULTY and administrators would later exemplify Eugene Trani's commitment to the idea of one university with recollections of him correcting them an instant after they said "MCV" rather than "VCU." Trani was a stickler for the inclusive nomenclature, but unless VCU's people experienced one university in practice and reality, rules about nomenclature mattered little. The university's strategic planning process engaged faculty, administrators, and staff in putting the university on the rise.

In early 1992, President Trani assigned what would become the VCU strategic plan to Provost Charles P. Ruch. The planning began in the midst of VCU's case in support of that fall's bond issue, of its value to both the city and the state. In contrast to the recently abandoned master site plan, the new strategic plan conceived of VCU as an engaged urban university.

THE FIRST step was appointment of the Commission on the Future of the University. The commission included a dozen faculty members, two members of the Board of Visitors, two students, and seven administrators (including five deans), along with four vice presidents as ex-officio members. Each of the schools at the university had representation, but all members of the commission received instructions "to deliberate and act from the perspective of the entire University."[1]

This injunction cut two ways, for it meant not only that the plan would speak for the university but also that any specifics in the plan about individual schools must also serve the university, rather than being seen as the result of "logrolling" by self-seeking commission members. In addition, commission members would learn from one another, returning to their own leadership posts with informed understanding of challenges and opportunities confronting other units of the university. Demonstrating this spirit, Michael Brooks, the dean of the School of Community and Public Affairs, served as the provost's special assistant for the plan and, as such, oversaw the plan's dissolution of that school, including relocation of the Department of Urban Studies and Planning from that school to the College of Humanities and Sciences, to which he returned as a faculty member at the close of the planning process.[2]

Brooks introduced the planning process and the commission members to the Faculty Senate in February 1992. VCU would, willy-nilly, be a different university in just a decade, he said, but planning would enable active management of resources, rather than drift. The plan also addressed "key issues that cut across the campuses—size, enrollment mix, organizational structure, the role of technology, and the desirability of new academic programs." He did not need to mention that any realistic plan must also assume continued budgetary limits.[3]

Provost Ruch departed in February 1993 to become president of Boise State University, and Grace Harris, his successor, guided the commission through the rest of its work. The draft report went to the board and the university in March 1993. *VCU Today,* on 5 March 1993, published the draft plan as an insert to the regular issue and requested responses for publication (typed, and no longer than a page). Trani reiterated the invitation for comments, declaring that "strategic planning is our most important internal priority." The hearings at both campuses would continue into the middle of May, giving all an opportunity to speak.[4]

It was a busy spring at VCU, with accomplishments highlighted by the University Libraries' acquisition of its "one millionth volume," an honorary degree conferred on Mikhail Gorbachev, the last president of the Soviet Union, and commencement ceremonies for nearly four thousand graduates. The Commission on the Future of the University worked hard through those months. In addition to the commission's two dozen meetings, members studied more than two hundred letters and memoranda from the university community and convened thirty-eight hearings for public discussion. When classes ended in May, the commission met in two day-long sessions to consider all the ideas and suggestions and then subdivided into five committees to focus on issues not yet settled: technology, the "programs affected by the plan," graduate education and research, student affairs, and, as Brooks put it, "all of the smaller issues not encapsulated by the other four committees." The plan would go to administrators and then to the Board of Visitors for approval in September.[5]

Trani later emphasized the effectiveness of Dr. Grace E. Harris on the strategic planning process. He named Harris as Provost Ruch's interim successor in early 1993. At the time of the appointment, she was the vice provost for community affairs and continuing education, and previously

Dr. Grace E. Harris served VCU
as faculty member, dean,
provost, and acting president.
(Virginia Commonwealth
University Libraries)

dean of the School of Social Work and a faculty member since the 1960s.
Harris originally applied for graduate study to RPI's School of Social Work
after graduating from Hampton University in 1954, but the state's white
political leaders' shift to "massive resistance" to desegregation of public schools caused nervous RPI officials to turn her away, even though
African Americans had previously studied graduate social work at the
school. Harris then attended Boston University before transferring to RPI
for her MSW degree in 1960, and, after joining the RPI faculty in 1967, for
her doctorate from the University of Virginia. Trani first met Harris just
after being appointed president, when she was a candidate for the vice provost position. Trani interviewed both candidates himself and enthusiastically recommended her to the Board of Visitors. In summer 1992, not
long before Ruch announced his departure, Trani accepted an invitation
to accompany Harris and Dr. Thomas M. Kerkering, a specialist in pediatric AIDs research, on a trip to Africa, where he would discuss possible
exchange programs with universities on that continent. The time spent

together left Trani even more impressed with her abilities, and he readily proposed that she become the interim provost and vice president for academic affairs, filling a term ending on 1 July 1995. In early March 1994, the Faculty Senate presented to him an unsolicited resolution endorsing Harris's work as interim provost, and Trani then obtained a waiver from the university's Office for Equal Opportunity before recommending to the Board of Visitors that Harris be appointed to the permanent position, foregoing the search. The board agreed and appointed Harris to the position she already filled.[6] But that came after her leadership for the strategic plan.

The confidence and engagement displayed in the planning process belied the daunting array of problems that VCU faced in the near term. The commission had access to a large body of documentation about the sociopolitical environment, from which a shorter "environmental scan" became Appendix C of the published report. VCU's external environment, as perceived in 1993 and looking several years ahead, makes a good starting point for discussion of the plan.

For one thing, Virginia's population was growing and becoming more diverse, while an aging faculty prepared for mass retirements. How big should VCU become? And, with population growth in the region "increasingly suburban," should VCU plan for a "distributed campus"? What then of VCU's "social responsibility as an urban university"? Where would VCU be located in the future?

Next, as Gorbachev's visit in April reminded, the end of the Cold War and the emergence of international electronic communications promised "a global economic environment," yet the shift to "a peace economy" would also force changes in Virginia from defense to "technology-based industries." Education had to keep up with that changing economy, but with less funding from the federal and the state governments. Generating revenues from tuition and fees, however, burdened students and their families. VCU would have to "do more with less," by setting priorities, eliminating duplicate programs, and sharpening "its definition of educational mission."

Equally challenging was the future of health care, buckling under "the dramatic increase" in costs along with the lack of health insurance for many Americans. Yet, within that daunting context, the report was forthright: "VCU must examine how to build upon the presence of a major health care center for the benefit of the entire University." Finally, the university faced, as it had since its founding, issues of "computers and information technology." The commission could hardly have predicted the World Wide Web (that software being just released into the public domain in 1993), but the report predicted correctly that technology would "impact personnel in virtually every function of the university" as well as "increase the options students have in accessing education."[7]

The official plan repeated the assumptions that guided the process: the goal was "the best interest of the university as a whole," which required "regular and frequent communication" with the "wider university community." If the task was large, the timetable was ambitious. The plan had "a six-year life," to be implemented in full by September 1999.[8]

The completed report, as approved by the Board of Visitors at its September 1993 meeting, contained fifteen "strategic directions," ranging from students and education to faculty and staff development, and covering all aspects of the university's operations. Making VCU one university was not one of the fifteen, but cross-campus collaboration, communication, and connection came up often enough to be a definite subtheme. The tone throughout was confident and determined.[9]

By contrast, the news coverage of the board's approval emphasized the plan as VCU's response to continued hard times, reflected in predictions of 15 percent cuts for higher education in Governor Wilder's last budget proposal and of declines in enrollment, including in business and the arts, which Trani explained as "fiscal attrition." The *Times-Dispatch* report called the strategic plan "a sweeping restructuring plan that calls for the elimination of duplicative courses and programs and for slashing administrative spending." The *CT* also described it initially as a restructuring plan, but recognizing the plan's significance for students, it provided a series of articles giving more detail about the plan's implications for all the proposed strategic directions. John Moeser, professor of urban studies and planning and a member of the plan's commission, told the *CT* that his service was a privilege. "Rather than aimlessly drift into the future, the plan determines the destiny of VCU."[10]

One important piece of the future received only passing mention in the plan. Under strategic direction number 4, which called for enhancement of numerous existing programs with potential for excellence, the reader found item 4b, a simple statement: "The University should support the establishment of an undergraduate engineering program, relying heavily on private sources of funding for the start-up costs of the program."

The newspaper report noted the proposal with the skeptical observation that "Virginia already has several engineering schools turning out more graduates than nearby states."[11]

The final version of the *Strategic Plan for the Future of Virginia Commonwealth University* closed with a chart of the fifteen strategic directions and the "Responsible Person(s)" for each. This procedure enabled a decentralized development of the university but with accountability. Nowhere in the chart was mentioned the proposed school of engineering or the partnership with the biotechnology research center. Those projects, which became main themes in VCU's advancement across the strategic plan's lifetime, presumably were the president's responsibility.[12]

Work was underway already on the Virginia Biotechnology Research Center. The consultant's report, in fall 1991, was enthusiastic but realistic, for success would require various public-private partnerships. In November 1991, following the Board of Visitors' endorsement of the consultant's report, a steering committee formed, with its membership sending a message of corporate and governmental endorsement: William W. Berry, chairman of Dominion Resources Inc.; Robert C. Bobb, city manager; Lawrence Framme, state secretary of economic development; William H. Goodwin Jr., president of CCA Industries Inc.; and G. Gilmer Minor III, president and chief executive officer of Owens & Minor Inc. President Trani would be committee chairman. At the same time, Trani announced that Richmond Renaissance's executive director, Robert E. Olson, would be the project's director. Although a university employee, his first year's salary would come from Richmond Renaissance.[13]

Olson set about studying the organization of other biotechnology research parks and recommended the legal structure of an authority, which in Virginia required legislative approval and a board with members appointed by the governor. The success of the bond issue in November 1992 was still fresh when Trani announced that the park would seek authority status in the 1993 session. By then, the park had attracted financial support from local corporations and the Retail Merchants Association of Greater Richmond, and city and county governments were behind the project, too. The enabling legislation passed easily, and the Virginia Biotechnology Research Park Authority came into being in July 1993 and created a nonprofit corporation to operate the park.[14]

Thus, the biotechnology park might have seemed well underway even before the strategic plan itself started in fall 1993. The bond issue provided funds enough for what would be an administrative office building, but the park needed a structure to house actual biotechnology enterprises. First, school officials calmed down parents angry that the new biotech center would occupy the site of the MCV childcare center, with assurances that the ground floor of the parking deck to be constructed at the north end of Eighth Street would house a brand-new childcare center. Then, they convinced the Board of Visitors and the state that VCU should finance construction, for $15–16 million, of a shell building adjoining the center, to be called Biotech One. This was a gamble, as the state's Department of General Services strongly warned, and success depended on securing tenants.[15]

A gamble, but park leadership also saw building Biotech One and securing tenants as a necessity for the research park's future. At the groundbreaking for the center and Biotech One, on 17 May 1994, the governor and mayor were among those who heard park director Olson's announcement that the building was already 40 percent leased. The future occupants included start-up firms connected to VCU faculty, but as a group they better fit the model of an incubator, with expectations that success would lead to acquisition by a larger firm or removal to a larger facility. That was in keeping with Richmond Renaissance's long search for a business incubator, but VCU needed a closer, more stable relationship with the research park.[16]

For Trani, there was more to it than the park's identity with VCU. "What you eventually need is faculty champions for every idea, because if it is viewed as Trani's idea or Trani's folly, given the natural push and pull between faculty and administration, people will fight it like crazy," he later explained. "So, I knew right away I needed some champions from the Medical Center, and I got some faculty champions from the Medical Center, faculty members who thought this would be a good idea, potentially for commercialization of some of their ideas."[17]

One such was Donald J. Abraham, chair of the Department of Medicinal Chemistry in the School of Pharmacy and founder of the Drug Design and Development Center (later the Institute for Structural Biology and Drug Discovery), and the other was Kenneth Kendler, director of the Psychiatric Genetics Research Program in the Department of Psychiatry, who combined his laboratory's work with that of the Psychiatric Genetics Research Program, under Lindon Eaves, of the Department of Human Genetics, also in the School of Medicine. In 1996 the two programs took the name Virginia Institute for Psychiatric and Behavioral Genetics. As important, with the latter came the Virginia Twins Registry, a large-scale gathering of data from twins for research into patterns of genetic inheritance founded in the 1970s at the medical school by Walter Nance and Linda Corey. The two institutes and the Mid-Atlantic Twin Registry (so named after adding North Carolina data in 1997 and South Carolina data in 1998) continue as tenants of Biotech One. Biotech One was well on the way to being fully occupied when it opened in November 1995, but the institutes and the twin registry became invaluable anchor tenants.[18]

For similar reasons, VCU and the city worked with the outgoing administration of Governor Wilder to move the Office of the State Medical Examiner and the state's Department of Forensic Sciences from outmoded facilities to the research park. In early 1994 the new administration of Governor George F. Allen contemplated instead sending the medical examiner and forensic laboratories to the Elko Tract, in eastern Henrico County, where some had sought to locate VCU thirty years earlier. Governor Baliles's administration had floated a plan to move state health and medical agencies to the tract, but nothing happened. Now it seemed revived. Trani and City Manager Bobb went to the office of Donald C. Williams, director of the Department of General Services under Allen, to ask for reconsideration. Trani recalls that Williams met with them in his office, rather than in his conference room, and the screensaver on Williams's computer monitor over and over flashed the injunction: "Remember, this is the Allen Administration!" Despite this unpromising start, they managed to bring the medical examiner's office and forensic sciences to the research park, where those agencies continue to occupy Biotech Two.[19]

This agreement was crucial, for the city provided the site for Biotech Two, thus giving convincing evidence that both the state and the city stood behind the Virginia Biotechnology Research Park. Moreover, with the Biotech Center and Biotech One at one end and Biotech Two at the other, the park now had a visible presence. The arrival of the Office of the State Medical Examiner had special meaning then, too, for novelist Patricia Cornwell's best-selling crime stories featured Kay Scarpetta, a fictional state medical examiner of Virginia, and the cutting-edge work of forensic sciences. Thanks to Cornwell, the occupants of Biotech Two brought name recognition and, indeed, sexiness to the Biotechnology Research Park.[20]

VCU's PROPOSED school of engineering also figured prominently in larger economic development plans for the region, and its development paralleled

Richmond's slow but steady economic rebuilding in the 1990s. In early February 1993, the Metropolitan Economic Development Council (MEDC) convened its annual meeting with the good news that investment in the Richmond region "by relocating or expanding companies more than tripled in 1992," and jobs created doubled, compared to 1991. Richmond and the surrounding counties created the MEDC in 1978 to market the region—both to attract new businesses and to retain those already here. President Trani then spoke to the 150 leaders present about planning for a school of engineering at VCU. As he would say many times in the coming year, the Richmond metropolitan region was the largest in the United States without an engineering program. That had cost the city new businesses in the past, and the lack hampered MEDC's efforts in the present. Representatives of an accreditor of engineering programs would visit in March to help university administrators and faculty evaluate the feasibility of a program there. The form was uncertain—a separate school, a collaboration with community colleges, or a consortium with existing engineering programs at other state universities—but, it seemed clear, Trani himself was certain that engineering was coming to VCU.[21]

Three presidents of universities with engineering schools consulted with VCU in March—just as the draft VCU strategic plan went out for comments—and issued their report in mid-April. They agreed that "'the most viable alternative'" would be to develop the program as VCU's from the beginning. By then, Trani had acquired formal endorsement of the program from the Metropolitan Chamber of Commerce and local governments. At the end of April, the city manager requested that city council authorize the purchase of land at the corner of Belvidere and Broad Streets, to the northeast of the Academic Campus, to donate to VCU if the school of engineering went forward.[22]

One week later, a delegation of leaders from the Richmond region headed to Jacksonville, Florida, to study that city's successful economic development. Trani was among the travelers (he recalled the amusement among the Richmonders when the Jacksonville hosts declared their intention of attracting a franchise in the National Football League; in November 1993 the NFL awarded Jacksonville the franchise). Jacksonville's city leaders were in the midst of developing a school of engineering at the University of North Florida, and they told the Richmonders how essential they considered it to be for the city's future. Even before departing for Richmond, the group agreed that the engineering school was a project it would support, and one of the business leaders invited Trani and a few others to return aboard his corporate plane. On the way home, Trani pressed the advantage. That Richmond was the largest metropolitan area in the country without an engineering school had become a civic and economic problem needing remedy.[23]

Context mattered, too, for the Jacksonville trip occurred in the midst of fallout from release of a consultant's report, privately commissioned by Richmond business leaders, titled *Back to the Future: Richmond at the Crossroads*. James A. Crupi, a highly regarded city planner, interviewed fifty Richmond leaders in December 1992 and January 1993, and his report mixed his general vision of the future for American cities with scathing criticism—based on his informants' words—of Richmond's business, political, and newspaper leadership. There was consensus on the problems, but none on solutions. "It is a community commentary that Richmond's two most exciting projects (Valentine Riverside and Biomedical [sic] Research Park) are being led by a historian and an educator," he declared. The report asserted that, in particular, out of the past decades of racial politics in Richmond, the business leadership (white) and the political leadership (African American) distrusted each other, with metropolitan paralysis as the consequence.[24]

This context provided Trani and VCU with opportunity. Trani had no history in Richmond, and, if VCU did not yet stand very high in their estimations, neither political nor business leaders had reason to distrust the university. Moreover, as demonstrated by the visit to Trani in August 1990 that set off the Biotechnology Research Park, local leaders interested in action could bypass the local paralysis by working with the university. To be sure, Trani and VCU had to earn the trust and respect of both business and political leaders, something that the Biotechnology Research Park went far to accomplish. In fact, in mid-March 1993, the *Times-Dispatch* editorialized that the research park was "not the only excitement at VCU these days." The editorial commended the draft strategic plan, recently released. "And to think," it concluded, "three years ago pessimism was widespread that VCU—having incurred the wrath of its neighbors for a master plan of expansion into residential areas—was fresh out of options and destined to stagnate."[25]

How then to create a school of engineering at a state university without using state funds, as the strategic plan proposed? It is important to realize, too, that Trani also saw engineering as a means toward the goal of one university. Biomedical engineering already existed as a graduate program at the medical school, with little interest then in connecting to the Academic Campus, but for Trani, engineering as a school would involve scientists at the Academic Campus and earn respect from the MCV Campus as it brought both campuses into engagement with the research park. It is telling that Trani envisioned the school's engineering specialties in biochemical fields, rather than the more traditional civil engineering. In approaching outside donors to support the school, Trani had to persuade them also to back his vision for VCU.[26]

As planning went forward, VCU decided not to put the engineering school at the Belvidere and Broad site, although the change of plans did not shake the city government's preference for VCU construction at the site. All agreed that it was an important gateway to the city, with the adjacent exit ramps from the interstate highway directing traffic there. In addition, ever since the abandonment of the master campus plan in 1990, planners on campus and at city hall foresaw VCU moving north and thus aiding in upgrading that portion of the decrepit Broad Street corridor. For the time being, the city and university expected eventually to use that property, but the engineering school would go elsewhere, although exactly where was unknown.[27]

Even though his advisory committee, as well as the president of the University of North Florida, had recommended that VCU go it alone, the university had to consider the politics of higher education in Virginia, where Old Dominion University, George Mason University, the University of Virginia, and Virginia Tech already had engineering schools. The key person was Dean Paul E. Torgersen, of Virginia Tech's engineering school, who had a long-standing interest in advancing engineering education in the Richmond area. Tech also had a policy of supporting only graduate programs off-campus, with all undergraduate education being residential in Blacksburg, but Torgersen determined that a joint arrangement with VCU, by which Virginia Tech's engineering school would help to develop the new school's faculty and curriculum, did not violate that policy. In fall 1993, Trani and Provost Harris flew to Blacksburg to seal the agreement, only to find the airport fogged in. Trani insisted that their pilot circle until clear enough for landing, and the timing of the meeting proved propitious. After finalizing the agreement between VCU and Virginia Tech about engineering that day, Torgersen left for a press conference to announce his appointment as the latter school's next president. With Virginia Tech's new president behind the plan, it would move successfully through the State Council of Higher Education.[28]

On 10 February 1994, at a ballroom at the Commons, President Trani, for VCU, and President Torgersen, for Virginia Tech, announced their collaboration to create an undergraduate engineering school in "the Richmond area." Henry A. McGee, former chair of chemical engineering at Tech, would lead the effort, now as VCU's associate provost for engineering. In addition to chemical engineering, the school would offer degrees in electrical, mechanical, and biomedical engineering. The latter graduate program at the MCV Campus was expected to stay there. The site for the other programs had not yet been determined. Location would become its own story.

It was a proud day for the university. An anonymous VCU faculty scientist gave $250,000 to endow a biomedical engineering professorship. Endorsements from the Metropolitan Chamber of Commerce, the Central Richmond Association, and the Virginia Society of Professional Engineers supported the donor's confidence. City Manager Robert Bobb declared the school "essential for our business recruitment and business retention programs."[29]

The highlight of the ceremony, though, was Trani's announcement that an anonymous donor, committed to the Richmond business community and convinced that a school of engineering would be invaluable to that community, had made an unrestricted gift of $10 million (to be matched by other contributions) to start the school. This was the largest single gift to VCU ever. The donor, William H. Goodwin, shunned self-promotion, but his role was crucial. An engineering graduate of Virginia Tech, he went on to an MBA degree from the Darden School of Business at the University of Virginia and then to business success. His CCA Industries Inc. owned several high-profile enterprises, and success enabled him and his wife, Alice Goodwin, to support causes they cared about. One was the eradication of cancer, and they strongly backed the Massey Cancer Center. Goodwin had served for a decade on the board of the MCV Foundation when he became its president in May 1993. He also agreed to serve on the inaugural steering committee for the Biotechnology Research Park, though he was not one of the park's strongest champions.[30]

The proposed school of engineering caught his interest, and Goodwin, too, spread the news that Richmond was the largest region to lack one. There was another connection to VCU. Peter Wyeth, vice president for advancement, came to VCU from the Philadelphia Orchestra Association, but he had previously worked with donors at Hampden-Sydney College and at the University of Virginia. At Virginia he got to know Goodwin as a board member for the Darden School. There Goodwin pioneered a plan to use an independent foundation to create and own a new campus for the business school, which would then lease it at nominal rent to the school. The independent foundation could manage investments with far greater freedom, and better returns, than could more conservative state entities, and he brought that idea to the engineering school's planners. Wyeth helped Goodwin convince Trani that an engineering foundation was the solution to founding a school of engineering without state funds, and Goodwin's anonymous gift announced in February 1994 started the foundation well.[31]

As important, Goodwin helped to recruit to the foundation the region's business elite. The School of Engineering Foundation not only made that school possible, it also engaged people of means and power with VCU, almost all of whom, like Goodwin, were alumni of other schools. Goodwin also took a delegation, all businessmen, to see Governor George F. Allen, who also became a backer of the school. Indeed, after leaving the governorship Allen joined the foundation's board. Goodwin also recruited businessman and philanthropist C. Kenneth Wright to serve as a trustee of the School of Engineering Foundation, and Wright and his wife became major donors to VCU as well as the school.[32]

The ambitious 1994 timetable projected approval from the State Council of Higher Education in 1995, the first students to enroll in 1996, and the collaboration with Virginia Tech, assuming the fledgling school's successful flight, to end in 1999–2000. The *Times-Dispatch* endorsed the project editorially as "VCU's wave of the future." The editorial stated that the "most exciting aspect of an engineering school at VCU is the prospect of its collaboration with MCV." Here was Trani's vision of the engineering school as a bridge between the two campuses, contributing to the making of a single, unified university. "Biotechnology is the wave of the future," the editorial declared. "And a VCU School of Engineering could be Richmond's chance to ride it."[33]

The agenda for the March 1994 meeting of the Board of Visitors was crowded, as had become the norm, but the board agreed to launch a fundraising campaign for the new engineering school. The goal was $20 million, and VCU already had more than half that amount committed. The academic plan for the school would be ready for the board's approval in the fall, with submission then to the State Council on Higher Education. The biggest news from the meeting was the purchase of three properties on Broad Street, on the northern edge of the Academic Campus. One site, at Harrison and Broad, was slated for the new convocation center (discussed below). The second property was just to the west of that site. The third site, a former car dealership at Broad and Belvidere, at the northeast corner of the Academic Campus, had once been considered as the site for the engineering school. The newspapers reported that "school officials say that plan is now dead."[34]

So, where would the engineering school be located? In July, Trani announced that VCU had selected a location on Cary Street, on the southern border with the Oregon Hill neighborhood. VCU sought no repetition of the controversy with that neighborhood about expansion. When the Advance Electric Supply Company, at the southwest corner of Cary and Belvidere, had closed not long before, the owners offered to sell the property to VCU, and the VCU Real Estate Foundation considered accepting, but Trani said no; he opposed expansion south of Cary into the neighborhood. Logically, then, a site on the north side—the VCU side—of Cary Street for the school would be acceptable to Oregon Hill.[35]

Trani had hardly confirmed that VCU would purchase the property at the northwest corner of Cary and Belvidere, occupied by Carneal & Johnson Architects, before the Oregon Hill Home Improvement Council (OHHIC) hand-delivered a letter to his office protesting the decision. The problem was parking, the letter said, with the Gladding dormitory already producing congestion. VCU scoffed: there was already a large parking deck just to the west on Main Street, and a new deck was to go up on Broad Street, along with surface parking at the new property at Broad and Belvidere. Parking was a nonissue, and VCU already occupied much of the north side of Cary Street. The Oregon Hill group countered by announcing plans to take its concern to the state's Department of General Services and the Art and Architectural Review Board, which had to approve the VCU building plan (even though private money funded the project). Kelley Lane, of OHHIC, also noted that the state's Department of Historic Resources would have to approve the planned destruction of the Carneal & Johnson building, which dated to the 1840s and, more important, was listed as a contributing structure in Oregon Hill's designation on the state and national Registers of Historic Places. Those entities had opposed the VCU master plan and perhaps would do so again.[36]

That OHHIC turned immediately to state agencies to stave off VCU's engineering school, rather than seeking support from adjacent neighborhood associations and city council members, as it had done in fighting the master plan five years earlier, measured the effect of Trani's decision in 1990 to abandon the master plan and to seek cooperative relations with VCU's neighbors. A week after the July 1994 board meeting, the *Times-Dispatch* carried a lengthy analysis of Trani's first four years at VCU and cited that decision as "an astute move that won community kudos and set a powerful tone for his presidency."[37]

Another sign of change at VCU came in August with news that the university had received in 1993–94 the highest level of private gifts in the school's history. The largest portion, including the anonymous founding gift to the engineering school, came from outside the university family, an indication of Trani's success at engaging Richmond-area businessmen in VCU's plans. But alumni contributed nearly 30 percent more than in the previous year, and the membership of the MCV and VCU alumni associations had grown proportionately.[38]

In Oregon Hill, admiration for Trani's administration was muted at best. In September 1994, Dulaney Ward, OHHIC's director, announced that construction of the engineering school was acceptable if VCU saved the house located at 610 West Cary Street, soon to become known as the Jacob House. Like the building occupied by the architectural firm, the destruction of which OHHIC now seemed to expect, the Jacob House appeared in Oregon Hill's historical register records as a contributing structure. Trani responded that VCU well knew that it had three options for the house: destruction, incorporation into the engineering building (OHHIC's preference), or moving it.[39]

The *Times-Dispatch* chimed in with an editorial chiding OHHIC for making too much of the commonplace people who had resided at the house ("They weren't Robert E. Lee," OHHIC's Ward had conceded): "Sentimental attachment is not enough reason to deter progress." VCU should just move the house to another site, it concluded. VCU officials had the wit not to follow the paper's lead and dismiss the house's past residents as nobodies, for the stature of the house and its occupants soon began to rise.[40]

The year, one of VCU's best, ended with the State Council of Higher Education approving the engineering school. The consent was contingent on raising "the bulk of the $20 million" in private funds needed by April 1996 (the school was to open in fall 1996). VCU also promised not to seek more than $2 million in state funds for annual operating costs (estimated to total more than $7 million annually, the *Times-Dispatch* said, with "research grants and tuitions [*sic*]" covering the remainder). In return, VCU would be freed to set tuition at higher rates (the state's law schools already had that permission). The agreement also freed the school of the state's cumbersome approval process for new buildings. That meant that VCU might not need approval from the state's historic preservation officials to demolish or move the Jacob House. Trani said that no decision had been made, but "it will be an important test case."[41]

JUST ONE month earlier, on 17 November 1994, the Board of Visitors accepted a consulting architect's plan for development of Broad Street between Belvidere on the east and Harrison Street on the west. The plan was audacious, with the existing streetscape of warehouses and an abandoned automobile dealership to be replaced by a tree-lined thoroughfare within the northern side of the Academic Campus, which by way of Broad Street to the east connected to the Medical College of Virginia Campus. The board also voted to attract a national college bookstore to set up on the ground floor of the parking deck planned for the south side of Broad Street between Shafer Street, the consultant's proposed main entrance to the Academic Campus, and Harrison Street. The parking deck, welcome in itself, was a necessary precondition for the effective functioning of the planned convocation/recreation center slated for the north side of Broad.[42]

Michael Dennis, MIT professor and planner, whose Michael Dennis and Associates drafted the plan, acknowledged its boldness and the need for collaboration with the city and the neighborhoods for its success, yet VCU could do no less. "The part of Broad Street that passes the VCU academic campus," his report stated, "is currently the most derelict and forlorn portion of its entire length." Rejuvenating those blocks would make the northern gateway to VCU a destination. Already, meetings with the city and neighborhood leaders had been positive.[43]

Back on 5 November 1991, the *CT* reproduced a letter to all students from President Trani on the work of the Neighborhood and University Recreational Development Study Committee, one of the entities created as part of his community initiatives in September 1990. The committee included university and community representatives, and the university backed its work by hiring an architectural consultant from California to review the university's recreational facilities at both campuses. The report described VCU as "one of the least equipped universities" in Virginia and the nation. VCU needed new swimming pools at both campuses, "an array" of indoor and outdoor recreational spaces, and an "assembly area for 2,500–3,000 persons." Fortunately, the Academic Campus had potential space for development at "the areas north on Broad Street." Trani promised students that the proposals would receive his "personal attention and commitment."[44]

The only way for VCU to build an on-campus facility for sports events was as a convocation and recreation (co-rec) facility, with access for students in addition to scholarship athletes, enabling it to be built with bonds to be paid by student fees. Yet, students' hopeful expectations of departing VCU long before the center opened made a hard sell out of winning them over to a hike in fees for the benefit of future students. So, when university officials headed to New Orleans to visit Tulane University, where students and the basketball team shared a new co-rec center, Trani arranged for the 1991–92 president of the Student Government Association, Michelle L. Andryshak, to come along. The facility won her over, and she helped win over the SGA to support a fee increase for a co-rec center. In April 1992, VCU announced that tuition and fees would rise by 15 percent, including an additional $60 fee ($50 for the co-rec center, and $10 for the fine arts center). By the SGA's agreement, the fee would jump another $50 in two years. Trani defended the hike with reference to new facilities at Louisville and Tulane, both members of the Metro Conference like VCU and both urban universities, which he declared had "dramatically changed campus life."[45]

The co-rec center did not figure prominently in the strategic plan, though strategic direction 12, under the heading of developing "a strong sense of campus community," called for continued development of "recreation facilities that respond to student needs." More than a year before, in April 1992, the VCU Real Estate Foundation had moved to purchase the property on the north side of Broad Street, across from Shafer Street, and Athletic Director Richard Sander declared it "first choice for the recreational facility."[46]

Even before the strategic plan's adoption in fall 1993, the future of the co-rec center came to involve the future of the basketball program. In early 1993, Sander announced the good news that the state had okayed $2 million for planning and land acquisition for the proposed VCU convocation and recreation center. The site had shifted a block westward from the property previously acquired, and even though Sander was optimistic that it might open in 1996, the project would require substantial fundraising. Student fees alone were insufficient. Not only that, but the Student Government Association had almost immediately questioned the commitment of student fees to such projects in a time of ever-rising costs for students. The consequence was a determination to raise private funds for the center, too, which also resulted in a much finer building than originally conceived.[47]

Sander's announcement included the statement that the center would become the home court for the VCU basketball team. Years before, games moved from the cramped Franklin Street Gymnasium to the downtown Coliseum. Sander, seconded by Coach Sonny Smith, said that the problem with the Coliseum was that VCU could not control scheduling there. As an example, the 1992–93 team played seven of its final eight games on the road. Home court advantage truly existed in college basketball, and VCU's team would benefit from playing on campus.[48]

The problem was that Sander and Smith failed to convince the person making the final decisions. The *Times-Dispatch* reported at the end of July 1993 that Trani still saw the downtown Coliseum as the basketball team's home. With VCU playing in the Metro Conference, he looked forward to attracting large crowds to games at the Coliseum, larger than the seating capacity planned for the campus building. No doubt the virtue of supporting the city by using the Coliseum also mattered. Moreover, the Coliseum was adjacent to the future Virginia Biotechnology Research Park, and the viability of the Coliseum was a benefit to the research park, and vice versa. Trani and Sander had discussed the Coliseum situation before, and one strategy had been to gain national exposure by attracting collegiate championship events to Richmond and the Coliseum. In addition to early-round games in the men's basketball tournament, Sander managed to secure the 1994 women's basketball championship. That proved a dramatic success for the fans, as the University of North Carolina won on a last-second three-pointer by Charlotte Smith, but it became evident that the Coliseum (and VCU and Richmond) could not compete for such events with other cities with newer facilities. Sander held his ground about the team playing on campus, and, according to sportswriter John Markon, had a strategic argument: the best way to get fans of VCU basketball to contribute to the fundraising for the building was to promise them home games there.[49]

Trani came around, but it took time. One year later, in September 1994, a major fundraising drive got underway for the VCU convocation and recreation center. The cochairs of the drive were famed basketball player Charles Barkley, who had played for Coach Sonny Smith at Auburn University, and Stuart Siegel, cofounder of S&K Apparel, a discount chain that had clothed innumerable VCU students for job interviews, not to mention their professors. Siegel made a major donation of his own, and the Board of Visitors voted in October to name the center for him. The women's basketball team was slated to play all its home games at the Siegel Center when it opened, now in 1998, but Trani and Sander still disagreed about the home for the men's team. That did not poison their relationship, for VCU had just extended Sander's contract, but Trani liked the Coliseum. The team had a nearly 75 percent winning record there, he said. "Why would anybody walk away from that wonderful facility?" Sander responded, as he had previously, that the Coliseum was too often unavailable. "I've been here eight years, and the Coliseum has never been available in February," he said.[50]

In the process that led to the on-campus convocation and recreation center, a quiet turn away from a key element of the strategic plan occurred. The notion of satellite campuses, to accommodate the suburbanization of the Richmond region (and hollowing out of the city), went by the way. The Siegel Center was a resource intended for a residential university. VCU needed more full-time students for the revenues, but the state's university-age population was on the rise, too. Rather than satellite campuses, with large parking lots for students and faculty to come and go, the years after the strategic plan saw an undeclared but definitive shift to a residential campus and to the city, with the Biotechnology Research Park, the School of Engineering, and the Siegel Center anchoring the urban university.

THE BUDGET cuts had hit the MCV Campus just as forcefully as at the Academic Campus, although the School of Dentistry's and the School of Nursing's centennial celebrations in 1993 went off as planned. The VCU strategic plan that year proposed a major organizational change at the Medical Campus, with the School of Basic Health Sciences to be merged into the School of Medicine. An external advisory group, comprised of medical school administrators, concurred. Only one other university medical school in the United States separated basic sciences from medicine, and the growing research focus of both VCU schools made the merger logical. The Board of Visitors agreed to the merger at its July 1993 meeting. Soon thereafter, Vice President for Health Sciences John Jones announced that Dean

Stephen Ayres, of the School of Medicine, had asked to step down after eight successful years as dean (Ayres's final column in the Alumni Association's *Scarab* as dean strongly urged the merger). Dean Gaylen Bradley, of the School of Basic Health Sciences, soon stepped down, too, to return to teaching.[51]

All seemed amicable, but, even so, many involved naturally feared the consequences of change. Trani announced that Vice President for Research and Graduate Studies William Dewey would serve as interim dean for basic sciences, and Hermes Kontos, professor of internal medicine, would be the interim dean for medicine. Kontos's appointment reassured worriers. He received his MD from the University of Athens and, having decided on a career in academic medicine, went on to get a PhD in physiology at MCV. He had served as interim chair of two departments in the medical school. He was experienced, respected, and blessed with a calm temperament. In the long run, the merger's opportunity for Kontos to take a larger administrative role was perhaps as valuable to VCU as the merger.[52]

The MCV Hospitals still faced dire financial problems. As President Trani explained in the *Scarab*, state regulations hamstrung MCV Hospitals' actions to become more competitive. The legislature had offered a bit of relief with a bill "permitting limited joint venturing" by the hospitals, which Trani described as "an important step toward improving the competitive position of MCV Hospitals."[53]

Alumni returning to the MCV campus in spring 1994 would nonetheless see changes underway. The new Ambulatory Care Center, connected floor-by-floor to the Nelson Clinic, was under construction for April 1995 (Sheryl Garland, head of ambulatory care, declared that the facility had been needed for at least a decade). A few blocks to the northwest, the Virginia Biotechnology Research Center was scheduled to open in summer 1995, and back on the MCV Campus, the new medical sciences building was also rising on Marshall Street across from the Main Hospital where the East and Dooley Hospitals had once stood, to open in summer 1996.

Then, on 19 June 1994, the *Washington Post* published, in its commentary and opinion section, a story titled "Burning Secrets." The story, by Cliff Honicker, a longtime researcher into radiation experiments on human subjects in the years after World War II, described a secret laboratory at MCV in the 1950s where "imbued with Cold War zeal and scientific arrogance, doctors conducted a series of potentially dangerous experiments on hundreds of unaware human subjects, most of them poor and African American." Honicker's purpose was to argue for the declassification of the records of such experiments in general, and he thus painted the activities at MCV in lurid colors, though he acknowledged a concern at MCV at the time for patient consent and that the project ensured that the patients healed. He also quoted Hermes Kontos, interim dean of the School of Medicine, affirming that no such experiments could occur at MCV in the present day.[54]

President Trani could not let the story pass, even if it concerned matters of four decades ago, for the story damaged VCU's reputation. That it was a Sunday and Father's Day made no difference, as he put together a response team. He pulled in Vice President John Jones and set medical archivist Jodi L. Koste to work to document what happened at MCV back then. The action was so swift, and the record was so clear, that VCU's initial response to the *Post*'s story appeared in the *Times-Dispatch* the very next day. The experiments were limited, controlled, and hardly secrets, for the *Richmond News Leader* had carried stories about them, and the physicians published the results of the experiments in scholarly journals. Two weeks after the Honicker article, which Trani called "irresponsible journalism that must be rebuked," Trani's bylined response for MCV and VCU appeared in the *Post*. He challenged the first article point by point. "In all," he concluded, "the *Post* article's 'investigation' of the Medical College of Virginia's burn unit misreads the record, misrepresents the work of the scientists and moralizes about past research practices." Because of the potential damage to the school's reputation, and the fears that the article might cause former patients and their families to sue VCU, Trani later explained in the *Scarab*, he had to set the record straight.[55]

Reports of medical experiments involving radiation elsewhere had led President Bill Clinton to appoint an Advisory Committee on Human Radiation Experiments. A member of the commission, Susan E. Lederer, a historian at Pennsylvania State University, was going to do research at the MCV campus anyway, and she looked into the record of the burn project. She was present on 25 July in Washington when Trani testified before the commission that the MCV experimenters did not "take advantage of vulnerable populations." Lederer supported his contention: "In my review, I saw no evidence to support the report in the newspaper."

The commission nonetheless requested further documentation from the MCV archives about the experiments as it prepared to make its final report. Honicker appeared at more than one commission meeting to complain that it was giving insufficient attention to the MCV story he had exposed, although university officials assuredly disagreed. The commission's final report, issued in October 1995, stated that the radiation research done in the 1950s at the medical school would violate present-day federal standards for informed consent by human subjects, but MCV was hardly more than a footnote in a 900-page document. Whatever its effects on MCV's reputation, the episode demonstrated Trani's grizzly-like response to what he perceived as unfair and uninformed criticism of his university.[56]

In November 1994, President Trani was named the recipient of the first Leadership Metro Richmond Distinguished Leadership Award, presented by the National Association for Community Leadership. Also that month, at the same meeting where the plan for the future of Broad Street was presented, the Board of Visitors created procedures for naming an acting president. The action was prudent in general, but its specific purpose was to prepare for President Trani's planned research sabbatical in summer 1995. The sabbatical also might have been viewed by all involved—VCU and Richmond—as a chance finally to catch a breath. As 1994 ended, Virginia Commonwealth University was moving forward with a purpose and a strategic consensus.[57]

9

Building One University, 1995–1999

IN RETROSPECT, the late 1990s might appear to be an age of technological innovation and economic growth, but at the time, public universities struggled to find effective solutions to budgetary uncertainties. Historian John R. Thelin declared, "The flagship state university presidents of the 1990s were all singing the same chorus: 'We used to be state supported; then we were state assisted; and now we are state located.'" The example of Virginia, he continued, backed that complaint as Republican state administrations failed to restore the budget reductions of the early 1990s. VCU and other schools responded creatively by seeking private donors, creating independent foundations, and making special economic and reporting arrangements within the state system. At the same time, campus disputes over inclusion and civility provoked scrutiny from outside, subsumed under the perjorative label of "political correctness," and roiled universities, VCU among them. The public attention to "political correctness" on campus belied the diminished public support for the universities.[1]

In Richmond, VCU maintained the commitment it had made to the city as an urban university. Thelin contends, perhaps with tongue near his cheek, that the nineteenth century's "A&M," the agricultural and mechanical universities, changed to a twenty-first-century A&M, of athletics and medicine. Many Richmonders then primarily associated VCU with those activities—far more than with the humanities and sciences—and putting both on a healthy basis mattered for VCU's efforts to build one university.[2]

ON 6 JANUARY 1995, the basketball team opened its Metro Conference season at the Richmond Coliseum with an upset victory over the powerful University of Louisville. The defeat—and his team's play—displeased Louisville's coach, Denny Crum, but he declared that the Rams "deserved the game." The victory was VCU's fifth in a row, albeit all at the Coliseum, the home court downtown, and gave the team a shiny record of 10–3, which was especially sweet after being predicted to bring up the rear in the conference.[3]

The sweetness quickly turned sour. Louisville and all the other members of the Metro Conference had plans to depart for a new, larger conference, leaving VCU and Virginia Tech behind. The "complicating factor," as Athletic Director Richard Sander explained, was that the conference bylaws specified that each departing school owed an indemnity of $500,000, to be divided among the remaining schools. As things looked then, VCU and Virginia Tech stood to receive $2.5 million each, plus by continuing as a two-team Metro Conference they could divide funds pooled for the conference from the National Collegiate Athletic Association.[4]

That prospect pleased no one. President Trani flew to the NCAA convention to propose to the presidents of schools forming the new conference that VCU be included, but received little encouragement. VCU prepared to go to court to make the departing schools pay exit fees, if necessary. Meanwhile. rumors had Tech moving to the Atlantic 10 Conference, and the Colonial Athletic Association (CAA) offered to admit either or both schools.[5]

VCU received its answer in the form of a fax sent after business hours on Friday, 13 January, from the chancellor of the University of North Carolina–Charlotte. The other five members of the Metro had decided instead to invite seven new schools to join the Metro, and to expel VCU and Virginia Tech. Fourteen schools in the conference would be just two too many. Trani responded angrily: "The American public believes that greed, cynicism and unscrupulousness dominate collegiate athletics. This will do little to dissuade them." The conference was a good fit for VCU, he continued. "There's a similarity: medical centers, urban universities, diverse student bodies." The *Times-Dispatch* joined Trani's call for the NCAA to mediate.[6]

The NCAA did not move to mediate, and the Virginia schools turned to the lawyers. Just one day prior to the lawsuit's preliminary hearing, all parties agreed to mediation. VCU and Virginia Tech departed the Metro Conference with a settlement of $1.135 million each. The five remaining Metro schools also agreed to play VCU at Richmond one time over the next five years. The next issue was the future conference homes for the two Virginia schools, and President Trani and President Paul Torgersen, of Tech, were so happy that they spoke about entering a new conference as a twosome.[7]

As it turned out, Virginia Tech joined the Atlantic 10 Conference, and VCU settled into the Colonial Athletic Association. The CAA, which then included the University of Richmond, meant less expensive trips to games and new rivalries. Trani and other officials made the best of the situation, and VCU fans were excited about future success in what they hoped was the less competitive CAA, after a final mediocre season in the Metro.[8]

Trani remained angry about the mistreatment of VCU, and faulted the National Collegiate Athletic Association, supposedly the governing body for intercollegiate sports, for staying on the sidelines through the controversy. He told readers of the *Chronicle of Higher Education* that the public too often associated college athletics with "hypercommercialism, cynicism, and unscrupulous practices," and the shuffling of conferences justified the association. College sports needed reform, he declared, and reform needed the backing of the NCAA.[9]

As hoped, the CAA proved more accommodating than the Metro, and the 1995–96 basketball team managed a record of 24–9 and earned a berth in the NCAA tournament. The next year proved more difficult, as the team fell back to 14–13 and defeat in the first game of the conference tournament. With four of the CAA's coaches fired after the 1996–97 season, Coach Sonny Smith now boasted the longest tenure at his school of all the conference's basketball coaches.[10]

Construction of the Siegel Center, on Broad Street at Harrison, was far enough along that, as Athletic Director Sander pointed out, the Athletics Department's recruiters could bring prospective student athletes there to excite them about the future. President Trani saw multiple uses for the center, ranging from high school graduations to concerts and conventions. Funding for the center had just benefited from the "windfall," as Trani put it, of $8 million from a contract with the Pepsi-Cola Company for "beverage exclusivity." All agreed that with the center within walking distance for many students, and with the parking deck across Broad Street slated to open in 1998, crowds could easily get to the events there.[11]

ALTHOUGH VCU had successfully pushed back against charges of malpractice in radiation experiments in the 1950s, the present-day problems of the MCV hospitals continued. In April 1995, Louis F. Rossiter, professor of health administration and director of the Office of Health-Care Policy and Research, explained the larger context in the *VCU Voice*. The "gridlock" in Washington notwithstanding, he said, "managed care is here to stay." Already, the legislature had mandated that Virginia's Medicaid patients be enrolled in health maintenance organizations, and businesses, especially in Northern Virginia, were doing the same for their employees. HMOs, Rossiter explained, expected to reduce spending on health care by keeping subscribers healthy and by providing financial incentives to health care providers to limit services to actual need. The changes all led "to a single question: In health care, what works?" On the bright side, Rossiter noted, grant funds for research to evaluate new health care policy had increased significantly.[12]

On 18 May 1995, the new Ambulatory Care Center opened at Eleventh and Clay Streets, the corner once occupied by the Alumni House, now relocated across the street. It was the first new building "designed specifically for rendering outpatient care" on the Medical Campus in twenty-five years. The facility reflected improved medical procedures that enabled patients to recover at home rather than in a hospital, which accorded with the strategies of the new health management organizations, but the shift away from inpatient care also added to the financial stresses bedeviling the MCV Hospitals.[13]

At the end of August 1995, the *Richmond Times-Dispatch* ran a three-part series on the dire financial situations of the MCV Hospitals and the University of Virginia Hospital. The headline for the first article in the series also conveyed the university's message: "MCV in Fragile Financial Health." Competition from other local hospitals, the new limits insurance companies placed on payments, and the expenses imposed by indigent care were just the beginning. Even with an outpost at Stony Point on the city's southwestern border, the Main Hospital's city location put off suburbanite patients with insurance. Despite surveys showing patients were very satisfied with the care they received, the "belief that all of Richmond is a dangerous place to be," as John Jones, vice president for health sciences, put it, remained a barrier.

If those were not enough problems, the hospitals also had to comply with state regulations, unlike their competition. A year earlier, Columbia/HCA, a private investor in hospitals, had initiated discussions with MCV Hospitals, causing a flurry of attention, but VCU officials now declared that no private suitor would consider an investment unless the state's regulations went away. To reinforce the point, in October, VCU and UVA reported that the cost of educating a physician was nearly $80,000 per year, with the state covering less than 30 percent. Revenues from clinical practice at the hospitals subsidized the remainder, but the same competitive forces confronting the hospitals, especially the pressure on fees from the spread of managed care programs, meant that those revenues could not be depended on for the future.[14]

In mid-October 1995, the news leaked out that the Allen administration had under consideration a plan to sell the MCV Hospitals and the University of Virginia's hospital. Another option was to create private foundations, tax-exempt, to run the hospitals, though that would remove state oversight and the state's sovereign immunity—a legal protection of Virginia agencies, universities, and their employees from suits for tort liability. The two universities favored a third option: "the creation of quasi-governmental authorities to take over the hospitals' management." They also fully opposed the sale of the hospitals.[15]

Hardly had the news gone out than Governor Allen announced emphatically that the hospitals would not be sold: "I am not for it. My Cabinet secretaries are not for it. It's without merit." The authority option had advantages, he continued. Accountability to the state would continue, as would Medicaid funding for medical care for the indigent. Under the plan, nurses, technicians, and other workers, although not the physicians, would no longer be state employees, but the authority option would enable them to remain in the state's pension system. According to the *Times-Dispatch*, the immediate outcry against the sales, especially from the governor's fellow Republicans in Albemarle County, home of the University of Virginia medical school, inspired the governor's announcement on the verge of legislative elections.[16]

The process would be political, to be sure, but VCU officials expected to benefit from proximity by standing arm-in-arm with the University of Virginia. The Allen administration proposed in early December 1995 to submit legislation to create authorities to oversee and manage the hospitals. State law permitted such authorities, but the legislature itself would define how the entities would operate. The issues were complicated—an unnamed state official said setting up the authorities might "take several years." John Jones was more optimistic: "I think in several months that it could be completed."[17]

Then, the University of Virginia's board of visitors pulled out of the agreement. At the end of the year, that board asked for exemptions from state regulations for the hospital but without any changes to its management structure, and the Allen administration declared that option unacceptable. At VCU, dismay at the older university's decision became determination to seek authority status without an ally. Fear persisted that the medical schools' now-divided paths would lead neither to the greater freedom both sought. And, some supporters in the legislature wanted "to know why MCV couldn't live with the U.Va. bill," as one of them said.[18]

The authority bill—thirty-two pages long—went to the legislature as February began, and VCU leaders emphasized the unique situation of the MCV Hospitals in Richmond. The hospitals' charity care cost $88.5 million in 1994, nearly twice that at the University of Virginia. The Richmond market was full of competing hospitals, unlike in Charlottesville, with several offering sophisticated services. The MCV hospitals had lost top physicians to them, revenues were down, and jobs had been cut. The authority legislation was essential to the hospitals' future, and President Trani and Donald Gehring, vice president for external relations, convinced a dozen local legislators to cosponsor the bill. The authority board would include sixteen members—VCU's president, the dean of the medical school, and four members named by the legislature, five by the governor, and five from the Board of Visitors (also appointed by the governor). Trani and Gehring assured legislators that this board would give the state more, not less, authority, and the University of Virginia board's rejection of the plan for that reason gave credence to the assurances.[19]

Once lawmakers got a look at the legislation, modifications swiftly followed. Both schools revised their respective bills to promise to continue to provide health care to the indigent, and VCU also promised that indigent care would continue at the downtown Medical Campus. Just a few days later, legislators pushed a compromise bill, eliminating the authority proposal to make the hospitals an independent state agency. As such, it would have most of the freedoms sought under the original bill, but the hospital employees would continue as state employees, and the legislature would retain oversight of large capital outlays, such as those for new buildings. The lawmakers had hardly completed drafting the compromise when lawyers pointed out that the MCV Hospitals, if it were an independent state agency, could not, under the state's constitution, "incur debt or enter into joint ventures," and such partnerships were essential, VCU leaders said, to the hospital's financial survival. Thus, before the second bill came to the lawmakers, a third one, returning to the semi-independent authority status, was being written.[20]

Another issue was that the authority also involved substantial exemptions from the state's disclosure laws, a protection of proprietary information "in today's volatile health-care market," said VCU officials. Legislators expressed concern about the nondisclosure, especially that the hospital's finances might deteriorate even further, but now without anyone the wiser until too late. President Trani reminded them that the health authority's board would include members chosen by the legislature. "This is going to be a very public corporation," he declared.[21]

The legislation moved forward. On 9 February a key House committee endorsed the authority setup, with two revisions. The first was that hospital workers would retain state employee status and the other allowed for legislative review of any construction projects of $2 million or more (that is to say, for all significant projects). The version of the legislation in the Senate did not include those requirements, but no one expected a problem in resolving the differences.[22]

That seemed the right moment for VCU to explain the reasons for seeking the new arrangement for the hospitals, and an essay, under President Trani's name, appeared in the *Times-Dispatch* on 11 February. The MCV Hospitals (MCVH) and the University of Virginia Medical Center both remained committed to the "threefold mission" of teaching, medical care, and research, but the "changing health-care marketplace" required new, more competitive arrangements. State regulations complicated that, as with the requirement that MCVH use the state's procurement process to contract with the MCV Associated Physicians "its own faculty practice plan." MCVH provided about $100 million in indigent care in 1995 (about a third of such care in the entire state), with $30 million of that not reimbursed. The authority would give the flexibility to continue such ventures as Commonwealth Care of Virginia Inc. to connect local primary-care physicians and low-income patients, and the satellite facilities, such as at Stony Point at the southwestern side of the city where an ambulatory surgery center was planned. The mission remained the same, he indicated, but the administrative means needed to change.[23]

The next day, both House and Senate voted to permit VCU to create the health authority, with the bill approved by each going to the other for what turned out to be significant revision. Two weeks later, in early March, the battle continued behind the scenes. At last, on 9 March, the bill won final approval from both houses of the legislature. Trani conveyed both the exhilaration of the moment and the strain involved in getting there when he called the health authority bill "the most important piece of legislation" for VCU since the 1968 merger.[24]

The new Medical College of Virginia Hospitals Authority Board met for the first time at the end of August 1996. As expected, Trani was elected to chair the new board, with Robert M. Freeman, chairman of Signet Banking Corporation, vice chair; State Senator Benjamin J. Lambert III, of Richmond, secretary; and Dr. Lindley Smith, a member of the Board of Visitors, treasurer. The officers reflected the quality of the different appointments to the authority's board, as planned. The authority was "in the early stages of a critical transition," Trani said, but all were pleased with the prospects.[25]

In October 1996, John E. Jones, vice president for health sciences, announced that he would step down after six eventful years in that post. He had come to VCU from West Virginia University as an early and important hire for the Trani administration. Jones oversaw the merger of some two dozen physician plans into one, the merger of the Schools of Basic Health Sciences and of Medicine, and most recently the creation of the MCV Hospitals Authority. His successor was Hermes Kontos, dean of the School of Medicine, which post he would retain as part of an administrative reorganization.[26]

ON THE day in May 1994 when the Board of Visitors approved the dissolution of the School of Community and Public Affairs and the merger of the Schools of Basic Health Sciences and of Medicine, as recommended in the strategic plan, the board also named Joyce Wise Dodd the interim director of the School of Mass Communications. Dodd, a veteran of fourteen years at Mass Comm, recently headed an unsuccessful effort to hire a new director for the school. The school now operated under provisional accreditation after an outside review committee found "ineffective" leadership, a "fractious" faculty, and poor relations with the alumni. The unhappy struggles of the School of Mass Communication need not be detailed here, but the school as it was then helped to give rise to the innovative AdCenter (later Brandcenter) (and the innovative Entrepreneurial Programs Tuition agreements).[27]

In addition, conflicts at VCU over "political correctness" and "affirmative action" efforts to ensure gender and racial equity, especially heated in the early 1990s, featured Ted J. Smith, a journalism professor at the school and the university's leading antagonist of both issues. The national battle lines had been drawn up during President Ackell's tenure. Alan Bloom's bestseller from 1987, *The Closing of the American Mind: How Higher Education Has Failed Democracy and Impoverished the Souls of Today's Students*, seemed to ride both the wave of budget cutting (and consequent questioning of university activities) and the wave of ascendant conservatism in opinion. The title of Bloom's book betrayed an assumption about a unified American mind, with consensus as its default setting, when national discourse had shifted, as scholar Henry Louis Gates Jr. put it, to "the matter of cultural pluralism in our high school and college curricula and its relation to the 'American' national identity." If the outside critics roiled the humanities, so, too, did the simultaneous furious discourse over the meanings of postmodernism, the "cultural turn," and, especially in literary studies, the intrusions of theory, or as detractors preferred, "French theory," in which the slippery text displaced the once-central author. Rather than responding to critics of political correctness in terms that the critics employed, humanities scholars seemed instead to erect rhetorical barriers to understanding by laymen. These developments, evidence of the intellectual vitality of the humanities from one perspective, seemed to prove the critics' case from another.[28]

Finally, to make the storm perfect, at universities across the country, student groups once in the unheard minority now had numbers and arguments to demand that university cultures give them respect. Prohibitions on discriminations on the basis of race and gender flowed outward and clashed with such college behaviors as fraternity brothers at George Mason University parading in drag for an "ugly woman" skit, with one brother adding blackface to the stereotyping. The parade resulted in suspension of the fraternity by the university, as well as a subsequent suit by the American Civil Liberties Union that successfully challenged the university's action. Critics painted efforts by university administrators to maintain what they saw as necessary civility on campus as heavy-handed assaults on freedom of speech.[29]

President Trani had a policy of nonintervention in faculty and departmental affairs, and he stayed out of the managerial and accreditation matters, but political correctness and then the AdCenter kept him aware of the School of Mass Communications. Trani brought with him to VCU a commitment to diversity and civility on campus, founded on his own international experiences and the University of Wisconsin system's ambitious "Design for Diversity." Trani had already proposed a similar policy for VCU when in 1991 the courts found in the case of *UWM Post v. Board of Regents of University of Wisconsin* that the speech restrictions were unconstitutionally too broad.[30]

As the complaints about political correctness at universities gathered force, Trani tried to calm the local waters with an essay in the *Times-Dispatch* at the end of July 1991, proposing that the controversy trivialized the serious issues of inclusion and multiculturalism, and that critics mistook maintaining conditions for open debate on campus for restrictions. The newspaper quickly published a response by journalism professor Ted J. Smith, the incorporator of the Virginia Association of Scholars, a branch of the National Association of Scholars, founded in 1987 "to confront the rising threat of politicization of colleges and universities and to summon faculty members back to the principles of liberal education and disciplined intellectual inquiry." Trani could hardly have asked for better evidence that political correctness had not stifled debate at VCU than Smith's essay, which declared political correctness both a threat to free speech and a scheme to silence critics of affirmative-action policies.[31]

Smith also was the leader of the five VCU male faculty members who sued the university after a 1991 salary study concluded that female faculty members were unfairly paid less than male faculty members and the university provided those women faculty members with raises to make salaries more equitable. The case began with the *CT*'s publication of all faculty salaries in 1988; female faculty members compiled statistical evidence from it to demonstrate a distinctly gendered disparity in salaries. Their study came to the Faculty Senate only in April 1991, and that body asked for a new, up-to-date investigation. That second study, released at the end of October 1991, found that on average, women earned $1,345 less than their male tenure-eligible counterparts. University lawyers proposed a solution: a salary equity fund would provide an across-the-board raise of 2.25 percent to all tenure-eligible females, and female faculty might also submit applications for one-time salary adjustments if needed for equity.[32]

Smith and his fellows then filed suit, claiming that other, more meritocratic factors, such as hours taught, books and articles published, and previous service as administrators, might just as well explain the consistent, overall salary differences as gender bias. The males took their complaint first to the Equal Employment Opportunity Commission for an investigation, which found the university in compliance with the laws, and they then went to court and on to the appeals court. A three-judge panel ruled in August 1995 that there should be a jury trial. VCU and the five males then agreed to settle the lawsuit. The financial settlement was ordered secret, but VCU agreed that it would "never again award pay raises without measuring merit and performance will be used in any future study of salaries." Said Smith, "We are in favor of pay equity, we just think it has to be done correctly."[33]

Meanwhile, on the political correctness front, a VCU task force headed by Peter Vallentyne, chair of the Department of Philosophy and Religious Studies, drafted a revised policy on harassment. The Faculty Senate debated the policy in January 1992, and by a strong vote of 24 to 8, advised against imposing the code. Trani told the *Times-Dispatch* that the final policy would "be heavily influenced" by the senate's voice, and he had yet to decide whether to submit to the Board of Visitors any of the proposed changes to the existing policy. The *Times-Dispatch* asked editorially, "Does the Trani administration believe in academic freedom or not?" Trani fired off an angry response—the faculty vote was exactly how universities ought to operate—copied to leaders of the Faculty Senate and Faculty Council of the University Council.[34]

Trani's backing for the "politically correct" speech code was sincere. He expressed empathy with students subjected to verbal harassment, and he emphasized that VCU's student body was going to become more multicultural in the future. Nonetheless, he knew when to cut his losses. In September 1992, he withdrew the proposed non–sexual harassment code, telling the newspapers, "It may have been one idea too many I brought from Wisconsin." The *Times-Dispatch* praised his decision. "It helps to have the speech-code distraction out of the way," the paper concluded.[35]

In 1995, finally, the School of Mass Communications received welcome news that outside evaluators had recommended the school's provisional accreditation be lifted, and not long after, interim director Joyce Dodd was rewarded with appointment as the school's director. During this period also, a young instructor of advertising, Diane Cook-Tench, had an idea for a new graduate school. She came to VCU from the Martin Agency, a Richmond advertising firm with a national clientele, where she had risen to a top leadership position at age thirty-five and then left to have more time for her family and to teach others. Filled with ideas and hard to dissuade, Cook-Tench wanted to create the best graduate advertising program in the country, an ambition sure to resonate with Trani. Existing programs were either university-based, turning out researchers, she explained, or proprietary schools, turning out portfolios. Cook-Tench proposed a program

based on actual industry workings, with attention to the future of advertising, and thus committed to diversity in a diverse nation. In addition
to Dodd's support, Cook-Tench also had endorsements from advertising
leaders with local connections, and they then helped to bring together what
Trani later called a "dramatic" national board of advisors.[36]

"She just came to see me out of the blue," Trani recalled, "and out of the
blue, I gave her permission." She needed money, of course. Tuition would
cover all operating costs, she promised, including rent on space in downtown Richmond, adjacent to the new headquarters of the Martin Agency
in Shockoe Slip. "In effect," Trani said, "I gave her a cash advance against
tuition."[37]

The budgetary logic was more formal. Under what became known as
Entrepreneurial Programs Tuition (EPT) agreements, new or significantly
expanding programs could receive a large portion of the tuition paid by
enrollees in those programs, with that increased funding used to cover
operating costs. Cook-Tench's AdCenter was a prototype for EPT agreements that enabled VCU to enlarge other academic offerings, including
from the Schools of Business, of Education, and of Engineering through
the 1990s and beyond.[38]

On 28 September 1995, a week after the AdCenter received approval
from the Board of Visitors, the center's board convened in Richmond to
announce the new graduate program. Classes would begin in fall 1996, and
already ad agencies had donated significant funds and talent to announcing the new program. It would seek an initial class of sixty students,
advancing to one hundred, with a goal of 20 percent of the students being
minorities. Reflecting the EPT agreement, tuition would be the same for
in-state and out-of-state students, unlike the difference that was the norm
for academic programs at VCU. Trani cited the center, along with the
Virginia Biotechnology Research Park and the School of Engineering, as
an example of "'universities taking down their walls, intellectually if not
physically, to link up with the talent of the community and the resources
of the community.'" The center's slogan was simpler, but just as ambitious:
"We're not out to save the world, just advertising." Soon after the AdCenter welcomed its first students, in October 1996 VCU announced the public phase of "Partners for Progress," a new capital fundraising campaign.
The goal was $120 million, double the amount raised in the previous cam-
paign, with some $80 million already pledged. The chair of the campaign
was Richard T. Robertson, "a 1967 VCU alumnus and president of Warner

Brothers Domestic Television Distribution," as the *Times-Dispatch* put it. Technically, he had graduated from the Richmond Professional Institute, of which he had fond memories, but the personable Robertson had reconnected with VCU in the 1990s, first by joining the Alumni Association. He strongly supported his alma mater's new vigor, with particular interest in the School of Mass Communications, which honored him in 1994 as outstanding alumnus. Outside donors, such as William H. Goodwin Jr. and Stuart Siegel, had lifted VCU, but the university's long-term support depended on the alumni, and Robertson's generous enthusiasm set a valued precedent for the entire university. The campaign eventually raised $167 million.[39]

THE CENTER for Public Policy also emerged from the strategic plan in March 1994 with the dissolution of the School of Community and Public Affairs, which, in turn, traced its heritage to VCU's very beginnings as an urban university. Heading the center was political scientist Robert D. Holsworth, a faculty leader well-known to local newspaper readers as a ready source for commentary on politics. The new center formally got underway in July 1994, with a university mission to bring together expertise in public policy issues from both campuses to serve the community and the state.[40]

Then came the announcement that former governor L. Douglas Wilder would join the center and teach classes at VCU. He had chosen not to return to the practice of law after leaving office and instead began a syndicated radio talk show, through which he displayed his political intelligence and provocative wit. Those qualities promised success in the classroom, too, but his academic connections had seemed closer to his alma mater, Virginia Union University, where a new library took his name and housed his personal papers. He and Trani had traveled together to China on a trade mission in 1993, the former looking after the state's interests and the latter looking after VCU's, but Wilder came to VCU to engage with students, not merely as a favor to a friend.[41]

In addition to teaching courses in contemporary politics, Wilder would also help organize symposia on policy issues for the center, with the center, in turn, providing him with a home for his activities. President Trani welcomed Wilder's hiring as a coup that would win the center national attention. Holsworth agreed, and he foresaw Wilder's classes attracting students not only from both VCU campuses but also from other area

Professor L. Douglas Wilder, former governor of Virginia, speaks on health policy and politics to students at the MCV Campus, March 1996. (Virginia Commonwealth University Libraries)

universities. Wilder was equally enthusiastic, and the three men would build professional and personal relationships in the coming years.[42]

Wilder began teaching in fall 1995, and the first Wilder Symposium opened on 26 January 1997 at the Medical College of Virginia Campus. The theme was "Race and Health Care as We Approach the 21st Century," with Dr. Jean Harris, the first African American woman to graduate from the Medical College of Virginia and a former secretary of human resources for Virginia, joining Wilder, her childhood neighbor, as a moderator. The next symposium, in April 1998, concerned the Richmond public schools, evidencing the center's commitment to investigating the most trying of public policy issues. A year later, Grace Harris retired as provost and she also came to the Center for Public Policy to build a program to develop faculty skills for academic leadership, which became the Grace E. Harris Leadership Institute.[43]

MEANWHILE, GOVERNOR ALLEN's administration cited support for the engineering school as an example of its increased higher education funding in the 1994–96 budget, but its main budgetary theme was controlling tuition increases. That would include approving salary increases for faculty and staff conditioned on the colleges and universities themselves finding savings enough to fund the raises. This confidence in the power of economic incentives fit well into a larger trend, soon decried by academic observers under the label of neoliberalism, to trust market forces to produce efficiencies in higher education. If creating the engineering school involved playing up the roles of private donors and tuition funding, VCU was ready to do so.[44]

The larger part of the university's argument for the engineering school was that it would bring benefits—"jobs, taxes, and educational opportunities"—to the city and region. In mid-February, Richmond's city council pledged $100,000 annually for the school's first five years. A handful of defenders of the Jacob House, an antebellum structure on Cary Street slated for demolition, attended that council meeting to protest. Trani promised to seek state review before demolishing the house, but he also pointed out that the property belonged to the VCU Real Estate Foundation, a private entity not bound by state regulation. Councilman Richardson, who had once stood with Oregon Hill against the VCU master plan, now spoke about the engineering school's potential for increasing the numbers of minority engineers, and council approved the funding.[45]

The fate of the Jacob House divided the region's groups engaged in historic preservation. On one side was the Historic Richmond Foundation, which declared the engineering school a "greater good" that "far outweighs the preservation of these buildings." Countering that view were several groups, including the National Trust for Historic Preservation. As the Association for the Preservation of Virginia Antiquities put it, destruction "would send the wrong message to the VCU community" by seeming to value "the working class heritage of the Oregon Hill Historic District" less than the homes of the wealthy that VCU had already preserved on Franklin Street. The state's Department of Historic Resources found a middle ground of its own, recommending that VCU preserve the buildings, but if that was impossible, then to move them; and if that was impossible, at least to document their features before destruction. Legally, VCU could do as it pleased, the *Times-Dispatch* observed, but "community relations" were "another matter."[46]

Public perceptions mattered. Having decided not to incorporate the house into the new engineering building, VCU offered to move it. In April 1995,

Trani announced that private moving funds would be available to any group that could provide a home to the house. The proposal came two weeks prior to the Department of Historic Resources' review board's meeting about placing the house on the National Register of Historic Places. Trani's proposal noted somewhat grumpily that before VCU's plans for the property, "there seemed to be no public interest in saving this structure." Because the Oregon Hill Home Improvement Council (OHHIC) lacked funds to purchase a lot for the house, it dismissed the offer as "a slick P.R. move." Maybe, but the offer also came with $105,800 in moving expenses.[47]

As expected, the historical review board did designate the Jacob House for the National Register of Historic Places, but by then the story of the engineering building had transformed. On 12 April 1995, Trani announced that the state's package of incentives to Motorola Inc. to build a manufacturing plant to fabricate semiconductors in Goochland County, west of Richmond, included $16 million to expand the engineering school for special training in microchip manufacturing. In the mid-1990s, Virginia set out to use state incentives—some "$153.7 million in tax credits, grants, and worker training," was the *Washington Post*'s estimate in 1996—to attract semiconductor manufacturers. The Motorola project, "the largest single capital investment" in that company's history, received the most attention, especially in central Virginia, but IBM and Toshiba opened a "fab," as the microchip factories were known, in Manassas in November 1995. A third fab, a joint Motorola/Siemens project, later opened in eastern Henrico County. Scholar Jan Mazurek pointed out that although the fabs made chips in clean rooms, they used toxic chemicals and vast quantities of water. Writing in 1999, she said that the industry was too new and too swiftly changing to assess long-term environmental impacts. Even so, she concluded that "when measured against other economic development strategies, such as giving $200 million sports stadiums to billionaire team owners, development strategies based on microchip manufacturing look pretty good."[48]

Several months earlier, with the identity of the corporation interested in a high-tech plant in central Virginia still secret, Wayne Sterling, the state's director of economic development, began meeting with Trani and other VCU officials. The promise of the new engineering school became important to the campaign to bring Motorola to Virginia, with Trani's emphasis on the school as a trainer of future employees of Richmond companies given specific application. The inducements that the state now offered to Motorola would include a second engineering building housing a ten thousand-square-foot clean room where students could receive special training in manufacturing semiconductors. The remainder of the new funds would endow professorships in semiconducting engineering.[49]

The *Times-Dispatch* declared the Motorola announcement "stupendous news" for the entire region, with the company planning to invest $3 billion and eventually to employ five thousand people. The project benefited the engineering school and complemented the biotech research park. Local columnist Robert Holland couldn't help gloating, "Research Triangle of North Carolina, eat your heart out!"[50]

In that context, the counteroffer from OHHIC to pay for the renovation of the Jacob House on its original site went nowhere. The Greater Richmond Chamber of Commerce soon after sent a batch of local business and governmental leaders on a third annual visit to another city for briefings on economic development. The destination in 1995 was Minneapolis–St. Paul, and presenters there focused on the University of Minnesota's impact on the region through engineering and health sciences research. According to the newspaper, this focus was the Richmond group's "calculated move" in support of President Trani's "efforts to increase VCU's role in Richmond's economic development." So little impact did OHHIC's renovation offer have that the *Times-Dispatch* editorialized on 16 May, shortly after the Minnesota trip, that the only options for the Jacob House were moving or demolition.[51]

Then the terms of the discussion changed another time. The house, given its name from John Jacob, its first resident and an early superintendent of the then-nearby penitentiary, had been constructed by George Winston, a Quaker and an employer of free men of color as masons and carpenters. That not only engaged members of the Richmond Friends Meeting, but also enabled the house to be identified with the long history of African Americans in Richmond. The Quaker connection even conjured up possibilities that the house might have been a station on the Underground Railroad. Richmond Quakers joined representatives of the NAACP and others on 20 May to protest VCU's plans.[52]

In early June 1995, VCU announced the house would be moved, preferably to a site across Cary Street from its original location. Trani noted that VCU accepted the historical significance of the house, which was why the house would be moved and not demolished. The preservationists agreed that the preferred site was better than the alternatives. Work got underway in August, with the move planned for September. Quaker activist Alan

Schintzius tried to protest the move on 7 August by sitting in a bulldozer's scoop at the construction site; the police arrested him quietly, and the workers from Expert House Movers Inc. continued their preparations.[53]

As the fall semester got underway, Motorola announced its purchase of 230 acres west of Richmond in Goochland County for the semiconductor fabrication plant, and the Jacob House, freed from its foundation, moved across Cary Street to its new site. On the moving day, the Central Virginia Association also convened its forty-fourth annual meeting. The 350 business and government leaders heard the keynote speaker, President Trani, predict that the Richmond area was on the brink of a boom. It might be twenty years before the full effect of Motorola's plant will be known, he said, but in the interim, VCU was in the midst of "the biggest expansion in its history." The region had plenty of assets, he continued, "tourism assets, historic assets, transportation assets," but the "core," the city of Richmond, must be "safe, inclusive, and vibrant."[54]

The story of the Jacob House and Oregon Hill continued after the move in 1995. Developer Stephen Salomonsky began building dormitory-style apartments along Cary Street just west of the Jacob House in the late 1990s, and purchased the Jacob House in 2001. To the outrage of Oregon Hill activists, Salomonsky then proposed another apartment building attached to the Jacob House. In early 2003, the Oregon Hill Neighborhood Association informed him (and dozens of public officials and preservation organizations) that it would "adamantly oppose" the proposal. With that threat in the air, Alan Schintzius, the local Quaker activist who had climbed onto a bulldozer to try to block the moving of the Jacob House in 1995, contacted Salomonsky about allowing the house to serve the community and honor its past. Negotiations followed, and the developer quietly arranged for the Richmond Friends Meeting to manage the process of doing that. A commission of fifteen people, including historians, preservationists, and community members, with Dave Depp, clerk, and Betsy Brinson, historian, of the Friends Meeting, facilitating the Quaker method of decision by consensus, decided that the Oregon Hill Home Improvement Council made the best proposal for using the house and had the resources to help preserve it. In turn, Salomonsky's gift of the house and other concessions won the neighborhood's support for his apartment project. OHHIC celebrated its occupancy of the Jacob House on 8 June 2004 with the unveiling of a state highway historical marker. On the first floor was a permanent exhibition on the early history of Quakers in Richmond.[55]

Meanwhile, Motorola Inc. recorded declines in sales of semiconductors—thanks to a seemingly glutted cell-phone market—and decided in spring 1996 to postpone construction at the site in Goochland County. Local backers made lemonade by declaring that the postponement gave area schools, including the soon-to-be-born engineering school, more time to prepare local people for employment with Motorola. Confidence returned in May with news of the corporation's plan, in partnership with Siemens A.G., to build a factory employing up to two thousand at the Elko Tract in eastern Henrico County, which county officials had hoped in 1968 to make the home of VCU.[56]

The engineering school was already burgeoning. In March VCU announced plans to triple the size of the school and double the estimated cost to $40 million. That day's ceremonies included announcements of a gift of $500,000 from the Philip Morris Companies (now Altria Group), expansion of the Motorola clean-room laboratory, and construction of two more classroom buildings, with the complex now slated to occupy the entire block.[57]

That meant that rather than renovating, as promised, the old Victory Van Warehouse, then occupied by the School of the Arts' crafts programs, VCU would tear it down. The day's announcements included not only the news about the engineering school but also a plan to invest some $16 million in a new building for the fine arts. The site was left open, but the likeliest location was on Broad Street, where VCU had been acquiring property. The Board of Visitors and the School of Engineering Foundation reached agreement on 21 March for the foundation to acquire the warehouse site, to reimburse VCU for renovations already made there, and to acquire a new site for the new fine arts center. Trani noted that members of the arts faculty welcomed the news, even though the proposed new building would have less space than the warehouse. "Nobody was happy with the renovation of that old building," he said. "This gives them a brand new building that they design from the get-go."[58]

THE ANNOUNCEMENT also seemed to shift public attention from Cary Street and the Jacob House north to Broad Street. A committee of top administrators had already begun development of a master site plan for the two campuses, to replace the plan that Trani had withdrawn back in 1990. By February 1996, when the preliminaries of that plan went before the University Council, VCU leaders already had consulted successfully with the university's neighbors. The plan proposed a consistent, urban design for VCU's future, with buildings built to the perimeters of their sites, along the streetscape, a marked difference from the suburban look of earlier buildings, such as the 1975 Business Building (later Harris Hall). The university's largest land acquisitions—fully twenty-one acres—were at the MCV campus. The new steam plant, parking decks, and the Biotechnology Research Park would fill the spaces there. Finding funds to make the new master plan a reality remained uncertain, but Donald C. Bruegman, vice president for administration, was confident that "there are creative ways to finance things through public-private partnerships."[59]

Even before the plan's formal approval, VCU celebrated the groundbreaking for the new Siegel Center, a facility for student recreation and for university convocations and other events. A photograph of the ceremony shows Trani; Henry Rhone, vice provost for student affairs; Richard Sander, the athletic director; the presidents of the student government associations at both campuses; and Barbara Abernathy, of the Carver Area Civic Improvement League. The latter group, and other organizations from the Carver neighborhood to the north of Broad Street, had been consulted and involved in the revitalization project from its beginning, reflecting lessons learned from the long fight with Oregon Hill.[60]

The VCU-Carver Partnership was unveiled on 31 July 1997, and the project received a grant of $400,000 from the U.S. Department of Housing and Urban Development in September to carry out plans for revitalization of the neighborhood, located just north of VCU's developments on Broad Street. There were five "partnership strategies": develop Carver Elementary School into a community school with expanded hours and services, provide enhanced health and social programs to residents, create a community plan with the expertise of the Department of Urban Studies and Planning, include faculty from the Schools of Arts and Business in job-training initiatives, and expand the VCU Police Department for community policing in the neighborhood. The university's matching funds for the grant more than doubled the amount needed, reflecting the good relations already nurtured between VCU and the Carver Area Civic Improvement League. Barbara Abernathy, president of the league, explained that she and Trani had met a year before to plan the VCU-Carver partnership, and Trani had volunteered the promise that VCU would not move north of Marshall Street so long as he was president. The good relations between neighborhood and university meant that the neighborhood okayed the use of the Biggs Building, a onetime furniture factory, on the north side of Marshall Street, as temporary quarters for the Ceramics and Sculpture Departments until the fine arts center was built.[61]

The Board of Visitors concluded a busy academic year in May 1996 with a focus on construction matters, including viewing architects' rendering of the planned engineering building and approving construction of the School of Fine Arts building. That building would stand on Broad at the northern end of Shafer Street, and officials already envisioned that street as a hub for student activity from the arts building south to Cabell Library.[62]

The board at that meeting also honored Donald C. Bruegman, senior vice president for administration, who was retiring from VCU after eighteen years of engagement with master plans, neighborhood relations, and construction. Two other major figures in VCU's development as a university also retired that summer. John S. Ruggiero, the dean of the School of Pharmacy since 1984, and Thomas C. Barker, the only dean ever of the School of Allied Health Professions, stepped down in July. Barker had joined MCV in 1967, prior to the merger creating VCU, as head of the School of Hospital Administration.[63]

The board's personnel decisions at the July meeting also deserve attention. Richard Toscan, dean of the School of Theater at the University of Southern California, was named dean of the School of the Arts. One year before, Dean Murry N. DePillars resigned to become an executive vice president at Chicago State University. DePillars, a painter and jazz aficionado, came to VCU in 1971 as assistant dean and became dean in 1976. His two-decade tenure saw the School of the Arts become one of the largest and most highly regarded public art schools, but Chicago was his hometown, and he felt the call to return. It may say something about the quarters the School of the Arts had occupied that DePillars's parting comment was, "I'll miss the people more than the buildings." It fell to Thomas DeSmidt, interim dean, to manage the change in direction from renovating the warehouse on Belvidere to constructing a new building on Broad Street.[64]

The other board appointment that day was the successor to Bruegman. Back in April, VCU's furious real estate and construction activity provoked a critical editorial from the *Times-Dispatch* that wondered where funds came from to pay for "such conspicuous growth." As VCU moved into an era of market solutions, public-private partnerships, and quasi-public entities, like the MCV Hospital Authority, the editorial warned that opportunities abounded for missteps and the appearance of missteps.[65]

On this occasion, Lois Trani spoke up. Trani paid attention, for she rarely commented on administrative matters. She told him that a university president might surmount any number of missteps but leading a university into financial problems was a career-ending mistake. He needed a first-rate financial manager. Her advice led to an offer to Paul Timmreck to become senior vice president for administration and finance. Timmreck had two decades of high-level experience in state government as staff director of the State Senate Finance Committee, budget director for Governors Robb and Baliles, and secretary of finance for Governors Wilder and Allen. He knew state finances intimately and had the respect of leaders in both parties. Hiring Timmreck away from Governor Allen's administration was a coup for VCU, and for the next decade he provided invaluable leadership as the university continued to grow.[66]

With Timmreck on board, Trani had an important addition to his senior leadership team, which included Grace Harris as provost, Hermes Kontos as vice president for health sciences, Donald Gehring for government relations, Peter Wyeth for advancement, and Sue Ann (SAM) Messmer for university relations and then as chief of staff. Trani's team was capable and long-serving, which allowed Trani to concentrate on projects that fostered the development of the university.[67]

The Richmond Real Estate Group named the Virginia Biotechnology Research Park its 1996 project of the year for making "a significant contribution to the Richmond real estate market." Unlike the site of the engineering school, where the fates of existing buildings became flash points, the research park built on property where destruction had already occurred, leaving nothing but "a series of low-cost parking lots" with no one to protest the new construction. The Virginia Biotechnology Center opened in January 1996, and the attached Biotech One building finished construction in the summer (with the prospect of being 70 percent leased by January 1997, said Trani). In the fall, groundbreaking took place for Biotech Two, which would house the Virginia Division of Forensic Science and the Office of the State Medical Examiner. The research park, and the university, promised benefits for the city and for the region, an encouragement for further cooperation between the city and the suburban counties surrounding it.[68]

A year later, the research park named Robert T. Skunda, the secretary of commerce and trade under Governor Allen, as president and chief executive officer. He had made a strong record in state government of convincing corporations to invest in Virginia, and the *Times-Dispatch* described him as "a prize catch" for VCU. His move also suggested the Allen administration's commitment to the park's expansion, which had not been as evident just a few years earlier. Skunda declared that "biotechnology" might be too narrow a term as he proposed to market the park in "the field of general life sciences."[69]

As EXPECTED, the Board of Visitors approved the new master site plan at its July 1996 meeting. There were signs already that the action on campus aided in recruitment of students. After declining freshmen enrollments in recent years, the class of 2000 would total 1,900 students, the largest since 1987, and the "academic quality" of the students was up, too. Applications in 1997 jumped another 15 percent. VCU also had the second-safest campus in Virginia by 1996. That report counted only incidents reported on campus to university police, but the crime rate in Richmond, including the highly publicized homicide rate, also began to abate. It is hard to estimate the impact of crime, and a reputation for crime, on enrollments over the years at VCU, but it seems obvious that perceptions of a safer campus would encourage more students to live there.

Board member Clarence Townes observed at the time that parents now wanted students to live on campus, a trend that the ever-larger portion of the student body originating in Northern Virginia reinforced. According to Henry Rhone, vice provost for student affairs, VCU had total space for only 2,400 students. There were insufficient rooms yet for a residential campus. The usual public-private arrangements for constructing student housing, moreover, involved a university providing the land and a developer building the housing and leasing it to the university. VCU had no extra land to provide. "We don't have one bit," said Rhone.[70]

As early as January 1995, assessments of the strategic plan, not yet two years old, emphasized the accomplishments so far: "new programs, organizational changes and policy enhancements that will position VCU for success." The strategic plan had worked well—some 90 percent of the 160 items in the original plan reported progress if not successful achievement—and that, combined with changes in the external environment for VCU and for higher education, made revision worthwhile. Teams of top administrators managed this process, unlike the conscious effort in 1992–93 to engage everyone at both campuses, which also suggested the confidence that the university's expansion had inspired.[71]

In November 1997, *VCU Voice* published the draft revision of the strategic plan as a supplement, and a set of university forums followed for comments. The plan remained ambitious about VCU as an urban research institution, but the continued difficulties of the MCV Health System, as "a quality health services provider in a highly competitive market-place," stood out as one of the plan's five new "strategic themes." After a final meeting with students, staff, and faculty in early January 1998, Trani presented the revised strategic plan to the Board of Visitors for its approval. The plan, as published in March 1998, looked ahead while also reflecting the achievements of the previous years at VCU, with two confident declarations on the cover of the brochure: "The decade of the 1990's [*sic*] has been a vigorous period of university-building" and "VCU approaches the end of the century secure in its mission and guided by an ambitious vision for its future."[72]

By summer 1996, thanks partly to VCU's expansion, the *Times-Dispatch* concluded that "the shape of downtown may be changing." Richmond was unusual in that its commercial/retail districts and financial/business districts had long been separated by hilly distance that kept office workers from regular shopping on Broad Street. Two decades before, conflicts over priorities for development along Broad Street's retail district versus development in the Main Street financial district added fuel to the city's racial tensions. Since then, development south of Main Street had gone forward, while stores closed along Broad Street and the Sixth Street Market Place changed from positive initiative to painful reminder. The newspaper took some justifiable pride in the announcement that its parent company, Media General Inc., had committed to construction of a new complex to house the company's and the newspaper's offices at Fourth and Franklin, two blocks south of Broad Street. This came as welcome news, indeed, for just a few years before, the newspaper's printing and production operations moved to suburban Hanover County, and rumor had the rest of the *Richmond Times-Dispatch* soon to depart its city, too. Publisher J. Stewart Bryan hoped the paper's decision might be a spark for change. "I can look out my window and see Miller & Rhoads gone. The John Marshall. Thalhimers. There's nothing here," he lamented. Other recent projects inspiring hope included Ethyl Corporation's construction on Belvidere, on the site of the old penitentiary across from Oregon Hill. James H. Boykin, chair of the Department of Real Estate Studies at VCU, welcomed the projects but warned that the western part of downtown, nearest to the Academic Campus, needed more. "'There has to be some incentive for people to want to work and play and be educated and live in a place," he said.[73]

The other side of those incentives for residents in downtown emerged in summer 1996, with the unsuccessful efforts of the Daily Planet, an agency providing services to the homeless, among others, to move from its building on Canal Street, adjacent to Ethyl Corporation's new construction. Planned moves to a neighborhood on the north side of town and then to a site in Jackson Ward, just north of the Broad Street retail district, fell before local opposition. Ethyl Corporation had promised to cover half the cost of a generous purchase of the agency's property, but the delays led to the offer being rescinded. Then, in July, word got out that an anonymous donor offered $2 million to move its Canal Street center to another location, and the donor insisted on a veto over that new location. Speculation had it that VCU was behind the offer, with the new engineering school going up just a few blocks to the west, but a spokesperson for the university said that no such offer had been made. The problem in Richmond of the homeless, often panhandling and otherwise present in public spaces, as in other U.S. cities then, proved divisive, with some advocating for the social services obviously needed and others convinced that bringing residents back to the downtown districts required reducing the presence of the homeless. With each side convinced the other's policy made the problem worse, the issue would flare up again.[74]

VCU's ascent in the 1990s coincided with political doldrums for Richmond's city government. In December 1995, longtime city councilman Chuck Richardson, a respected and candid friend to VCU, fell victim to drug addiction and received a jail sentence for distributing heroin. A year later, both the superintendent of public schools and the director of the public library were removed from their jobs. Meanwhile, a series of revelations about a onetime aide to city councilman (and mayor 1994–96) Leonidas Young that involved drug sales and then bank fraud led ultimately to a prison sentence for Young. The continuing saga played out in the press from the mid-1990s to the decade's end. Meanwhile, in late 1997 City Manager Robert C. Bobb, a strong supporter of the Biotechnology Research Park, accepted a new position in Oakland, California, and a few months later,

Clarence Townes, a member of the VCU Board of Visitors and a founder of Richmond Renaissance in 1982, announced his retirement as executive director of that organization, which had united black and white leaders behind economic development projects, such as the research park.[75]

The consequence was an unexpected leadership vacuum in Richmond. Times had changed, though, and a new factor was Virginia Commonwealth University. In 1997, Trani became chairman of the Greater Richmond Chamber of Commerce. The city and region still seemed on the rise, as did VCU.[76]

On 23 October 1997, groundbreaking took place for the future fine arts center on Broad Street. In addition to housing the School of Arts' Departments of Sculpture, of Crafts, and of Painting and Printmaking, the building would boast studios, woodshops, a foundry, kilns, and a welding shop, which required the building to include specialized ventilation systems. Dean Richard Toscan called the fine arts center a major boost toward the school's goal of being one of the country's five best. Construction

Eugene P. Trani at West Broad Street, 2001. Across from the West Broad Street parking deck is construction of the Edmund F. Ackell Residence Center and beyond it is the Siegel Center. (Courtesy of *Richmond Times-Dispatch* and The Valentine)

continued for the Siegel Center and the parking deck/bookstore nearby, and Trani reiterated VCU's commitment to revitalizing that stretch of Broad Street, at "the heart of our region."[77]

ON 7 NOVEMBER 1997, VCU provost Grace Harris conveyed the university's "extreme disappointment" at the State Council of Higher Education's denial of permission for the university to go forward with plans for a degree-granting African American studies program. This came after SCHEV staff members had seemed to welcome the proposal and reflected continuing ideological divisions that had previously led to the forced resignation of the agency's longtime chief, Gordon Davies, in 1995.[78] The decision dismayed students and faculty at VCU and came in the midst of controversy in the newspapers about funding for the School of Engineering.

The *Times-Dispatch*'s negative coverage of VCU engineering began a year before, when stories unexpectedly took the wind out of the new engineering school's sails as the first 103-member class started the fall semester. VCU had provided scholarships to half the engineering students, or, as reporter Ruth Intress put it, "one third of all merit scholarship money given to Virginia Commonwealth University's 1,968 freshmen this fall is going to 50 students." Although VCU officials played down the significance of the financial aid, Intress reported that "talk has been circulating for months" that VCU was having difficulty in recruiting students "to its new and untried program." In fact, Dean Henry A. McGee Jr. said, so many students applied that additional scholarship money had to be found. Another story in that day's paper, also by Intress, noted that VCU "had nothing but promises and a glossy brochure to show prospective students." Regardless, groundbreaking for the first engineering building took place in mid-November 1996.[79]

In late October 1997 controversy flashed again after VCU requested a revision in the appropriation act that created the engineering school to permit using funds from student tuition for operation and maintenance costs. That act, passed prior to the advent of Motorola and the addition to the project of a microelectronics program in a second building, restricted payment of those costs to private funds. Articles in the *Times-Dispatch* on 30 and 31 October treated the request as VCU's reneging on a promise not to seek state funding for the engineering school. The charge angered Trani, of course, and he responded on 9 November with a long explanation, published on the editorial page, which emphasized that Virginia institutions "commonly use tuition revenue for the upkeep of academic buildings," that "the Commonwealth expanded the mission of VCU's engineering school," and that the recent request "is entirely consistent with the appropriation act." The newspaper proudly separated its editorial and news department, but in an unusual move, the news department published a response below Trani's letter on the editorial page. It referred to Trani's pledge on 22 December 1994 that VCU "would raise private sums—not seek state funding—to cover the operating costs of an engineering school," a pledge that won SCHEV's approval. Not only that, it said, but VCU officials well knew, as other state officials did, as early as May 1994, that Motorola was considering a move to Virginia. Trani had been angry before, but that response, which in effect called him a liar, infuriated him. As is usually the case when tilting with the press, he got no satisfaction from the editors, but he did inform the paper that he would no longer grant interviews to the reporter who wrote the offending stories.[80]

That controversy contrasted with the *Times-Dispatch*'s usual supportive coverage. In fact, an editorial in June 1997 declared that "contrary to popular perception, downtown Richmond is going gangbusters," and credited VCU for an "impressive—even staggering—portion" of that growth. A national business magazine agreed. In its issue of 24 November 1997, *Fortune* magazine named Richmond as one of "North America's Most Improved Cities." Economic times were good in general then—President Clinton had bragged at a meeting of world leaders, "America's economy is the healthiest in a generation and the strongest in the world"—and, the magazine said, consequently nearly every city could claim improvements. Being *Fortune* magazine, its list focused on cities that, "in short, have made the kinds of improvements that attract business, ensuring their long-term viability." Richmond, at number ten, was in very good company, joining Atlanta and Raleigh-Durham as the southern cities on the list. The magazine stated that VCU was central to that improvement: "Richmond has bolstered its image as a technology center thanks in large part to a corporate-led campaign to strengthen Virginia Commonwealth University, which now has an engineering school as well as a biotechnology research park adjacent to its medical school. Twenty-three companies have already set up shop in the park, which opened in 1992."[81]

Eugene Trani was the subject of the cover story for the December 1997 issue of Richmond's own *Inside Business* magazine, and that article began with him reading happily the passage quoted above from the article in

Fortune. "The actual description couldn't have been more accurate," he said. "That's it to a T." *Inside Business* added a qualifier: "Trani and his team" had been pushing VCU forward just as much as the corporate leaders had pulled it up. As evidence that Trani had been a bridge between education and business in Richmond, the magazine also cited his chairing of the Greater Richmond Chamber of Commerce. Trani said that universities "can't be islands. They've got to enter into partnerships." But, he continued, VCU was also "a major part of the infrastructure," which made Richmond attractive to future business investment. "Universities are clearly as important as superhighways and airports."[82]

That success was enough for *Style Weekly*, in early 1999, to name him "1998 Richmonder of the Year," declaring that he "had transformed the face and the future of Richmond." The story, titled "Trani-Vision," covered all that had occurred at VCU since his arrival in 1990 and closed with reference to the 1997 article in *Fortune* that endorsed Richmond's direction: "Many in Richmond would argue that while Fortune wrote the words, it was Trani who wrote the fortune."[83]

IN AUGUST 1997 Mack McCarthy, the successful basketball coach at the University of Tennessee–Chattanooga, resigned. Soon, rumors spread that he would come to VCU as an assistant coach to Sonny Smith, with whom he had worked in the past, and take over as head coach after Smith's retirement. Athletic Director Richard Sander saw the arrangement as a way to smooth the transition when Smith retired, and the latter declared that he would depart a year earlier than expected if the arrangement could be made. McCarthy declared that the new basketball facility, "the last piece of the puzzle," had made up his mind for VCU.[84]

Once practice got underway, Smith happily deferred to McCarthy, who in turn insisted that he was merely an assistant to Smith, who needed just six victories to be VCU's winningest basketball coach. That proved a near thing, for the team finished the season in March 1998 with only nine wins. Nonetheless, Smith departed to praise from local sportswriters who had found him not only accessible but almost always in joking good humor no matter the numbers on the scoreboard. Meanwhile, Coach McCarthy and his team looked forward to the expected opening of the Siegel Center in the 1998–99 season. Instead of the planned first game against the University of Virginia, however, construction delays forced the team to play home contests at the Richmond Coliseum and the University of Richmond's Robins Center.[85]

McCarthy refused to use the team's itinerant status as an excuse for its mediocre record, but in February 1999, when VCU announced Alltel Wireless as the arena's corporate sponsor, he did admit that there would be "comfort" playing at home. The official opening of the Siegel Center to the public occurred in early June 1999, but, as President Trani had promised, since March students had shared the weight room and the courts on the recreational side of the center with varsity athletes. "Maybe if we had football, it wouldn't be that way," said Athletic Director Sander, "but this is a VCU building built to the needs of VCU." The center connected with the community, too, as Hanover and Henrico Counties held 1999 high school graduations there, and local high school basketball tournaments scheduled games for the arena, too. The Siegel Center brought many area residents to the VCU Academic Campus (and downtown Richmond) for the first time, advertising the school to prospective students and their parents and serving both university and city.[86]

Finally, on 19 November 1999, the day came. The women's basketball team christened the building by playing West Virginia at the Siegel Center at 5:00 p.m., and the men's team again faced powerful Louisville at 8:00 p.m. The women fell to the Mountaineers, but the men recovered from a twenty-point deficit to pull out a highly satisfying victory. As McCarthy said after the game, "It couldn't have worked out any better." Louisville's coach Denny Crum won far more games than he lost, but, once again, he had to watch as VCU fans rushed the court to celebrate a Rams victory.[87]

Also in 1999, Roderick J. McDavis succeeded Grace Harris as provost. McDavis, like Harris, was African American, but unlike Harris, he was new to VCU. McDavis had previously been dean of the University of Florida's School of Education. After five effective years as provost in Richmond, he returned to his undergraduate alma mater, Ohio University, for a long tenure as its president.

10

Virginia's University, 2000–2004

A SPECIAL report appeared in the *UniverCity News* at the end of August 1998, titled "Richmond at the Crossroads: The Greater Richmond Metropolitan Area and the Knowledge Based High Technology Economy of the 21st Century." This report, with its title echoing that of consultant James Crupi's harsh report on the city in 1992, set an agenda for VCU. It was the fruit of a sabbatical for President Trani at St. John's College, Cambridge University, from April to July 1998 (Provost Grace Harris served as acting president in his absence). Albeit pointing to the future, the report also revealed how VCU's progress remained rooted in its mission as an urban university, and specifically as a university located in Richmond, Virginia.

Trani's vision for the region's future centered on VCU, and the life sciences, specifically, but what gave credence to that vision was VCU's development as a residential campus and simultaneous evidences of revival in downtown Richmond neighborhoods. By century's end, signs of urban vitality were widely visible, and analysts of the upturn often credited urban universities and medical centers as the foundations for improvement. VCU became one of the cited examples of an urban university engaged with its city.[1] In contrast to the inward-looking, commuter school of two decades before, however, VCU, and Richmond, now welcomed students from across Virginia.

PERHAPS THE vision always had been there—with the Biotechnology Research Park and then the engineering school as major steps along the path—but the immediate source of "Richmond at the Crossroads" was Trani's sabbatical at Cambridge. That began in 1996 with a visit to Richmond and the Biotechnology Research Park by Christopher M. P. Johnson, fellow and former bursar of St. John's College. Through Johnson's own interest in what Richmond might accomplish, Trani then traveled to Cambridge, in his own words, "to understand the Cambridge Phenomenon, as it has come to be called—that is, the growth of the high-technology industry in this university town."[2]

At Cambridge, Trani interviewed several dozen people, including university administrators, consultants, entrepreneurs, venture capitalists, and faculty members, about the swift rise there of some one thousand high-tech industries employing twenty-eight thousand workers, in an area about as populated as Chesterfield County, Virginia. He returned with two convictions for VCU. The first was that Cambridge's development had been from the bottom up, not driven by plans from above, and it followed then "that strong departmental and institute-level leadership at the University is essential." Trani began a practice of meeting with new department chairs to impress on them the strategic importance of their jobs for VCU. The second conviction came from the scientists he interviewed there in fields such as chemical synthesis, microelectronic technology, and biotechnology. They would say, Trani told the *Times-Dispatch*, "You don't understand. They're all the same technology. They're all coming together." He returned to VCU convinced of the centrality of the life sciences, a meeting place for all these fields, and a meeting place that might also bring closer integration of the MCV and Academic Campuses.[3]

As the title of his report, "Richmond at the Crossroads," indicated, Trani looked beyond VCU to the metropolitan region—as the *Times-Dispatch* put it, "with all the calm of a freight train." Richmond had the beginning ingredients for a high-tech future—the Motorola and White Oak semiconductor fabs, VCU's medical and engineering schools, the Biotechnology Research Park, and several corporate research facilities—but Trani argued that the region needed a strategy "to the next level." One great advantage that Richmond had over Cambridge was land for development, as well as the interstate highway corridors already envisioned as regional assets. The problem, along with a lack of venture capital, was that that the plan required regional cooperation, still a sticking point despite a quarter century of planning documents demanding it.[4]

Trani expressed confidence that the Metropolitan Area Projects Strategies (MAPS) planning process, then underway, might endorse his "focused incubators" and otherwise move the region forward along the lines of the Cambridge Phenomenon. The creation of Rick Horrow, a consultant and sports enthusiast, MAPS began in 1993 in Oklahoma City as a project to develop the infrastructure of that city's depleted downtown district by way of a dedicated sales tax, narrowly approved in a referendum. Success there led to some 250 similar planning projects across the country, for the promise was that combining projects desired by different constituencies into one basket would facilitate both regional development and the voter approval for needed tax increases. Horrow himself came to a meeting in April 1998, hosted by Hanover County's board of supervisors, to kick off the process, although a group had been meeting since September 1997 to identify potential projects to bring under the MAPS umbrella.[5]

By the end of October 1998, the local MAPS list had grown to 125 submitted projects, but the recent rejection of a MAPS tax increase by referendum at Birmingham, Alabama, and the need in Virginia for legislative approval for any such local referendum caused leaders to caution that MAPS would take time to complete. As it happened, the MAPS process in Richmond foundered first on the legislature's resistance to new taxes (Governor James Gilmore having won his state office in 1997 on a promise to eliminate the local property tax on automobiles) and then on the state's slide into budgetary impasse on funding the repeal of the "car tax." As a local journalist put it five years later, MAPS "couldn't gather any political momentum and it dissipated."[6]

As the fate of MAPS indicates, the lifting got heavier after 1998, for the region and for VCU, but the university's ambitions never shrank. First things first: The 1998–2000 budget, enacted in March 1998 not long before Trani departed for Cambridge, included funds for the life sciences building. Groundbreaking for the building occurred in January 1999, and by then Trani had wrapped the building into his vision of scientists and other scholars engaged in interdisciplinary research in the life sciences. Trani drew a laugh at the ceremony's close when he promised that the delayed Siegel Center really would open before the life sciences building.[7]

Two MONTHS before, on a chilly day in November 1998, the 21st Century News Center opened on the first floor of the T. Edward Temple Building (until 23 October known as the General Purpose Academic Building), with its director, Joyce Wise Dodd, promising seminars and workshops for working journalists right away and a graduate degree in "multiple-media journalism" by fall 2000. By then, the wheels had come off at the School of Mass Communications. The interim director, June Nicholson, after a year, wanted to return to teaching and her own programs to increase women and minorities in journalism. Stephen Gottfredson, dean of the College of Humanities and Sciences, just a year on the job himself, stepped in. He canceled the coming accreditation renewal, created an internal study of the school, and agreed that the school would suspend enrollments into graduate programs to concentrate on undergraduate training.[8]

The internal committee made its report in April 1999. It found a lack of leadership, a lack of vision, and a lack of morale. Dean Gottfredson suspended the search for a new director and appointed two interim associate directors to manage for the next two years. Roger Lavery, a faculty member in the AdCenter, would oversee the advertising instruction, and Terry Oggel, a member of the English Department and former president of the Faculty Senate, would handle journalism instruction. Though the announcement emphasized that the 21st Century News Center would continue, the charge of poor leadership angered Dodd, who had been the school's director before Nicholson. She also disliked no longer reporting to the provost but rather internally to an associate director. In October 1999, Dodd resigned. No doubt, controversy within the School of Mass Communication contributed to the center's difficulties, but the model for the center—fundraising rather than the EPTs that bottomed the VCU AdCenter—made for a steeper climb, too. The News Center's programs merged into the regular curriculum, to its benefit.[9]

President Trani stayed out of the fray, but the *Richmond Times-Dispatch*'s editorial comment on conditions at the school undoubtedly came to his attention. Trani's commitment to growth was fine, the editorial declared, "but construction should not proceed at the expense of—to the detriment of—academic programs." In fact, the school's problems preceded Trani's arrival at VCU, and nothing in the internal committee's critical review suggested that the problems resulted from university priorities. Nonetheless, the editorial's charge must have resonated with anyone harboring a disagreement with university priorities. That VCU's growth, both in ambitions and physical plant, might come at the cost of quality in academics would become a regular discordant subtheme in the local news media's usually positive coverage of the university in the next decade.[10]

Meanwhile, the AdCenter's program won accolades (and jobs for graduates) from the advertising industry, but its founder, Diane Cook-Tench, announced in summer 2000 that she would leave the directorship to start up at the school a continuing educational program for advertising and marketing professionals. Taking her place would be Patricia Alvey, from the faculty at the University of Texas' advertising program. Finally, in August 2001, VCU announced the appointment of Judy VanSlyke Turk as director of the School of Mass Communications. Turk was the founding director of the College of Communications and Media Sciences at Zayed University, in the United Arab Emirates, but she had been on the faculty at the University of South Carolina, and, in April 1993, she had come to VCU as a consultant to help the School of Mass Communications gain accreditation. With Turk's return, a circle closed.[11]

Clearly, not everything that people at VCU tried in the 1990s turned to gold. Moreover, making changes in schools and departments guaranteed dissent, from articulate and independent-minded academics, about the directions and the costs of change. Even so, if the previous chapter's narrative about the School of Mass Communications began with challenges to university policies on gender equity and political correctness from Ted J. Smith III, professor of journalism and the university's most ardent and eloquent conservative advocate, the full story of Mass Comm in the 1990s also demonstrates consistent female leadership with commitments to making the media more diverse and inclusive.[12]

IF THE life sciences provided a vision for the university's growth after 1998, the swiftly expanding student body, no longer overwhelmingly commuters, made new construction necessary. Back in 1989, the evening school had accounted for about 25 percent of all credit hours earned, reflecting a student body attending part-time and commuting to classes. Many of those students had worked before entering (or returning to) higher education, as evidenced by the average age of twenty-seven.[13]

Three years later, the student body was "bigger than ever and brighter than last year." The latter reference was to improved scores on the Scholastic Aptitude Test for new students, a predictor of performance and a status marker for universities, but what with state funding and revenues from tuition dependent on enrollments, the increased numbers—up from 21,608 in 1991 to 21,857—made administrators happy. Thus, the enrollment declines in 1993 and again in 1994 caused budget shortfalls that might have been worse had Vice Provost Sue Ann Messmer not been able quickly to expand off-campus continuing education programs. A year later, SCHEV adjusted downward its forecast of future enrollments in Virginia. Because university budgets rested on enrollment forecasts, shortfalls had financial consequences, as VCU could testify to once again. The expected shortfall for 1995–96 had to be met via budget cuts, for the contingency funds used to cover shortfalls the previous two years were exhausted.[14]

Then, just as quickly, enrollments reversed. VCU saw the 1996 incoming freshman class totaling 1,850 students, compared to 1,690 the year before. Predictions were for even more students enrolling in the next years. Credit went to both the rising number of students in secondary schools nationwide and to Virginia's own population growth. In 1997 the freshman class exceeded 2,000, beating the previous record of 1,925 set in 1987, and the total enrollment passed 22,000, also a record. In September 1998, VCU welcomed another record number of students: 22,850, up 150 students over the previous year. President Trani predicted 1,000 more students in the next three years.[15]

The economic good times brought a call from Governor James Gilmore for rolling back tuition by 20 percent—this following a tuition freeze under his predecessor—with the state making up the funding difference from its now seemingly ever-burgeoning coffers. Gilmore had won the previous year's election with a similar promise to eliminate the unpopular property tax on automobiles, which went to localities, with state funds. "There is more than enough money to do this," Gilmore stated. University officials publicly expressed agreement that students and their families would appreciate the relief, estimated at $636 per VCU student in 1999–2000, but noted that, in fact, the measure provided no additional funding for the universities. The freshman class in 1999 set another record, for the third year in a row, and was up by 51 percent over 1995's freshman class.[16]

That summer, construction began on a new dormitory on the north side of Broad Street between the School of the Arts and the Siegel Center, which would boast nearly four hundred beds, in two- and four-bedroom apartments. The building would have space for retail stores on its ground floor as well as a community space for the use of the adjacent Carver neighborhood. Most important, though, was that the dormitory was for "upperclassmen" rather than freshmen. VCU was becoming a residential campus through student demand.[17]

In 1997, barely half of the fewer than two thousand freshmen lived in residence halls; five years later, VCU expected nearly three thousand freshmen to arrive and 68 percent of them—more than the entire freshmen class of 1997—to live on campus. In addition to constructing dormitories on Broad Street, with a new one scheduled for the corner at Belvidere Street, the university purchased the onetime Capitol Medical Center on Grace Street and converted it to student housing. As preparation for the new master site plan loomed, an issue now for planners was how much housing to

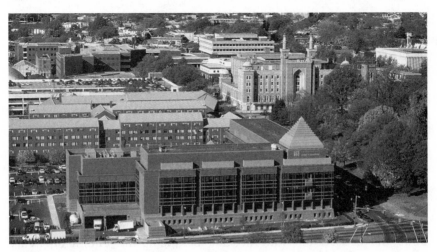

The original engineering building, opened in 1998, with Gladding Residence Center behind on left, Monroe Park on the right, and Altria Theater behind the park, 1999. (Virginia Commonwealth University Libraries)

provide for the future, especially as private developers also seemed interested in meeting the demand.[18]

The university celebrated not only record enrollments but increasing competition for admission, as evidenced by rising grades and test scores for admitted freshmen. As important was the demographic profile of the student body, of which in 1998 25 percent were African American, 10 percent were Asian, and the number of Hispanic students had doubled since 1994. "Students come to VCU because they want to be in the real world," Trani declared that year, "and the VCU enrollment reflects that American population in general." Since 1991, freshman enrollment had increased by 60 percent. VCU was no longer a commuter school, and construction in the next decade reflected that change.[19]

ON 1 JULY 1998, the city of Richmond's health department transferred responsibility for clinical services to the Medical College of Virginia Hospitals, an arrangement already in effect at the South Richmond Health Center. Although it was at the expense of nearly forty city jobs, the move enabled the city to use the savings for other areas of public health such as preventive care that might help indigent patients avoid ending up in the hospitals. Richmond differed from many other cities in that it operated no public hospital of its own. Not that long before, with the waves of white flight to the suburbs pulling other hospitals out of the city, the MCV Hospitals seemed on the way to becoming the de facto public hospital, where only the poorest and uninsured came for treatment. Instead, through innovative health programs and focused research, such as that of the Massey Cancer Center, the hospitals remained places where patients of all classes came for lifesaving care. That is the big story about the VCU Health System after 1998, and its successful conclusion depended on finding solutions to the long-running problem of provision of health care to people without health insurance.[20]

As happened every year then, VCU included a request for $5 million to pay for indigent care in its 1999 budget submission to the legislature, out of a total of $13.7 requested in new funding. The university pointed out that the hospitals provided $18 million in care for which there was no reimbursement, treating more than one-third of the state's indigent patients. Even though the arrangement for the state to accept federal Medicaid funds, made at the beginning of the 1990s with Governor Wilder, still held, that provided only 80 percent of the actual costs of care, with the hospitals and MCV Physicians covering the remainder. The hospital's margin between revenues and costs was perilously narrow. Meanwhile, the university also needed funds to maintain the new engineering building—an oversight by the legislature, Trani reasserted—and state appropriations had failed to keep up with the university's growth.[21]

The request for funds for indigent care received editorial endorsement from the *Times-Dispatch*, too, but of the additional funds requested, the editorial said that legislators "should ask why existing hikes in appropriation do not suffice." VCU had been treated generously in recent years, "and let us remember: VCU recently has added (a) an engineering school, (b) a fine arts center, and (c) a recreation center." The tone of the editorial was new, perhaps an outgrowth of the dustup in 1997 over promises about funding the engineering school, but it seemed to say that VCU's ambitions unbefitted its proper place. "Beyond the supplement for MCV," the editorial concluded, "is more money for VCU really necessary?" The attitude of the editorial notwithstanding, it stated the problem that funding for indigent care posed for Donald Gehring, vice president for governmental relations, and for other VCU administrators working with legislators and the governor: winning funds for indigent care tended to leave state officers convinced that they had treated VCU generously enough, and the school's other funding requests would then go by the wayside.[22]

By the time that the legislature met in early 1999, the amount needed to fund indigent care had grown. As Hermes Kontos, dean of the medical school, explained, cost-cutting insurance companies, especially through managed care, no longer reimbursed enough for paying patients to help cover care for those without insurance. Carl Fischer, CEO of the MCV Hospitals, agreed, reporting a 25 percent reduction in the rates paid by insurers and managed-care companies. Without profits enough, there could be no investments to modernize and expand facilities, and if there were losses, then some patients—the working poor, Trani emphasized, in jobs without insurance coverage—would be turned away. So, too, did the medical school and the faculty teaching there depend on the financial health of the MCV Hospitals.[23]

For many observers, the solution to ever-increasing medical costs was through organizations to manage care. Medical College of Virginia Hospitals stepped into the field of managed health care in fall 1995 when University Health Services Inc., an arm of the hospitals created by the legislature (and soon blended into the MCV Health Authority) to enable the hospitals to enter into agreements with other entities, purchased an interest in Virginia Chartered Health Plan, a health maintenance organization, an HMO. Through the remainder of the decade the state and federal governments expanded mandates that recipients of Medicaid be enrolled in managed-care plans. In October 1998, VCU's University Health Services purchased the entirety of the Virginia Chartered Health Plan, and by spring 1999, it was the third-largest enroller of Medicaid patients in central Virginia.[24]

In fact, as Sheldon Retchin, head of the MCV Physicians, observed in January 2000, the rise of managed care "severely disadvantaged academic health centers" (AHCs). The HMOs relied on primary care physicians to serve as gatekeepers for care by specialists, but most AHCs had limited primary care capacity and emphasized specialty practices. Most AHCs, like VCU, combined "two major clinical components, teaching hospitals and faculty practice plans." After reductions in Medicare funding in 1997, conditions had deteriorated for many such institutions, with some university teaching hospitals sold and Allegheny University in Philadelphia declaring bankruptcy in 1999. Many AHCs chose to expand primary care capacity, which VCU did by partnering with community physicians ("an 'affiliation' strategy," which had the benefits of smaller capital investments and operating costs while "bridging town-gown relationships"), and to invest in their own HMOs, balancing the financial risk against the promise that "the growth of managed care would lead to population-based care through large integrated delivery systems." The recent backlash against the gatekeeping functions of HMOS, Retchin noted, had resulted in relaxing some constraints and reduced "the demand for primary care at AHCs."[25]

By 2000, Virginia Premier Health Plan operated in eighty counties and enrolled about 130,000 Medicaid patients. In November of that year, a team at the Medical Center created Virginia Coordinated Care, which enlisted nearby primary-care physicians to provide continued health care for uninsured patients who first entered the system via the Medical Center's emergency rooms or the ambulatory care center. The economic logic of the plan was that coordinating better care for the uninsured would reduce expensive use of the emergency department and other hospitalizations. The plan proved no panacea, but results—in terms of health care and costs—were valuable enough to continue. Those who envisioned VCU as an urban university in service to its community would have approved.[26]

That positive work went on behind the scenes, but problems became public. Such was the case in January 2000 when the Office for Protection from Research Risks (OPRR) suspended nearly 1,500 clinical trials at VCU involving human participants. The Food and Drug Administration and the National Institutes of Health had determined in December that VCU's management of human-subjects research did not meet federal guidelines. The failures were procedural, without the immediate risks that had seemed possible in the long-ago research into radiation burns that had been publicized in 1994. On 12 January, Trani emailed faculty that no one had been harmed, that patients enrolled in clinical trials would receive treatment, and that a proper review process was a priority. The directive from Washington arrived that evening, and by afternoon of 14 January, Trani had a task force of fifteen people on hand for a lengthy meeting to start the process of resuming the clinical trials. In the meantime, VCU contracted with an independent institutional review board (IRB) from the state of Washington to review and approve both new and existing projects.[27]

The OPRR had called for resignations of the members of VCU's institutional review board as part of its demands for lifting the suspension, and that caused Vice President for Research William Dewey to step down from his vice presidency, too. Francis L. Macrina, a former interim director of the Massey Cancer Center and current director of the Institute for Oral and Craniofacial Molecular Biology, became acting vice president. Dewey had planned to step down in June, but he determined it was in the best interests of the university not to wait.[28]

The task force moved quickly, and at the end of January OPRR "approved and reinstated VCU's revised formal agreement, called a Multiple Projects Assurance, that lets the university conduct research on humans." The agreement included continued contracting with the independent IRB until VCU's own IRB was operational again after mandatory training. Trani explained to the Board of Visitors at the February meeting that VCU had to expand administrative support to meet the demands arising from expanded research. The expense was unexpected, he said, but far better than the imposed hiatus on research.[29]

Some eight months later, in late August 2000, as classes began, the *Times-Dispatch* asked whether VCU's medical research was "losing ground." Once VCU ranked in the top third of recipients of research money from the National Institutes of Health, but for several years now that support had remained "flat," and VCU's medical school dropped in the rankings from thirty-fourth to fifty-eighth. The newspaper story assigned a variety of causes to the stagnation in research, but most prominent was the complaint that VCU's focus on growth and construction neglected the needed infrastructure to carry on research functions. The problems with research protocols were symptomatic. In addition, reductions in patient-care income from new managed-care programs caused physicians to devote more time to seeing patients and less to research, a problem compounded at VCU by the added costs of indigent care.[30]

On 1 July 2000, the Medical Center undertook another change to operate, as the *Times-Dispatch* put it, "in a market less and less accommodating to the special needs and issues of teaching hospitals." The MCV Hospitals Authority combined business operations with the MCV Physicians, the physicians' practice, to operate as the Virginia Commonwealth University Health System Authority. The legal structure—the authority—remained the same, but the merger was intended to reduce costs. The operating margin for the hospitals in 2000 fell below $2 million, and that slightly positive result depended on the state's supplement for indigent care. Hermes A. Kontos, the chief executive officer of the new entity, and Sheldon Retchin, president of MCV Physicians, agreed that the alliance could benefit all, and the physicians voted overwhelmingly in favor of the change.[31]

VCU pushed hard for funding for indigent care in early 2001, including an eloquent editorial by university Rector Edward L. Flippen about his experiences as an uninsured patient at MCV Hospitals forty years before, after an auto accident. Eloquence bumped against harsh budgetary conflict between Governor James Gilmore, protecting his plan to cut the property tax on automobiles, and the legislature, protecting the state's financial stability. Fortunately for the VCU Hospitals, the governor had okayed technical allocation of state funds for indigent care, enabling the hospitals to draw full matching funds from the federal government, a fiscal maneuver that finally relieved the annual burden of seeking funds for indigent care as a line item in the state's budgets. Moreover, the VCU Health System, as an authority of the state, now enjoyed exemption from the hiring freeze and large budget cuts that the impasse over paying for the governor's car-tax reduction had produced.[32]

As the fiscal year closed in June 2001, the VCU Health System set about cutting costs again, as the year's slim operating margin—less than 1 percent more than what was spent—required economies, the governor's aid with funding indigent care notwithstanding. The goal was a profit of 2 percent in the next year, with those funds targeted for capital expenses. Good intentions gave way to necessity after the disasters of 9/11, when the hospitals cleared space for expected burn victims from the attack on the Pentagon, losing $2 million in potential business to the patriotic inactivity.[33]

The new presidential administration of George W. Bush had begun its tenure in early 2001 with an emphasis on tax cutting, a theme that roiled Virginia politics that year, too. The state legislature declined to implement Governor Gilmore's promised elimination of the property tax on automobiles at the level he preferred, and the governor balked at compromise. Gilmore now contended that "rising energy costs and a weakening economy" justified tax relief, after having promised as a candidate in 1997 that the state's booming economy would make the tax relief painless.[34]

In that context, the state's political impasse forced budget cuts, including a freeze on both hiring and discretionary spending at colleges and universities. Vice President for Finance and Administration Paul Timmreck explained in 2000 that VCU faced significant reductions in the coming year, also, but that current projects, including new student housing construction, could continue. The situation was dire enough that a possible budgetary compromise between governor and legislature merited full front-page coverage in the *CT* on 9 April 2001.[35]

The budget impasse persisted, with Gilmore unwilling to abandon his prized tax cuts, and a bipartisan coalition in the legislature equally unwilling to push the state to financial disaster. Thus, in November 2001, just four years after Republicans won the three top state offices and claimed a strong majority in the legislature, voters elected Democrats Mark Warner governor and Tim Kaine, a former Richmond mayor, lieutenant governor. Until then, though, the budgetary impasse, and Governor Gilmore's attention to his other post as chair of the Republican National Committee, made for a quiet, albeit frustrating, summer in government.[36]

On Monday, 10 September 2001, the *CT* reported complaints from residents in the new dormitory that the promised cable television was not yet available, and the VCU Alumni Association asked for suggestions of a new name for the Academic Campus. The annual convocation, opening the academic year, was the front-page story, with faculty members honored for excellence, and an address by President Trani. He reported that the enrollment had reached 24,500 students, another record, with nearly 40 percent of the total being minority students. VCU, as an urban university, he said, had three great advantages: it focused "on the right fields for the 21st century," it looked "like America in terms of diversity," and it required "involvement in the community."[37]

The next morning, terrorists in hijacked airplanes brought down the World Trade Center towers, crushed one side of the Pentagon, and caught the horrified attention of the world. At VCU classes continued, officially, through that day. Many students stayed glued to the news, some faculty members canceled classes, and the Commons offered "town meetings" for conversation. Evening classes did suspend (to keep students off the highways; classes would resume the next morning), and a large crowd gathered for a candlelight vigil on campus. President Trani and other university officials attended, and speakers included the president of VCU's Muslim Student Association. Trani declared to the crowd that diversity was an American strength and called for all there to support one another. At the Medical Campus, the MCV Hospitals prepared immediately after the attack on the Pentagon for possible arrival of injured persons, which proved unnecessary.[38]

The attacks postponed the dedication of the new life sciences building (Trani had noted at the convocation that already one in five VCU undergraduates majored in a life science). At the groundbreaking in 1999, Trani had emphasized life sciences as defining the future of science, referring to his experiences in Cambridge. The building also reflected the development of the sciences on the Academic Campus, it facilitated integration of the two campuses, and it encouraged collaboration in teaching and research. "It will also serve," he declared, "as a testament to the capacity of this university community to come together to think strategically about where VCU should be in the next decade."[39]

On Thursday, 6 April 2000, the roof of the under-construction life sciences building caught fire. The Richmond fire department had it out in fifteen minutes, with little damage, but the smoke spread across the Academic Campus and justified a front-page story in the *CT*. On the same day, a private corporation announced that it had successfully sequenced a human genome, work that had already contributed to hearty predictions of what the life sciences might soon achieve. The official announcement, at the White House, came on 26 June 2000. President Bill Clinton marveled at the potential that this first survey of the entire genome promised: "Without a doubt, this is the most important, most wondrous map ever produced by humankind."[40]

Two weeks after the fire and the first announcement of the genome's sequencing, Thomas F. Huff, a professor of microbiology and immunology and director of the Institutional Grants Program at the Massey Cancer Center, became the first vice provost for life sciences. His charge was to lead cross-campus development of research and education in life sciences. Trani announced the appointment and declared that soon, VCU students would be able, via life sciences, to study with top researchers on the MCV Campus as well as with those on the Academic Campus.[41]

As construction continued, Trani and Huff presented their vision for life sciences to faculty at a meeting at the MCV Campus on 27 September 2000. "'It will literally consume us for the next five years,'" Trani declared. Huff concurred, saying that VCU, as a national research university with a comprehensive health center, had an obligation to develop interdisciplinary programs for education and research in life sciences. As important, Trani explained the life sciences program as "the culmination of a 10-year, $400 million investment in the infrastructure for the life sciences, engineering, biotechnology, health-care education, and research and patient care." Rather than taking a sudden new direction, VCU had arrived at a destination: the study across disciplines and across the campuses of "biological complexity," to use Huff's term.[42]

"Biological Complexity" was the cover story for the summer 2001 issue of *Shafer Court Connections*. Vice Provost Huff declared that the sequencing of the human genome was a scientific accomplishment comparable to sending humans to the moon, and VCU life sciences could put VCU in the thick of these exciting developments in addition to attracting new students, faculty, and research funding. The happy convergences multiplied, for VCU announced that summer the creation of the Inger and Walter Rice Center for Environmental Life Sciences on a 342-acre property, rich in biodiversity, along the James River, just a half hour's drive away from the urban university. VCU agreed never to sell the property and to respect all its ecosystems. Inger Rice had studied interior decoration at the Richmond Professional Institute, and that connection made her gift even sweeter. Biology already was second only to psychology in the number of undergraduate majors, and the life sciences building and the Rice Center made the field even more attractive at VCU.[43]

Thus, the dedication of the life sciences building on 15 November 2001 provided a rare celebratory moment that fall. Located at the intersection of Harrison and Cary Streets, at the southwest corner of the Academic Campus, the building featured two lecture halls, seven classrooms, more than forty laboratories, and three greenhouses. The Board of Visitors honored the president by naming it the Eugene P. and Lois E. Trani Center for Life Sciences. The recognition seemed appropriate, though he would have joined Huff in emphasizing the obvious practical necessity of preparing VCU students for the "scientific explosion" occurring around them.[44]

One of the promises of life sciences was that students would engage with researchers from across the university, and the opening ceremonies included symposia where experts from VCU engaged with audiences. One session reflected the headlines, as speakers, including Richard P. Wenzel, an expert of infectious diseases, and Karen M. Kester, an entomologist, discussed the role of physicians and other scientists in combatting bioterrorism. Fears that terrorists might also use smallpox as a weapon had caused federal officials to plan purchases of a quarter-billion doses of smallpox vaccine to hold in readiness of an attack. Wenzel questioned the wisdom of mass vaccinations, given the likelihood of side effects for some persons and the fact that people vaccinated in the past retained some immunity. Wenzel became a spokesman for calm during the next year, even as the vaccine purchases went forward, and federal officials fretted that the government of Iraq, albeit not involved in the 9/11 attacks, had accumulated smallpox and other biological weapons. Thanks to Wenzel's counsel, when the federal government recommended smallpox vaccinations for all health care workers, the VCU Health System declined to administer them.

It took some courage to resist in that atmosphere of fear, but, as Wenzel argued, the physician's obligation remained, "Above all, do no harm."[45]

Another concern in the anxious months after 9/11 was the possible danger facing the thirty faculty, staff, and family members at VCU-Qatar's Shaqab College of Design Arts at Doha, the capital of Qatar, on the Persian Gulf. A new emir took power in 1995, and that year established the Qatar Foundation for Education, Science, and Community Development, which began planning for Education City, a large campus near Doha, where branches of universities and research institutions from around the world could locate. The search for partner universities led in 1997 to VCU's School of the Arts. Dean Richard Toscan headed the negotiations, and in summer 1998, the Board of Visitors agreed to a contract for VCU faculty to establish in Qatar undergraduate programs for female students in three design fields: fashion, interior, and communication arts. The School of the Arts' high ranking in the United States caught the attention of the Qatar Foundation, and the plan was for a three-year development of what would become a full branch of VCU, with the foundation covering the costs and making overhead and other payments to the university in Richmond. The Shaqab College of Design Arts, operated by VCU and with Paul Petrie, a professor of interior design, as founding director, opened in fall 1998 with twenty-nine female students "enrolled in the equivalent of the Art Foundation program."[46]

All went as planned, and in spring 2001 VCU's proposal for a baccalaureate program at VCU-Qatar successfully received approval from the Board of Visitors, the State Council for Higher Education of Virginia, and the Southern Association of Colleges and Schools, VCU's accreditor, and waited on the legislature. Then came 9/11 and questions about the safety of Americans in Qatar. Toscan visited the campus himself at the end of October and reported back that the university's representatives there felt safe. Legislative approval of VCU's creation of a "full degree-granting branch campus in Qatar" followed in early 2002. As the U.S. military invasion of Iraq loomed, the campus at Qatar remained safe enough, and VCU's other study abroad programs continued to flourish. A year later, Dean Richard Toscan credited the VCU School of the Arts' rise since his arrival in 1996 to the top of the rankings of university arts schools in part to funds received from the branch in Qatar, which enabled scholarships, innovative curricula, and other support for teachers and students in Richmond.[47]

Meanwhile, VCU had an unexpected boost to its reputation when John Fenn, research professor in the Department of Chemistry since 1994 and an affiliate professor of chemical engineering, received the 2002 Nobel Prize in Chemistry. At a press conference on 9 October, Fenn spoke warmly about the students and his colleagues at VCU, and President Trani praised Fenn's deserved honor as recognition for VCU, too. "The award is not only a validation of his research, but of VCU's leadership in a post-genomic era, which we have invested in with VCU life sciences," he said.[48]

VCU received more national attention soon after, when a Florida traveler, stopping for a meal just north of Richmond in Ashland, was shot in the abdomen by the roving snipers whose evil exploits terrified Maryland, Washington, D.C., and Virginia that October. Fortunately, he was rushed to the VCU Health System trauma center, where a team of professionals, led by Rao R. Ivatury, director of trauma and critical-care surgery, saved his life. In late November he left the health center after "five surgeries that removed his spleen, part of his pancreas and two-thirds of his stomach," with every expectation of eventual recovery. The care he received at the Medical Center—the region's only Level One trauma center, staffed twenty-four hours a day—brought national attention from such outlets as "ABC's 'Good Morning America,' NBC's 'Today' show, CNN, and National Public Radio."[49]

Those successes brought warmth at a gloomy time of chilling budget problems for the state. In October 2002 Governor Mark Warner told student reporters that "the state's business plan in the late '90's was similar to that of the dot-coms—and just like the dot-coms, the state went down the tubes." Voters in the state elections in November 2002 did approve some $850 million in bond funds for higher education. Of VCU's $77 million share of the bond funds, the Medical Campus would receive $40 million toward construction of a medical sciences building, renovations to Sanger Hall, and, most important, a major addition to the Massey Cancer Center. Virginia's budgetary crisis persisted through 2003, and Governor Warner mandated budget cuts across state government that averaged 11 percent, and then employed necessity to convince the legislature to pass a bipartisan tax increase in 2004. The gloom was evident at the August 2003 meeting of the Board of Visitors: there was little prospect of increased funds for programs and operations, and the only strategy seemed to be, once again, to seek "maximum tuition and fees flexibility and avoid any future cuts to the budget."[50]

Even so, VCU's forward motion continued. In fact, the board, at its meeting in May 2003, approved a school of world studies and a school of government and public affairs, both within the College of Humanities and Sciences. The Board also approved life sciences as an academic unit and a new PhD program in integrative life sciences, described in the minutes as fitting responses to the vision of one university in the VCU strategic plan.[51]

Back in 2002, Patricia Alvey, executive director of the AdCenter, had resigned after two years in Richmond to return to Texas and a new advertising institute at Southern Methodist University in Dallas. In November, just after the bond referendum for higher education received approval from the voters, VCU announced that Rick Boyko, copresident and chief creative officer of Ogilvy & Mather Worldwide Inc., in New York, would retire from the industry to head the AdCenter. The move got national attention; Mike Hughes, chair of the AdCenter's advisory board, declared that every professional in advertising studied Boyko's work and "for a relatively small group of graduate students to have daily access to such an accomplished professional is probably unprecedented in advertising education." Boyko would join the AdCenter, then based in Shockoe Bottom in downtown Richmond, in July 2003, and he was ready for heavy lifting, too, telling *Adweek* in June 2003 that he wanted to help make the AdCenter "the Harvard of advertising."[52]

So much was happening by fall 2003 that some successes gained little notice. African American studies had been left unmoored after the politicized rejection of departmental status by the State Council of Higher Education in 1997. A procedural change at SCHEV that permitted council staff to approve proposals for new majors based on courses already taught at a university enabled the new degree-granting Department of African American Studies to get underway, at long last, in fall 2003. Political scientist Njeri Jackson became the founding chair, and sociologist Anne Creighton-Zollar and historian Norrece T. Jones, both veterans of the program, proudly welcomed the new majors.[53]

THE NEW Gateway Building, which got underway in July 1999, reoriented the medical campus and enhanced the experiences of patients and their families. As any visitor to the old Main Hospital could testify, its entrance—a narrow doorway to the street—was neither evident nor welcoming. In addition to occupying what had been Twelfth Street itself between Marshall and Clay Streets, the university successfully requested that Twelfth Street between Broad and the Gateway Building at Marshall Street be made a two-way street for a more efficient traffic pattern at the entrance, which would include both drop-off lanes and lanes for valet parking. As Donna Katen-Bahensky, the chief operating officer for the health system, enthused, "For the first time, patients and their families will be welcomed to MCV Hospitals through one door."[54]

The new Gateway Building unquestionably made the MCV Hospitals more attractive to patients and their families, but it proved no financial lifesaver. During earlier restructuring intended to improve finances at the hospitals, President Trani had several times declared, "We don't want David Hunter coming here." Hunter headed a hospital consulting firm, called the Hunter Group, with a reputation, as the *NewYork Times* put it in 1999, "as a slash-and-burn cost-cutter who can do the dirty work that floundering hospitals cannot bring themselves to tackle on their own," and, as Trani's comments suggest, a hospital's hiring of the Hunter Group often signaled financial desperation. Trani now explained that the Hunter Group also worked with hospitals in good-enough shape but concerned about planning for the future. The VCU Health System was in that latter group, and, as CEO Hermes Kontos explained, the goal was to get to an operating margin of 3 percent to 5 percent, rather than barely meeting expenses. Without a larger margin, the system would be hard-pressed to respond to future needs.[55]

The 2002 fiscal year ended with the health system in the black, but with the margin less than predicted. Dominic J. Puleo, executive vice president for corporate finance, noted that among other unanticipated expenses, the clearing of the hospital's beds in the expectation of patients surviving the 9/11 attacks had cost the system $2 million. He also noted that representatives of the Hunter Group were present at the Medical Center every day, with a final report due in the fall.[56]

At the end of July 2002, Katen-Bahensky, the hospitals' COO, left to direct the University of Iowa Hospital and Clinics; "It's been a tough four years," she said, with her focus, of necessity, "so much on the financial side." VCU installed in her place William Kerr, a former CEO of a university medical center but now the leader of the Hunter consulting team at VCU. Another member of the consulting team, MarieAnn North, also a former CEO of a health care organization, became interim CEO of the MCV Physicians, which the consultants had recommended strengthening. Hermes Kontos and Sheldon Retchin remained executive officers of the health system, but the consulting firm had just delivered a report of more than one thousand pages, and the appointments would help VCU to make the recommended changes.[57]

Rumors, naturally, accompanied the consultants' work, among them that the A. D. Williams Clinic, housed in a building from 1938, would close. The rumors proved accurate, for space in the newer Nelson Clinic and Ambulatory Care Center made a consolidation of clinics there more efficient. On the day of the consultants' final report, Hermes Kontos, CEO of the VCU Health System, announced that he would retire in 2003. The system's board endorsed the direction of the Medical Center by elevating Dr. Sheldon Retchin, the executive vice president and chief operating officer, who had been prominent in unifying the hospitals and the physicians' practice, to CEO.[58]

And, there was the Hunter Group's report, all 1,200 pages of it. The report proposed that by cutting expenses and improving revenue, the system could find $130 million. The report called for reducing labor costs, but no immediate plans for layoffs existed, as a reassuring email message to employees indicated. The report also assumed that the state of Virginia would fully pay for the cost of indigent care at the hospital and that levels of hospital use would remain steady. If implemented, the report promised an operating margin of 3 percent to 6 percent by the end of June 2005. With hospital "costs spiraling," Retchin said, "we also have to look for ways to optimize growth."[59]

In April 2003, John Duval became CEO of MCV Hospitals, replacing William Kerr, from the Hunter Group, as the consultants stood down. Duval would start work on 1 June 2003, and he arrived to good news that grew better. The VCU Health System would not only end the year with a profit, but the amount continued to grow as accountants watched, and the fiscal year ended on 30 June 2003 with a margin of $19.6 million, as compared to $3.9 million in 2002 and just $300,000 in 2001. The goal had been for a profit margin of 5 percent to 6 percent, and this result was 2.5 percent, but the budgetary momentum was in the right direction.[60]

The health system's profit margin remained positive, enabling improvements to go forward. Behind the scenes, MCV Hospitals and other academic hospitals had emerged from the hyper–cost-cutting era of health management organizations (HMOs) to negotiate higher returns from health insurers. The era when academic health centers could charge premium prices for health care to support medical education and clinical research was gone, but, said Retchin, "I think we are back in a range that's fair and reasonable." By 2004, finance-related hospital issues—indigent care, computer systems, and capital construction—that had worried VCU's leaders from the university's founding seemed finally under control. Everyone involved knew that no solutions were permanent, but it was a relief after several years of hard effort to look ahead with some confidence.[61]

In 2005, the School of the Arts published a hardcover book of more than 250 pages with an eye-catching graphic design, titled *VCUArts*. It stated proudly: "VCUArts is the #1 public university school of arts and design in the nation." The book gave information about the school's fifteen departments and programs, from art foundation to theatre, mixed with stories about sixteen students representing those departments and programs. The volume made a splendid testimonial for why VCUArts merited that ranking.

The book also included eighteen feature stories about Richmond, the "community." Just a decade after an epidemic of homicidal violence and a downtown commercial district in serious decay, *VCUArts* invited new students to explore the city, which as presented here was a place of films, live performances, art, thrift stores, bike shops, and restaurants (both for "when you are picking up the tab" and "when you are not picking up the tab"). A map of the city at the book's close marked the places described, and though centered on the school's Broad Street home, the dots ranged from Shockoe Bottom in the east all the way west through Carytown and beyond. By 2005, not only was Richmond being transformed, but VCU's perspective had expanded from the relative safety of the campuses to view the city as a resource and educational environment. To be sure, the volume was more advertisement than muckraking exposure, but it nonetheless revealed the changed and positive environment in Richmond, a result for which VCU administrators, faculty, staff, and students could take some credit.[62]

In 2005 also, journalist Bob Rayner described the differences between the VCU campus he encountered in 1988 as a graduate student in the School of Mass Communication and the campus seventeen years later. The campus in 1988 "seemed cramped and pedestrian," he recalled, but now the students filled the campus west of Belvidere, which had grown north across Broad and prepared to spread east across Belvidere from the School of Engineering on Cary Street. "Pull it all together and it feels like progress— relentless and unyielding," he concluded. "Just what the old city needs."[63]

Rayner was not the only observer during those years to see VCU's expansion as "relentless and unyielding," but from President Trani's perspective, the heavy lifting had occurred in phases and the processes differed from one campus to the other. To be sure, the physical expansion of VCU since 1990, when Trani withdrew the master plan, might seem obvious in retrospect. Fiscal necessity, as declining state budgetary support required increased tuition revenues and consequently made increased numbers of students not just desirable but essential, meant that the campus would expand. The question then arose, however, where would VCU go?

At the Academic Campus in the 1990s, the first phase had involved the move north to Broad Street, with the new School of Engineering building on Cary Street sending the School of the Arts there. The move depended on fostering a mutually respectful relationship between VCU and the Carver neighborhood. Then, thanks to the work of the VCU Real Estate Foundation, two new dormitories, one between the School of Arts and the Siegel Center and the other at the corner of Broad and Belvidere, brought student residents to Broad Street. The student population then attracted restaurants and other retail businesses, making the larger neighborhood attractive to other student residents. During the same period, private developers renovated three large buildings for student apartments, and a shopping area, with a large home-improvement supply store and a grocery store, opened just to the west. A once-decrepit stretch of the city's main thoroughfare had come back to life, with more private projects underway.[64]

On the southern boundary of the Academic Campus, too, entrepreneurs perceived that demand for housing there would rise following construction of the School of Engineering and the life sciences building. In addition to the apartment houses erected on the Oregon Hill side of Cary Street, developers snapped up properties southwest of the campus along both Main and Cary Streets. A news story in July 2003 quoted the declaration of one that "the university inviting private enterprise to come and help shoulder the burden" had attracted the investments. Another concurred: "The anchor is VCU." A third developer interviewed was Ed Eck, an early arrival who'd renamed his multihued, renovated section of West Main Street "Uptown," and he, too, credited VCU's growth for the changes. "Everybody who went downtown this way saw how bad the conditions were," he said. "Now that's all changing."[65]

This record ensured widespread support for the university's announcement in late spring 2003 of a dramatic plan to construct a new campus, featuring an extension of the School of Engineering and a new building for the School of Business, along with dormitories and a parking deck, east of Belvidere Street and southeast of the Academic Campus. At this point it was a vision—a residential campus "perhaps modeled after Cambridge University or Yale"—but VCU's impact along Broad Street, Main Street, and Cary Street convinced city officials to endorse the plan. It would transform a part of downtown Richmond, as the *Times-Dispatch* put it, "now largely composed of parking lots, open land, abandoned buildings, offices and scattered residences." Support for the plan also came from businessmen William H. Goodwin Jr., leader of the campaign for the School of Engineering, and Steve Markel, vice chairman of Markel Corp., an insurance company, and a member of the Board of Visitors. Markel took a particular interest in a new School of Business building. The new buildings for engineering, arts, and life sciences had exposed the 1975 business school building (later named Harris Hall), he said, as a facility for business students "that might not be as good as their high schools."[66]

Just before that announcement, in early May 2003, at practice for the NASCAR race at Richmond International Raceway, driver Jerry Nadeau crashed his car into a wall. A helicopter carried him to the VCU Medical Center in critical condition. As had happened the year before with the victim of the snipers at Ashland, the physicians successfully set Nadeau on a road to recovery. As had happened the year before, too, the name of the medical center where he received that first-rate treatment went out incorrectly via the Associated Press to a national audience of worried race fans as the Medical College of Virginia Hospital. This was the third time in a year that national media left out VCU's name in positive stories.[67]

It was bad enough that the *Richmond Times-Dispatch* persisted in identifying the Medical Campus as "MCV," at least in headlines, but the *New York Times*, in a recent story about the high prices of cancer drugs, identified Thomas J. Smith as "an associate professor of oncology at the Medical College of Virginia Commonwealth University." President Trani had had enough. The official name, from now on, for all the university's "health-care entities" was the VCU Medical Center, and signs using nomenclature of the past were to come down. An email about the name went to faculty and staff, and local media received similar information. The campaign helped, for when Nadeau returned in early September 2003 to thank everyone for his care, the *Times-Dispatch* used the proper name, although the newspaper's headline writer could not yet abandon the space-saving shorthand of MCV. Later in the fall, the VCU Health System's chief, Sheldon Retchin, told a meeting of the MCV Alumni Association that the name was in keeping with the practice of academic medical centers across the country. Even so, an alumnus and former faculty member appealed to the courts, unsuccessfully, to retain the full MCV name.[68]

Nomenclature mattered at the Academic Campus, too, for VCU officials had dubbed the proposed eastward expansion at the Academic Campus the "Monroe Campus," according to reports provided to the Board of Visitors in November 2003. The project had grown a little larger with reports that the AdCenter eyed the old Central Belting Building, on Canal Street, as a new home nearer to the university than its space downtown at Shockoe Bottom. Not only that, but VCU also proposed taking over the little-used Canal Street entrance to the Downtown Expressway, a move as audacious as the closing of Twelfth Street for the Gateway Building at the Medical Center. To the *Times-Dispatch*, university leaders stressed the project "as entrepreneurial and as a creative private-public partnership," with the state picking up only a small portion of the tab. To the *Commonwealth Times*, university officials emphasized the importance of expanding facilities to meet the growing student enrollments (fall 2003 saw the fifth consecutive year of increased numbers of freshmen). Regardless, VCU needed more space, said Trani.[69]

The Monroe Campus changed its name to the Monroe Park Campus Addition when the board agreed in June 2004 to rename the Academic Campus the Monroe Park Campus. Trani expressed relief, for the name vexed him from his arrival, with its suggestion that academic work occurred only there and not at the MCV Campus, which would retain its name. In fact, Trani had asked the VCU Alumni Association in September 2001 to solicit suggestions from the alumni for a new name for the Academic Campus, and no competitive alternative emerged then to naming it the Monroe Park Campus.[70]

The change of name also signaled a new prominence for the park, which was (and is) a part of the city, and not owned by the university, in VCU's future planning. In addition to the School of Engineering on the south side of the park, the existing and planned student housing adjacent to the park meant that some three thousand student residents would share Monroe Park with other residents, including a shifting population of the city's homeless. During the battle over the master plan back in 1989–90, neighbors had rejected plans giving a large responsibility for the park to the university. Trust had returned under Trani, but VCU's regular maintenance and other care for the park was informal rather than official.

In May 2004, City Manager Calvin Jamison included $100,000 in the city budget for improvements to the park, and City Councilman William Pantele declared his support for the park, too. A project to add landscaped medians to Belvidere Street, along the park's eastern boundary, was scheduled for that summer. Brian Ohlinger, the associate vice president for facilities, declared that VCU sought only an improved and welcoming park for all. "Monroe Park is a green oasis in the midst of the urban fabric," he said.[71]

With the renaming of the campus in June 2004, VCU hired arborists to remove eighteen dying trees in the park and shore up fifteen others. Park visitors may have been even happier with the improvements VCU made to the restrooms. Funds from the city were on the way, but VCU's actions got the upgrades off to an early start, while also demonstrating that the university and city could cooperate in managing the park. By October, Pantele's efforts brought funding, an advisory council, and a foundation to support the park. The renovated Monroe Park fountain, with four tiers and featuring gargoyles spouting water, returned to service as a crowd cheered. The Fan District Association paid half the refurbishing costs, and representatives from Oregon Hill served on the park's advisory council and endorsed the improvements. Not only that, but the nonuniversity residents from the neighboring apartment and condominium towers backed the park. VCU and its neighbors had moved far from the fraught relations of the past.[72]

IN AUGUST 2004, the Board of Visitors approved the new campus master site plan, presented in an oversized book filled with color illustrations and titled *VCU 2020*. Assuredly, the title referred to clarity of vision more than to a sixteen-year commitment, but it did measure a hard-won confidence about the future for VCU and Richmond. As the planners stated, the relationship between the new plan and the 1996 master plan was "evolutionary, not revolutionary." Planning began in June 2003, and included "over 66 interviews" and presentations to "over 51 groups," including university bodies, neighborhood associations, and city and state agencies.[73]

The Monroe Park Campus had transformed from "serving a local, part-time, non-traditional commuting undergraduate student population in the arts and business" to serving now "a broad spectrum of programs to a full-time, traditional, resident undergraduate and graduate student population engaged in leading academic and research pursuits." The college-age population in Virginia continued to grow, and VCU envisioned some thirty thousand students by 2008, with more of them seeking a residential experience. Already, VCU enrolled more students from Fairfax County, in Northern Virginia, than from adjoining Chesterfield and Henrico Counties. VCU had added some 1,500 dormitory beds in recent years, and a new dormitory, Brandt Hall, named for the university's first president, was rising next to Rhoads Hall on the northern edge of Monroe Park. The plan declared the park "the New 'Gravitational Center' of the Monroe Park Campus." Even better, it stated, "Monroe Park is uniquely suited to VCU: urban, historic, and shared with both the City and the community."[74]

Unlike the Monroe Park Campus, which looked to expand horizontally to the east, the MCV Campus looked to vertical growth. The Gateway Building, at Twelfth and Marshall, was now the crossroads of that campus, with a new critical-care hospital and replacement of North Hospital with a hospital extension of the Massey Cancer Center planned to the east of the Gateway Building. The rest of the MCV campus was mixed up with historic buildings and hemmed in. "This combination of factors has produced a very dense campus with few remaining development options that do not involve demolition of existing structures." The plan was frank: the outmoded A. D. Williams Clinic and the West Hospital would be demolished.[75] That proposal led to a very public fight with a new generation of preservationists, who were as committed to a positive vision for Richmond's future as VCU's leaders were.

More than anything else, though, the driver of the master plan was the expanding student body at VCU—an increase between 1997 and 2007, projected to total seven thousand students—with growth expected to continue through 2010. As higher education across the nation came to depend more and more on tuition, this was good news, but it also meant "increased demands for everything the university provides." To be sure, VCU still lagged behind other Virginia schools in enrolling higher-paying students from other states, but the university now enrolled more Virginia students than any other state school. The plan declared proudly, "VCU has become 'Virginia's University.'"[76]

11

Opportunity University, 2005–2009

As VCU NEARED its fortieth anniversary, conditions for higher education in Virginia and the nation changed. State legislation in 2005 ratified the long-term trend toward less state support for public higher education and ever-larger tuition charges for students. Soon after, the shocks of the "Great Recession" tested all institutions. VCU's mission—its commitment to the city of Richmond and to educating Virginians, most of them without wealth and often first-generation college students—survived the ups and downs. But those few years after 2005 were rocky for VCU and other universities, and observers saw that conditions for higher education, in Virginia and the nation, had changed by 2009.

PRESIDENT TRANI had earlier used the phrase "Virginia's University" in a newspaper story from February 2004 that combined discussion of nomenclature changes, campus expansion, and urban economic development to highlight a newfound "institutional pride" at VCU. Evidence of that pride abounded, including the common sight of students and others wearing clothing with VCU logos and colors. In addition, the story noted, the VCU basketball team was enjoying a highly successful season.[1]

Coach Jeff Capel was in his second season in charge of the basketball program, becoming the youngest head coach in the country when he took over for Mack McCarthy in March 2002 at age twenty-seven. Capel had been an assistant coach on McCarthy's staff after a playing career at Duke University, and his ability to communicate with the players had impressed both Athletic Director Richard Sander and President Trani. Capel's hiring would also mark a change in philosophy from a preference for experienced, older coaches, like Sonny Smith and McCarthy, to taking chances on younger, less-experienced coaches capable of climbing the professional ladder. That Capel's teams did well set that pattern.[2]

The 2003–4 team went 23–8, winning the Colonial Athletic Conference tournament (at the Richmond Coliseum) over George Mason University by a single point. It had been eight years since the team's last championship.

The Rams then faced the higher-ranked Wake Forest team in the NCAA tournament and put up a good fight before falling by a score of 79–78. The youthful coaching staff of the university's flagship sport fit well with the fresh look of campus construction and the diverse crowd of students out and about in the city, an urban university in action.[3]

IN THE early years of the century in Richmond, one commonly encountered narrative gave VCU credit for aiding the city in pulling itself out of a nadir in the late twentieth century. There was truth behind that narrative. For example, Richmond's population, which had plummeted from about 250,000 in 1970 to just less than 200,000 a quarter century later, remained steady at that low level into the next century. Without the growth of VCU's enrollments, the population would have continued its decline. Yet, a negative narrative about the city also emerged in 2002, when former governor L. Douglas Wilder and former congressman Thomas Bliley joined forces to advocate for a change in Richmond's city charter to permit a mayor directly elected by the voters and with executive power over city government. Their contention, presented forcefully by Wilder, was that the city had long suffered from a lack of leadership, with neither the mayor elected by the council nor the city manager able to take charge. Wilder, a Democrat, and Bliley, a Republican, brought great authority to their proposal and, together, framed it as nonpartisan.[4]

The Wilder-Bliley proposal for citywide, at-large election of the mayor also reopened memories of past schemes to dilute black voting power. "The racial implications surrounding the issue are still too volatile to toy with," columnist Michael Paul Williams wrote. Even so, he agreed that Richmond needed a mayor "with some real clout" and a vision for the city's future.[5]

VCU faculty members John Moeser and Rutledge Dennis, the latter now teaching at George Mason University, had years before analyzed the politics of annexation in Richmond, and in 2002 they led a group of local leaders in proposing a "friendly amendment" to the Wilder-Bliley proposal. Moeser's analysis of the 1998 city election showed that high turnouts in just three majority-white districts could carry a citywide election—exactly what the courts had stopped in 1977 with elections by district. Moeser, Dennis, and company proposed that the elected mayor would have to carry at least five of the city's nine districts. The Richmond Crusade for Voters, longtime electoral organization for blacks in the city, endorsed the amendment.[6]

A year before, President Trani had become the chair of Richmond Renaissance, an organization first formed to be a solution, by way of economic development, to the racial and political conflicts between the white business elite and black elected officials after 1977. In October 2002, Richmond Renaissance convened for its annual meeting, with Wilder as the main speaker. Announced as speaking on his experience with budget balancing as governor, in light of the state's increasingly dismal budget situation, Wilder inevitably turned instead to his proposal for a strong mayor, arousing loud complaint from, among others, Henry Marsh, now state senator and a fervent opponent of Wilder's proposal. Trani defended the invitation, pointing out that Wilder had attracted a larger audience than usual. When asked whether he had discouraged Wilder from discussing the mayoralty, he declared, "I am the last person in the world to tell a member of the faculty of Virginia Commonwealth University what they're allowed to talk about and what they are not allowed to talk about." Clarence L. Townes Jr., a founder of Richmond Renaissance and former member of the VCU Board of Visitors, also defended Wilder's invitation. Both men acknowledged that they favored the reform.[7]

That fall saw the Wilder-Bliley team and the Richmond City Council, whose memberships conspicuously did not overlap, create separate commissions to study the issue. The former moved forward, thanks in part to financial support from Richmond businessmen, to announce a proposal for an elected mayor, with the Moeser-Dennis amendment that a candidate must carry five of the nine council districts included. They then collected ten thousand signatures to place the measure on the ballot in November 2003. As the election impended, Trani, as head of the sponsoring Richmond Renaissance, welcomed some two hundred people to a public forum on the mayoralty, with presentations on Richmond history and government by Njeri Jackson, chair of the Department of African American Studies, and John Moeser, from the Department of Urban Studies and Planning, preceding the debates. A few weeks later, the measure received the voters' approval by a 4–1 margin and went on to the legislature. With that body's agreement, in November 2004, Richmond proceeded to elect a mayor, giving Wilder, a VCU professor and professed reluctant candidate, a landslide victory in which he carried all nine city districts. Earlier that year, on 21 May 2004, VCU renamed its School of Government and Public Affairs, which could trace its heritage back to VCU's founding as an urban university, to become the L. Douglas Wilder School of Government and

Public Affairs. Inevitably, the new mayor's relationship with VCU, and vice versa, became an issue.[8]

As mayor, Wilder proved to be decisive (imperious, some would say). He met in late November with his transition team, a meeting that the *Times-Dispatch* described as "heavily flavored with the presence of top officials from Virginia Commonwealth University, as well as by VCU graduate students." In addition to creating the new post of city administrator, replacing the city manager under the former charter, Wilder wanted the transition team to advise him on a new chief of police. In late January 2005, Rodney D. Monroe, chief of police at Macon, Georgia, became the new chief in Richmond. A veteran of the force in Washington, D.C., before going to Georgia, Monroe promised "community-based policing." His appointment would prove to be one of the signal successes of Wilder's mayoralty.[9]

Meanwhile, and connected, as the mayoralty campaign got underway in 2004, VCU announced plans for major construction at the MCV Campus, setting off a lingering controversy with historic preservationists. In August 2004, on the heels of the drafting of a master plan, the Board of Visitors accepted proposals for the razing of three older—and, it turned out, much loved—buildings on the MCV Campus. Originally, the plan had been to tear down Cabaniss Hall (1928), the School of Nursing's building on Broad Street, and then to renovate adjacent West Hospital (1941) for a new home for nursing. But the cost of renovation proved too great. Instead, VCU proposed to demolish not only Cabaniss Hall, with the School of Nursing to gain a new building on Leigh Street, but also to pull down both West Hospital and the nearby A. D. Williams Clinic (1938) to construct a new, large-scale medical sciences building. No funding was yet available for that project, and the School of Nursing building would require additional fundraising, too, so the exact timetable remained uncertain.[10]

Regardless, the plan sparked protest from Richmond's articulate historic preservationists, especially about the prospect of losing West Hospital. William T. Sanger considered construction of the building one of the greatest achievements of his presidency of the Medical College of Virginia, enabling MCV finally to boast of a state-of the-art medical center. Time and technological change took a toll, and when David Hume and other surgeons marched in 1972 on the governor's office to insist on better state support for the Medical Center, the inadequacy of West Hospital was one of their complaints. Since then, construction at the Medical Center had occurred elsewhere, with West Hospital an architectural survivor, its art deco mass looming over Broad Street. As part of the announcement in August 2004, the university provided documentation of an agreement in 1992 between VCU and the Virginia Department of Historic Resources (DHR) giving the university permission to tear down West Hospital, with VCU promising, if it did so, to salvage the ornamental fixtures that gave the building a period identity.[11]

Style Weekly immediately featured an essay by architectural writer Ed Slipek Jr., a VCU graduate, condemning DHR for not safeguarding West Hospital and imploring the Board of Visitors to vote no on its destruction. West Hospital, he contended, was one of the few buildings at VCU "both brilliant architecturally and rich in institutional memories." Sharing his outrage were the leaders of the Association for the Conservation of Historic Richmond Neighborhoods (ACORN). Unlike the Historic Richmond Foundation, with its more elite focus on fine architecture and the city's grand past, ACORN advocated renovation of existing buildings to stabilize neighborhoods and to encourage new residents to join those already there in the city. ACORN's leaders, who included VCU graduates, organized a walking tour at the Medical Campus to publicize the buildings and then, the next day, attended the August meeting of the Board of Visitors, distributing a flyer portraying VCU as an evil surgeon about to cut a vital organ from an unwitting patient. It was to no avail. President Trani explained the options facing the MCV Campus, but all that he asked of the board at the August meeting was approval of the master plan, with the priority being the Monroe Park Campus Addition and with details at the MCV Campus yet to be determined. The board approved the master plan; ACORN's leaders left the meeting vowing to fight on.[12]

One month later, Mayor Rudolph C. McCollum Jr., elected by his fellow councilmen under the old system and a candidate for mayor in the upcoming at-large election in November, called for a moratorium on destruction of buildings downtown, including West Hospital. He condemned VCU's plans along with the state's plans to tear down two government office buildings—both former hotels—near Capitol Square. His larger complaint was that the state (and state agencies, like VCU) could obtain permission from DHR to demolish state-owned buildings in the city, without the city having any say in the process. Trani responded angrily, for VCU had shared its plans months before without complaint from the city. As he had argued to the Board of Visitors, the priority was "to create a modern academic center," but now he went on to point out that the VCU Medical

Center provided $47 million of indigent medical care for Richmonders, without the city "paying one penny of that."[13]

These events marked a collision of two forces for revitalization of the city: urban universities and historic preservation. The latter's modern era dates from the mid-1960s, with a gradual shift from preservation of the best from the past to renovation and reuse of older buildings to stabilize declining neighborhoods and to invite new residents (a process often criticized using the derogatory term "gentrification"). Thanks to the federal program of tax credits in return for rehabilitation of historic properties, Richmond developers had worked with preservationists and neighborhood organizations across the city on projects that included renovations and reuse. The preservationists and their allies, led by ACORN, believed that they had found ways to protect and improve the city's older neighborhoods without tearing down the buildings. As in the cases of Oregon Hill and the Carver neighborhood, adjacent to VCU's Monroe Park Campus, conflicts between neighborhood preservation and economic development certainly could arise, but until 2004, VCU and the preservationists had followed parallel paths to the betterment of Richmond. The campaign for a mayor elected by the citizens had aroused memories of older, racially inflected antagonisms that set the neighborhoods against the businessmen, and as the controversy over West Hospital entered partisan politics, the relationship between VCU/economic development and historic preservation/neighborhood revival seemed to slide into that older antagonism that posited one side as destructive and the other as obstructive.[14]

Immediately after L. Douglas Wilder became the new mayor, political columnist Jeff E. Shapiro noted that Wilder remained a member of the VCU faculty, and the university faced local opposition to its demolition plans at the MCV Campus. He asked, "What will Wilder do if this becomes a legal and/or regulatory fight?" At an early press conference, Wilder dismissed the issue, but *Style Weekly* returned to it. "Will VCU receive special treatment when downtown issues arise?" As it happened, West Hospital remained upright, and the mayor never had to consider recusing himself, but the idea that Mayor/Professor Wilder and VCU's President Trani had a special, behind-the-scenes connection would persist. In the short run, VCU faculty, including Robert Holsworth, dean of humanities and sciences, William Bosher, dean of the School of Education, and Paul Timmreck, vice president for finance, advised the mayor's transition process. Trani repeated his conviction, supported by Wilder's own record of thorough independence, that the mayor was his own man, point-ing out that Wilder had not asked him either before running for mayor or now before inviting VCU faculty to serve. Despite Wilder's sweeping victory, *Style Weekly* named Jennie Knapp Dotts, the executive director of ACORN, its 2004 Richmonder of the Year.[15]

WHILE ANTICIPATED construction set off controversy, actual construction went forward on a research addition that would double the size of the Massey Cancer Center. Thanks to funding from the previous November's state bond issue and the generosity of philanthropists, notably William H. Goodwin Jr. and Alice Goodwin, who alone gave $25 million to the center, work began in summer 2003 with the demolition of Randolph-Minor Hall next door. An architecturally undistinguished dormitory built in 1952, Randolph-Minor Hall sparked no protest from preservationists but none-theless was a rare building at VCU in that its name honored two women, pioneer nursing graduates Agnes Dillon Randolph and Nannie Jaqueline Minor. The name survived by way of its transfer to the old First African Baptist Church building on College Street just to the south, which later housed the Department of Clinical Laboratory Sciences.[16]

One unexpected consequence of the destruction was the opening of a dramatic view, looking west from Church Hill, of the Egyptian Build-ing and behind it the medical sciences building, named in March 2003 to honor Hermes Kontos. That proved fortuitous. President Trani was in the habit of gathering up all his grandchildren for a Saturday brunch and then driving with them around town to check on VCU construction proj-ects, or, as the family called it, "Gene-land." Descending Church Hill on Broad Street one Saturday, the group took in the new vista at the Medi-cal Campus. Trani noted as he drove that the planned Massey addition would leave some open space, and he returned from the excursion to pro-pose pushing out the plan for the cancer research center to occupy the entire available site. When it opened in May 2006, the addition, named the Goodwin Research Laboratory, included eighty thousand square feet of research space, more than double what had been planned in 2003, with seventy-two laboratories and a parking deck for patients.[17]

Meanwhile, construction got underway on the Critical Care Hospital in early 2005, and even with five of its planned sixteen floors underground, the tower would loom over the Museum of the Confederacy (MOC). The MOC included both the modern museum building, adjacent to where

View of the Egyptian Building from Church Hill before expansion of the Massey Cancer Center, 2003, with Kontos Medical Sciences Building behind. In the background is the dark brick of West Hospital and the Richmond City Hall. (Virginia Commonwealth University Libraries)

the ambulances arrived at the hospital's emergency room, and the White House of the Confederacy, a fine house built in 1818 and occupied by Jefferson Davis during the American Civil War. Despite assumptions that its name encouraged, the museum had earned a reputation for honest presentation of the past, including a pioneering exhibition on slavery in the South. Visitation, however, declined steadily, and even accounting for the institution's name as a marketing problem, the MOC's location in a busy, confusing medical center made it a difficult destination for visitors. To be sure, the relationship was not fraught, and VCU provided parking and steam heat to the museum. Nonetheless, as VCU prepared to begin construction of the Critical Care Hospital, the MOC declared that it faced economic disaster and must consider moving.[18]

There was a problem. If the White House of the Confederacy moved from its original site, it would lose its designation on the National Register of Historic Places. The move of the Alumni House (Maury-Maupin House) to permit construction of the Ambulatory Care Center had cost it its listing on the register. Even so, the Museum of the Confederacy began preparing to relocate. The MOC's saga continued for several difficult years, before it finally merged with the American Civil War Center to become the American Civil War Museum. The White House of the Confederacy remained at the Medical Center. The campus master plans had assumed the house's permanence at the MCV Campus, yet VCU could not avoid again being cast in public as Godzilla encroaching on the tiny besieged site. The situation seemed to ratify the narrative of heedless destruction of history that preservationists out to save West Hospital had put forward.[19]

That narrative could be flipped to emphasize how VCU had transformed the city of Richmond for the better, and such assessments also abounded by 2005. In April, Philip Morris USA announced plans to build a major research center at the Biotechnology Research Park, nearly doubling the size of the research park and employing as many as seven hundred people. "After years of small steps," the *Times-Dispatch* said, "it was as though the Virginia BioTechnology Park had suddenly scaled the Matterhorn." Trani and others recounted the park's climb since 1990, and the news stories noted the cigarette manufacturer's long connection to VCU (and its predecessor institutions), including an endowed chair in the School of Business and current funded research studies to the amount of $4.4 million. In June construction began for the new nursing building, at Eleventh and Leigh Streets on the northern side of the Medical Campus, replacing the building on Broad Street next to West Hospital. Groundbreaking in November came for the Critical Care Hospital and the Monroe Park Addition.[20]

These events celebrated VCU's future, but they also celebrated the generosity of donors who backed VCU's future. Front and center at the groundbreaking for the Monroe Park Addition was William H. Goodwin Jr., whose most recent gift, to the engineering expansion, was the largest in VCU's history. Goodwin told the crowd about a conversation he had with President Trani in which he talked about the benefits of his training in both engineering and business. Soon after, he received a call from Steven Markel, head of an insurance company, who said that Trani had told him about combining business and engineering in the new addition. They went golfing together to talk about the plan, and, Goodwin said, provoking laughter from the crowd, it cost Markel mightily, too. Thanks to their generosity, and that of many others, VCU had a record fundraising year in 2005.[21]

The president's steady presence at VCU may have relieved some observers, for other important leaders prepared to depart. Heber H. (Dickie) Newsome Jr., dean of the School of Medicine, retired after forty years at VCU, with Jerome F. Strauss III, from the University of Pennsylvania, taking his place as dean and head of MCV Physicians, the physician-faculty group practice of the VCU Health System. Paul Timmreck, senior vice president for finance and administration, who had ensured that VCU's expansion would be fully financed, and legal, during a period of steady reductions in state support for higher education, announced in July that he would retire in 2006. John Bennett, state secretary of finance, a post Timmreck once held, agreed in November to take over the vice presidency at VCU. And, after twenty years, Richard L. Sander, athletic director, announced his retirement. He would stay on for a few years in an advisory role with the SportsCenter, the graduate program in sports leadership that he had created. He expressed pride in the Siegel Center and in the breadth of competitive success for student-athletes at VCU, totaling thirty conference championships in the decade since VCU joined the Colonial Athletic Association.[22]

As THOSE retirements took effect, so, too, did new legislation with the potential to transform higher education in Virginia. The process began a few years earlier with discussions about the volatility of state funding among leaders of the state's three dominant universities—University of Virginia, Virginia Tech, and the College of William and Mary, the "Big Three," to use analyst Lara K. Courturier's term. Although the authority status secured by the VCU Health System in the mid-1990s provided a precedent of sorts, what the Big Three proposed was a new status as "chartered universities," with the autonomy, among other things, to set their own tuition and fees. Technically, the schools' boards of visitors already had that power, but Governor George Allen's tuition freeze and Governor James Gilmore's tuition rollback exposed the limits of that power. By 2003, the Big Three saw that their best way out of the budgetary volatility was to become Commonwealth Chartered Universities, with the key provision that they would now be political subdivisions of the state, akin to counties and cities. As Courturier explains, that meant an exemption for the Big

Three from the requirement "that state agencies deposit all non-general funds monies, which includes tuition and fees, into the state treasury."[23]

The state's budget impasse in the legislative session of 2003 and the consequent priority in the 2004 session to craft a bipartisan tax increase postponed action on the proposed legislation until 2005. In the interim, though, Governor Mark Warner, whose backing for the bond bill in 2002 showed his commitment to higher education, got involved. He organized several town hall meetings across the state in fall 2004 to discuss the charter proposal. At the first meeting, convened at VCU on 25 October 2004, Warner declared that higher education must serve the state's needs, and thus any legislation needed accountability as well as autonomy.[24]

VCU officials played little role in the politics of charter universities. The problem, from VCU's perspective, was not only that the Big Three could increase tuition without badly discouraging student applicants, but also that they enjoyed a substantial out-of-state enrollment of students paying the full cost of their education, as state policy mandated. VCU, as "Virginia's University," lacked the out-of-state students, and its Virginia students did worry about the costs of their educations.[25]

Meanwhile, VCU and the state's other higher education institutions, through the Council of Presidents, moved from fears of bad effects for them to a proposal to "make autonomy available to public colleges on three levels of increasing freedom." Presidents of the Big Three acknowledged political reality. They accepted the governor's accountability standards as part of the price of autonomy and went along with the other schools' three-tiered system as the remainder of that price. They also agreed to remain state agencies. The legislation—then-Virginia secretary of education Peter Blake described it as "a complex, 32-page bill that amended 13 sections of the Code of Virginia and added 45 sections and three subchapters"—moved remarkably efficiently to passage. The universities received "additional operational autonomy" in return for meeting eleven (later twelve) "basic state policy objectives." The Restructured Higher Education Act of 2005 won plaudits in Virginia and attention across the country. The product of competing interests, it bore little resemblance to the original charter proposal. Paul Timmreck, vice president for finance, told Lara Courturier that "many wondered whether the increased accountability is matched by an appropriate degree of increased autonomy and decentralization."[26]

Observers also agreed that the accountability measures restored power to the State Council for Higher Education of Virginia that had been lost in its politicization in the 1990s, and made boards of visitors far more directly responsible for university decisions. Back in 1997, Trani had published an essay in the *Chronicle of Higher Education* responding to worries that controversies over "political correctness" and other issues had encouraged trustees and government officials to challenge the authority of presidents. He proposed that VCU's example, with community advisory boards, five private foundations, the research park, and the health authorities, showed that "a broader model of shared governance" best served to mitigate possible partisan interference at the university. In Trani's model, all of these governmental/constituent entities revolved around the president, not the board of visitors, and no matter that the model had worked well for VCU, how the board would operate under the new legislation remained to be seen.[27]

The Board of Visitors met in May 2005 and announced that Trani had agreed to extend his presidency to 2010, when he would be seventy (the board made the invitation, and, after consultation with Lois Trani, he accepted). He looked forward to engagement in a variety of areas, but specifically mentioned the impact of Philip Morris USA's research complex just announced for the Virginia Biotechnology Research Park the month before. The facility would nearly double the size of the research park, and though company officials were "tight-lipped" about the planned research there, one suggested more focus on basic science than product development. Both Thomas Huff, vice provost for life sciences, and Francis Macrina, recently appointed vice president for research, expressed pleasure at the prospects for research partnerships between VCU and the park's new arrival.[28]

Construction was already underway for the Philip Morris research center when the *Richmond Times-Dispatch* published a set of stories about "Who Runs Richmond" on 14 August 2005. For all the changes in Richmond's economy and government since the 1960s, the newspaper found that "a small circle of closely connected men who have the power to make their visions Richmond's destiny" dominated the city. A hard-nosed civic responsibility characterized the city's elite generally, and that made leaders receptive to Trani's advocacy for VCU. "They all understood that a major research university is an essential building block for a modern community in the technological world," he told the newspaper.[29]

BACK ON campus, the fall semester 2005 got underway with warnings about safety, as a murder victim's body had been found that summer behind the

Temple Building at the Monroe Park Campus. Henry Rhone, vice provost for student affairs and enrollment services, told students that VCU was their neighborhood, and they must look out for one another. More worrying to many students was the new, and slower, email system, but campus attention soon shifted to Hurricane Katrina's pounding of New Orleans and the feckless response of the federal government to the disaster. VCU administrators proudly announced another record freshman class, more than double the size of the 1996 class.[30]

On 5 September, a security camera recorded one of those freshmen, Taylor Marie Behl, of Fairfax County, departing her dormitory with a man in his late thirties named Benjamin Fawley. She did not return. Two days later, a VCU police officer telephoned Behl's mother, Janet Pelasar, to inform her of their search for her daughter. Two days after that, VCU announced Behl's disappearance to the press. On 15 September, Richmond Police Chief Rodney Monroe announced that the city had taken over the case, which it now considered a criminal investigation. Aiding would be the VCU Police Department, the Virginia State Police, and the FBI. The focus narrowed to Fawley, who finally admitted to being with Behl when she died of asphyxiation and pointed detectives to the location of her body in a shallow grave in Mathews County. President Trani announced the sad conclusion to the search. Behl "was part of our university family and we feel her loss."[31]

The case, involving sex and a murder mystery, attracted television true-crime shows. Behl's mother also published a memoir about her daughter and the case, which concluded a year later with Fawley receiving a thirty-year sentence for the homicide. Several counts of child pornography, from a search of Fawley's computer during the investigation, were then dropped.[32]

As those dropped charges suggest, the Behl investigation moved from physical evidence to clues left behind on the internet by Fawley, Behl, and others. Behl's pages at then-new social networking sites like LiveJournal and Myspace disturbed older observers for what they saw as guileless vulnerability. In retrospect, the case presaged the wholesale embrace of online social media, made possible by internet-connected smartphones, with profound and still-emerging effects on higher education and society. In the aftermath of the iPhone, introduced in January 2007, students found it increasingly difficult to stop texting, posting, and streaming even in the classroom, and entrepreneurial administrators dreamed of new forms of distance learning and "hybrid" classrooms.[33]

The murder shadowed the semester, but there was celebration again in November, as VCU began the month with groundbreaking ceremonies for the extension of the Monroe Park Campus. In addition to the new School of Business, the expansion of the School of Engineering, the parking deck, and the student housing, the announcement came that the award-winning AdCenter would move into the adjacent Central Belting Building, a historic structure built originally as the carriage barn for the Jefferson Hotel. Two weeks later, groundbreaking took place at the MCV Campus for the new Critical Care Hospital, the largest capital project ever at that campus. Appropriately, one of the dignitaries wearing a hard hat and breaking the ground was a six-year-old girl who had spent the first few months of her life in the neonatal ICU at the hospital. A few days later, the *Times-Dispatch* discussed VCU's impact on Richmond in general, citing creation of the engineering school as when the figurative snowball began rolling downhill. "Now it's a snowball that's caught on fire," declared Jim Dunn, the president of the Greater Richmond Chamber of Commerce.[34]

Elections in 2005 brought Tim Kaine, former Richmond mayor and lieutenant governor in the Warner administration, to the governorship, and his inauguration in January 2006 started another legislative session. Warner's final budget left VCU seeking additional funding from the legislature, as usual, but it did include construction money for the second medical sciences building, a companion to the Kontos Medical Sciences Building and slated for the site on Broad Street vacated by the School of Nursing, whose new building, Cabaniss Hall, was going up on Leigh Street. That spring, the Goodwin Research Laboratory at the Massey Cancer Center opened to researchers. The building boom would continue for several years. "More space, modernization and technology attracts more qualified scientists and clinical experts," explained Sheldon Retchin, chief executive officer of the VCU Health System. When the second medical sciences building opened in April 2009 its name had become the Molecular Medicine Research Building, although it was still connected to the Kontos Building. As important, the university had worked with the Historic Richmond Foundation to make the new building a good neighbor to Monumental Church next door. In fact, its restrooms would be open for visitors to the historic church.[35]

For all the satisfaction that VCU's acceleration of construction provided after 2004 (the *CT* welcomed back students in fall 2006 with a two-page spread mapping all the projects, planned and underway), it is likely that the basketball team's successes did as much to foster pride at VCU and in the community. Coach Jeff Capel's team followed the championship season of 2003–4 with nineteen wins in 2004–5 and a postseason berth in the National Invitational Tournament. The 2005–6 season ended with a defeat in the Colonial Athletic Conference tournament and, a month later, with Coach Capel's move to the University of Oklahoma. As sports writer John Packett noted in the *Times-Dispatch*, the coach's departure put pressure on President Trani, for VCU was also hiring a successor to Richard Sander as athletic director. April 2006 was stressful but also highly successful as VCU hired first Norwood Teague, associate athletic director at the University of North Carolina, as athletic director and then introduced the new head basketball coach, Anthony Grant, the associate head coach of that year's national championship team, the University of Florida. At the press conference to announce Teague's hiring, Trani stated again that there would be no football program at VCU as long as he remained the president.[36]

Grant's first season was one of the very best for the Rams, as the team claimed twenty-eight victories and the 2007 CAA tournament championship. The team then went to the NCAA tournament with the dubious assignment of playing the perennially tough Duke University Blue Devils. The game came down to the final seconds, with the ball in the hands of the Rams' star guard Eric Maynor. His jump shot from near the free throw line seemed to take forever to drop smoothly through the rim for a 79–77 victory. The tournament gave little time for celebration, and VCU next faced the powerful Pittsburgh Panthers, forcing overtime but unable to repeat the magic of the Duke game. It took almost as long for fans' blood pressure to return to normal as for Norwood Teague to sign Coach Grant to a six-year contract extension.[37]

By then, Richmonders, if asked, would associate VCU with basketball, the hospitals, and with construction projects across the downtown. It is ironic that President Trani's own long-standing passion was less visible than the sports trophies and new buildings. Long before he came to VCU in 1990, Trani was an avid world traveler, convinced that global connections were a fundamental aspect of higher education. In October 2006, he departed for India, with Mayor Wilder, to establish exchange programs with selected Indian universities. Trani and Wilder enjoyed one another's company and exploration. In fact, Wilder had accompanied Trani to the summer 2006 commencement ceremonies at VCU-Qatar.[38]

Trani came to VCU after holding a Fulbright professorship in the then-Soviet Union, establishing academic exchanges with China, and traveling abroad whenever possible. At VCU he found numerous academic connections established with the world but nearly all of them depended on the continued efforts of a single faculty member. To be sure, the medical school had long attracted outstanding foreign-born students and physicians, but the student body at the Monroe Park Campus became notably more ethnically and internationally diverse after 1990, thanks in large part to the increased enrollment from the rapidly diversifying suburbs of Northern Virginia. In 2003, Trani convinced Peter Kirkpatrick, cofounder of the French Film Festival, to head the Office of International Education, and Kirkpatrick negotiated relationships with some twenty international universities. He sought urban universities with medical schools to make a good fit with VCU and particularly looked to schools in the so-called BRIC nations—Brazil, Russia, India, and China—then seen as on the rise. Trani's India trip with Wilder produced "memorandums of understanding with the India Institute of Technology in Kharagpur, one of India's leading technology schools, and the Post Graduate Institute of Medical Education and Research in Chandigarh," and Trani followed the trip with an op-ed essay for the *Times-Dispatch* on India's rise to economic prominence. In November 2007, he and the mayor departed for visits to universities in England and Russia, and he returned with agreement to a relationship with Harris Manchester College of Oxford University. He remained committed to "building a culture of internationalization for our VCU students."[39]

Back in Richmond, a short-lived eruption of conflict with advocates for the Oregon Hill neighborhood echoed the past but also marked differences between VCU in 1990 and in 2007. The university proposed expanding the Cary Street Gym by one hundred thousand square feet to meet the demand for recreational facilities from a student body of thirty thousand, up 40 percent in a decade and expected to rise. Student fees would pay for the expansion, but in contrast to their resistance to the campaign Trani and others waged to win student backing for the Siegel Center, students now endorsed the fees. Brian Ohlinger, associate vice president for facilities, and John Bennett, vice president for finance, met with neighborhood groups about the project, too. In November 2006 they proposed two options to leaders from Oregon Hill and thought they had won support for an option that required demolition of two aged stables. The remainder of the construction site would be properties that VCU had owned since the 1970s and 1980s. This time, when condemnation of the destruction of the stables came, the neighborhood was not united against VCU. Despite numerous fiery comments in the press and online, the stables' defenders did not garner significant backing, for VCU's plans respected the existing gymnasium building—once the City Auditorium—and now included moving one of the former livery stables. In late September 2007, the construction along Cary Street received approval from the state of Virginia.[40]

In early December 2007, the Virginia Minority Supplier Development Council held its annual awards celebration to recognize people and entities in the Richmond region demonstrating commitment to contracting for services with minority-owned enterprises. The main award went to Philip Morris for contracts to construct its new research building at the Biotechnology Research Park. The President's Award went to Eugene Trani, representing VCU. The award noted that 19 percent of contracts for construction of the Critical Care Hospital went to minority businesses, and a minority-owned firm was the primary contractor for renovation projects at the Monroe Park Campus. Pamela Lepley, the university spokesperson, declared, "None of our projects get off the ground without Dr. Trani asking how we're going to assure there's significant minority participation."[41]

That policy was of no small significance, given VCU's ongoing construction program and Richmond's history. Thirty years before, the advent of a black majority on Richmond's city council exposed political, racial, and economic conflicts, which policies of economic development, endorsed by the city council and newly founded Richmond Renaissance, helped to mitigate. In 1983 city council agreed to an ordinance requiring that 30 percent of city contracts be set aside for minority-owned businesses. That policy provided a degree of peace and encouraged new businesses in the city, but it fell prey, in the case of *City of Richmond v. J. A. Croson Co.*, to a conservative Supreme Court in 1989. That decision, prohibiting quotas, or "set-asides," set off a national scramble to meet the Court's more stringent requirements for affirmative action policies.[42]

Trani arrived at VCU in 1990 just after the *Croson* decision, but he was committed to ensuring that VCU's contracts for goods, services, and construction encouraged minority participation. In 1991, VCU started an annual minority vendor networking event and business card exchange to acquaint vendors with VCU's procurement policies and procedures. Development of the Biotechnology Research Park also demonstrated that commitment, with the park's planning, legal and financial services, and construction work designed to encourage minority participation.[43]

One court-approved strategy employed by VCU has been to encourage prime contractors to use minority- and women-owned business enterprises as subcontractors. Early on, a prime contractor was discovered to have hired a minority subcontractor for the sole purpose of giving cover while writing the checks to the actual white-owned subcontractors. On learning of it, VCU immediately put a stop to the subterfuge, and when Brian Ohlinger joined the university as associate vice president for facility management, Trani warned him about that episode. "Always in the back of my mind," Ohlinger recalled, "was that . . . he was serious . . . that he wanted true minority participation." Under Ohlinger, VCU strove to use contracts framed as "construction manager at risk," which gave the university greater opportunity to work with and monitor prime contractors. In addition to encouragement for minority subcontracting, VCU also pushed established contractors to mentor new firms that could soon become successful subcontractors themselves. Those results were not as highly visible as VCU's buildings going up across Richmond, but the effort was another way for the urban university to serve Richmond. Trani accepted the award in December 2007 with pride.[44]

One month prior, before a crowd of five hundred at the Siegel Center, James A. Crupi presented the follow-up to the harsh report he had made for city leaders in 1992. This report, also commissioned by an unnamed group of leaders, found more to commend in Richmond than Crupi's 1992 report did, including VCU's expansion and the rise of the Virginia Biotechnology Research Park. Fifteen years on, however, problems persisted. The public schools needed improvement, regional cooperation remained elusive, and issues of race still hampered honest dialogue. President Trani liked the report but observed that nowhere did Crupi acknowledge that Richmond was the state's capitol, with a state government that should also play a supportive role in the city's development. The report provoked much further commentary locally, but largely undiscussed was Crupi's observation that the region faced imminent changes, with important leaders, among them President Trani, scheduled for retirement, with an aging workforce, and with increasing in-migration of ethnically and culturally diverse people.[45] Much had changed for VCU and Richmond between 1990 and the end of 2007.

THE SPRING semester 2008 was sweet at VCU. It began in January with the new buildings on the eastern addition to the Monroe Park Campus ready for students and faculty, even though the ceremonial opening would wait until April. The School of Business' new building was named in honor of Thomas G. Snead Jr. and Vicki M. Snead, alumni of the school who headed the successful capital campaign for the campus extension, and the graduate program in advertising had changed its name from the AdCenter to the Brandcenter, responding to industry trends but also appropriate as it prepared to move into the renovated Central Belting Building adjacent to Snead Hall.[46]

The Board of Visitors that spring approved a dozen new academic degree programs, six of them doctoral, including an interdisciplinary PhD in nanoscience and nanotechnology. The much-discussed *U.S. News and World Report*'s rankings of "Best Graduate Schools" showed the sculpture and nurse anesthesia programs retaining their no. 1 positions, with the School of the Arts at no. 4 nationally. In the top fifty nationally among their peers were the Schools of Education, Nursing, Pharmacy, and Social Work, with several other programs ranked, too. The basketball team did almost as well as the year before, and VCU successfully signed Coach Anthony Grant to another contract extension after other schools came seeking his services. Men's tennis coach Paul Kostin won the eight hundredth victory of his coaching career, which included sixteen straight invitations for his VCU teams to the NCAA tennis tournament, and students formed a campus "muggle quidditch team" to play a game described in J. K. Rowling's popular "Harry Potter" books.[47]

The new School of Business building—Snead Hall—and the East Hall of the School of Engineering had a formal dedication on 9 April, after being used for classes since January. Speeches that day from Governor Kaine, Mayor Wilder, and President Trani emphasized two themes. They noted first, that the proximity of the two buildings encouraged cross-disciplinary collaborations and innovations, and second, that VCU's growth served the Richmond community.[48]

More support for the latter theme came at month's end with the release of the city's new Downtown master plan, which emphasized, among other elements, urban architecture, respect for history, access to the James River, and economic diversity. The plan marked a sea change in attitudes since the days of destructive urban renewal just forty years before. The *Times-Dispatch* devoted its Sunday commentary section on 27 April to the plan, with essays endorsing the plan from Mayor Wilder and President Trani. The latter pointed out that VCU's strategic plan and the city's plan "acknowledge a symbiotic relationship," and the newspaper noted in its editorial endorsement of the master plan that VCU had "earned a reputation as a powerful force for revitalization—one that is sensitive to the needs of its neighbors." Making it all sweeter was the fact that 2008 was the fortieth anniversary of VCU's founding, and both the university and the city had moved far since then. At the business-engineering dedication earlier in the month, then-state senator Donald McEachin announced that the General Assembly had declared 1 July 2008 "VCU Day" in Virginia. On that day also, VCU would join the University of Virginia, Virginia Tech, and the College of William and Mary as "a Level 3 institution" under the provisions of the state's restructuring of higher education, with approval "to negotiate a management agreement with Cabinet secretaries" for the future.[49]

The spring semester 2008 ended, as usual, with the joy of commencement ceremonies and the departure for summer of most students and some faculty, with administrators and staff remaining to enjoy the campus with shorter queues and easier parking. In mid-May the Board of Visitors convened to approve faculty promotion and tenure decisions, an annual responsibility, and President Trani prepared for another summer sabbatical, this one at the Taubman Center for State and Local Government at Harvard University. Attention in Richmond those first weeks in May, however, focused on the recruitment of Police Chief Rodney Monroe by the city of Charlotte, North Carolina. Monroe had proved a fine chief, reducing crime in the city while earning respect and trust from boardrooms to the neighborhoods. The city wanted Monroe to stay, with Mayor Wilder and the city council arguing over who loved him more, and the *Times-Dispatch* calling him a "hero" and asking citizens to email him to stay. Nonetheless, in the middle of May, Monroe took the job in Charlotte. A day later, Mayor Wilder announced that he would not seek reelection.[50]

The public courting of Monroe, and his prospective departure from Richmond, seems to have been the occasion for someone, using the pseudonym "harry potter" and the email address "cleanupvcu," to send a series of accusatory email messages to the news media, to Rector Thomas Rosenthal's wife, and to Belle Wheelan, a former Virginia secretary of education and then president of the Commission on Colleges of the Southern Association of Colleges and Schools, VCU's accreditor. The gist of the messages was that VCU, under corrupt pressure from high administrators, had violated its own procedures in awarding Chief Monroe a bachelor of independent studies degree, with a minor in criminal justice, in 2007. The accusations gave a negative spin to facts about his student career at VCU that had been reported positively in the press then.[51]

Rector Rosenthal retrieved the message from his wife's email on 18 May and learned that, according to "harry potter," university officials, including President Trani and Mayor Wilder, had pressured lower-level administrators to permit Monroe to graduate without having fulfilled the university's requirement that at least thirty credit hours be done at VCU. He had, in fact, taken just two courses at VCU, for six hours, as the 2007 story about his graduation noted. Rosenthal contacted Richard O. Bunce Jr., director of the Department of Assurance Services at VCU, to start an investigation, and informed Provost Stephen Gottfredson and President Trani, the latter recusing himself from the investigation. With Bunce present, Gottfredson then informed Robert Holsworth, his successor as dean of the College of Humanities and Sciences, and Jon Steingass, the founding dean of the University College, of the emailed allegations. As a later report stated, "The responses of the two deans at this meeting, as described by both the director of assurance services and the provost, suggested that allegations of inappropriate influence might have merit and needed to be further investigated." The executive committee of the Board of Visitors met on 22 May and endorsed the investigation of a conspiracy and, because of the nature of the charges, approved hiring investigators from a consulting firm to aid in the process. A small notice appeared in the newspaper on 23 May of a VCU inquiry into whether an unnamed student received a degree fraudulently.[52]

When the vice presidents gathered for their weekly meeting on 27 May 2008, not only were they aware of those charges, but all must have shared a sense of bitter irony to read the agenda item about a "Tobacco Free Medical Center." Five days earlier, the New York Times revealed "a contract with extremely restrictive terms that the university signed in 2006 to do research for Philip Morris USA, the nation's largest tobacco company and a unit of Altria Group." The contract barred publishing the results of the research without the corporation's permission, required silence if contacted by the media about the research, and gave all intellectual rights in the research to the corporation. Vice President for Research Francis Macrina acknowledged to the Times the restrictive language but said that such contracts were balancing acts, and VCU had concluded that it could accept the agreement. As the article indicated, the larger context for the story was the tobacco industry's long suppression of scientific evidence that cigarettes harmed people and the issue of whether a medical center ought to work with a tobacco manufacturer in the first place.[53]

VCU officials responded immediately. The next day's *Richmond Times-Dispatch* reported that the research services agreement with Philip Morris was one of a half dozen such agreements between VCU and private corporations, agreements like those at other universities, and the article mentioned eight such schools by name. Vice President Macrina explained that the agreement was less restrictive than the *Times* story suggested, and the funded research did not involve cigarettes. Finally, as the *Times* had conceded, he noted that the funding from Philip Morris constituted less than 1 percent of the research grants garnered by the health center that year.[54]

Meanwhile, the degree investigation went forward, with tensions escalating behind the scenes. Monroe departed for Charlotte in mid-June, and the investigators made their report to the Board of Visitors two weeks later. The day before the board met, Dean Holsworth sent a long and angry letter to Bunce about the investigation, in which he charged that interrogators had threatened faculty members with retribution during interrogations and had operated from the start with the assumption that only a corrupt conspiracy explained the special treatment of Monroe. He declared, "It would be the oddest conspiracy I've ever witnessed for the purported perpetrators to announce what they've done in great detail on the front page of the *Times-Dispatch* and then follow it up with public celebration of Monroe in front of 10,000 people at commencement." The investigators were frustrated, in turn, with what a later report described as lack of cooperation, conflicting statements, and faulty memories. The report, as announced on 27 June, found no systematic problems with VCU's graduation procedures, nor any evidence of involvement by President Trani, but Monroe had received special and inappropriate treatment. Because VCU had no procedure for revoking a degree, he remained a legitimate graduate. "Monroe's reputation remains intact," the *Times-Dispatch* declared. "VCU's has suffered."[55]

By telephone from Boston and his sabbatical, President Trani promised that the university would examine its degree processes, though he endorsed the board's decision that Monroe would retain his degree. Trani also promised that a task force to investigate the university's research contracts with Philip Morris would hold public meetings, with the first one scheduled for the Kontos Building at the Medical Campus on 16 July 2008.

Trani was nearby that day but unable to attend, for he had suffered a bout of chest pain late the week before that took him to the VCU Hospitals and emergency quintuple coronary artery bypass surgery. He had not suffered a heart attack, and the prognosis was good, but the surgery was a shock. Trani, a "workhorse," had heretofore never missed a day of work because of illness. Now he faced six to eight weeks of rehabilitation.[56]

The Board of Visitors had assigned to Provost Gottfredson responsibility for the university's response to the investigators' report, but with the receipt of Dean Holsworth's letter of protest, the board asked the provost to review the investigation itself. On 3 July 2008, he reported that the investigation "does *not* contain material errors of fact or of conclusion." Five days later, the provost informed the board that he had accepted the resignation of Dean Steingass, who was departing to another position in another state, and proposed to accept Holsworth's resignation from his deanship. They did not go quietly. On 22 July, the same day that President Trani went home from the VCU Medical Center, the paper reported the angry resignations of Steingass and Holsworth, both critical of the board's investigation, along with the resignations in sympathy with them of Michael Pratt, interim director of the Wilder School of Government and Public Affairs and director of the Center for Public Policy, and, soon after, of William H. Parrish, codirector of the VCU Public Safety Institute.[57]

The *Times-Dispatch*'s coverage, especially of the Philip Morris contracts, had been limited since its initial article giving VCU's response, although reporters did cover developments with the Board of Visitors. Filling that space was more speculative reporting online by bloggers, such as Richmonder James A. Bacon in his blog *Bacon's Rebellion*. Bacon and local freelancer Peter Galuska published essays about VCU's problems at *Bacon's Rebellion* and at *Richmond.com*'s online business section. Meanwhile, two medical bloggers with onetime connections to the VCU Health Center— Michelle Kienholz, of the *Medical Writing, Editing & Grantsmanship* blog and formerly director of the Women's Health Research Core program at VCU, and Roy M. Poses, a former faculty member at the medical school and founder of the *Health Care Renewal* blog—reported regularly about the contract with Philip Morris. The blogs kept the story alive, and, at their best, the writers called on VCU to meet its own highest standards. The town hall–style meeting convened in July 2008 by the university's task force on the research contract heard twenty speakers from VCU repeat the concerns expressed online.[58]

The *Times-Dispatch* obtained, and on 3 August published, the text of Holsworth's June letter of protest to Richard Bunce about the investigation. That made public the charge that an investigator for the board had warned Monroe's advisor, an untenured assistant professor, that noncooperation might negatively impact her future case for tenure. That threat provoked retired faculty member Alan Briceland, a founder of the faculty senate and jealous defender of the faculty's role at VCU, to demand that the senate conduct its own investigation. In fact, though, faculty, staff, and administrators had been relegated to the sidelines as the investigation went forward, leaving people uneasy and dismayed.[59]

On 14 August 2008, a small group of VCU officials gathered by invitation for a press conference called by President Trani. He told them that concern about his health after bypass surgery had convinced him to move his retirement up a year, to depart VCU at the end of June 2009. Although he declined to comment on the summer's events, Trani did express dismay at reports that "there is an air of fear and intimidation at VCU." He declared, "That's not the VCU I know." On being told the news, Governor Tim Kaine, a former mayor of Richmond and, according to speculation, a candidate to follow Trani at VCU, declared Trani "the best thing to happen to Richmond in the last 20 years."[60]

Every decade in the United States, some five thousand persons serve as presidents of colleges and universities, with terms of office "averaging less than seven years." By 2009, about twenty-five of them annually "resigned, retired prematurely, or were fired." As the head of a complex institution, with consensus about direction a rarity and with constraints unlike in a corporation, the university president is a public target for all criticism of the institution he or she heads.[61] As presidents under attack can testify, painful circumstances reveal one's true friends. That summer, the silence in defense of VCU's administration was deafening.

To be sure, Trani's announcement that he would retire a year early was no apology, and it neither satisfied the critics nor closed the investigations. It was a telling sign of his priorities that he ignored critical newspaper columns about his own presidency, but when columnist Michael Paul Williams chided VCU for falling behind George Mason University in the *U.S. News and World Report* rankings by sacrificing academics to "unbridled growth," Trani responded. Not only did VCU stand high in other rankings, he asserted, but "VCU provides more access—more opportunity—to Virginia students than any other institution of higher education in the state."[62]

The fall semester's start coincided with a meeting of the Board of Visitors, and controversy continued. Board member, alumnus, and novelist David Baldacci condemned the investigation into the Monroe diploma, charging that the investigators had assumed a conspiracy and tried to create one when the evidence did not support that conclusion. The rest of the board heard him out and then accepted the report of the investigation and authorized the provost to make the university's report to SACS, the accrediting agency. That report, more detailed than the board's previous statements to the press, also went to the press in early September and inspired a front-page headline in the *Times-Dispatch* on 6 September: "Rules Broken for Monroe." The Southern Association of Colleges and Schools reviewed the report, noting in its conclusion that this was the only inappropriately awarded diploma out of thousands checked and that the university promised safeguards to prevent a recurrence, including creating an independent university ombudsman in July 2008. SACS imposed no sanctions. Journalist Michael Martz, who had covered the story from its beginnings, summed up the conclusion well: "In the end, there is no agreement on the crime or the punishment—only a blemish on VCU's reputation." That result was not satisfactory to longtime state legislator Lacey E. Putney, chairman of the House Appropriations Committee, and on 9 September he requested that the Joint Legislative Audit and Review Commission (JLARC) conduct its own investigation, with, he hoped, suggestions for processes that all boards of visitors in Virginia might adopt.[63]

On 15 September, former dean Steingass gave an interview to the *Times-Dispatch*, with further confusion of who said what to whom, but that day the stock market collapsed, and the investment firm Lehman Brothers filed for bankruptcy, the largest ever. Economists would later determine that the United States entered an economic recession in December 2007, and signs of distress had grown obvious enough by May 2008 for President Trani to publish an editorial essay in the *Chronicle of Higher Education*, titled "Even in Hard Times, Colleges Should Help Their Communities." Even so, the bottom dropping out in mid-September shook everyone.[64]

The Task Force on Research Contracts at VCU made its recommendations on 1 October, emphasizing standardized contracts, with transparency, rather than the special arrangements negotiated with Philip Morris, and President Trani promised a swift institutional review, with the new rules in effect by the end of the academic year. Less than a week later, the Board of Visitors learned that Governor Kaine had ordered VCU and all other state agencies to develop plans for budget cuts of up to 15 percent, on top of the 5 percent cut he had previously mandated. The economic crisis and the presidential election campaign commanded attention then, but VCU also celebrated the opening of the new Critical Care Hospital on 8 October. Almost as exciting was the simultaneous announcement that the international design firm I. M. Pei Partners had contracted to help design the new School of Medicine building to be constructed on the site of the A. D. Williams Clinic. With the new building, the enrollment of the medical school would be able to grow from 750 to 1,000 students.[65]

Two weeks later, the House Appropriations Committee summoned Rector Rosenthal, President Trani, and Provost Gottfredson to the state capitol to discuss the just-released JLARC report on the degree awarded to Rodney Monroe. The report "largely backed VCU's internal findings," including finding no evidence involving Trani, but the committee members wanted more, specifically that VCU rescind the degree, with Chairman Putney pointedly noting that the legislature oversees the boards of visitors. Rosenthal, apparently the only VCU representative to speak, was conciliatory but insisted that the contretemps was not of Monroe's own making. A month later the Board of Visitors revised the university policy to read, "The university reserves the right to revoke any degree, certificate or other university recognition for cause," but did not revoke the degree.[66]

Back in July, albeit largely overlooked, VCU officials announced that for its fortieth anniversary, the university would celebrate "all things VCU" through a festival at Monroe Park, open to all, in October. One of the anniversary events would be the dedication of a monument to the Richmond Professional Institute, "a triple helix made up of 52 cast-stone discs," each representing a year from the school's founding in 1917 to the merger with the Medical College of Virginia. The sculpture, created by sculpture MFA graduate Charles Ponticello and now located just west of Ginter House on Franklin Street, joined sculpture faculty member Lester Van Winkle's "Truth and Beauty," an assemblage of desks and easel honoring RPI's founding dean Henry Hibbs, outside the Hibbs Building. But unlike the twentieth-anniversary events in 1988, the "Fortieth and Forward" commemoration in 2008 focused on the postmerger history of VCU.[67]

A drizzle of rain on 25 October did not keep people away from Monroe Park and the celebration of VCU at age forty. The sound of live music—the bands chosen online by ninety thousand voters—attracted some, and there were also booths representing international students, health and wellness programs, and the adjacent neighborhoods, including Oregon Hill. The day before, officials dedicated four historical markers, for the St. Philip School of Nursing and the pioneering cardiac transplantation program at the MCV Campus, and at the Monroe Park Campus for Founders' Hall and the Shafer Street Stage. "VCU can be gritty; it can be sublime," the *Times-Dispatch* editorialized. "We are glad it is here."[68]

VCU students and other Richmonders might be forgiven then for looking past the festival in Monroe Park to the impending presidential election. Just three days before the Monroe Park Festival, candidate Barack Obama himself visited Richmond for a rally at the Coliseum downtown. Obama's victory two weeks later saw celebrations across Richmond, but nowhere more public than on Broad Street outside the Siegel Center, where students and others filled the street and then marched east to downtown.[69]

There was one more fortieth-anniversary event. Two days after Coach Anthony Grant's basketball team defeated Western Michigan at the Siegel Center, a crowd filled the facility for an evening with actor, comedian, and activist Bill Cosby. He had been scheduled for the Siegel Center a decade earlier, but construction delays prevented his appearance then. This evening began with former mayor Wilder introducing his friend Cosby, for "the first presentation in the new L. Douglas Wilder Lectureship Series." Cosby mixed humor with admonitions and inspiration in his address, the university presented him with an honorary doctorate, and the audience expressed approval for it all. It measures just how wrong so many things went for VCU in 2008 that several years later, after charges of sexual assault against Cosby, the university considered rescinding that degree.[70]

The new year began with *Style Weekly* naming the whistleblower "harry potter" its Richmonder of the Year, albeit more for the resignations and turmoil than for anything positive. For President Trani, the degree and contracts with Philip Morris were mistakes that procedural improvements could remedy, but the charge that people at VCU felt "a climate of fear" distressed him. In addition to the earlier announcement of an independent ombudsman, VCU announced on 13 January, at a campus forum on ethics, the creation of a private "tip line" for anyone to report ethical violations at VCU.[71]

Meanwhile, the search for VCU's next president proceeded. Governor Kaine, mentioned prominently as a possible successor to Trani, removed himself from consideration because Trani's decision to resign a year early left him, as governor, unable ethically to accept the presidency. Even with the governor's warm feelings for VCU, the harsh fiscal environment meant deep budget cuts for VCU and Virginia higher education. Vice President for Finance John Bennett told the Board of Visitors in mid-February that VCU's state funding "dropped from $8,812 per full-time student in 2000" to $6,130 in the coming fiscal year ("equivalent to $4,243 in 2000 dollars, Bennett said"). Hindsight is always clearer, but observers even then sensed that the Great Recession changed the conditions for higher education. President Trani left the board meeting early to go to the Senate chamber at the capitol building, where he received a framed copy of the legislature's resolution of appreciation for his service to the university, city, and state, and the senators rose to give him "a sustained standing ovation."[72]

One week later, on 20 February 2009, the Board of Visitors announced that Michael Rao, since 2000 the president of Central Michigan University, would follow Eugene Trani as president of Virginia Commonwealth University. "Mike and VCU are about the same age, and they both are just now hitting their strides," said Ed Bersoff, former rector and chair of the presidential search committee. Rao himself noted the attraction of VCU's "great momentum," and Trani declared that the search committee had "found the right person to continue VCU's transformation as a world class university and academic medical center." In truth, so much had changed at VCU and in Richmond and the nation in the year past that his arrival did mark a new era for the university. VCU was now a tier-three institution with a new, more autonomous relation to the state, and the city of Richmond had a new mayor with fewer and different connections to VCU. The nation continued to stagger economically, with the depth of the Great Recession orders worse than previous times of budgetary austerity. The future was darkly uncertain, but VCU and its city had strengths enough now for confidence going forward.[73]

VCU BASKETBALL fans soon got a taste of markets and salaries in action. That year's team won the Colonial Athletic Association title for the third year in a row and easily won the conference tournament. That secured a berth in the NCAA tournament, where the Rams put up a fight against elite UCLA before falling by a point. Success made Coach Anthony Grant a desirable commodity, his contract extensions notwithstanding, and at the end of March, he accepted a new job at the University of Alabama. Athletic Director Norwood Teague was prepared for the loss and slated interviews with prospective coaches right away. In the final major decision of the Trani era, VCU hired Shaka Smart, thirty-two-year-old assistant coach at the University of Florida, a decision that Trani endorsed as "a 3-point shot." At his first press conference as coach, Smart memorably promised, "We are going to wreak havoc on our opponents' psyche and their plan of attack."[74]

Later in April 2009, the *Richmond Times-Dispatch* filled its Sunday opinion section with articles and editorials about President Trani's legacy after nineteen years. Philanthropist William H. Goodwin Jr. enumerated the achievements—the Biotechnology Research Park, the School of Engineering, the Siegel Center and School of the Arts on Broad Street, the expansion of the Monroe Park Campus eastward, and the new research and clinical facilities at the MCV Campus—and Todd Woodson, president of the Oregon Hill Home Improvement Council, lamented the destruction of historic buildings and the expansion of the Cary Street Gymnasium. Faculty member George Munro, a scholar of Russian history, again stated that Trani's, and the university's, focus on growth had stretched resources for teaching and research, but also praised him for his commitment to scholarship and agreed on the lasting value of the president's accomplishments. Indeed, with eighteen thousand employees and thirty-two thousand students, VCU was "more populous than 90 percent of the localities in Virginia," and the university calculated that it had invested more than $2.1 billion in the city since 1990. As the paper's editorial said, "The eye cannot miss his legacy." The semester's final issue of the *Commonwealth Times* carried a last interview with President Trani. He expressed confidence in VCU and his successor but also great concern that the state underfunded higher education and had forced universities to rely on student tuition, which presented problems for the future at "an opportunity university" like VCU.[75]

VCU's fortieth commencement ceremony took place at the Richmond Coliseum on 17 May 2009. Some four thousand students "from 116 Virginia cities and counties, 37 states and the District of Columbia, Puerto Rico, the Virgin Islands and 41 countries" received professional, graduate, and undergraduate degrees that spring. Unlike at VCU's first commencement, in 2009 there was no controversy about nomenclature or demands for separate ceremonies. Back at VCU's founding, Edward A. Wayne, chair of the commission that created the school, had predicted that the merger of RPI and MCV would solidify into a university by 1980 or 1985. Events proved his timeline optimistic, but he was right about the university's future.[76]

At the commencement, Lois Trani was awarded the Edward A. Wayne Medal for her service to VCU. Giving up her own career as a nurse anesthetist, she hosted countless events to build support for VCU. In addition, through the MCV Hospitals Auxiliary of the VCU Health System, she volunteered for more than two thousand hours at the hospitals, mainly at the Massey Cancer Center, earning her the Auxiliary Founders Award, and the center named the patient resource library at its Stony Point site in her honor.[77]

Two days before the commencement, a statue of Eugene P. Trani was unveiled quietly at the Eugene P. and Lois E. Trani Center for Life Sciences. The memorial project began a few years earlier, funded by donors, and Trani had agreed to it on two conditions. He asked that he be represented with a world globe, reflecting his commitment to international education. And his other condition: that the bronze statue be life-sized.[78]

BEFORE THE Great Recession hit, VCU concluded another capital campaign. Charlotte Roberts and lawyer James C. Roberts joined alumni Thomas and Vickie Snead to head the campaign, which raised more than $400 million, making a total of $735 million in gifts to VCU since 1990. The campaign attracted 42,000 new donors, with significant growth in support from VCU alumni. Exemplary was alumnus and former rector W. Baxter Perkinson Jr., who also gave funds for a new dental building opening in 2009. Alumni who had grasped opportunities at VCU now provided the means for new generations of students to do the same at their opportunity university.[79]

Epilogue

As VCU's fiftieth anniversary year began, on 28 January 2018, the *Richmond Times-Dispatch* published a front-page article titled "How VCU's Footprint Is Expanding in Richmond" with accounts of a half-dozen current construction projects. Similar stories, with similar titles, had appeared in the local press numerous times in the previous half century as Virginia Commonwealth University and the city of Richmond rose together. Three days earlier, President Michael Rao delivered his annual state of the university address, with proud reports of VCU's record of research productivity and provision of access and opportunity for a highly diverse student body. He mentioned that fifty years had passed since VCU's creation and quoted President Warren Brandt's statement at the first convocation: "VCU will become a name that will mean a great deal in years to come." What sounded plaintive then had proven predictive. Rao went on to describe VCU in Richmond as an "anchor institution." This concept became a term of art for urban planners in the wake of the Great Recession, the national economic collapse that Rao faced on his arrival at VCU in 2009. It identified urban universities and urban hospitals—"eds and meds," as the phrase had it—and similarly local-based institutions as essential sources of social and economic stability for communities rocked by corporate and financial ups and downs.[1]

Members of the Wayne Commission in 1967 and all the university's presidents since then assuredly would have embraced Rao's description of VCU, with its thousands of employees, students, and alumni, as an "anchor institution." After his retirement from VCU's presidency, Eugene Trani completed, in collaboration with former dean Robert D. Holsworth, the research project about universities in the twenty-first century that he had begun in summer 2008, before his health emergency interrupted his sabbatical. Published in 2010, *The Indispensable University* cited VCU in Richmond, among the schools it described, to show colleges and universities "indispensable to economic and community development," anchor institutions in all but the name. No one who lived through the previous half century in Richmond would dispute that conclusion. The promise made in 1968 had been fulfilled.[2]

MICHAEL RAO's presidency came as a different era for higher education got underway, as did the beginning of a new chapter for VCU and Richmond, a story for another, later, historian to recount. Yet, one major event that occurred after 2009 closes this narrative. In 2009 VCU's new basketball coach Shaka Smart had promised teams that would wreak havoc on the court, and his 2010–11 team, running and pressing, exemplified havoc in action. Different observers would later see the magic descending at different points in that season, but magical it proved.

Smart's first season had resulted in a record of 27–9, but defeat in the Colonial Athletic Association's tournament precluded an invitation to the postseason NCAA tournament. When the National Invitational Tournament, a consolation prize for teams passed over by the NCAA, scorned the Rams, too, the team accepted an invitation to the relatively new College Basketball Invitational. The tournament featured the usual single-elimination games, with losers departing and winners advancing, but the championship required winning two games. The team did just that, taking down St. Louis University twice for the championship, with guard Joey Rodriguez named the tournament's most valuable player. The experience gained would matter a year later.[3]

It looked like another rejection from the NCAA tournament in 2011 as the Rams fell to Old Dominion University in the CAA tournament championship game. On Sunday, 13 March, the NCAA selection committee, in its wisdom, selected VCU as one of the very last teams included, with a Tuesday "play-in" game in Dayton, Ohio, against the University of Southern California, before the tournament really got underway at week's end. VCU's invitation offended the television basketball pundits—if the tournament was a beauty contest, Dick Vitale complained, why did the selection committee choose ugly VCU over more beautiful teams from major universities—and the victory over Southern California was sweet revenge. The Rams then faced Georgetown University on Friday. Before the game, Coach Smart showed the team a clip of another national sports pundit scoffing at the Rams' chances, and Georgetown fell by a score of 74–56, with the VCU crowd at one point happily chanting the name of a third skeptical broadcaster.[4]

On Sunday, the confident, overachieving Rams defeated Purdue University to advance to the tournament's final sixteen teams, a first for VCU. What made the achievement even sweeter was the similar success of the University of Richmond's team, giving jubilant Richmonders two teams still to cheer for. "No other city in the country can make such a claim," columnist Paul Woody, a VCU alumnus, happily declared. "This week the eyes, cameras and all manner of multi- and social media of a nation will be on Richmond." Even the *Roanoke Times,* out where fans of Virginia Tech had earlier believed that their team better deserved VCU's place in the tournament, declared that the two Richmond schools had "done their city and state proud."[5]

To honor the accomplishment, the city of Richmond sponsored a joint pep rally for both schools at Shockoe Bottom, near where the Brandcenter had its beginnings. President Rao and President Edward L. Ayers, of UR, arrived at the rally by canalboat, and with Mayor Dwight Jones they lifted a banner proclaiming Richmond the "Hoops Capital of the World." The teams' success, wrote Michael Paul Williams, "triggered the rare outbreak of unabashed civic pride." Too often Richmonders let excessive caution and internal conflicts block concerted action. "If VCU and UR can make the Sweet 16," he asked, "why can't the region successfully tackle poverty, educational inequity and regional discord?"[6]

Both teams would play in the same regional final at San Antonio, Texas. A crowd of more than one thousand outside the Siegel Center on 23 March cheered the Rams' departure for Texas. There the VCU pep band, the brassy Peppas, boarded a boat on San Antonio's Riverwalk and serenaded spectators along both banks. On Friday, the game with Florida State went to overtime. The Rams had possession down by a point with less than ten seconds to go. Joey Rodriguez tried to get the inbounds pass to sharpshooting Brandon Rozzell, who stumbled out of a screen from Jamie Skeen. Rodriguez then spotted Bradford Burgess open and got the ball to him for a quick layup. Seven long seconds remained as Florida State hustled up court, but Rob Brandenburg blocked a final desperate shot as time expired, with VCU up 72–71. The University of Richmond fell to top-ranked Kansas, a disappointment but a relief to many that the city's teams would not have to face each other to get to the coveted Final Four. Instead, as reporter Michael Martz put it, the tournament successes "brought together the two universities as the public champions of a city that is getting unprecedented national attention for all the right reasons."[7]

Fans in Richmond and San Antonio had hardly recovered from celebrating Friday night's victory by the time that Sunday's game with powerful Kansas began. The Rams again could not be stopped, even when Kansas came back from a fourteen-point halftime deficit, and the team pulled ahead for a 71–61 victory. Students watched the game at the Siegel Center and, as they had done after the Florida State game, poured out to flow down Broad Street toward Monroe Park, as thousands of others filled Floyd Avenue on the way to join them. In contrast to the scene forty years before at the Grove Avenue Republic, the police stood by, happily monitoring the situation. VCU's advance to the tournament's Final Four was national news, with congratulations from congressmen and the governor and a story prominent on the front page of the *Washington Post* the next day. As Mayor Dwight Jones, in San Antonio for the games, declared, "VCU projects Richmond in a way no slogan can."[8]

After the Rams beat Kansas, the two most popular internet searches were "Virginia Commonwealth University" and "VCU." The VCU homepage received eleven million hits (after making the Sweet Sixteen

VCU fans arrive at Monroe Park to celebrate the men's basketball team's victory over the University of Kansas to go to the Final Four, 27 March 2011. (Virginia Commonwealth University)

the Sunday before, there had been four million hits). "Between Friday, March 25, and Monday, March 28, VCU was mentioned or featured by the media at least 3,200 times," the *Washington Post* reported. "Typically, the university only gets about 300 mentions in that time period." University officials said there had been no attention like this since John Fenn won the Nobel Prize in 2002. "One thing I can measure is Google hits," President Rao declared happily. The university's strategic plan called for outreach to the public and closer connections to alumni. Rao said, "This will help with that."[9]

On Monday, 28 March, a line of alumni and students stretched from the VCU bookstore out to the sidewalk on Broad Street waiting for the arrival of the Final Four T-shirts, printed overnight in Florida. The bookstore expected to sell thirty thousand of them. Governor Robert McDonnell, whose daughter was an alumnus, announced that he would be in Houston for the games, as did Congressman Eric Cantor. It was a happy and capacious bandwagon. By that afternoon, more than 1,000 of the 3,250 non-student seats given to VCU for the Houston finals had already sold, and the Athletics Department prepared to conduct a raffle for the 884 tickets allotted for students.[10]

One of the lucky students was Nan Turner, a journalism major who wrote later about her experiences. Not only was the city abuzz with excitement, and the stores sold out of black and gold VCU regalia, but her phone trilled incessantly from friends and family wishing luck to the Rams. On arrival in Houston, she and her companions hurried to Reliant Stadium, the seventy thousand-seat site of the Final Four, where huge banners advertised the games, with VCU's logo prominent among them. Scott Day, Assistant Athletic Director for Athletic Communications, also described the thrill of seeing the VCU logo displayed on the stadium. Neither mentioned how much that logo, and nomenclature, had changed since the university's earliest years.[11]

Alas, the magic was exhausted, and on Saturday, 2 April 2011, VCU fell to Butler, which then fell in turn to Connecticut in the Monday championship game. The VCU game ended in Richmond with students pouring once again out of the Siegel Center into Broad Street. This time, a portion of the crowd, perhaps one hundred out of a thousand people, exploded fireworks and set afire trash containers. Policemen in riot gear moved in to direct the peaceable majority toward Monroe Park and to quell the resistors. The price of VCU's fame was that news of the postgame disruption on Broad Street now went out to the nation via the Associated Press.[12]

The disorderly conduct was small potatoes compared to the positive impression VCU fans and players had made. "This group of guys won't understand tonight, but down the road, we'll be able to look back and realize, that they changed not only VCU basketball, but the whole university," Coach Smart said after the Butler game. "A whole lot of people around the world now know what a great university this is."[13]

For the historian returning to those exciting, inspiring days in March 2011 through the documentary record, it is striking how often then the media quoted VCU students and VCU alumni about the university, their university. To name but a few of those expressing themselves in 2011: students Clare F. Anderson, Brian Gresca, Alaina Jacoby, Adele McClure, Asha Patel, Chris Peck, Geral Staten, and Drew Tolley; and alumni Dee Anderson, Taylor Early, Chelse Greaux, Melissa Harreld, Jessica Oberholtzer, and Bill Schwartz. Indeed, the *Albany Times-Union* (NY) found two VCU alumni in upstate New York happy to talk about the Rams and their alma mater. Those students and alumni, along with the confident basketball team and its charismatic coach, and all the people at both campuses wearing black and gold, represented VCU well.[14]

Eugene Trani had been a basketball fan since childhood, and he was present in 2011 as VCU became the first team ever to reach the Final Four by winning five straight games. Two years before, at the 2009 commencement, he spoke to the graduates and family and friends for the last time as president. He did not talk about VCU's campus expansion or Richmond's economic development. Nor, even though he shared the stage with graduation speaker Dr. Francis Collins, former director of the National Human Genome Research Institute, did he talk about the life sciences and the convergences of medicine, engineering, and the sciences that had guided building up one university. Rather, he thanked the graduates and declared, "The real test of our institution will be the quality of your success."[15]

Across the years since 1968, the students at VCU—from freshmen dormitories to the hospitals—give energy and spirit to the continuing work of teachers, researchers, staff, and administrators. From VCU, students go out to the city, state, nation, and world to make families, to work usefully, and to "make it real." Faculty member, musicologist, and unlikely punk rocker Dika Newlin once described herself in terms that might apply to all

VCU's people: "It is hard to find out about me because I'm involved in so many different things." One thing for certain, we all go out from VCU, the urban, research, comprehensive, Virginia, opportunity, and anchor university in downtown Richmond. As Coach Shaka Smart told his players in 2011, "We're from right here—the middle of the city."[16] In that, too, the promise of 1968 truly had been fulfilled.

NOTES

Abbreviations

BofV   Board of Visitors, James Branch Cabell Library
  CT   *Commonwealth Times*
 JBC   James Branch Cabell Library, VCU
 LVA   Library of Virginia
  NL   *Richmond News Leader*
NYT   *New York Times*
  TD   *Richmond Times-Dispatch*
TMC   Tompkins-McCaw Library, VCU
VHS   Virginia Museum of History and Culture
 WP   *Washington Post*

Introduction

1. Diner, "How Universities Migrated." Diner's essay summarizes his thesis in *Universities and Their Cities*. Although Dorn in *For the Common Good* is not focused on urban universities as such, he does close his history with the example of the University of South Florida, a relatively new urban university (175–99).

2. Diner, *Universities and Their Cities*, esp. 111–33. Other recent discussions include Acolin, Voith, and Wachter, "City and Suburbs"; Owens, "Urban Revitalization." On the University of Richmond, see UR Downtown, https://downtown.richmond.edu/.

3. Diner, *Universities and Their Cities*, provides background (14–16) but does not discuss academic medical centers in the body of the book. On mergers of academic medical centers and universities, see Azziz et al., *Strategic Mergers*, 17–18. See also Azziz, "What Is the Value?"

4. Gray, *Searching for Utopia*, 67, 79.

5. Bowen and Tobin, *Locus of Authority*, 82, 86, 135, 152–54.

6. Thelin, "Success and Excess," 109. For a contemporary warning about the economic crisis facing higher education in the early 1970s, see Cheit, *New Depression*.

7. VCU's first president, Warren Brandt, warned the faculty in his end of year report in May 1972 that "a 'superboard' to control the entire state system of higher education is 'out there, brewing.'" The General Assembly might

consider such action in its 1973 session, he said, but its effect would be unpredictable. "People who have lost faith in higher education want it," he noted ("Brandt Discusses VCU's Future with Faculty," *CT*, 18 May 1972).

8. "Virginia Colleges Waste Put at $80 Million," *WP*, 23 Jan. 1974; "Shaner Report May Benefit VCU," 24 Jan. 1974. See Musick and Cribbs, *Virginia Higher Education*, and see also "State Colleges Attack Shaner Report," *Cavalier Daily* (University of Virginia), 5 Feb. 1974; Hamilton, *Serving the Old Dominion*, 113–14; Strother and Wallenstein, *From VPI to State University*, 366–67.

9. "Refusal to Merge Colleges Pays Off, State Official Says," *Fredericksburg Free Lance–Star*, 22 Oct. 1987. On North Carolina's system, see Link, *William Friday*.

10. On Virginia politics in the late twentieth century, see Atkinson, *Dynamic Dominion* and *Virginia in the Vanguard*.

11. See, for example, Hayter, *Dream Is Lost*. On the RVA branding, see Cushing, "Sticking It to Richmond."

12. Veysey quoted in Ogren, "Sites, Students," 189.

13. Clark, *Distinctive College*; Dabney, *Virginia Commonwealth University*; James Sweeney, review of *Virginia Commonwealth University*, by Virginius Dabney, *Journal of Southern History* 55 (May 1989): 361.

14. Tuchman, *Wannabe U.*

15. Mattingly, "Introduction," 577–78, 577.

16. Bowen and Tobin, *Locus of Authority*, xv. For an early warning to historians about this evidence gap, see Rosenzweig, "Scarcity or Abundance?," 735–62.

1. THE MERGER

1. Carruth, *Medical College of Virginia Story*, 48 (statistic), 56 (quotation), 58. See also Dabney, *Virginia Commonwealth University*, 141–66. Not all the alumni opposed MCV's direction, as indicated by an enthusiastic declaration in the *Scarab* 12 (May 1963): "The Medical College of Virginia in the past one-third century has passed from a 'cubby hole' college to true university status" (1). On the history of medical education in the United States, see Starr, *Social Transformation*; Rothstein, *American Medical Schools*; and Ludmerer, *Time to Heal*.

2. Dabney, *Virginia Commonwealth University*, 171–214 (quotation p. 180). See also Hibbs, *History of the Richmond Professional Institute*.

3. Hibbs, *History of the Richmond Professional Institute*, 123–31. The school's annual yearbook took the name *Cobblestone* in 1956.

4. Tarter, "Lloyd Campbell Bird."

5. Dabney, "Albertis S. Harrison, Jr.: Transition Governor," in Younger and Moore, *Governors of Virginia*, 361–72.

6. Wallenstein, *Cradle of America*, 344–80. See also Wilkinson, *Harry Byrd*, and Pratt, *Color of Their Skin*.

7. Wallenstein, *Cradle of America*, 368–69.

8. Ibid., 367–68; Dabney, "Harrison."

9. Wallenstein, *Cradle of America*, 372–78. See also Wallenstein, "Black Southerners."

10. *Biennial Report of the State Council of Higher Education to the Governor and General Assembly of Virginia, 1962–1964*, ix, Harrison Papers, Box 108, Folder "Council of Higher Education, January–June 1964," LVA.

11. "Senate Joint Resolution No. 30" (typescript), Harrison Papers, Box 108, Folder "Council of Higher Education"; 'We Shall Fight," *Proscript*, 14 Feb. 1964; "Bill of Rights," *Medicovan* 17 (Feb. 1964): 8.

12. Dabney, *Virginia Commonwealth University*, 222; "RPI Increases Buildings and Faculty," *Proscript*, 20 Sept. 1963; "Speak or Spray," *Proscript*, 15 Nov. 1963; "Rally Round for RPI," *NL*, 19 Nov. 1963.

13. "Governor's Plan Would Also Trim Operating Funds," *Proscript*, 10 Jan. 1964; "Dr. Oliver Warns against March," *Proscript* 17 Jan. 1964; "Kicking RPI Around," *TD*, 14 Jan. 1964, quoted in Griggs, "Influence of Accreditation," 29.

14. "Gifts and Grants for Fiscal Year over 3 1/2 Million," *Medicovan* 16 (Sept. 1963): 1; "Newcomen Dinner," *Medicovan* 16 (Oct. 1963): 1, 8; "Gifts and Grants for Fiscal Year over Four Million," *Medicovan* 17 (Sept. 1964): 3; [Hoke], "First 125 Years."

15. Caravati, *Medicine in Richmond*, 40; Carruth, *Medical College of Virginia Story*, 45–47 (on Hume), 52. See also Hume's account in "The Department of Surgery," *Scarab* 15 (Feb. 1966): 1–12, and Lee, "David M. Hume," 111–19.

16. Carruth, *Medical College of Virginia Story*, 52.

17. Ibid., 52–54; "Man of the Year," *Scarab* 12 (May 1963): 17; "Dr. Kinloch Nelson Will Head Medical School July 1," *Medicovan* 16 (May 1963): 1.

18. Temple to Harrison, 24 June 1964; Otto H. Olsen, president of the state AAUP, George Mason College, to Harrison, 17 Apr. 1964, all in Harrison Papers, Box 108, Folder "Commission on Higher Education." Members of the commission are given in Russell, *Report of the Higher Education Study Commission*.

19. Lloyd C. Bird to Albertis Harrison, 16 Sept. 1964; Harrison, "Remarks at Organizational Meeting of Virginia Commission on Higher Education," 18 Sept. 1964, all in Harrison Papers, Box 108, Folder "Commission on Higher Education"; "Registration Tops 6.370; Enrollment Largest Ever," *Proscript*, 25 Sept. 1964; "Education School Is Unique," *Proscript*, 29 Oct. 1965.

20. Bird to Dr. William F. Quillian, 23 Dec. 1964; Bird to Harrison, 23 Dec. 1964, all in Harrison Papers, Box 108, Folder "Commission on Higher Education."

21. Senate Joint Resolution No. 30, introduced 7 Feb. 1964. On expenses, see Bird to Harrison, 12 May 1965; Harrison to Bird, 14 May 1965; Harrison to U.S. Senator A. Willis Robertson, 7 July 1965; Robertson to Harrison, 8 July 1965, all in Harrison Papers, Box 108, Folder "Commission on Higher Education"; Prince B. Woodard, Director, SCHEV, to presidents of colleges and universities and chairs of Boards of Visitors, 21 Sept. 1964, Harrison Papers, Box 109, Folder "Council of Higher Education—Director, Prince B. Woodard," LVA.

22. "Dr. Oliver, Governor, Hold Holiday Meeting," *Proscript*, 8 Jan. 1965; Editorial, *Proscript*, 26 Mar. 1965.

23. "Enrollment Tops 6,370," *Proscript*, 25 Sept. 1964; "All-Time High," *Proscript*, 24 Sept. 1964; "RPI Claims Biggest On-Campus Enrollment," *Proscript*, 10 Dec. 1964; "University Status Seen for College," *Proscript*, 8 Oct. 1965.

24. "MCV Estimates Future Enrollment," *Medicovan* 19 (Jan. 1967): 2; "New Clinical Center under Way," *Medicovan* 18 (Oct. 1965): 1; "Hospitals Re-Designated as North, South, East and West," *Medicovan* 18 (Nov. 1965): 1.

25. "Community Colleges Given Top Educational Priority," *Danville Register*, 26 Dec. 1965; "Highlights of Commission Report," *TD*, 26 Dec. 1965.

26. Russell, *Report of the Higher Education Study Commission*, 39–45.

27. Godwin to Smith, 25 Jan. 1966, Godwin Papers, Box 149, Folder "Medical College," LVA (all quotations); Oliver to Godwin, 1 Feb. 1966, Godwin Papers, Box 151, Folder "Richmond Professional Institute," LVA.

28. "RPI Seeks $16.9 Million," *Proscript*, 7 Jan. 1966; "RPI Unveils 14-Year Master Site Plan," *Proscript*, 18 Feb. 1966; Editorial, *Proscript*, 25 Feb. 1966. There are two maps of the campus site plan in the Godwin Papers. The first, dated January 1966, showed a campus extending from Grace Street south to Main Street. The second, dated February 1967, reflected the site as ultimately described by the Wayne Commission, stretching from Broad Street on the north across the proposed Downtown Expressway to Albemarle Street on the south, far into the Oregon Hill residential neighborhood. See Godwin Papers, Box 151, Folder "Richmond Professional Institute."

29. "Individuality of RPI in Merger Stressed," *Proscript*, 4 Mar. 1966; "$16 Million Allocation Approval Seen," *Proscript*, 11 Mar. 1966; "15-Member Study Commission Approved," *Proscript*, 18 Mar. 1966.

30. "E. A. Wayne Dies," *TD*, 5 Dec. 1990.

31. Undated list of names, headed "(Suggestions by C. O. L.)," including "14. Negro preferably an education [*sic*] 15. Woman," Godwin Papers, Box 106, Folder "Comm. Establishment University Richmond Metropolitan Areas and Recomm.," LVA.

32. "Dr. Oliver Will Retire Next Year," *Proscript*, 23 Sept. 1966; Markham D. Auman, president of student government, RPI, to Godwin, 9 Jan. 1967, Godwin Papers, Box 289, Folder "Richmond Professional Institute," LVA.

33. "School of Dentistry Receives $2 Million Grant for Addition," *Medicovan* 19 (Jan. 1967): 1; "MCV Surgeons Transplant Dog Hearts," *Medicovan* 20 (Feb. 1967): 1; "Richard Lower Dies at 78; Transplanted Animal and Human Hearts," *NYT*, 31 May 2008; McRae, *Every Second Counts*, 135–36, 156–64. See also "Heart Transplants Gained Part of Vital Beat at MCV," *TD*, 14 Jan. 1968.

34. "Early University Start Hoped," *TD*, 22 Jan. 1967, reprinted in *Scarab* 16 (Feb. 1967): 7, 17. Wayne emphasized that the interview conveyed his impressions, not those of the commission.

35. Memorandum, Kinloch Nelson to Administrative Council, 7 Feb. 1967, Dabney Papers, 7690-a1, Box 2, Folder 1, UVA; Memorandum, Kinloch Nelson to Faculty, School of Medicine, 28 Apr. 1967, 8, 10, photocopy in Kneebone's possession; Griggs, "Influence of Accreditation," 52. See also Flexner, *Medical Education*.

36. Memorandum, 28 Apr. 1967, 11; Griggs, "Influence of Accreditation," 52–54.

37. "Board Endorses Wayne Commission Recommendations," *Medicovan* 20 (Jan. 1968): 1; "Governor Signs Bill Creating University with MCV as Component," *Medicovan* 21 (Apr. 1968): 1.

38. "Richmond's Crime," *Proscript*, 14 Apr. 1967; "Barriers Erected on Shafer Street," *Proscript*, 22 Sept. 1967.

39. "Beards, Long Hair, Cut Short in Court," *Proscript*, 18 Nov. 1966; "New President Gives Opinions," *Proscript*, 22 Sept. 1967; "Two Negroes Named to Fulltime Faculty," *Proscript*, 29 Sept. 1967. On Harris, see "Grace E. Harris, Ph.D. (1933–2018)," Virginia Commonwealth University, 29 May 2019, https://gehli.vcu.edu/the-institute/grace-e-harris/.

40. Moeser and Dennis, *Politics of Annexation*.

41. Williams, "In Search of a Home." The Wayne Commission's own "Site Evaluation for a Metropolitan Richmond University" declared that the potential for an "urban-oriented" university only existed within the city (1), and the district it identified as "Mosque/Oregon Hill" in the city had the "greatest potential" (5). J. Sargeant Reynolds Papers, Mss1 R2265 a FA2, VHS (the site evaluation is dated 7 Nov. 1966).

42. "College Names President," *Proscript*, 10 Feb. 1967; "Dr. Nelson Defines Role of Urban University," *Proscript*, 24 Feb. 1967; "New President Gives Opinion," *Proscript*, 22 Sept. 1967; "Dr. Nelson Discusses Urban Age," *Proscript*, 6 Oct. 1967; "Dr. Nelson Emphasizes Need for Unifying Campus and City," *Proscript*, 10 Nov. 1967.

43. Parkerson to Wayne Commission, 18 Oct. 1967; Parkerson to Godwin and General Assembly, 25 Nov. 1967, both in Godwin Papers 1966, Box 106, Folder "Central Virginia University," LVA. Another (short-lived) proposal was for the new university to take over the University of Richmond's campus on the western edge of the city. The idea reflected the Baptist university's financial difficulties at the time more than the attractiveness of the location. See Archibald A. Campbell to Edward Wayne, 3 June 1967, Godwin Papers 1966, Box 106, Folder "Comm. To Plan Establishment Proposed State Supported Univ. Richmond Metro," and Alley, *Richmond*.

44. See O'Mara, *Cities of Knowledge*, esp. chap. 2, "'Multiversities,' Cities, and Suburbs," 58–93; and Diner, *Universities and Their Cities*, 2–4, 129–33. Charles Dorn shows that the University of South Florida set up on the outskirts of Tampa, which gave it a choice of urban issues to address, but the school also later had to scramble to establish itself within the city proper (Dorn, *For the Common Good*, 184).

45. "University Is Proposed," *Proscript*, 1 Dec. 1967; "Proposed Merger Creates Mixed Ideas," *Proscript*, 8 Dec. 1967.

46. J. Sargeant Reynolds to Mrs. C. Lathrop Reed, 8 Mar. 1968, Reynolds Papers, Folder 18, VHS.

47. "RPI-MCV Consolidation Given Assembly Approval," *Proscript*, 16 Feb. 1968. The Wayne Commission had quietly resolved the question of retaining accreditation for the new university in summer 1967. MCV's reaccreditation would have come in 1969, but if the university were founded before then, the medical school would be folded into the expected self-study and accreditation confirmation four years after the founding (Gordon W. Sweet, Southern Association of Colleges and Schools, to Wayne, 7 July 1967, Godwin Papers, Box 106, Folder "Commission to Plan Establishment").

48. BofV Minutes, 30 Apr. 1968, 24, 27 May 1968, JBC. See also Dabney Papers, 7690-m, Box 28, UVA.

49. "Courage by All," *Medicovan* 21 (June 1968): 2. See McRae, *Every Second Counts*, 277–81, and Lederer, *Flesh and Blood*, 170–78.

50. BofV Minutes, 10 June 1968, JBC; "Academic Chief Appointed," *TD*, 12 Apr. 1968; "Nelson Quits for Position outside State," *TD*, 14 June 1968; Nelson to Godwin, 24 July 1968, Godwin Papers, Box 289, Folder "Richmond Professional Institute"; BofV Minutes, 24 June 1968, 2 July 1968, JBC.

51. BofV Minutes, 24 June 1968; BofV, Executive Committee Meeting Minutes, 24 June 1968 (quotation), JBC. See also Dabney, *Across the Years*, 309–10.

52. "Acting Provost Has Dual Roles," *Proscript*, 20 Sept. 1968.

53. Dabney to Wygal, 25 June 1969; "Duties and Responsibilities of the Executive Administrator," undated typescript, both in Fred O. Wygal Papers, Box 2, Folder 10, M154, JBC (also, Dabney Papers, 7690-al, Box 2, Folder 2, UVA).

54. Wygal to Smith, 3 July 1968, Brandt Papers (RG-2), Box 6, Folder "Executive Administrator (Fred O. Wygal)," JBC; "Provost Smith Granted Leave; Colonel Heil Named Acting Provost," *Medicovan* 21 (Nov. 1968): 1; "Dr. R. Blackwell Smith, Jr., Resigns as Provost," *Medicovan* 21 (Jan. 1969): 1, 3.

55. Wygal to Andrew J. Brent, 11 July 1968, Brandt Papers (RG2), Box 6, Folder "1968 Coordinating Committee," JBC; "Suggested Areas of Planning and Action for Developing the Virginia Commonwealth University," undated memorandum, Brandt Papers, Box 6, Folder "Executive Administrator (Fred O. Wygal)"; "Acting Provost Has Dual Roles," *Proscript*, 20 Sept. 1968.

56. "Dr. Smith of MCV Is 'At Home,'" *Proscript*, 27 Sept. 1968; "President of MCV Student Government Sees No 'Visible' Changes since Merger," *Proscript*, 18 Oct. 1968.

2. Setting Out, 1968–1969

1. "Student Take-Over at Union," *Richmond Afro-American*, 6 Apr. 1968; "4,000 Pay Tribute to Dr. King at State Capitol," *Richmond Afro-American*, 13 Apr. 1968; "Reaction to Slaying Continues in State," *TD*, 6 Apr. 1968.

2. Allen and Daugherity, "Recovering a 'Lost' Story," 25–44; Moeser and Dennis, *Politics of Annexation*.

3. "VCU Urban Role Aired," *Proscript*, 27 Sept. 1968. That issue of the *Proscript* also reported the hiring of Oliver Paris as director of admissions at the Academic Campus. Heretofore admissions had actually been largely the responsibility of individual departments, as befitting a professional school. VCU would now follow standard procedures for university admissions ("Admissions Director and Policy Are New," *Proscript*, 27 Sept. 1968).

4. Kelso interview, 26 June 2012.

5. Editorial, "Puppy Burning," *Proscript*, 11 Oct. 1968; "'Puppy Burn' Slated by Student Organization," *Proscript*, 18 Oct. 1968; Kelso interview. A protest via threatened puppy burning was also carried on in the same way at the University of Cincinnati; see "Campus 'Puppy Burning' against the War Called Hoax," *WP*, 12 Nov. 1968.

6. "School Officials Bar SLG Rally Plan," *Proscript*, 25 Oct. 1968; Kelso interview.

7. "School Officials Bar SLG Rally Plan"; "Students Hold Off-Campus Rally," *Proscript*, 1 Nov. 1968.

8. "Students Meet with Renneisen," *Proscript*, 8 Nov. 1968.

9. Williams, "In Search of a Home," 38.

10. "Students Prefer Nixon in Presidential Poll," *Proscript*, 18 Oct. 1968; "How Glad We Are," *Proscript*, 8 Nov. 1968.

11. BofV Minutes, 26 Sept. 1968, JBC; Proposal, Schechter and Luth, Inc., in RG11-2.1.11, Box 1, University Advancement, VCU Logo Materials, 1968–1990, JBC.

12. Griggs, "Influence of Accreditation," 48–50.

13. Alley, *History of the University of Richmond*, 254. In 1952, UR and MCV agreed to a combined degree program in medical technology, and UR had joined MCV and R-MC in protesting to the governor after 1940 that RPI ought not to develop a collegiate program in Richmond (239–40, 254). According to "University of Richmond Comes of Age," *Richmond Mercury*, 19 June 1974, fully 50 percent of Richmond attorneys had graduated from UR's School of Law and 25 percent of the local physicians were alumni.

14. John Heil to Joann Spitler, 4 Mar. 1969, Folder "VCU Identification Committee Correspondence, 1969," RG11-2.1.11, Box 1, University Advancement, VCU Logo Materials, 1968–1990, JBC; Spitler to Warren Brandt, 19 Mar. 1969; James L. Dunn to Brandt, 21 Mar. 1969, both in RG2, Presidents' Papers, Box 8, Folder "Identification," JBC.

15. "New Afro Group Has Specific Goals," *Proscript*, 8 Nov. 1968.

16. "Harvest Queen Is Serious Actress," *Proscript*, 2 Dec. 1966; "The Observer," *Proscript*, 9 Dec. 1966.

17. McLeod interview; "Afro-American Group Recognized by SGA," *Proscript*, 8 Nov. 1968.

18. "Floyd B. McKissick to Speak," *Proscript*, 7 Feb. 1969. See also "Study of Blacks Advocated," *TD*, 20 Feb. 1969. On Baraka's 1987 visit, see "Baraka Visiting VCU," *TD*, 8 Oct. 1987.

19. "Group Petitions for Courses in Afro-American Culture," *Proscript*, 20 Dec. 1968; "Virginia Colleges Beginning to Offer 'Black Studies,'" *Richmond Afro-American*, 26 May 1969; "Afro Courses Not Needed," *Proscript*, 11 Apr. 1969.

20. Biondi, *Black Revolution on Campus*, 207. For the SAAP demands, see "Report of the Ad Hoc Grievance Committee," 30 Apr. 1969, Dabney Papers, 7690-m, Box 34, UVA.

21. "Committee Studies Demand Proposals; Open Student Meeting Held Yesterday," *Proscript*, 2 May 1969; McCormick, *Black Student Protest Movement at Rutgers*, 4.

22. "Ouster of Rector Requested by Negro Students at VCU," *TD*, 29 Apr. 1969; Editorial, "We Want . . . Now!" *Proscript*, 2 May 1969.

23. McLeod interview.

24. "VCU Students Demand the Boot for Dabney," *Richmond Afro-American*, 3 May 1969.

25. "New Post Created in Urban Studies," *Proscript*, 25 Apr. 1969.

26. "Committee Studies Demand Proposals," *Proscript*, 2 May 1969; McLeod interview.

27. "Committee Studies Demand Proposals"; "Activists at VCU Are Relatively Few," *TD*, 4 May 1969.

28. "Black Students Demand Rights," *Proscript*, 7 May 1969; Briceland interview, 2 Aug. 2011.

29. BofV Minutes, 29 May 1969, JBC.

30. Briceland interview; "VCU Appears to Have Met Blacks' List," *TD*, 6 Sept. 1969. Dabney elaborates on his resignation as rector in *Across the Years*, 310–11, and *Virginia Commonwealth University*, 237.

31. Hitz, *Never Ask Permission*, 195.

3. A UNIVERSITY EMERGES

1. "Enrollment Reaches More Than 11,650," "Afro-American Courses Added for Fall, Spring," and "Chairman Named to Student Court; Convention Begins," all 1, and Editorial, "Let's Be Consistent," 4, all in *CT*, 19 Sept. 1969.

2. *Scarab* 18 (Aug. 1969): 2, 15, 19, 26.

3. Cheit, *New Depression in Higher Education*; Thelin, *Going to College in the Sixties*, 114–15, 167–68.

4. "Dr. H. I. Willett Named to Join Education Faculty," *Proscript*, 8 Nov. 1968; "Recommendation to the Board of Visitors from the General Academic Division Virginia Commonwealth University," 30 Oct. 1968, RG2, Box 2, Folder "Board of Visitors," JBC. Walter R. Coppedge, hired then as assistant vice president under Brooke, recalled that the two campuses were so separated that they did not even share the same telephone service (Coppedge interview, 2 July 2015).

5. Dabney, *Virginia Commonwealth University*, 236; "Dr. Warren Brandt Named to Head VCU," *Radford News Journal*, 30 Jan. 1969; Strother and Wallenstein, *From VPI to State University*, 28–30; "'Challenging Situation' at VCU Attracts President, Dr. Brandt," *Proscript*, 7 Feb. 1969. Lloyd C. Bird commended the choice of Brandt to Rector Virginius Dabney, and Dabney responded that Brandt had but one deficiency, a lack of urban experience. Fortunately, he went on, H. I. Willett would be able to provide that perspective for the new president. See Bird to Dabney, 3 Feb. 1969, and Dabney to Bird, 5 Feb. 1969, Dabney Papers, 7690-al, Box 2, Folder 3, UVA.

6. Brandt interview, 32–33; Strother and Wallenstein, *From VPI to State University*, 30, 76–77.

7. Brandt interview, 18 Sept. 2007, 34; Brandt to Blackwell Smith, 3 Feb. 1969, RG2, Box 5, Folder "Congratulatory Letters on Position VCU President," JBC; Brandt to John H. Wessels Jr., 14 Apr. 1969, RG2, Box 7, Folder "Governor's Office—Misc.," JBC.

8. Minutes, BofV, 3 Oct. 1968, JBC; "University Seal, Colors Adopted," *Proscript*, 7 Feb. 1969; Agenda, 16 Jan. 1969, RG2, Box 5, Folder "Coordinating Committee, 1968," JBC; Schechter & Luth, Inc., "Development of a Total

Identification System for Virginia Commonwealth University," 16 Sept. 1968, RG11-2.1.11, Box 1, University Advancement, VCU Logo Materials, 1968–1990, JBC.

9. "University Seal, Colors Adopted" (Brandt himself gamely struggled to explain the new seal: "It's a symbol—a new symbol of a new university and it will mean what VCU is"); "VCU Adopts Seal, Colors, Unit Names," *TD*, 31 Jan. 1969; "VCU: The World at Its Doorstep," reprinted from *Commonwealth Magazine* in *Medicovan* 23 (Mar. 1970): 8.

10. *Medicovan* 22 (Feb. 1969): 3, 5; BofV, Executive Committee Minutes, 20 Mar. 1969; BofV Minutes, 27 Mar. 1969, both in JBC; "MCV Campus Now Known as VCU Health Sciences Center," *Medicovan* 22 (May 1969): 4.

11. BofV, Executive Committee Minutes, 17 Apr.; BofV Minutes, 24 Apr. 1969, JBC.

12. BofV Minutes, 24 Apr. 1969, JBC; Memorandum, Brandt to Faculty of VCU, 24 Apr. 1969, RG2, Box 1, Folder "Administrative Structure—VCU" (also in RG2, Box 6, Folder "Faculty—Misc. Correspondence 1968–1971"), JBC.

13. Brandt to "Faculty, Health Sciences Division," 28 Apr. 1969, RG2, Box 6, Folder "Faculty—Misc. Correspondence 1968–1971," JBC.

14. Godwin to Brandt, 2 June 1969; Brandt to Godwin, 13 June 1969, RG2, Box 7, "Folder "Governor's Office (Important)," JBC.

15. Heil to Brandt, 17 June 1969, RG2, Box 9, Folder "MCV—V-P for Health Sciences, John H. Heil," JBC.

16. "Report of the Survey of Medical College of Virginia," by a survey team representing the Liaison Committee on Medical Education of the Council of Education of the American Medical Association and the Executive Council of the Association of American Medical Colleges, RG2, Box 10, Folder "MCV Report of the Survey of September 8–11, 1969," JBC.

17. "MCV School Accredited for 2 Years," *TD*, 11 Mar. 1970. The Medical Education Building was renamed in honor of William T. Sanger, president of MCV from 1925 to 1956. See "Medical Building Named in Honor of Dr. Sanger," *CT*, 15 Apr. 1970.

18. "The Annual Meeting," *Scarab* 18 (Aug. 1969): 16–17.

19. Brandt to "Dear Colleague," 22 Aug. 1969, RG11-2.1.11, Box 1, University Advancement, VCU Logo Materials, 1968–1990, JBC; "Spotlight Dimming on the Name MCV?," *TD*, 30 Aug. 1969; "What Do You Think? Have You Returned Your Card?," *Scarab* 18 (Oct. 1969): 1–2.

20. Brandt to James M. Miller, Drew University, 19 June 1969, RG2, Box 4, Folder "Congratulations to Dr. Brandt and Acknowledgements," JBC.

21. "'Moratorium Day' March to Follow Teach-in Near Here," *CT*, 15 Oct. 1969; Caravati, *Medicine in Richmond*, 47–48, reproduces the competing advertisements; "Report of the Survey of Medical College of Virginia."

22. "Nixon's Vietnam War Policy Draws Support from Faculty," *CT*, 7 Nov. 1969; "So Many . . . [*sic*] and It Was Peaceful," *CT*, 20 Nov. 1969; "Ever Curse the Day You Were Born?," *CT*, 3 Dec. 1969.

23. "Students and Faculty to Aid in Decisions" and "Two Free Parking Areas Available to VCU Students," *CT*, 3 Oct. 1969; "Senate Debates University Council," *CT*, 17 Oct. 1969; "Equal Seating Rejected: SGA Threatens to Dissolve" and "An Open Letter to the President," *CT*, 12 Nov. 1969; "Brandt Defends Stand," *CT*, 13 Nov. 1969; "Candlelight Ceremony Held to Protest Assembly Seating" and "Senate Backs Equal Seating," *CT*, 14 Nov. 1969.

24. "Meeting Disrupted by Local Residents," *CT*, 12 Nov. 1969.

25. Blake to Members of the University Assembly, 3 Dec. 1969, RG2, Box 17, Folder "University Assembly 1969," JBC; "Assembly Rejects Equal Representation Motion by Senate," *CT*, 4 Dec. 1969.

26. Brandt to Linwood Holton, 5 Dec. 1969, Holton Executive Papers, 1970, Box 165, Folder "Virginia Commonwealth University," LVA.

27. "Memo—Subject: Identity of the Medical College of Virginia," *Scarab* 19 (Feb. 1970): 1–14.

28. Brandt, "Report from the President," *Scarab* 19 (Feb. 1970): 15, 22.

29. "President's Report," *Scarab* 19 (Aug. 1970): 15; Editorial, "What's in a Name?," *TD*, 8 Mar. 1970. The MCV graduates, in addition to Smith, were Carl E. Bain and R. Maclin Smith, pharmacy, and Randall O. Reynolds, dentistry.

30. "The Academic Senate of Virginia Commonwealth University, A Brief History," ca. 1970, RG2, Box 1, Folder "Academic Senate," JBC; Memorandum, B. W. Haynes and Elizabeth Reynolds to the Faculty of Virginia Commonwealth University, 3 Feb. 1970, RG2, Box 17, Folder "University Assembly 1970," JBC; "University Senate Formed," *CT*, 18 Feb. 1970.

31. Brandt to Faculty and Staff, 17 Oct. 1969; John Weeks, Llewelyn-Davies Associates, to Brandt, 5 Jan. 1970, RG2, Box 18, Folder "VCU Master Plan 1969–1970," JBC.

32. BofV Minutes, 3 Aug. 1970, JBC; Minutes of a Special Meeting of the Art Commission, 19 and 20 Feb. 1971, RG2, Box 18, Folder "VCU Master Plan, 1971–1973," JBC.

33. Brooke to "All Members of the Academic Division," 31 July 1969, RG2, Box 3, Folder "Brooke, Francis, 1972–1974," JBC.

34. "Unitary Nonracial Schools Sought Here by Court Petition," *TD*, 11 Mar. 1970; Pratt, *Color of Their Skin*, 41–46.

35. Pratt, *Color of Their Skin*, 48; Moeser and Dennis, *Politics of Annexation*, 135–42. See also Hayter, *Dream Is Lost*, esp. 63–110.

36. "Meet Dr. Brandt," *CT*, 8 Jan. 1970; "Elam Wins Presidency in Run-Off Election," *CT*, 10 Apr. 1970; "VCU, Reynolds Plan Earth Projects," *TD*, 22 Apr. 1970.

37. *Richmond Chronicle* 2 (May 1970) (courtesy of Dale Brumfield). Novelist Lee Zacharias wrote in 1981: "It was in the same block as the Grove Avenue Republic, a three-story house occupied by a band of post-hippies who had proclaimed their independence from the war machine otherwise known as the United States and celebrated their secession by blocking off Grove Avenue at night, opening their windows so the whole Fan could hear 'The Lonesome Death of Hattie Carroll' while they cavorted in the street, exploding beer bottles and passing joints. It was early afternoon, and I presumed the Republic was sleeping." See Zacharias, *Lessons*, 250–51.

38. "MCV to Present Expansion Master Plan," *TD*, 23 Apr. 1970.

39. "Black Panthers Hold Meeting in Rhoads Hall" and "First Edition to Perform Here," *CT*, 1 May 1970.

40. Strother and Wallenstein, *From VPI to State University*, 298–99; Dabney, *Mr. Jefferson's University*, 517–18.

41. Dabney, *Virginia Commonwealth University*, 237–38; "Cambodia, Killings in Ohio Spur Demonstrations in State," *TD*, 6 May 1970; "VCU Boycott Opposition Is Growing," *NL*, 6 May 1970; "Three-Day Strike Advocated" and "Faculty Says No to Strike," *CT*, 6 May 1970. "We ask that you join us in our outrage, that you refuse to attend classes for the remainder of the week as a symbol of your anger," declared flyers distributed on 5 May, which also publicized the Tuesday noon meeting on Shafer Street. See RG2, Box 17, Folder "Student Unrest," JBC.

42. "Minor Fire Drives Students from U. Va. ROTC Building," *TD*, 7 May 1970; "Memorial Held," *CT*, 7 May 1970.

43. "Student Groups to Confer with Governor Monday," *CT*, 8 May 1970; Brandt to "Ladies and Gentlemen of the Board," 9 May 1970, RG2, Box 17, Folder "Student Unrest," JBC. On Monday, Brandt sent letters of thanks to administrators, the local media, and city officials. In particular, he thanked Milton I. Wallace, director of buildings and grounds, for coping with "many false alarms and bomb scares." Brandt to Wallace, 11 May 1970, RG2, Box 17, Folder "Student Unrest."

44. "Delegation Urges Firing of Brandt," *CT*, 13 May 1970; "Governor 'Opens Doors,' Listens to Student Groups," *NL*, 11 May 1970; "Student Leaders Talk with Holton," *TD*, 12 May 1970; "Holton Warns Protesters Taxpayers May Revolt," *TD*, 13 May 1970. See also Temple to Holton, 12 May 1970; "Summary of Conference with Concerned Students, VCU (Pro-Establishment)," 12 May 1970, Holton Executive Papers 1970, Box 165, Folder "Virginia Commonwealth University," LVA.

45. *NL*, 8 May 1970, p. 21. The Board of Visitors, at its meeting on 4 June 1970, proposed a resolution of appreciation for Brandt, the faculty, and the students during those days in May, but Brandt suggested that such a resolution

was not well advised yet, and the board put it off until a later date. See BofV, Minutes, 4 June 1970, JBC.

46. "Vice President MCV Approved" and "Vice President MCV Hospitals Approved," *Scarab* 19 (May 1970): 2–3.

47. BofV, Minutes, 4 June 1970, JBC; BofV, Minutes, 23 July 1970, JBC; *Scarab* 19 (Aug. 1970): 16. Dr. Wyndham Blanton, a member of the Board of Visitors and an alumnus of MCV, told the meeting of the Alumni Association two days later that the board devoted nearly two hours to discussing the resolution. *Scarab* 19 (Aug. 1970): 18.

48. Pratt, *Color of Their Skin*, 48–49 (Supreme Court quoted on p. 46).

49. Ibid., 49–50, 59–61.

50. See RG2, Box 18, Folder "University Libraries, 1968–72," JBC, esp. Brandt to G. Gilmer Minor Jr., 29 Sept. 1970.

51. "Grove Avenue Republic!," *CT*, 15 Apr. 1970; "Grove Ave. Republic to Meet Tonight," *CT*, 17 Apr. 1970; "Hearings Continued for 17 in Melee," "Ginsberg Readings Applauded by 1500," and "Holton, Brandt Express Reactions on Disturbance," *CT*, 14 Oct. 1970.

52. "Summary of Deans' Reports on Involvement of Their Particular Schools in the Community, July 1, 1969-June 30, 1970," RG2, Box 18, Folder "Willett, Dr. H. I., 1971–1974," JBC.

53. "Brandt Is Inaugurated, Cites VCU's Urban Role," *TD*, 11 Nov. 1970; Dabney, *Virginia Commonwealth University*, 239.

54. Draft Termination Policy, Brandt to All Employees, Apr. 1970; Wilson to Wright, 4 May 1970, RG2, Box 19, Folder "Wright, Vincent F., Termination."

55. All documents found in RG2, Box 19, Folder "Wright, Vincent F., Termination," JBC.

56. Pratt, *Color of Their Skin*, 54; John V. Moeser, "Founding Member of VCU's Department of Urban Studies and Planning Looks Back on the Program Turning 30," *VCU News*, 10 June 2003.

57. "Wright Appeal Goes to Board" and Editorial, "Dean Wright," *CT*, 21 May 1971; Earl E. Wheatfall to Brandt, 21 May 1971, RG2, Box 19, Folder "Wright, Vincent F., Termination," JBC.

58. "Wright May Appeal Firing," *Petersburg Progress Index*, 28 May 1971; "VCU Named in $125,000 Damage Suit," *Danville Bee*, 16 Sept. 1971; Appeal hearing transcript, 24 May 1971, RG2, Box 16, Folder "PF-13" and Folder 1, "440–444," JBC; Handwritten statement in unknown hand, RG2, Box 17, Folder "Student Affairs, 1970–1972," JBC.

59. Pratt, *Color of Their Skin*, 56–66.

60. "VCU Named in $125,000 Damage Suit," *Danville Bee*, 16 Sept. 1971; "Wright Sues for His Job," *CT*, 17 Sept. 1971; Flyer in RG2, Box 19, Folder "Wright, Vincent F., Termination," JBC.

61. "Extensive Fire Damage Still under Investigation" and "19th Century Paper, Paintings Destroyed in Fire," *CT*, 8 Oct. 1971.

62. On the Pollak Building, see Louis W. Ballou to William O. Edwards, 15 Sept. 1971, RG2, Box 18, Folder "University Relations—Correspondence (William O. Edwards) 1968–71," JBC. On Theresa Pollak, see Pollak, *Art School*.

63. Brandt to Holton, 13 May 1970, Holton Executive Papers 1970, Box 165, Folder "Virginia Commonwealth University," LVA.

64. Ibid.

65. Hume to Brandt, 9 June 1970; Brandt to Hume, 22 June 1970, RG2, Box 8, Folder "Health Sciences Division—Miscellaneous, 1968–70," JBC.

66. Willett to Brandt, 17 June 1971, RG2, Box 18, Folder "Willett, Dr. H. I., 1971–1974."

67. BofV Minutes, 23 Mar. 1972, JBC; "Study Report on New Hospital Nears Completion," *VCU Today* 1 (May 1972): 1.

68. "Group to Hear Voices of MCV Employees," *TD*, 22 Apr. 1972. See also Holton Executive Papers 1972, Box 114, Folder "Virginia Commonwealth University Problems," LVA.

69. "'Serious Problems' at MCV Disclosed," *TD*, 19 Oct. 1972, summarizes the sequence of events. For the board's role, see also BofV, Minutes, 15 May 1972, 20 July 1972; Minutes, Executive Committee, 1 Aug. 1972; Minutes, 21 Sept. 1972, 16 Nov. 1972, JBC.

70. "'Serious Problems' at MCV Disclosed," *TD*, 19 Oct. 1972. Another sign of progress was the groundbreaking on 16 Nov. 1972 for the new 1,700-space parking deck behind the North Hospital, which would be the largest parking deck in the city. That was not enough for the authors of the *Self-Study*, who declared that "the parking situation for patients and their families is beyond belief." It went on: "Visitors coming into this area of town are frightened by the lack of safety, and many patients will not come to this Hospital because of this glaring inadequacy." *Virginia Commonwealth University Self-Study*, 414, 415.

71. "Extensive Renovation Is Outlined for MCV," *TD*, 30 Nov. 1972; "Deck Begun at MCV Campus," *VCU Today*, 22 Nov. 1972; "New MCV Hospital Proposed," *VCU Today*, 14 Dec. 1972.

72. "MCV 'Secession' Move Alleged," *TD*, 29 Nov. 1972; David M. Hume to Richard A. Michaux (copy), 30 Nov. 1972, Holton Executive Papers, 1973, Box 104, Folder "Medical College Problems 1972–3," LVA.

73. *Virginia Commonwealth University Self-Study*, 315, 404.

74. Imirie to Edward A. Willey, 23 Jan. 1973, RG2, Box 18, Folder "H. I. Willett, Consultant to the President, 1971–1974," JBC.

75. "House Approves Pike, MCV Bills," *TD*, 6 Feb. 1973.

76. Brandt to VCU Faculty and Staff, 13 Mar. 1973, RG2, Box 10, Folder "Neal, M. Pinson, Jr.," JBC. The memorandum also is in the Linwood Holton

Executive Papers, 1973, Box 108, Folder "Virginia Commonwealth University," LVA. Former Dean Kinloch Nelson told Brandt that the appointment of a provost was "an excellent step forward" (Nelson to Brandt, 19 Mar. 1973, RG2, Box 8, Folder "Health Services Division—Miscellaneous, 1971–74," JBC). To match Provost Neal at the Medical Campus, in September 1973 Brandt named Francis Brooke provost at the Academic Campus. The appointment of T. Edward Temple, former secretary of administration for Governor Holton, as vice president for development and university relations and professor of urban studies was announced at the same time. See "Temple, Brooke Get New VCU Posts," *TD*, 21 Sept. 1973.

77. Edward E. Willey to Brandt, 26 Feb. 1973, RG2, Box 7, Folder "Governor's Office (Complaints)," JBC.

78. Ibid.

79. Brandt to Blanton, 2 Mar. 1973, RG2, Box 7, Folder "Governor's Office (Complaints)," JBC.

80. "David M. Hume," 111–17 (quoted passages are on pp. 114, 116). See also "MCV Transplant Pioneer Dies in West Coast Crash," *TD*, 21 May 1973.

81. BofV, Minutes, 21 Feb. 1974, JBC. At the June 1974 meeting of the MCV Alumni Association, President Rufus P. Ellett Jr. declared that the association had been "making progress" on nomenclature. "President's Report," *Scarab* 23 (Aug. 1974): 18.

82. BofV, Minutes, 21 Feb. 1974; Minutes, 21 Mar. 1974, JBC.

83. Brandt to Neal, 25 Feb. 1974, RG2, Box 10, Folder "Neal, M. Pinson, Jr.," JBC.

84. Keyser to Godwin, 12 Aug. 1974, Godwin Executive Papers, 1974, Box 85, LVA.

85. "Millions Lost on MCV Computers," *Richmond Mercury*, 27 Aug. 1975.

86. Brandt to Faculty and Staff, 2 Nov. 1973, RG2, Box 4, Folder "Computer Center 1973–1974," JBC.

87. "Computer System Threatens MCV," *Harrisonburg Daily News Record*, 17 Aug. 1974.

88. BofV, Minutes, Executive Committee, 29 May 1974; Minutes, Executive Committee, 25 July 1974.

89. Booz Allen Hamilton, Inc., to M. Pinson Neal, 26 Sept. 1974, RG2, Box 10, Folder "MCV Hospitals: Study on Replacement and Renovation of Facilities," JBC. See also "$87.9 Million MCV Project Linked to Fiscal Changes," *TD*, 18 Oct. 1974, 1, 4.

90. Dabney, *Virginia Commonwealth University*, 250–51. See also, "Brandt to Leave VCU for 'Other Challenges,'" *TD*, 16 Aug. 1974.

91. "Brandt Had Conflicts at Virginia," *Carbondale Southern Illinoisan*, 29 Oct. 1974. The Richmond informants noted—and Professors Blake and Briceland from history and J. Ives Townsend at the Medical Campus were

quoted—that Brandt brought a quartet of faculty members to argue against him at the Board of Visitors' meeting. Nonetheless, they agreed that he considered the board's failure to approve his quota system "a major defeat." See "He'll Be Concerned about and Available to Students," *Carbondale Southern Illinoisan*, 31 Oct. 1974. Dabney in *Virginia Commonwealth University* (251) judges Brandt "able, but stubborn and opinionated," yet concedes that "Warren Brandt left Virginia Commonwealth University a distinctly better institution than it was when he became its first president."

92. "The Brandt Years Brought Growth, New Image to VCU," *VCU Today* 4 (29 Aug. 1974): 1.

93. Simon recalled in his memoir that Trani "drove me around in his little VW bug" as he campaigned for Congress. See Simon, *P. S.*, 128.

4. T. EDWARD TEMPLE AND THE COMPREHENSIVE UNIVERSITY

1. Dabney, *Richmond*, 356–57; Sorrell and Vlk, "Virginia's Never-Ending Moratorium," 1–8.

2. Dabney, *Richmond*, 358, 361.

3. "City-Suburb Dispute Grows," *WP*, 28 Jan. 1971.

4. "Richmond's School Merger Spawns a New Melting Pot," *WP*, 17 Jan. 1972.

5. Dabney, *Richmond*, 339; Ryan, *Five Miles Away*, 101–4.

6. Dabney, *Richmond*, 363–64, 369.

7. Ozmon and Craver, *Busing*, 11–16, 31.

8. "Streaking Barred in Capitol Square," *Fredericksburg Free Lance–Star*, 9 Mar. 1974.

9. "Sore Heads and Bare Bottoms: Cops and Streakers at VCU," *Richmond Mercury*, 27 Mar. 1974.

10. Zacharias, "End of the Counterculture," 143.

11. Gutek, *Education in the United States*, 317.

12. "Brandt to Leave VCU for 'Other Challenges,'" *TD*, 16 Aug. 1974; "Committee Heads University While President Sought," *VCU Today*, 29 Aug. 1974; "While Search Committee Organizes," *CT*, 6 Sept. 1974. On Temple's arrival at VCU, see "Temple, Brooke Get New VCU Posts," *TD*, 21 Sept. 1973.

13. "Temple, Hahn Eyed for Top VCU Spot," *TD*, 20 Aug. 1974; Dabney, *Virginia Commonwealth University*, 252; "Today's People," *VCU Today*, 27 Feb. 1975, 4; "Temple Named President," *CT*, 14 June 1975.

14. RG2, Box 36, Folder "Temple, T. Edward," JBC.

15. "Is Half a Library Better Than None?," *WP*, 25 Sept. 1960; "Library Sets Up Formal Sit-Down," *WP*, 30 Nov. 1960; "Mayor [*sic*] Resigns." *WP*, 4 Oct. 1966; "New Planning Chief," *WP*, 6 Dec. 1966; "Holton Will Keep Temple as

Virginia Plans Chief," *WP*, 13 Jan. 1970; "Holton Names 6 to New Cabinet," *WP*, 28 June 1972.

16. "Temple Named President," *CT*, 14 June 1975.

17. "Top Cabinet Aide Picked by Godwin," *WP*, 14 Dec. 1973; "T. Edward Temple: VCU's Second President," *VCU Magazine* 4 (Aug. 1975): 22. See also employment-related correspondence in RG2, Box 36, Folder "T. Edward Temple Vice President for Development and University Relations," JBC.

18. BofV, Minutes, 12 Sept. 1974, JBC.

19. Briceland to Temple, 27 Sept. 1974, Temple to Briceland, 3 Oct. 1974, Neal to Briceland, 9 Oct. 1974, and Brooke to Briceland, 15 Oct. 1974, all in RG2, Box 18, Folder "University Interim Administrative Committee 1974," JBC; Governor's Office to Heads of All State Agencies, 2 Dec. 1974, RG2, Box 27, Folder "Governor's Office 1970–1974," JBC.

20. "Urban University with Dual Roles," *TD*, 13 Oct. 1974.

21. "Two at VCU Being Eyed as President," *TD*, 19 Apr. 1975; BofV, Minutes, 17 Apr. 1975, JBC. On Sanger, see also "Dr. William T. Sanger Dies," *Scarab* 24 (May 1975), and "Dr. William T. Sanger: A Tribute," *VCU Magazine* 4 (June 1975): 12.

22. "Offices Displace 909 Residents," *CT*, 2 May 1975.

23. "Graduation Ceremonies Announced," *CT*, 2 May 1975; "Temple Chosen VCU President," *TD*, 29 May 1975.

24. "Temple Chosen VCU President."

25. "Your Introduction to the President of VCU," *Scarab* 24 (Aug. 1975): 1, 25–26.

26. "Ever Hear of RPI/VCU?," *CT*, 11 Apr. 1975, p. 4.

27. "Temple Named President."

28. "Temple Chosen VCU President"; "Temple Named President"; "Temple Talks on Unity, Image," *VCU Today*, 6 Aug. 1975.

29. See RG2, Box 29, Folder "Image Reports," JBC.

30. BofV, Minutes, 19 June 1975, JBC; William R. George, with Bruce Reuben, "Guidance Counselors" (May 1975), 84, 85; George, with Joseph Harman and Howard Shaffer, "Study of Richmond Residents" (June 1975), 40, both in RG2, Box 29, Folder "Image-VCU," JBC; "Further Evening Shopping Downtown Called Unlikely," *TD*, 3 Feb. 1976.

31. "Drop in Area Crime Rate Not Seen in Future," *TD*, 15 May 1975, 1, 4.

32. "A Library with Room to Grow," *VCU Magazine* 4 (Nov. 1975): 21–23.

33. "MCV Hospital Bond Denied," *CT*, 2 May 1975; "Temple Talks on Unity, Image," *VCU Today*, 6 Aug. 1975; "Temple Presents Budget to Committee," *VCU Today*, 29 Oct. 1975. For the initial Booz Allen Hamilton report, see "$87.9 Million MCV Project Linked to Fiscal Changes," *TD*, 18 Oct. 1974, 1, 4.

34. BofV, Minutes, 17 July, 18 Sept. 1975, JBC; "Budget Problems: MCV Hospital vs. General Assembly," *CT*, 26 Sept. 1975; "Temple Presents Budget to Committee."

35. "An Inauguration," *CT*, 12 Dec. 1975.

36. BofV, Minutes, 19 Sept., 18 Dec. 1975; "New Assistant Provost Appointed," *Scarab* 25 (May 1976): 16.

37. BofV, Minutes, 15 Jan. 1976; "Hospital Is Critical but Breathing Easier," *VCU Today*, 28 Jan. 1976; "Governor Godwin Recommends MCV Hospital Project," 18, and "Update, School of Medicine," 20–21, in *Scarab* 25 (Feb. 1976).

38. "School of Dentistry," *Scarab* 23 (Nov. 1974): 21.

39. Dunning, *Principles of Dental Public Health*, 442–43. Dunning noted that as of 1973, there were seventeen dental schools with TEAM grants.

40. "Va. Low-Cost Dental Plan Held in Peril by State Unit," *WP*, 16 Oct. 1975; BofV, Minutes, 16 Oct. 1975, JBC.

41. BofV, Minutes, 20 Nov. 1975, 18 Dec. 1975, 15 Jan. 1976, JBC; "Executive Council Actions in Brief," *Virginia Dental Journal* 53 (Apr. 1976): 38–39.

42. "Governor Godwin Recommends."

43. Temple to Edward E. Lane, 15 Feb. 1976, RG3, Box 10, Folder "Temple, T. Edward, President," JBC; BofV, Minutes, 19 Feb. 1976, JBC.

44. "VCU Votes Key Changes In Administrative Posts," *TD*, 19 Mar. 1976.

45. BofV, Minutes, 17 Mar. 1976, JBC; "Temple Outlines VCU Overhaul," *Scarab* 25 (May 1976): 14, 16.

46. "Temple Outlines VCU Overhaul," 16; "President of MCV/VCU," *Scarab* 25 (Aug. 1976): 23.

47. Temple to Susan E. Scovill, 7 July 1976, RG2, Box 35, Folder "Student Complaints," JBC.

48. "President of MCV/VCU," *Scarab* 25 (Aug. 1976): 23.

49. "President of MCV/VCU," 23; "VCU Annual Fund Report 1975–1976," *VCU Magazine*, 5 (Winter 1976): [20]. A draft statement, "Virginia Commonwealth University: A Comprehensive, Contemporary University for Virginians," prepared by William Edwards for Temple and dated 26 April 1976, makes the case for VCU as a comprehensive university and details the 1976 legislature's shabby treatment of the university. See RG2, Box 55, Folder "President's Staff Retreat," JBC.

50. "VCU Trims Projected Enrollment by a Third," *NL*, 24 Mar. 1976, reprinted in *Scarab* 25 (May 1976): 19–20; "President of MCV/VCU," 22–23.

51. BofV, Minutes, 20 June 1974, JBC.

52. "VCU Hiring Plan Rejected," *NL*, 1 June 1976; "VCU Is Ordered to End Hiring Plan Based on Sex," *TD*, 2 June 1976.

53. Temple to "Vice Presidents, Deans, Department Heads and other Administrative Personnel including Search Committees," RG3, Box 10, Folder

"Temple, T. Edward, President," JBC; "VCU to Appeal Judge's Ruling On Hiring Plan," *TD*, 24 June 1976.

54. Deslippe, *Protesting Affirmative Action*, 2–6. He discusses the Cramer case on p. 146.

55. "Discriminating to End Discrimination?," *CT*, 31 Jan. 1977.

56. "Homosexuality: A Normal Life Style," *CT*, 27 Sept. 1974. The American Psychological Association followed the psychiatrists in declassifying in 1975. On the APA's decision and the controversy, see Bayer, *Homosexuality and American Psychiatry*.

57. Papers of the Gay Alliance of Students 1974–1977, M357, Folder "Application for Registration as a Student Organization Gay Alliance of Students," JBC; BofV, Minutes, 17 Oct. 1974, JBC.

58. "Gay Awareness Club Rejected," "Gays Talk about Gays," and "A Step Backward," *CT*, 1 Nov. 1974. A copy of the petition, with signatures, is attached to Memorandum, Richard I. Wilson, Vice President for Student Affairs, to Brooke, Neal, and Temple, 23 Jan. 1975, RG2, Box 35, Folder "Student Affairs (folder 2)," JBC.

59. D'Emilio, "Cycles of Change," 36; "Gay Group Sues VCU for 'Rights,'" *TD*, 10 Apr. 1975; "Pretrial Talks Due on Gay Alliance's Suit against VCU," *TD*, 22 May 1975.

60. Transcription, oral history interview with Stephen Michael Lenton by Katherine Randolph, 17 Aug. 2000, Lenton Papers, Series 26, Folder 140, VHS.

61. "4th Circuit Tells VCU to Recognize Gay Group," *TD*, 2 Nov. 1976. The ruling also applied to universities in all the southern states under that court's jurisdiction.

62. BofV, Minutes, 18 Nov. 1976, JBC; "Gay Alliance Wins Two-Year Court Battle," *CT*, 12 Nov. 1976; "College Homosexual Groups Ruled Valid," *Fredericksburg Free Lance–Star*, 1 Nov. 1976.

63. "A National Trend Becomes a Concern," *The Collegian* (University of Richmond), 9 Nov. 1978; "Gay Students Join Alliance at VCU," *Flat Hat* (College of William and Mary), 22 Apr. 1977.

64. "Temple Presents Budget to Committee"; Brooke to Temple, 23 Sept. 1976, RG3, Box 10, Folder "Temple, T. Edward, President," JBC.

65. On the East Virginia Toadsuckers, see Edward H. Peeples Jr. Papers, Box 25, Folder 3, JBC, vinyl record *The Worst of the East Virginia Toadsuckers*.

66. See "To Find a Cure: The Medical College Joins in the National Fight against Cancer," *VCU Magazine* 4 (June 1975): 13; Walter Lawrence interview, 25 Apr. 1996, TMC; *VCU/MCV School of Nursing*, 82; Jablonski, "Sparks to Wildfires"; Griggs, "History of the Virginia Commonwealth University School of Business," (undated, but the oral history interviews were from 1977); "Helping Out Where the Great Society Failed," *VCU Today*, 29 Sept.

1976, 5; John V. Moeser, "Founding Member of VCU's Department of Urban Studies and Planning Looks Back on the Program Turning 30," *VCU News*, 10 June 2003; "New Major Approved," *VCU Today*, 28 Mar. 1974; "A Display of Talent," *VCU Today*, 14 Jan. 1976. Meggs was chair of the Department of Communication Arts and Design from 1974 to 1987 and died, too soon, of leukemia in 2002 (see Carter, Meggs, and Wheeler, *Meggs*); "The Anderson Gallery," 24, and "Dance: All That Jazz, Tap, Ballet," 29, in *The Works: An Inside Look at Virginia Commonwealth University* (Richmond: VCU Print Shop, 1983).

67. A. M. Holst and *Encyclopedia Virginia* staff, "Kepone (Chlordecone)," *Encyclopedia Virginia*, 16 May 2014, https://www.encyclopediavirginia.org /Kepone; Woodlief, *In River Time*; Woodlief interview, 3 Aug. 2010.

68. "VCU Evening School Growing," *TD*, 12 Jan. 1976. See also Epps, *Community of Interest*.

69. "Evening College Now Largest in U.S.," *CT*, 17 Jan. 1977; "King of the Evening College," *CT*, 25 Apr. 1978. Mapp retired in summer 1978, to be succeeded by his longtime assistant, Rozanne G. Epps, who became director of the evening school and summer session. BofV, Minutes, 18 May 1978, JBC.

70. Brandt to Holton, 19 Oct. 1970, RG2, Box 7, Folder "Governor's Office—Misc.," JBC.

71. "Kirk Named Coach," *CT*, 12 Nov. 1976.

72. "Put Another Quarter in, Coach," *CT*, 19 Nov. 1976.

73. "Laying It on the Line," *VCU Today*, 8 Dec. 1976, 2.

74. "Mission" text, RG2, Box 10, Folder "Overall Goals—VCU/MCV," JBC.

75. "Blessed with Time Ahead," *CT*, 1 Mar. 1977. See also "MCV: Prestige, Step by Step," *CT*, 15 Feb. 1977; "RPI: Fifty Years On . . . ," *CT*, 22 Feb. 1977.

76. "VCU President, 61, Dies; Was Godwin, Holton Aide," *TD*, 7 Mar. 1977.

77. "In Memory of Hibbs and Temple," *VCU Magazine* 6 (Summer 1977): 1. The magazine also noted the death of Henry H. Hibbs, the founder and provost of RPI, who died on 4 April 1977 at age eighty-nine.

78. BofV, Minutes, 17 Mar. 1977, JBC. That mission, or purpose, statement remained in effect at the time of the university's second accreditation self-study in 1983, and the full statement is published there. See *Virginia Commonwealth University Self-Study* (1983), 3–5.

79. "Minutes of an Executive Session of the Executive and Property Committees of the Board of Visitors," 10 Mar. 1977, BofV, JBC; "VCU Unit Delays Decisions," *TD*, 11 Mar. 1977.

80. "H. I. Willett Dies Ex-School Chief Here," *TD*, 21 Mar. 1986. On his duties at VCU, see Brandt to Willett, 24 Oct. 1972, and Willett to Brandt, 18 June 1974, RG2, Box 18, Folder "Willett, Dr. H. I., 1971–1974," JBC; "Willett Accepts Temporary Role," *TD*, 18 Mar. 1977.

81. "Willett: Eight Months to Move Forward," *CT*, 5 Apr. 1977.

82. "Panel Searches for New President," *CT*, 12 Apr. 1977.

83. "RPI Founder, Provost Dies," *CT*, 12 Apr. 1977.

5. Edmund Ackell and the Comprehensive Research University

1. BofV, Minutes, 23 Mar. 1983, JBC.

2. Diner, *Universities and Their Cities*, 99–109; Smartt, *Urban Universities in the Eighties*, 37–42.

3. Moeser and Dennis, *Politics of Annexation*; Silver, *Twentieth-Century Richmond*; Drake and Holsworth, *Affirmative Action*. At least two VCU graduates—Robert A. Pratt, History BA, and Michelle D. Byng, BS and MS, Sociology—chose Richmond subjects for scholarly publications at the beginnings of their careers at, respectively, the University of Georgia and Temple University. Pratt examined school desegregation in *Color of Their Skin*, and Byng analyzed Richmond city politics in this era through a series of scholarly articles, among them, "Clash of Government Structure and Racial Politics."

4. *Virginia Commonwealth University Self-Study*, 3, 5.

5. BofV, Minutes, 19 May, 16 June 1977, JBC; Fanny Butler et al. to Wyndham B. Blanton Jr., 17 May 1977, RG2-8 (Beller) Provost for Administration, Box 1, Folder "Active Administrative Committee 1977," JBC.

6. Jane Bell Gladding, "Bikes, Books, and Frisbee: Chronology of Students," *VCU Magazine* 2 (May 1973): 14–17.

7. Horowitz, *Campus Life*, xii–xiii, 245–94.

8. "Appointments Board Created," *CT*, 4 Apr. 1974; "Student Government, Rights—Is Anyone Out There?" *CT*, 16 Jan. 1976; "Student Elections: A Constitutional Right—but, for Students?" *CT*, 30 Jan. 1976; "CUSA Adopts Proposal Supporting Student Elections," *CT*, 6 Feb. 1976; "Governance System Retreats into the Woods," *CT*, 12 Nov. 1976; BofV, Minutes, 16 June, 18 Aug. 1977, JBC; "The Students Who Thought They Could," *CT*, 13 Sept. 1977; Horowitz, *Campus Life*, 252, 280.

9. BofV, Minutes, 17 Nov. 1977, JBC.

10. Dabney, *Virginia Commonwealth University*, 262–63. See also "Dental Dean Is Named," *St. Petersburg Times*, 15 July 1966; "Climate Changes for New President," *VCU Today*, 6 Dec. 1977; "Edmund F. Ackell Dies; Led VCU," *TD*, 17 May 2014.

11. "A New President," *CT*, 22 Nov. 1977.

12. "Bond Issues," *CT*, 1 Nov. 1977; "MCVH Bond Agreement Final," *VCU Today*, 8 Nov. 1977.

13. "Tug of War over Budget," *VCU Today*, 8 Nov. 1977; "Prospects Dim for New Building," *VCU Today*, 24 Jan. 1978; "Pride of Virginia," *VCU Today*, 14 Mar. 1978.

14. "VCU's New President Hopes to Soothe Growing Pains," *TD*, 26 Mar. 1978 (all quotations are from this article); Ackell interview, 30 June 1995, TMC.

15. "Virginia Commonwealth University Fifth-Year Report for the Southern Association of Colleges and Schools," RG2, Box 60, Folder "Southern Association of Colleges and Schools," JBC.

16. "Interim MCV Official Asks Dr. Ackell to Replace Him," *TD*, 21 June 1978.

17. "Dr. Neal Quits as MCV Provost," *TD*, 1 July 1978.

18. "Top MCV Post Filled for Now," *TD*, 16 July 1978.

19. "Virginia Commonwealth University Request for Final Review/Approval of Reorganization of Controller's and Treasurer's Organization," RG2, Box 60, Folder "Reorganization & Supporting Documentation," JBC; "VCU Audit Says Many Didn't Pay, Got Credit," *TD*, 17 Nov. 1978.

20. "The Ackell Interview," *CT*, 29 Apr. 1980.

21. "Physician-Dentist to Be VCU Head," *Scarab* 27 (Feb. 1978): 1.

22. "My Fellow Alumnus," *Scarab* 27 (May 1978): 1.

23. Cover statement and "Our Alumni Comment," *Scarab* 27 (Nov. 1978): 4–6.

24. "Secretary's Report," *Scarab* 28 (Aug. 1979): 21–22.

25. "Medical College of Virginia Alumni Association of Virginia Commonwealth University," *Scarab* 28 (Nov. 1979): 1–4; Dabney, *Virginia Commonwealth University*, 265–67 (quotation on p. 266).

26. Wallenstein, "Desegregation in Higher Education in Virginia."

27. U.S. Commission on Civil Rights, *Black/White Colleges*, 2. For background on these developments and their implications for higher education in North Carolina, see Link, *William Friday*, 249–366.

28. "Va. Agrees to College Desegregation," *WP*, 18 Mar. 1978.

29. "Bakke Decision Won't Change Policies," *Harrisonburg Daily News-Record*, 30 June 1978; "HEW Says Bakke Ruling Won't Restrict Programs," *WP*, 23 Sept. 1978. On Ackell and the Minority Affairs Committee, see RG2-8, Beller Files, Box 1, Folder "Ad Hoc Committee on Minority Affairs," JBC.

30. "Reflection," and "Mayor Marsh Speaks," *Reflections in Ink*, Spring 1978, 1; Randolph and Tate, *Rights for a Season*, 244.

31. "Reflection," and "Mayor Marsh Speaks," 1; "Blacks Retain Control of City Hall in Richmond," *Baltimore Afro-American*, 9 May 1978; Moeser and Dennis, *Politics of Annexation*, 178–80.

32. Randolph and Tate, *Rights for a Season*, 251–52, Edds, *Free at Last*, 124–47; "Black Councilmen vs. White Manager: Richmond Political Fight Becomes Racial," *WP*, 29 Aug. 1978; "Richmond's Blacks Flex Their Political Muscle,"

WP, 7 Sept. 1978; Shelley Rolfe, "Its People—from Tea in the 'Gyarden' to Leisure Suits," in Beach, *Only Complete Guide to Richmond*, 13.

33. "As I See It," *Reflections in Ink*, Fall 1978, 11–12. Moeser and Dennis, *Politics of Annexation*, 180–82; Drake and Holsworth, *Affirmative Action*, 56–57 (the quotation appears on p. 57). See also Randolph and Tate, *Rights for a Season*, 251–53. The dramatic showdown in August 1978 between the white economic elite and the uncowed black majority on city council is recounted in Edds, *Free at Last*, 124–27.

34. "You Can't Stop Progress," *CT*, 24 Jan. 1977.

35. Roger L. Smith to Ackell, 13 June 1978, RG2, Box 52, Folder "Health Science Building/Baptist Church 1978," JBC.

36. Ackell to Larry E. Murphy, Senior Executive Assistant to the Governor, 9 Aug. 1978, RG2, Box 62, Folder "Health Sciences Building," JBC.

37. "Request to the Legislature," *VCU Magazine*, Dec. 1979, 24; Ware interview, TMC; "Robinses Give VCU $1 Million," *TD*, 10 Jan. 1980; "Pharmacy Building Named," *VCU Magazine*, Fall 1981.

38. *Faculty Senate Newsletter*, 30 Apr. 1976, May 1977, RG9-1, Box 5, Folder "Newsletters Faculty Senate 1968–1979," JBC.

39. Minutes, Faculty Senate, 18 Apr. 1978, RG2, Box 51, Folder "Faculty Senate 1978" [1], JBC.

40. "Senate Action on University Governance," *Faculty Senate News*, Nov. 1978, RG9-1, Box 5, Folder "Newsletters, Faculty Senate 1968–1979," JBC.

41. Stepka to Ackell, 21 Sept. 1978, RG2, Box 51, Folder "Faculty Senate 1978" [1], JBC; "Report/Task Force on Governance," *VCU Today*, Mar. 1980, 4.

42. "Senate Action on University Governance," *Faculty Senate News*, Nov. 1978, RG9-1, Box 5, Folder "Newsletters, Faculty Senate 1968–1979"; *Faculty Senate Newsletter*, Jan. 1979, RG9-1, Box 5, Folder "Newsletters, Faculty Senate, 1968–1979," JBC.

43. "Residents Plan to Fight VCU," *TD*, 15 Oct. 1978.

44. "VCU Officials Try to Reassure Fearful Residents," *TD*, 16 Dec. 1978.

45. Ackell, "Richmond's VCU: Urban University in Change," *TD*, 28 Dec. 1978.

46. "Door Shut on Foes of VCU Expansion," *NL*, 18 Jan. 1979; "90 VCU Students Applaud Expansion Plan Foe," *NL*, 30 Jan. 1979. See also *A Community Profile of Oregon Hill* (Richmond: School of Social Work VCU, [1976?]).

47. "Foes of VCU Find Climate Bad for Rally," *TD*, 16 Mar. 1979.

48. "900 Car Deck for VCU Gets Commission OK," *NL*, 21 Feb. 1979.

49. "The Ackell Interview," *CT*, 20–26 Mar. 1979.

50. "Ackell Interview Draws Reactions," *CT*, 27 Mar. 1979; *Faculty Senate Newsletter*, Apr.–May 1979, RG9-1, Box 5, Folder "Newsletters, Faculty Senate, 1968–1979," JBC. See also Minutes, Faculty Senate Meeting, 17 Apr. 1979, RG2, Box 51, Folder "Faculty Senate 1980," JBC.

51. "VCU-ACLU Calls for Ackell Apology," *CT*, 27 Mar. 1979; "Oregon Hill Unit Expands Battle," *TD*, 24 Mar. 1979.

52. "VCU Opts for Sunbelt," *Harrisonburg Daily News-Record*, 21 Mar. 1979; "Hello, Sun Belt," *TD*, 21 Mar. 1979; "Good News: Rams Join Sun Belt Conference," *CT*, 27 Mar. 1979.

53. "Good News"; "Bad News: Kirk Quits," *CT*, 27 Mar. 1979.

54. "His Game Hasn't Changed; for Barnett, Competition's Still the Key," *TD*, 27 May 1979; "New Head Ram," *VCU Magazine*, Fall 1979, 20.

55. "Lash to Direct Hospital," *VCU Magazine*, Summer 1979, 24; *Patient Information Handbook*, p. 4, RG2, Box 52, Folder "Hospitals General 1979," JBC.

56. "MCV Names Director, Creates Two Aide Jobs," *TD*, 10 Mar. 1979.

57. Ackell interview, 30 June 1995, TMC.

58. *The Virginia Plan for Higher Education* (Richmond: SCHEV, 1979); Diner, *Universities and Their Cities*, 91 (quoted phrase); Freeland, *Tranforming the Urban University*, 1, 4.

59. *Virginia Plan for Higher Education*.

60. See brochure "A Comprehensive, Contemporary University for Virginians," VCU, Office of University Relations/Publications, [1978].

61. President's Newsletter to Board of Visitors, May 1979, RG2, Box 55, Folder "President's Retreat," JBC; "I-A Institution," *VCU Magazine*, Fall 1979, 20, 22; "The Ultimate in Status Symbols," *VCU Today*, 26 Sept. 1979, 2.

62. Heilig and Mundt, *Your Voice at City Hall*, 31–32; Randolph and Tate, *Rights for a Season*, 152–63. The Bibos epithet, referring to wild oxen, was so arcane that author Donald P. Baker thought the term was "Bilbos," "a reference to the late Mississippi Senator Theodore G. Bilbo, a white supremacist." See Baker, *Wilder*, 131.

63. "Richmond Bond Sales Halted by Controversy," *WP*, 4 Jan. 1979; Richmond Independent Taxpayers Association, *The Taxpayers Report: Richmond's Taxes and Spending, 1970–1980* (Richmond: Author, 1979). See also *Report of the Capital City Government Commission*, Executive Summary, A3, 29 June 1981, William V. Daniels Papers, Mss1 D22709, Folder 1, VHS.

64. Michie and Mashaw, "Annexation and State Aid to Localities," 43; Sorrell and Vlk, "Virginia's Never-Ending Moratorium," 1–8.

65. "Richmond's Quiet Mayor," *WP*, 24 May 1979.

66. "VCU Won't Halt Oregon Hill Plan," *TD*, 21 Sept. 1979.

67. "Promises Made to Residents," *TD*, 22 Oct. 1979.

68. "Criticism of VCU Rejected," *TD*, 20 Nov. 1979; "Oregon Hill Touches Off Continued Controversy," *CT*, 20 Nov. 1979.

69. "The Students Who Thought They Could," *CT*, 13 Sept. 1977; "Campus Government," in Students of English 102-38, 102-50, and 102-75, *The Works*, 123–24; "Dr. Al Hangs It Up," *CT*, 9 Dec. 1980.

70. Briceland interview, 2 Aug. 2011; Notes, Meeting with Executive Committee of the Faculty Senate, 10 Sept. 1979, and Briceland to Ackell, 13 Sept. 1979, both in RG2, Box 51, Folder "Faculty Senate, 1980," JBC.

71. *Faculty Senate Newsletter*, Nov. 1979, RG9-1, Box 5, Folder "Newsletters, Faculty Senate 1968–1979," JBC. On the trend to contingent faculty, see, for example, Baldwin and Chronister, *Teaching without Tenure*; Donoghue, *Last Professors*; and Ginsberg, *Fall of the Faculty*.

72. BofV, Minutes, 20 Sept. 1979, JBC; "An Anniversary for the Times," *CT*, 18 Sept. 1979; "Extra! Extra! Read All about It!," *VCU Magazine*, Dec. 1979, 24.

73. "Report/Task Force on Governance," *VCU Today*, Mar. 1980; *Faculty Senate Newsletter*, Apr. 1980, RG9-1, Box 5, Folder "Newsletters, Faculty Senate, 1980–1991," JBC.

74. "Report/Biennial Budget Plan," *VCU Today*, 23 Apr. 1980; President's Newsletter to the Board of Visitors, May 1979, RG2, Box 55, Folder "President's Newsletter, 1979–1981," JBC; "Group Crashes Meeting at VCU," *TD*, 21 Mar. 1980.

75. "The Ackell Interview," *CT*, 29 Apr. 1980.

76. "Protection Given in Some City Races," *TD*, 2 May 1980.

77. "Political Pulse Quickens as Elections Draw Near," *WP*, 5 May 1980; "Most Attention Focuses on 8th District Today," *TD*, 6 May 1980; "Blacks Retain City Council Majority," *TD*, 7 May 1980. On McDaniel, see Drake and Holsworth, *Affirmative Action*, 58; "Claudette McDaniel, Pioneering Council Member, Dies," *TD*, 5 Nov. 2010.

78. *CT*, 29 July 1980.

79. *Faculty Senate Newsletter*, Sept. 1980, RG9-1, Box 5, "Newsletters, Faculty Senate, 1980–1991," JBC. See also "Task Force Studies Controversial University Governance Structure," *CT*, 21 Oct. 1980.

80. Minutes, 18 Sept. 1980, University Assembly, RG2, Box 61, Folder "University Assembly Meetings 1980," JBC.

81. *Faculty Senate Newsletter*, Oct. 1980, Feb. 1981, RG9-1, Box 5, "Newsletters, Faculty Senate, 1980–1991," JBC.

82. *CT*, 23 Sept. 1980; "A Consumer's Guide to Richmond Bands," and "Second Thoughts for a Second Issue," *CT*, 30 Sept. 1980. On Dickie Disgusting, see also Kollatz, *True Richmond Stories*, 146, and Soffee, *Snake Hips*, 142.

83. "Not for Sensitive Readers," *CT*, 7 Oct. 1980 (Ackell's letter appeared in that issue also). See also Brumfield, *Richmond Independent Press*, 87–89.

84. "Virginius Dabney and the History of VCU," *CT*, 5 Mar. 1985.

85. Newsletter, Oct. 1980, RG2, Box 55, Folder "President's Newsletter, 1979–1981," JBC; "Today's Chuckle," *CT*, 25 Nov. 1980; Fuller to Richard I. Wilson, 1 Dec. 1980, RG2, Box 60, Folder "Task Force on Student Media," JBC.

86. "Study Ordered of VCU Media," *TD*, 16 Jan. 1981; BofV, Minutes, 15 Jan. 1981, JBC; "Won't Be Public Relations Paper, VCU Editor Says," *TD*, 17 Jan. 1981; "Has the Punishment Begun?," *CT*, 27 Jan. 1981.

87. Brumfield, *Richmond Independent Press*, 86; "Sue Dayton Photographs the Hotel Jefferson," *CT*, 7 Oct. 1980; Herbert, *Jefferson Hotel*, 156.

88. "VCU Is Housing 573 in Hotels," *TD*, 31 Aug. 1978; "All You Need to Know about . . . Housing," *CT*, 30 Sept. 1980.

89. Minutes, University Assembly, 3, 15 Sept. 1981, RG2, Box 61, Folder "University Assembly Meetings 1981," JBC; BofV, Minutes, 24 Sept. 1981, JBC.

90. "Report of the Richmond Commission on Human Relations on Racial Polarization in the City of Richmond," 6–7, 31 Mar. 1981, RG2, Box 56, Folder "Richmond Chamber of Commerce," JBC (also found in William V. Daniels Papers, Mss1 D22709, Folder 6, VHS).

91. Harris, "Richmond," 46–52.

92. "Tensions in the Richmond Community: A Report of the Richmond Urban Institute," 10–12, 13–17, RG2, Box 56, Folder "Richmond Chamber of Commerce," JBC.

93. Minutes, Legislative Affairs Committee, 18 Nov. 1980, RG2, Box 56, Folder "Richmond Chamber of Commerce," JBC. See also *Report of the Capital City Government Commission*.

94. Minutes, Dialogues Group One, 16 Jan. 1981, William V. Daniel Papers, 1977–1984, Mss1D2270a, Folder 5 "Chamber of Commerce Dialogues on Racial Relations," VHS. See "Reflections on Reflections," *CT*, 14 Oct. 1980. Executive Editor Andrew Lee White said only that he "refused to waste any more energy than it takes to type these words to vindicate this publication." See "Viewpoint," *Reflections in Ink*, Oct. 1980, 2.

95. "Report of the Richmond Commission on Human Relations"; "Statement of Purpose Political Interaction Task Force Richmond Chamber of Commerce," 3 June 1981; and Bob Martin to Members of the Political Interaction Task Force, 18 June 1981, RG2, Box 56, Folder "Richmond Chamber of Commerce," JBC.

96. "A Joint Effort," *VCU Magazine*, Spring 1981, 22–23. See also "Revitalizing the Capital City," *VCU Magazine*, 1981–1982, [9].

97. "A Joint Effort," *VCU Magazine*, Spring 1981, 22–23; Schill and Nathan, *Revitalizing America's Cities*, 5, 24.

98. Schill and Nathan, *Revitalizing America's Cities*, 7, 45.

99. Ibid., 93.

100. "Demolition Dismembers Oregon Hill," *CT*, 14 July 1981.

101. "Revitalizing the Capital City," [9]; "Richmond Plans Convention Complex," *Harrisonburg Daily News Record*, 13 Feb. 1982. See also Drake and Holsworth, *Affirmative Action*, 60–61, 74–77.

102. "Decision to be Made on Redistricting Richmond," *WP*, 26 Aug. 1981; "Marsh-Backed Plan on Redistricting OK'd," *NL*, 31 Aug. 1981; "U.S. Backs Richmond Ward Setup," *WP*, 1 Sept. 1981; Moeser and Dennis, *Politics of Annexation*, 184–85.

103. "Revitalizing the Capital City," [9]; "Richmond Settles Suit Blocking Hilton Hotel Project," *WP*, 27 July 1981.

104. "Construction," *Scarab* 30 (Feb. 1981): 22–23; "Smith Honored," *Scarab*, 30 (Aug. 1981): 24; "Facilities Management: Medical Campus," *CT*, 8 Sept. 1981.

105. "Facilities Management."

106. "VCU Panel Backs Independent Student Media," *TD*, 11 June 1981.

107. Ackell to Crutchfield, 21 July 1981, RG2, Box 60, Folder "Task Force on Student Media," JBC.

108. "The 'World' According to Ackell: It's a 'Street University,'" *CT*, 8 Sept. 1981, 16–17, 27. On *ThroTTle*, see Brumfield, *Richmond Independent Press*, 123–42.

109. Minutes, University Assembly, 4 Feb. 1982, RG2, Box 61, Folder "University Assembly Meetings 1981–1982," JBC; "VCU Fee, Tuition Boost Approved," *TD*, 21 May 1982.

110. Jesse L. Steinfeld, "MCV's School of Medicine 1980," *Scarab* 29 (May 1980): 21–25. Dabney states that Ackell convinced Steinfeld to mute his antismoking views after an uproar followed his appointment (*Virginia Commonwealth University*, 283).

111. "The New Hospital: A Skyline Altered," *Scarab* 31 (May 1982): 3; "The Architectural Perspective: A Campus Revisited," *Scarab* 31 (Nov. 1982): 16; "A New Hospital for Virginians," *VCU Magazine*, Summer 1982, 19–20.

112. *VCU Today*, 8 Sept. 1982, gave the university protocol for Main Hospital: "The title should be used when giving directions to others or when making any reference to the new hospital" (3); Garrett Epps, "Impressions of a University," *VCU Magazine*, Summer 1983, 19–20. See also Lawrence interview, 25 Apr. 1996, TMC.

113. Hayter, *Dream Is Lost*, 216–19 (on Project One, see also pp. 172–73).

114. "Black Backed by Whites Is Richmond Mayor," *NYT*, 4 July 1982; "The Posture of a Leader: Mayor Roy West Tries to Sidestep a Tightrope," *CT*, 21 Sept. 1982; Silver, *Twentieth-Century Richmond*, 316–20; Drake and Holsworth, *Affirmative Action*, 61–64, 79–82; Byng, "Clash of Government Structure and Racial Politics," 79–80.

115. "First Honors Convocation," *VCU Today*, 20 Oct. 1982; "VCU's New Performing Arts Center Is Open," *VCU Today*, 8 Sept. 1982; "Secretary of the Year," *VCU Magazine*, Summer 1981, 24.

116. Ackell, "Challenge and Change," *VCU Today*, 20 Oct. 1982 (from a speech to the faculty in September); "From the Enclave of Power: Presenting VCU's President," *CT*, 14 Sept. 1982.

6. Hard Times, Hard Feelings, and Conflicts with the Neighbors, 1980s

1. Diner, *Universities and Their Cities*, 101–9; Dorn, *For the Common Good*, 183–84. See also Rodin, *University and Urban Renewal*, 30, 38.
2. Memorandum, Hall to Ackell, 18 June 1981, RG2, Box 67 (Ackell Additional), Folder "Financial Exigency Plan 1981," JBC.
3. "Legislators Say Tax Veto a 'False Hope,'" *Harrisonburg News Record*, 21 Oct. 1981. See also Atkinson, *Virginia in the Vanguard*, 17–46.
4. "Hike in College Standards Asked," *Harrisonburg Daily News Record*, 26 Mar. 1982; "Robb: Coppola Could Have Lived," *Winchester Star*, 19 Aug. 1982; "Opening Remarks from the President," *Faculty Senate Newsletter* 11 (Nov. 1982), RG9-1, Box 5, Folder "Newsletters, Faculty Senate, 1968–1979," JBC; "The Assembly: Money Will Be Session's Major Issue," *Winchester Star*, 8 Jan. 1983; "Despite Economy, Fewer Cuts Possible, Robb Says," *Winchester Star*, 12 Feb. 1983; "Tuition Costs Could Rise 10%," *Winchester Star*, 18 Oct. 1983.
5. "Honors Program Attracts Academic Excellence," *CT*, 20 Sept. 1983.
6. "MCV Takes New Strides in Fight against Cancer," *CT*, 6 Dec. 1983–23 Jan. 1984; Lawrence interview, 25 Apr. 1996, TMC.
7. "Commons Plans Festive Opening," *CT*, 6 Dec. 1983–23 Jan. 1984.
8. "Media Commission Recommended" and "Ron and Ed Have a Chat," *CT*, 1 Nov. 1983; "SMC Rejected by Committee on Student Affairs," *CT*, 22 Nov. 1983.
9. "Ackell and the Security of Silence," *CT*, 14 Feb. 1984.
10. "Political Science, Sociology in Limbo," *CT*, 31 Jan. 1984.
11. "Ackell: 'Some People Have Had to Suffer,'" *CT*, 21 Feb. 1984.
12. "Ackell Says Liberal Arts May Need Repackaging," *TD*, 12 Sept. 1984.
13. "No Photographers at Ackell Conference," *CT*, 11 Sept. 1984.
14. "A President Behind Closed Doors," *CT*, 18 Sept. 1984; "Richardson Terms Discrimination Intolerable," *CT*, 9 Oct. 1984.
15. "Ackell: Building an Image for an Urban School," *CT*, 26 Mar. 1985.
16. "VCU Emerges 'Stronger' from Four Difficult Years," *NL*, 20 Aug. 1985; "Ackell Praises Past; Sets Sights on More Money," *TD*, 21 Aug. 1985.
17. "Reaction to Budget for Colleges Mixed," *NL*, 21 Jan. 1986; "College Presidents Applaud Increases," *TD*, 21 Jan. 1986.
18. "Ackell Says Mills' Contract as AD Will Not Be Renewed," *TD*, 18 April 1986.
19. "Unlikely Scholars Often Beat Odds, Study Shows" and "First Five Semesters, Three Summers Little Help on Degree," *TD*, 25 Aug. 1985.
20. "How Much Help Can Tutors Give?," *TD*, 26 Aug. 1985; "Pollio Changes Tune on Academics," *TD*, 17 Sept. 1985; Townes interview, 3 June 2014.

21. "Love-Hate—Pollio Brings Emotions to VCU Coaching Job," *TD*, 15 Oct. 1985; "Winterfest—VCU Celebrates Its First Full Homecoming," *TD*, 14 Feb. 1986; "Neither Fans nor Rams Ever Gave Up," *TD*, 2 Mar. 1986.

22. "VCU President Says Change in AD Likely," *TD*, 31 Mar. 1986; "Friends' Ad, Contributors, Support Mills," *TD*, 8 Apr. 1986; "Mills' Time as Rams' AD Definitely Over," *TD*, 18 Apr. 1986.

23. "Sander Brings Bright Image to VCU," *TD*, 8 July 1986; "VCU Set to Name Sander AD," *TD*, 7 July 1986; "Fund Raising Key as VCU Hires Sander," *TD*, 8 July 1986.

24. "VCU Aligns with Schools That Offer Second Chance," *TD*, 14 Jan. 1987.

25. "VCU Will Seek $52 Million in First Full-Scale Fund Drive," *NL*, 14 Aug. 1986; "Charles Thalhimer to Lead VCU Drive," *TD*, 15 Aug. 1986; "VCU Raises $20 Million toward Goal," *TD*, 20 Nov. 1986.

26. "Maupin-Maury Campaign Moves Ahead," *Scarab* 35 (Nov. 1986): 2–6.

27. "Preliminary Figures Show VCU Fall Enrollment Down," *TD*, 26 Sept. 1986.

28. "Report Lists 26 Percent Decline in Crime at VCU," *NL*, 20 Nov. 1986; Alexia Cooper and Erica L. Smith, "Homicide Trends in the United States, 1980–2008," U.S. Department of Justice Bureau of Justice Statistics (NCJ 236018), Nov. 2011, p. 29, http://www.bjs.gov/content/pub/pdf/htus8008.pdf; "Uniform Crime Reports and Index of Crime in Richmond in the State of Virginia enforced by Richmond Police from 1985 to 2005," The Disaster Center, 2006, http://www.disastercenter.com/virginia/crime/13986.htm.

29. "Marketplace Opens amid Great Fanfare," *NL*, 18 Sept. 1985. For background to, and a critical analysis of, the so-called festival marketplaces, of which Sixth Street Marketplace was an example, see Bloom, *Merchant of Illusion*.

30. Hayter, *Dream Is Lost*, esp. chap. 5. On the Richmond set-asides—Richmond's Minority Business Utilization Plan of 1983—and the case of *Richmond v. Croson*, see Byng, "Clash of Government Structure," 77–91.

31. "VCU Seeking City Approval to Close More Streets," *TD*, 4 Aug. 1985.

32. "Ex-VCU Night School Chief Leaves 'Remarkable Record,'" *TD*, 14 July 1986.

33. "Debate Stirs Anew over Name for MCV," *TD*, 21 Oct. 1987.

34. "Ackell Gets Favorable Marks," *TD*, 19 June 1988.

35. "Disarray in VCU Buying Methods May Be Wasting Funds, Report Says," *TD*, 12 July 1987; "VCU to Try to Boost Purchasing Staff," *TD*, 14 July 1987.

36. "VCU Rules 'by Fear,' Letter Says," *NL*, 8 June 1988. See also "Facilities Management Employees Plan 'Sick-Out,'" *CT*, 25 Apr. 1988.

37. "Ackell Gets Favorable Marks," *TD*, 19 June 1988.

38. "VCU Employees Sent Questionnaires in Investigation," *NL*, 3 Aug. 1988.

39. "VCU Keeps Department for Now," *NL*, 9 Aug. 1988.

40. "VCU Employees Evaluating Report by Special Panel," *NL*, 12 Nov. 1988.

41. "School of Medicine: Alive and Well," *Scarab* 37 (Feb. 1988): 13–16.

42. "School of Basic Health Sciences: Smallest Is Largest," *Scarab* 37 (Aug. 1988): 22–25; "School of Dentistry: A Mandate for Redirection," *Scarab* 37 (Nov. 1988): 2–5; "Dr. Connell's Contract Not Renewed; Dr. Andrako Named Acting V.-P." *Scarab* 37 (Nov. 1988): 23.

43. BofV, Minutes, 19 July 1984, JBC; "Changing of the Guard," *Scarab* 33 (Nov. 1984): 22; "Dental Dean Joins Staff," 19, and "Medical Dean Appointment," 22, *Scarab* 34 (Aug. 1985); Ackell, "The Future of Health Care," *Scarab* 34 (May 1985): 19 (the quoted phrase came from President Ackell's address to the medical faculty in fall 1984).

44. Alastair M. Connell, "Address to MCV Campus Faculty February 5, 1985," RG9-1, Box 5, Folder "Reports, Addresses 1981–1985" [2], JBC; Connell, "How MCV Can Meet New Challenges," *TD*, 25 Nov. 1985; "MCV West Leaves a Proud Legacy," *TD*, 26 Oct. 1986.

45. "North Hospital Means New Era for MCV Care," *TD*, 19 Oct. 1986.

46. "MCV Officer Might Not Return," *TD*, 3 July 1988.

47. "MCV Top Official Seems Surprised by Quick Ouster," *NL*, 22 July 1988; "Academic Chief at MCV Removed," *TD*, 22 July 1988.

48. "Ousted MCV Official Calls for Openness," *NL*, 23 Aug. 1988; "MCV's Connell Prescribes Dose of Candor," *TD*, 24 Aug. 1988.

49. "Ackell Denounces Assertion of Faculty Problems at VCU," *TD*, 26 Aug. 1988; "Ackell: 'Candor' Talk Was 'Absolute Folly,'" *NL*, 25 Aug. 1988.

50. Connell, "A VCU Vice President Takes His Leave," Ackell, "The President Responds," and editorial, "End of Discussion at VCU?," *TD*, 27 Aug. 1988.

51. "VCU's Board Solidifies Power of Ackell to Oust Vice Presidents," *TD*, 16 Sept. 1988. See also BofV, Minutes, 15 Sept. 1988, JBC; "MCV Names Interim Official," *TD*, 20 Sept. 1988.

52. "Unity in Diversity—VCU Hopes Bash Will Strengthen Ties," *NL*, 3 Nov. 1988; Dabney, *Virginia Commonwealth University*, 392, 393.

53. "'Big Party' Wraps Up Anniversary," *CT*, 28 Mar. 1989; "Ram Dresses Up for Occasion When VCU Celebrates in Style," *TD*, 5 Nov. 1988; "VCU Celebration Is Just Beginning," *TD*, 7 Nov. 1988.

54. "VCU Celebration Is Just Beginning," *TD*, 7 Nov. 1988; "Happy 150th," *TD*, 29 Nov. 1988.

55. "VCU School of Medicine, Why?," *Scarab* 38 (Feb. 1989): 15–16.

56. "MCV's Alumni Association: Reviewing Yesterday, Examining Today, Looking toward Tomorrow," *Scarab* 38 (Feb. 1989): 13–14.

57. "Weathering a Winter of Discontent: 4 Alumni Look Forward to Brighter Days," *Scarab* 38 (May 1989): 24–27.

58. "VCU President to Retire in 1990; Baliles Mentioned as Successor," *TD*, 17 Mar. 1989; "Ackell Announces 1990 Retirement," *CT*, 28 Mar. 1989.

59. "VCU Tops Goal Ahead of Schedule," *NL*, 25 Oct. 1989; "VCU Says Fund Drive Tops Minimum Goal," *TD*, 26 Oct. 1989.

60. "VCU Campus to Expand," *CT*, 28 Mar. 1989.

61. Ibid.; "Master Plan Details Many New Changes," *CT*, 4 Apr. 1989.

62. "Residents Wary of VCU Expansion," *NL*, 23 Mar. 1989; "VCU's West Campus Proposal Calls for Buying 28 More Acres," *TD*, 23 Mar. 1989.

63. "Civic Groups, VCU Officials Meet," *TD*, 14 Apr. 1989.

64. "VCU Sees Chance to Capitalize on Status as an Urban University," *TD*, 7 May 1989.

65. "Residents' Views on VCU Blueprint Heard by Board," *NL*, 19 May 1989.

66. "Cohesive and Coherent," *NL*, 23 May 1989; "Up with VCU," *TD*, 24 May 1989.

67. "Concerns about VCU Plan Voiced," *NL*, 28 June 1989; "Coalition Asks Richardson to Postpone VCU Resolution," *NL*, 21 July 1989; "VCU Neighbors Are Heartened by Alternatives," *NL*, 16 Aug. 1989.

68. "Ask the Candidates," *TD*, 24 Oct. 1989; "Candidates in the 68th Agree VCU Should Not Expand into the Fan," *TD*, 26 Oct. 1989; BofV, Minutes, 16 Nov. 1989, JBC.

69. "VCU's Course," *TD*, 15 Nov. 1989; "VCU's Compromise," *NL*, 17 Nov. 1989; "VCU: A Community Asset," *TD*, 19 Nov. 1989.

70. See Jones, "Dynamic Social Norms," 281–84; Heller, "Introduction," 1–9. On the University of Virginia, see Leffler, "Mr. Jefferson's University," 56–87.

71. "Women's Network," Special Collections Vertical Files, JBC. Debates over the proposed Equal Rights Amendment to the U.S. Constitution also roused women to organize in support of (and opposition to) the amendment from the 1970s to its Virginia defeat in 1982. See Kierner, Loux, and Shockley, *Changing History*, 323–30.

72. "Afro-American Courses Remain Popular—Few Students Major in Subject," *NL*, 19 Feb. 1987; Bazin, "Gender Revolution," 67–68.

73. Kennedy, *Banking Crisis of 1933*; Kennedy, *If All We Did*, xiii. In 2009, Bo Lundgren, the Swedish minister who successfully managed a banking crisis in that nation in the 1990s, declared that Kennedy's book on the American banking crisis had been "one of the most useful" books to him at that time ("The Swedish Model," *The Economist*, 28 Jan. 2009).

74. In the mid-1990s, Scully conducted a survey of women's studies programs and departments for the National Women's Studies Association, which found that VCU's arrangement—an interdisciplinary program dependent on faculty formally assigned to departments (and thus to disciplines)—was typical, that such programs had less control over curriculum than traditional departments, and that despite much interdisciplinary scholarship and pedagogy in women's studies, programs remained multidisciplinary at best, with

the interdisciplinary ideal yet to be met. See Scully, "Overview of Women's Studies," 122–28.

75. Scully, "Program Celebrates 10th Anniversary," *Women's Studies News* 3 (Spring 2000): 1. See also Brinson and Hampton, "Women in Medicine," 50.

76. "Task Force Requests Women's Studies Program," *CT*, 25 Apr. 1988; interview with Alexis Ruffin, July 2015. According to the fall 1989 issue of *Women's Times*, the newsletter of the Virginia Women's Studies Association, a Funds for Excellence Grant from SCHEV provided the new program with start-up operating funds. See newsletter in Betsy Brinson Papers, Mss1 B7725b FA2, Series 12, Folder 138, VHS.

77. "Pollio Says the Talent Is Missing," *TD*, 11 Mar. 1987; "Mr. Bartow's Tournament Finally Comes to Richmond," *TD*, 22 May 1987.

78. "Baliles' Stand on Sports Backed," *TD*, 16 June 1987; "VCU Study Raises Graduation Worry," *TD*, 19 Nov. 1987; "Rams Big Winners on the Boards," *TD*, 22 Mar. 1988.

79. "VCU's Brown Collapses, Dies," *TD*, 3 Jan. 1989; "Rams Set to Resume Season after Service," *TD*, 4 Jan. 1989; "Pollio's Last Hurrah Deserves a Big Cheer," *TD*, 2 Mar. 1989; "VCU's Cursed Season Comes to a Merciful Close," *TD*, 6 Mar. 1989.

80. "Smith Eyes VCU Offer in Visit Here," *TD*, 18 Mar. 1989; "New VCU Coach Has Wit, Winning Attitude," *TD*, 21 Mar. 1989.

81. "State's Increasing Demand on Higher Education Cited," *TD*, 7 Jan. 1989; "Colleges Urged to Put Teaching before Facilities," *TD*, 15 Nov. 1989.

82. "Study Calls for Sharing with City," *TD*, 17 Feb. 1989.

83. "In Brief," *NL*, 17 Nov. 1989; "A Steep Decline in Richmond's Murder Rate," *Multimedia Journalism*, 16 Nov. 2011.

84. "Ackell to Step Down as President of VCU," *NL*, 16 Mar. 1989; "VCU Graduates Enter 'Real World,'" *TD*, 20 May 1990.

7. Playing through the Rain, 1990–1992

1. "... And Future," *TD*, 26 Sept. 1988; "Local Leaders Urged to Find Own Solutions to Problems," *TD*, 15 Mar. 1989.

2. "1986 in Review—the State," *TD*, 2 Jan. 1987; "Bobb's Team Facing Tough Choices in 1988," *TD*, 4 Jan. 1988.

3. "Virginia Colleges Jockey for Position in Race for Students of the Future," *NL*, 22 Aug. 1989; "Can VCU Facilitate Growing Student Population?," *CT*, 26 Sept. 1989; "Coming Soon: A New Mission for VCU?," *CT*, 19 Sept. 1989; "A 'Vision' for Universities," *TD*, 17 Nov. 1989.

4. "From the Presidential Search Committee," *VCU Voice*, 8 Sept. 1989.

5. "University Council Approves Mission," *CT*, 7 Nov. 1989; "University Site Plan Curbs Westward Expansion, Heads South," *CT*, 14 Nov. 1989.

6. Tyler-McGraw, *At the Falls*, 306–07; "Light Up the Night," *VCU Voice*, 27 Oct. 1989.

7. Herbert, *Jefferson Hotel*, 162–74; Pearsall, "Ellen Glasgow's Richmond," 142.

8. Edds, *Claiming the Dream*, 208. Jeffries, *Virginia's Native Son*, notes that Wilder remained silent about the Supreme Court's decision in *Richmond v. Croson* (1989) that the city's set-aside program for minority contractors on city construction projects was illegal (25). On Wilder's career through his first statewide victory, for lieutenant governor in 1985, see Yancey, *When Hell Froze Over* and Baker, *Wilder*.

9. "Ackell Calls VCU's Growth Plan 'Best We Can Do' to Meet Needs," *NL*, 16 Dec. 1989. See also BofV, Minutes, 16 Nov. 1989, JBC.

10. "VCU Approves Compromise Plan," *TD*, 17 Nov. 1989; "VCU's Monroe Park Takeover May Lose Richardson Backing," *NL*, 17 Nov. 1989; "VCU's Board Approves a New Master Site Plan," *VCU Voice*, 1 Dec. 1989.

11. "Change in Financing Education during Next Century Is Proposed," *TD*, 16 Nov. 1989; "Report on Colleges Draws Praise from U.Va., GMU Chiefs," *NL*, 16 Nov. 1989; "Educating Northern Virginia," *WP*, 5 Dec. 1989; BofV Executive Committee, Minutes, 15 Dec. 1989, JBC; "Baliles Pares Down Spending as View of Economy Clouds," *WP*, 19 Dec. 1989; "VCU Faces Two Percent Budget Cut," *VCU Voice*, 12 Jan. 1990.

12. "Three Contenders to Visit VCU for Interviews for Presidency," *NL*, 23 Feb. 1990.

13. Atkinson, *Virginia in the Vanguard*, 105–7; Schexnider, "Analyzing the Wilder Administration," 17; "Universal Ford Dealership Being Sold to Richmond Ford," *TD*, 23 Apr. 2013; BofV, Minutes, 18 Jan. 1990.

14. "Miller & Rhoads Closing Store Downtown Today," *TD*, 6 Jan. 1990; Dunford and Bryson, *Under the Clock*, 105–17; Howard, *From Main Street to Mall*, 8, 199–200. See also Rothchild, *Going for Broke*, 125n; "The R-Word Hit Home in Richmond Area in 1990," *NL*, 31 Dec. 1990.

15. "City Officials Ask Residents' Help in Driving Crime from Church Hill," *TD*, 10 Aug. 1990. On violent crime, see "Performance and Process Evaluation: Selected Neighborhood Action Patrol (SNAP) Program of the Richmond, Virginia, Bureau of Police," July 1987, copy in RG2, Box 72, Folder "City of Richmond 1986–1987," JBC. On drug arrests, see Parkhurst, "Expansion and Exclusion," 66.

16. "University-Wide Convocation to Honor Distinguished Faculty," *VCU Voice*, 16 Feb. 1990; "Ackell Praises 'Urban University' in Final Speech as President at Convocation," *CT*, 27 Feb. 1990.

17. "University Narrows Search, Presidential Prospects Begin Visits," *CT*, 27 Feb. 1990.

18. Trani interviews (the letter appeared in the Sept. 1956 issue of *Sport*).

19. On Ferrell, see Clifford and Wilson, *Presidents, Diplomats, and Other Mortals*, a festschrift honoring Ferrell with essays by his former students, including "A Tale of Two Kennans: American-Russian Relations in the Twentieth Century," 31–55, by Trani and his writing partner, Donald E. Davis.

20. Trani interviews.

21. Ibid.

22. Ibid.; Mitchell, *Delyte Morris of SIU*, and Harper, *University That Shouldn't Have Happened*; Sawyer, *Concerns of a Conservative Democrat*.

23. Trani, *Treaty of Portsmouth*; "39 Promoted to Full Professor Rank," *Carbondale Southern Illinoisan*, 19 Mar. 1971; Mitchell, *Delyte Morris of SIU*, 210–14; Axtell, *Making of Princeton University*, 352.

24. Trani, "Man and the Land"; Rodesch and Trani, "Paul Simon, Midwestern Progressive"; "21 SIU Faculty Promoted to Professor," *Carbondale Southern Illinoisan*, 10 Apr. 1975; Trani and Wilson, *Presidency of Warren G. Harding*.

25. "Physiology Department Chief Named," *Carbondale Southern Illinoisan*, 8 July 1976; Sample, *Contrarian's Guide to Leadership*; "Steven B. Sample, Former University President, Dies at 75," *NYT*, 30 Mar. 2016.

26. "Iowan Heads SIU-C Coal Center," *Carbondale Southern Illinoisan*, 10 Feb. 1977.

27. "NU Administrator Chosen for Post," *Omaha World-Herald*, 29 Apr. 1980; Trani interviews.

28. On Dimond, see Breo, "E. Grey Dimond, M.D." Dimond's interest in China was demonstrated in his book, *Inside China Today*.

29. Shaw, *Successful President*.

30. "Trani and VCU Aiming Even Higher—in His 4 Years, School Has Become New Kind of Urban University," *TD*, 24 July 1994.

31. "VCU Narrows Search to Trio," *TD*, 23 Feb. 1990; "University Narrows Search, Presidential Prospects Begin Visits," *CT*, 27 Feb. 1990; Trani interview, 19 Aug. 2010. Trani later explained the logic behind that approach to staffing his presidency: "There are presidents who come in and they throw half the crowd out. And half the crowd leaves friends who then spend the next five years waging a guerilla war against the president" (quoted in Zimpher and Howey, "President's Role in Educational Reform," 314).

32. "Coming Soon: A New Mission for VCU?," *CT*, 19 Sept. 1989; "University Council Approves Mission," *CT*, 7 Nov. 1989.

33. BofV, Minutes, 15 Mar. 1990, JBC; "Dr. Eugene P. Trani Is Appointed Fourth President of VCU," *VCU Voice*, 20 Mar. 1990; "Dr. Eugene P. Trani," *Scarab* 39 (June 1990): 36.

34. "VCU Choice Pledges Community Ties," *NL*, 15 Mar. 1990; "New VCU Chief Pledges Diversity," *TD*, 16 Mar. 1990; "University Board of Visitors Unanimously Approves Dr. Eugene Trani as New President of VCU," *CT*, 27 Mar. 1990.

35. "Trani Says VCU to Begin New Era," *TD*, 18 Mar. 1990.

36. BofV, Minutes, 20 Apr. 1990, JBC; *USA Today*, 20 Apr. 1990.

37. "ACLU Aiding Oregon Hill Group," *NL*, 14 Mar. 1990; "Top Officers Said to Direct VCU's Oregon Hill Move," *TD*, 1 May 1990; "VCU's Offer to Take Monroe Park Rapped," *TD*, 1 June 1990.

38. "Oregon Hill Group Loses Battle to VCU," *TD*, 12 June 1990.

39. "Meetings Scheduled on City Strategic Planning," *TD*, 8 May 1990; "City Seeks Visions of Future," *TD*, 3 June 1990.

40. "Richmond's Tomorrow," *TD*, 4 June 1990; "Improving Richmond Ideas Flow," *NL*, 7 June 1990; "Closer Ties with Area Counties Touted," *TD*, 8 June 1990; "Executives Voice Ways to Better City," *TD*, 10 July 1990.

41. "Success of Capital Campaign at VCU Not Limited to Dollars," *TD*, 1 July 1990.

42. Alvin J. Schalow Jr., "New Year, New Decade, New Century," *Scarab* 39 (Feb. 1990): 29, 37, and "University Surpasses Campaign Goal; Most Gifts Are for MCV Campus," *Scarab* 39 (Feb. 1990): 35.

43. "Dr. Eugene P. Trani," *Scarab* 39 (June 1990): 38.

44. "Presidents Sign Alumni House Land Transfer Agreement," *Scarab* 39 (Sept. 1990): 6.

45. Trani to "All MCV Campus Personnel," 9 July 1990 (in Trani Memos Folder, JBC).

46. "Dr. Trani," *Scarab* 39 (Sept. 1990): 14–15.

47. "1991 Layoffs Inevitable, Head of VCU Tells Board," *NL*, 28 Aug. 1990.

48. "Students Raise Voices, March, Meet with Governor," *CT*, 25 Sept. 1990; "Plan Aims to Make VCU Better Neighbor," *NL*, 13 Sept. 1990.

49. "A Conversation with Dr. Trani," *VCU Voice*, 7 Sept. 1990, 1, 7; "Trani Optimistic, Realistic toward First Years," *CT*, 1 Aug. 1990.

50. Agendas, President's Council, Trani Papers, JBC.

51. "Dr. Trani," 15.

52. "Plan Aims to Make VCU Better Neighbor" (first and second quotations); "VCU to Get 6 Proposals to Help Forge Better Ties with Neighbors," *TD*, 13 Sept. 1990 (third quotation); "Some Neighbors Pleased as VCU Votes to Foster Ties," *TD*, 14 Sept. 1990.

53. "Good Neighbors," *NL*, 20 Sept. 1990.

54. "Richmond's Tomorrow," *TD*, 4 June 1990; "Improving Richmond Ideas Flow," *NL*, 7 June 1990; "Closer Ties with Area Counties Touted—Meetings Produce Ideas for the Future," *TD*, 8 June 1990; "Executives Voice Ways to

Better City," *TD*, 10 July 1990; "Council-Created Group Targeting 5 Areas for Study," *TD*, 14 Sept. 1990.

55. Trani interviews. A typescript about the project, two pages in length and undated (though after Nov. 1991), gives the date of the meeting as Aug. 1990. See "Virginia Biotechnology Research Park," Richmond Renaissance Papers, Box A10, JBC.

56. "Wisconsin Bidding for Biotechnology," *Madison Wisconsin State Journal*, 16 Aug. 1987.

57. "Science, Technical Centers Proposed to Aid State Economic Development," *NL*, 24 June 1986; "Financing Available, but CIT May Get Just 2 of 3 Buildings," *TD*, 25 June 1986.

58. "Center Cultivating Skin Cells into Tissue for Transplanting," *TD*, 12 Aug. 1986; "ODU Chief's High-Profile Leadership Gratifies Some but Irritates Others," *TD*, 7 Sept. 1986; "Preliminary Figures Show VCU Fall Enrollment Down," *TD*, 26 Sept. 1986; "State High-Tech Center Heads for Next Challenges," *TD*, 11 Jan. 1987.

59. "City Officials Expect Only a Third of Requested Block-Grant Money," *TD*, 22 Jan. 1986.

60. "Incubation Plan for Helping Hatch Small Companies," *TD*, 13 Apr. 1987.

61. Trani interview, 10 Feb. 2015.

62. "Project GOLD Helps Middle School Students," *VCU Voice*, 2 Nov. 1990, 6. See also "The Touch of GOLD: Dr. Catherine Howard Empowers Kids," *VCU Voice*, 17 May 1991, 4.

63. BofV, Minutes, 2 Nov. 1990, JBC.

64. "Three Strikes," *NL*, 6 Nov. 1990.

65. "VCU Plan Retraction Is Urged[;] President's Move Comes as Surprise," *NL*, 15 Nov. 1990; "Trani Withdraws VCU Expansion Plan," *TD*, 16 Nov. 1990; "VCU Withdraws," *NL*, 16 Nov. 1990; "Good Will, Frustration behind VCU Decision," *NL*, 17 Nov. 1990; "VCU's Bright Future," *TD*, 18 Nov. 1990; Trani, "Reason Should Guide VCU Growth," *TD*, 18 Nov. 1990. Trani's phrase "a heart, a soul and a vision" echoed the charge by the chair of the Art and Architectural Review Board that the master plan lacked "vision and a heart and an aesthetic soul" ("Three Strikes?" *NL*, 6 Nov. 1990).

66. "Can Oregon Hill and VCU Harmonize?" *TD*, 16 Dec. 1990.

67. "VCU Considers Research Park," *Harrisonburg Daily News Record*, 17 Dec. 1990; Valentine interview, JBC. Richmond Renaissance also endorsed the consultant's report, and its executive committee "adopted the research park project as a priority in its program for 1992 and . . . provided support for the pre-development work." It named a subcommittee—City Manager Robert C. Bobb and Trani's visitors in summer 1990, T. Justin Moore and Henry Valentine—to spearhead its work. See "The Virginia Biotechnology

Research Park Project," undated typescript, Richmond Renaissance Papers, Box A10, JBC.

68. "R-Word Hit Home in 1990"; Smartt, "Thalhimers Department Store," 32–34.

69. "Warren and Williams Cost Lang," *CT*, 5 Mar. 1991.

70. "Metro's Gain May Take Toll—Sun Belt Could Be First to Feel the Heat," *TD*, 14 Feb. 1991; "Musical Conferences: Is VCU the Odd Man Out?," *TD*, 15 Feb. 1991; "Basketball, Conferences, NCAA and Bo," *CT*, 26 Mar. 1991.

71. "Metro Still Has Pulse—Barely," *TD*, 23 Jan. 1991; "VCU Tells Metro: Take Us, Please!," *TD*, 5 Mar. 1991.

72. "Rams' Affiliation Best for Both Parties," *TD*, 4 Apr. 1991; "A Done Deal: VCU in Metro's Fold," *TD*, 4 Apr. 1991. Metro Commissioner Ralph McFillen's assessment: "It was mainly through Dr. Trani's effort that VCU's stock went to a new level" ("A Done Deal").

73. "Presidential Inauguration," *CT*, 2 Apr. 1991.

74. "VCU Chief's Inauguration Set Saturday at the Mosque," *NL*, 2 Apr. 1991; "The Trani Inauguration," *TD*, 6 Apr. 1991; "VCU Expansion Is Inevitable, Wilder Says," *NL*, 6 Apr. 1991. See also "VCU Gets 4th President," *WP*, 7 Apr. 1991.

75. "Celebrating Our Individual and Institutional Excellence," *VCU Voice*, 22 Feb. 1991, 1–3. The distinction for urban universities between being "of" or merely "in" a community is discussed in Freeland, *Transforming the Urban University*, 3–4.

76. Trani, "The Future of the Academy and the Community: Virginia Commonwealth University and the Urban Mission," inaugural address, 6 Apr. 1991. A week later, the Lynchburg newspaper published an op-ed essay by Trani about VCU in which he made a similar argument, this time highlighting the new Community Associates Program, with seventeen projects approved, as exemplary (Trani, "Urban School Fits Special Niche," *Lynchburg News and Daily Advance*, 14 Apr. 1991). See also "Trani Is Inaugurated as VCU's Fourth President, Pledges 'Role Model of Urban University,'" *TD*, 7 Apr. 1991.

77. "Trani Is Inaugurated as VCU's Fourth President, Community Leaders Give Cautious Praise," *TD*, 7 Apr. 1991.

78. Richmond Tomorrow, *Citizens' Report*; "Task Force Offers Vision for City," *TD*, 25 June 1991; "Carpe Diem," *NL*, 25 June 1991 (quotation); "Carpe Diem II," *NL*, 26 June 1991.

79. "Victim of Times, Observers Say," *TD*, 5 Sept. 1991.

80. "Back to the Drawing Board—May Co. Pulls the Plug on Thalhimers, Putting Pressure on the City to Rethink Downtown," *NL*, 18 Nov. 1991.

81. "Convocation 1992: A Tradition of Honoring Faculty," *VCU Voice*, 6 Mar. 1992; "Bond Issues Delayed for Fine Arts Building," "Medical Sciences Building

on Hold," "Faculty and Staff May Receive Raises," and "King First Artist to Receive Faculty Award," *CT*, 25 Feb. 1992.

82. Trani, "'90s Higher Education: An Endangered Species," *TD*, 15 Mar. 1992.

83. "VCU Asks 'Friends' for Help," *NL*, 7 Feb. 1992.

84. Trani, Talking Points for Metropolitan Economic Development Seminar, 24 Jan.; Parents Council, 18 Feb.; Metropolitan Chamber of Commerce, 25 Feb.; Development Seminar, 2 Mar.; RPI Alumni, 1–2 May 1992, all in Trani Papers, JBC. See also Trani, "A Bond Bill for the Future of the Medical College of Virginia Campus—and Virginia," *Scarab* 41 (Summer 1992): 5.

85. "VCU Tuition, Fees to Rise 15 Percent," *TD*, 25 Apr. 1992; "Tuition Increases, University Budget Approved by Board," *VCU Voice*, 1 May 1992, 1, 7; Trani, "A Letter from President Eugene Trani," *CT*, 27 Apr. 1992.

86. "VCU Professor Wins $369,000 Award," *TD*, 16 June 1992; "So Far So Good for Local Arts in June," *CT*, 29 June 1992; "The Village Restaurant Gets Transplanted," *CT*, 6 Aug. 1992; "The Day It All Began," *CT*, 29 June 1992. Marshall, best known for *Brown Girl, Brownstones* (1959) and *Praisesong for the Widow* (1984), taught at VCU from 1984 to 1994.

87. "VCU Rejects May Co. Offer of Building," *TD*, 17 July 1992.

88. "VCU Board Names Gregory 1st Black Rector," *TD*, 17 July 1992; "Biotechnology Park Receives Boosts," *TD*, 16 July 1992; "Good News (2)," *TD*, 18 July 1992. See also Trani, "Biotech Park and Spinoffs Will Benefit City, State," *TD*, 7 Oct. 1992.

89. Trani interview, 19 Aug. 2010.

90. Trani to "Dear Colleagues," 10 July, 13 Aug. 1992, Trani Papers, Memos Folder, JBC; Trani, "The State of the University, Fall 1992," *VCU Voice*, 18 Sept. 1992; Talking Points, Combined Faculty Address, 11 Sept. 1992, Trani Papers, JBC.

91. "VCU Sets Expansion Strategy," *TD*, 4 Sept. 1992. See also "Study Reveals VCU's Effects on Area," *VCU Voice*, 18 Sept. 1992.

92. "State Cuts in Higher Education Lead U.S.," *TD*, 20 Oct. 1992. See also "Virginia's Spending on Colleges Dropped 13% in Past 2 Years," *Norfolk Virginian-Pilot*, 21 Oct. 1992.

93. "VCU Chief Disputes Data on Cuts," *TD*, 27 Oct. 1992; "Which School Hit Hardest by Virginia Education Cuts?," *TD*, 1 Nov. 1992.

94. "Bond Support Overwhelming, Education Reaps Benefits," *CT*, 5 Nov. 1992.

95. Frances Helms, "Visions of Change," *Richmond Surroundings*, Nov. 1992, 7–10.

96. "Realities Forcing College Changes," *TD*, 3 Dec. 1992. See also, for context, Trani, "SCHEV and the Quality of Education at VCU," *VCU Voice*, 30 Nov. 1992.

97. "College Presidents Blast Call for Restructuring," *TD*, 16 Dec. 1992; "U.Va. Faculty Backs Efforts by Casteen to Derail Changes," *TD*, 23 Dec. 1992; "State Agency, College Chiefs Hold Firm on Opposite Sides," *TD*, 6 Jan. 1993; "Education Board Backs Report on Restructuring," *TD*, 13 Jan. 1993.
98. Trani interview, 19 Aug. 2010.

8. Planning One University, 1993–1994

1. Commission on the Future of the University, *Strategic Plan*, 1.
2. "Founding Member of VCU's Department of Urban Studies and Planning Looks Back on the Program Turning 30," *VCU News*, 10 June 2003.
3. "Faculty Senate Reviews Strategic Issues, Debates Proposed Recreational Plan," *VCU Today*, 6 Mar. 1992, 1, 3.
4. "Responses to Strategic Plan Are Invited," *VCU Today*, 5 Mar. 1993; Trani, "Popular Perception vs. Higher Education," *VCU Today*, 26 Mar. 1993; "Strategic Plan Discussions Are Scheduled for March, April, May," *VCU Today*, 26 Mar. 1993.
5. "Gorachev Visits Campus, Accepts Honorary Degree," *CT*, 15 Apr. 1993; "VCU Library Presents Millionth Volume," *CT*, 19 Apr. 1993; "Sullivan Challenges VCU Graduates," *TD*, 23 May 1993; "Strategic Planners Face Final Revision Hurdles," *VCU Today*, 11 June 1993.
6. BofV, Minutes, 20 Apr. 1990, JBC; "Trani, 2 Other Officials of VCU Are Off to Africa," *TD*, 7 Aug. 1992; "Plan to End Remedial Classes Criticized," *TD*, 20 Nov. 1992. See also "2016 RTD Person of the Year Hall of Fame Inductee: Grace Harris, Retired Virginia Commonwealth University Administrator," *TD*, 12 Dec. 2016.
7. Commission on the Future of the University, *Strategic Plan*, 18–21.
8. Ibid., 22.
9. Ibid., 3–15; BofV, Minutes, 9 Sept. 1993, JBC.
10. "Restructuring Plan Targets Teaching, Services, Research," *CT*, 20 Sept. 1993; "Recruitment and Retention Strategies Gain Ground," *CT*, 27 Sept. 1993 (Moeser comment); "Task Force Evaluates Teaching-Learning Climate," *CT*, 4 Oct. 1993; "Feedback Sessions Induce Better Graduate Programs," *CT*, 11 Oct. 1993; "Commission Shapes University's Future," *CT*, 18 Oct. 1993 (only a passing mention of "a new Engineering program"); "Plan Seeks to Bolster Research Funding," *CT*, 25 Oct. 1993.
11. Commission on the Future of the University, *Strategic Plan*, 7; "Four-Year Schools Slow to Adopt Flexibility That Is Trademark of Community Colleges," *TD*, 13 Sept. 1993.
12. Commission on the Future of the University, *Strategic Plan*, 24.

13. "Project Maps Coliseum-Area Site for Research Park," *NL*, 27 Sept. 1991; "Research Park Gets Director," *TD*, 28 Nov. 1991; "Director, Committee Named for Research Park," *VCU Voice*, 13 Dec. 1991; Trani interview, 10 Feb. 2015.

14. "Research Park Board Turning to Counties," *TD*, 19 Nov. 1992; "Research Park Paper Signed," *TD*, 14 May 1993. See also Bonis, Koste, and Lyons, *Virginia Commonwealth University*, 119.

15. Trani, interview, 10 Feb. 2015. See also "Blueprints for BioTech—Research Park Is a Key to the Transformation of Downtown," *TD*, 30 Aug. 1993.

16. "Research Park Hopes to Break New Ground," *TD*, 18 May 1994.

17. Trani interview, 19 Aug. 2010.

18. On the Virginia Institute for Psychiatric and Behavioral Genetics, see its website at http://vipbg.vcu.edu/; on the Mid-Atlantic Twin Registry, see its website at http://www.matr.vcu.edu/.

19. Trani interview, 10 Feb. 2015. Trani perceived the conflict over the location of the laboratory as a symptom of the lack of cooperation in planning between the city, state, federal government, and the university (Trani interview regarding Oregon Hill, summer 2009).

20. "BioTech Park Coming to Life Downtown—Construction of First Buildings Proceeding and Space Quickly Filling Up with Tenants," *TD*, 11 Dec. 1994. On Patricia Cornwell, see her website at http://www.patriciacornwell.com/.

21. "'Beginning to See a Turnaround'—Development Council Here Reports Growth," *TD*, 5 Feb. 1993.

22. "City May Donate Land for VCU Engineering School," *TD*, 28 Apr. 1993.

23. Trani interview, 16 Feb. 2015; "Partnership Key, Richmonders Told," *TD*, 3 May 1993; "Trani Hears Words He Likes, Industry Followed Addition of College Program," *TD*, 4 May 1993.

24. Crupi, *Back to the Future*, 6.

25. "The Future VCU," *TD*, 18 Mar. 1993; Crupi, *Back to the Future*, 24.

26. Trani interview, 16 Feb. 2015.

27. "VCU Rules Out Belvidere, Broad Site for New School," *TD*, 10 Feb. 1994.

28. Trani interview, 16 Feb. 2015. See also "Virginia Tech Taps Torgersen," *TD*, 2 Oct. 1993.

29. "VCU Engineering School Plan Detailed," *TD*, 11 Feb. 1994.

30. "MCV Foundation Elects New President," *VCU Today*, 11 June 1993. See also "Wielding the Influence to Make Visions Reality," *TD*, 14 Aug. 2005.

31. Wyeth interview, 11 Jan. 2012. See also "Vice President for Advancement Named," *VCU Voice*, 1 May 1992; "UVA's Darden School Receives Its Largest Gift," *Business Wire*, 15 Nov. 1999.

32. Trani interview, 16 Feb. 2015. On Wright, see "VCU Donors to Be Honored," *TD*, 22 Apr. 2003; "VCU Gets Big Boost from Non-Alumni," *TD*, 10 Apr. 2005.

33. "VCU Engineering School Plan Detailed" and "VCU's Wave of the Future," *TD*, 11 Feb. 1994.

34. "Property Purchases Approved by VCU," *TD*, 18 Mar. 1994.

35. "VCU Negotiating to Buy Site for Engineering School," *TD*, 9 July 1994.

36. "Cary Street Site Opposed for School of Engineering," *TD*, 14 July 1994; "Oregon Hill Residents to Ask Review Groups to Reject Plan," *TD*, 15 July 1994.

37. "Trani and VCU Aiming Even Higher—in His 4 Years, School Has Become New Kind of Urban University," *TD*, 24 July 1994.

38. "VCU, Related Foundations Get $25.4 Million in Gifts," *TD*, 6 Aug. 1994.

39. "Second Building Stands in the Way of VCU Project," *TD*, 11 Sept. 1994.

40. "This Old House," *TD*, 25 Sept. 1994.

41. "Agency Approves School for VCU—Public, Private Funds to Go to Engineering," *TD*, 14 Dec. 1994; "SCHEV Approves VCU Engineering School Request," *VCU Voice*, 16 Jan. 1995, 1–2.

42. BofV, Minutes, 17 Nov. 1994, JBC.

43. "VCU Board Approves Broad Street Plan," *TD*, 18 Nov. 1994.

44. Trani to "Students of Virginia Commonwealth University," 30 Oct. 1991, in *CT*, 5 Nov. 1991.

45. Trani interview, 1 Apr. 2015; "VCU Tuition, Fees to Rise 15 Percent," *NL*, 25 Apr. 1992.

46. Commission on the Future of the University, *Strategic Plan*, 13; "VCU to Bid on Universal Ford Property," *CT*, 9 Apr. 1992.

47. "VCU Shoots for On-Campus Facility," *TD*, 20 Feb. 1993; Trani interview, 1 Apr. 2015.

48. "VCU Shoots for On-Campus Facility."

49. Trani interview, 1 Apr. 2015; "Opinions Differ on Use of VCU Facility," *TD*, 31 July 1993; "Arena for VCU: A Tough Sell Has Become a Tough Buy," *TD*, 31 July 1993.

50. "VCU Starts Drive for Sports Facility," *TD*, 14 Sept. 1994; "VCU to Name Center for Stuart Siegel," *TD*, 20 Oct. 1994; "Seating Plan Has Divided VCU Backers," *TD*, 17 Nov. 1994.

51. "VCU to Merge Schools of Medicine, Health Sciences," *TD*, 17 July 1993; "A Message from the Vice President," *Scarab* 42 (Summer 1993): 3; "School of Medicine": 19–20; Trani, "Strategic Organizational Change for the Medical College of Virginia Campus," *Scarab* 42 (Fall 1993): 6.

52. "Schools of Medicine, Basic Health Sciences to Merge," *Scarab* 42 (Fall 1993): 24–25; "Acting Dean at MCV Is Highly Touted," *TD*, 9 Aug. 1993.

53. Trani, "A Message from the President," *Scarab* 43 (Spring 1994): 1. See also Hoffman, "Emergency Rooms."

54. "Burning Secrets," *WP*, 19 June 1994.

55. "VCU Says Studies Sensationalized," *TD*, 20 June 1994; Trani, "No Burning Secrets," *WP*, 3 July 1994; "VCU President Fires Back in Research Rebuttal," *TD*, 4 July 1994; Trani, "Setting the Record Straight on Cold-War Radiation Studies," *Scarab* 43 (Summer 1994): 4.

56. "Panel Seeks More Data on MCV Radiation Studies," *TD*, 4 Sept. 1994; "Panel Urged to Query MCV Burn Subjects—Army-Funded Tests Conducted in '50s," *TD*, 13 Sept. 1994; "MCV Letter Conveys Fear—Radiation Research in 1951 Prompted Scientist's Worries about Bad Publicity," *TD*, 15 Feb. 1995; "Panel's Handling of MCV Study Criticized—Critic Says Cold War Burn Study Was Ignored," *TD*, 16 Feb. 1995; "Draft Report on '50s Burn Study Looks at MCV Role," *TD*, 11 May 1995; "MCV Defends Use of Prisoners in '50s Radiation Tests," *TD*, 5 Oct. 1995.

57. "Trani's Initiatives Cited in Recognizing Leadership," *TD*, 17 Nov. 1994; BofV, Minutes, 17 Nov. 1994, JBC.

9. BUILDING ONE UNIVERSITY, 1995–1999

1. Thelin, *History of American Higher Education*, 359–60. See also introduction in Smith and Bender, eds., *American Higher Education Transformed*, 7. On privatization at the University of Virginia, see Kirp, *Shakespeare, Einstein*, 130–34. These trends continued into the new century. See Sam Dillon, "At Public Universities, Warnings of Privatization," *NYT*, 16 Dec. 2005. For a rosier view of the 1990s and early 2000s, based on the demographics of the "baby boom echo," see McGee, *Breakpoint*, 12–17.

2. Thelin, *History of American Higher Education*, 381–85. See also Thelin, "New 'A&M.'"

3. "VCU, Crum Pleased with Victory" *TD*, 6 Jan. 1995.

4. "New Conference May Snub VCU, Tech," *TD*, 6 Jan. 1995; "VCU's Sander Hints Legal Action over Metro Conference Breakup," *TD*, 9 Jan. 1995.

5. "VCU Makes Pitch to Join New League—Trani Has Meeting with Presidents," *TD*, 11 Jan. 1995.

6. "Metro May Toss VCU, Va. Tech," *TD*, 15 Jan. 1995; "Mess in the Metro Is One for the Money," *TD*, 15 Jan. 1995.

7. "VCU, Tech Achieve Settlement with Metro," *TD*, 3 Feb. 1995.

8. "Only 70 Miles, but a World of Difference," *TD*, 10 Feb. 1995; "Smith Offers Unusual Silence on Subject of South Alabama," *TD*, 12 Mar. 1995.

9. Trani, "Distorted Landscape." For the larger context of intercollegiate athletics, see Thelin, *Games Colleges Play*.

10. "Few State Teams Make the Grade," *TD*, 20 Mar. 1996; "Smith Won't Fall Victim to CAA Coaching Purge," *TD*, 8 Mar. 1997.

11. "Siegel Center to Benefit Athletes, Students," *CT*, 17 Feb. 1997.

12. "Health Care: Asking Right Questions in a Time of Change," *VCU Voice*, 24 Apr. 1995, 9–10.

13. "Ambulatory Care Facility to Open for Patients in May," *VCU Voice*, 8 May 1995, 1–2.

14. "MCV in Fragile Financial Health," *TD*, 27 Aug. 1995; "Two Medical Siblings May Turn Competitors," *TD*, 28 Aug. 1995; "Doctors Upbeat Despite Pressures," *TD*, 29 Aug. 1995; "Virginia Undergraduate Medical Education Programs in Jeopardy," *VCU in the News*, Oct. 1995. The *TD* titled the series "The Med Centers: Coping, Costs, Competition," and VCU's University News Service then compiled the articles as a special issue of *VCU in the News*.

15. "MCV, U.Va. Hospitals Up for Sale?—It's One of 3 Options Being Discussed as Part of State Privatization Study," *TD*, 14 Oct. 1995.

16. "MCV, U.Va. Hospitals Won't Be Sold—Allen Rules Out Any Consideration of Idea," *TD*, 18 Oct. 1995; "Hospital Sale Idea Sank Fast—Plan Involving U. Va., MCV Found Few Takers," *TD*, 19 Oct. 1995.

17. "Privatization of Hospitals Endorsed—Proposal for U.Va., MCV to Go to Assembly," *TD*, 6 Dec. 1995.

18. "U.Va. Distances Itself from Authority Plan," *TD*, 28 Dec. 1995; "MCV, U.Va. Push Own Bills," *TD*, 23 Jan.1996.

19. "MCV Proposal Would Change Workers' Status—New Authority Plan Creates Unease," *TD*, 1 Feb. 1996.

20. "MCV Hospitals Authority Called Costly," *TD*, 2 Feb. 1996; "Privatization Plan Revised—Bill Makes MCV Hospitals 'Independent State Agency,'" *TD*, 6 Feb. 1996; "MCV Bill Undergoes Another Rewrite," *TD*, 7 Feb. 1996.

21. "MCV Disclosure Bill Gains," *TD*, 9 Feb. 1996.

22. "MCV Privatization Plan Clears Key House Hurdle," *TD*, 10 Feb. 1996.

23. Trani, "Medical Centers Need Relief from Red Tape—VCU Needs Freedom to Compete in Market," *TD*, 11 Feb. 1996.

24. "House Backs Motorola, MCV Plans," *TD*, 13 Feb. 1996; "MCV Plan Undergoes Last-Gasp Surgery," *TD*, 2 Mar. 1996; "Assembly Approves Semiprivate Group to Manage MCV," 10 Mar. 1996.

25. "VCU President Elected to Head MCV Board—Group to Set Policy for Hospitals' Authority," *TD*, 30 Aug. 1996.

26. "Jones to Step Down as Vice President," *CT*, 14 Oct. 1996.

27. "VCU Drops 2 of 13 Schools," *TD*, 21 May 1994.

28. Gates, *Loose Canons*, xi.

29. The incident at George Mason University is told in Kors and Silvergate, *Shadow University*, 157–58.

30. University of Wisconsin–Madison, "Design for Diversity,"Creating Community, [1988], https://diversity.wisc.edu/reports/reports/; University of

Wisconsin–Madison, "The Madison Plan," Creating Community, 9 Feb. 1988, https://diversity.wisc.edu/reports/reports/; David L. Hudson Jr. and Lata Nott, "Hate Speech and Campus Speech Codes," Freedom Forum Institute, last updated Mar. 2017, https://www.freedomforuminstitute.org/first-amendment-center/topics/freedom-of-speech-2/free-speech-on-public-college-campuses-overview/hate-speech-campus-speech-codes/. The decision of the U.S. District Court, Eastern District of Wisconsin, in the case of *UWM Post v. Board of Regents of University of Wisconsin*, is an appendix to Hoekema, *Campus Rules and Moral Community*, 193–96.

31. Trani, "Do We Really Know What PC Is About?," *TD*, 28 July 1991; Smith, "PC in Virginia: A Reply from the Resistance," *TD*, 4 Aug. 1991. Shields and Dunn, in *Passing on the Right*, find that many such faculty, despite feeling like a "stigmatized minority" (5), also feel indebted to the university and defend its traditions (4).

32. "On Publishing the VCU Salary List," *CT*, 8 Dec. 1987–24 Jan. 1988; "Study Finds Female Faculty Paid Less Than Males," *CT*, 29 Oct. 1991. The salary study and the proposed remedy preceded Trani's arrival at VCU, but, after seeking advice from the university's legal counsel, he approved the salary increases for female faculty members (Trani interview, 11 May 2015).

33. "Male Professors at VCU Act on Women's Pay Raises," *WP*, 8 Aug. 1992; "2 Universities Charged with Reverse Bias," *Chronicle of Higher Education*, 2 Sept. 1992; "EEOC Rules against Male Professors," *CT*, 11 Feb. 1993; "Virginia Commonwealth University Professors' Reverse-Bias Suit to Proceed," *Chronicle of Higher Education*, 8 Sept. 1995; "Court Reinstates Suit on Sex-Based Pay Increases," *NYT*, 14 May 1996; "Trial Ordered in Lawsuit over Pay Raises for Female Professors," *Chronicle of Higher Education*, 24 May 1996; "Male Professors, VCU Settle Discrimination Suit," *CT*, 30 Sept. 1996 (first quotation); "VCU, Male Professors Reach Deal," *TD*, 24 Sept. 1996 (second quotation).

34. "Proposed Harassment Policy Not Supported by Faculty Senate," *CT*, 28 Jan. 1992; "President Vows Close Study of VCU Vote," *TD*, 22 Jan. 1992; "VCU's Anti-PC Vote," *TD*, 23 Jan. 1992; Trani to Robert Holland (author of the editorial) and others, 23 Jan. 1992, Grimsley Papers, Accession #9379-a, Special Collections, UVA.

35. "The President's Candor," *TD*, 24 Sept. 1992.

36. "VCU School Clears Hurdle—Full Accreditation Urged for Mass Communications," *TD*, 11 Feb. 1995; "Dodd Is Named Director of VCU School," *TD*, 24 Feb. 1995; "VCU School Is Reaccredited in 'Quick Vote,'" *TD*, 7 May 1995; "Advertising Gets Its M.A. Degree," *NYT*, 14 Feb. 1999; "Agency Executives, Administrators Shaping Plans for VCU AdCenter," *TD*,

13 Mar. 1995. On the continuing commitment to diversity at the AdCenter, see "Celebs Help VCU Boost Minority Program," *Advertising Age*, 16 Feb. 1998.

37. Trani interview, 11 May 2015; "VCU Leases Space in Shockoe Slip as the Home for Its New AdCenter," *TD*, 1 July 1996.

38. "Guidelines for Entrepreneurial Programs Tuition Agreements (EPT Agreements)," last rev. 2004, are no longer operational. "Beginning in FY 2019, the redesigned budget model will replace these EPT agreements with a common, university-wide tuition allocation model that directs all tuition and fee revenue to the units" (https://budget.vcu.edu/budget-redesign/faq .html).

39. "VCU OKs Advertising Program," *TD*, 22 Sept. 1995; "Ad Executives Help Launch VCU Graduate Center," *TD*, 29 Sept. 1995; "One of a Kind: VCU AdCenter to Open in Fall 1996," *CT*, 29 Sept. 1995 (quotation); "AdCenter Ready to Open," *CT*, 5 Aug. 1996; "Adcenter's Driving Force—Cook-Tench Wants to Alter Perceptions of Her Profession," *TD*, 9 June 1998.

40. "VCU Drops 2 of 13 Schools," *TD*, 21 May 1994.

41. "Wilder Expected to Join Policy Center at VCU," *TD*, 10 Mar. 1995; "Wilder to Hit Moscow, Far East on Trade Trip," *TD*, 26 Sept. 1993; "Wilder Sees Big Potential with China," *TD*, 8 Oct. 1993; "VCU Chief Outlines Progress in China," *TD*, 9 Oct. 1993. See also Trani's op-ed analysis on their return, "Chinese Tortoise Passes Russian Hare," *TD*, 17 Oct. 1993.

42. "Wilder May Join VCU Faculty," *CT*, 22 Mar. 1995; "Wilder Expected to Join Policy Center at VCU," *TD*, 10 Mar. 1995; "It's Official: Ex-Governor Is Professor Wilder Now," *TD*, 24 Mar. 1995; "VCU Gets Wilder," *CT*, 24 Mar. 1995; "Wilder to Teach at VCU," *The Vine*, 4 Apr. 1995 (*The Vine* was successor to *Reflections in Ink*, 1994–2008).

43. "2-Day Symposium to Deal with Race and Health Care," *TD*, 26 Jan. 1997; "Wilder Symposia Opens at MCV," *CT*, 29 Jan. 1997; "VCU Sets Symposium on Richmond School System," *TD*, 14 Apr. 1998; "A Graceful Rise," *TD*, 1 June 1999.

44. "Governor Seeks Stronger Universities," *TD*, 8 Feb. 1995.

45. "VCU to Get City Money," *TD*, 14 Feb. 1995.

46. "VCU Is Urged to Save Houses," *TD*, 7 Mar. 1995. See also Pool and Ward, "Plainly Significant."

47. "VCU Offers Funds to Move 1817 House from School's Path," *TD*, 6 Apr. 1995.

48. "Board Finds Jacob House Merits 'Historic' Designation," *TD*, 19 Apr. 1995; Mazurek, *Making Microchips*, 2–5, 42–43, 93 (first quotation), 138 (second quotation), 222 (third quotation).

49. "Engineering School Plans Get a Boost," *TD*, 13 Apr. 1995; "Engineering School Could Advance under Motorola Plan," *VCU Voice*, 24 Apr. 1995. In

addition, Chesterfield County and Henrico County, on 12 April, each agreed to allocate $100,000 annually for five years to support the School of Engineering.

50. "Motorola Pact Has Marks of Winner," *TD*, 13 Apr. 1995; "High-Tech Future—Motorola Shows Linkage of Education and Jobs," *TD*, 19 Apr. 1995.

51. "Group Offers to Renovate House," *TD*, 28 Apr. 1995; "University Key to Area's Growth—Trani Sees VCU Playing Similar Role," *TD*, 6 May 1995; "The Jacob House," *TD*, 16 May 1995.

52. "Group Gets Help in Bid to Save Home—but VCU Wants to Tear Down or Move Jacob House," *TD*, 20 May 1995.

53. Ibid.; "VCU to Move Jacob House to Nearby Site, Trani Says—Neighborhood Group Assails Plan," *TD*, 9 June 1995; "Jacob House Given to Restaurant Owners—It Could Be Moved Sometime Next Month," *TD*, 11 July 1995; "Portion of House Is Razed," *TD*, 16 July 1995; "City Council to Hold Jacob House Public Hearing," *TD*, 20 July 1995; "Council Approves Jacob House Move," *TD*, 25 July 1995; "Man Opposed to Jacob House Move Arrested," *TD*, 8 Aug. 1995.

54. "Motorola!," *TD*, 8 Sept. 1995; "Moving Day," *TD*, 14 Sept. 1995; "Trani Sees Richmond on Brink of a Boom," *TD*, 14 Sept. 1995.

55. "The Jacob House," *Richmond Magazine*, Oct. 2003, 136; "Building a Reputation: Developer Stephen Salomonsky Works to Win Over a Neighborhood While Building around History," *Style Weekly*, 22 Oct. 2003; "Oregon Hill Backs Plan—Stephen Salomonsky Will Develop Roughly 60 Units along Half a City Block," *TD*, 25 Oct. 1995, and "The Jacob House" at https://www.richmondfriendsmeeting.org/the-jacob-house/. We are grateful to Betsy Brinson for an interview with Kneebone about the process, 6 Sept. 2016, and for providing access to documents in her possession, including the letter Charles Todd Woodson, Oregon Hill Neighborhood Association, to Salomonsky, 9 Feb. 2003, in which the quoted phrase appears.

56. "Motorola May Slow Plans Here," *TD*, 12 Apr. 1996; "We'll Be There, Motorola Says—Firm Postpones Building Plans About a Year," *TD*, 13 Apr. 1996; "Motorola Inc. Postponing Hiring Plans," *TD*, 28 Apr. 1996; "Chip Plant to Benefit Colleges—Incentives Include Grants for Education," *TD*, 17 May 1996.

57. Trani, "Medical Centers Need Relief," *TD*, 11 Feb. 1996; "VCU School Plan Grows—Engineering Complex Will Cost $40 Million," *TD*, 22 Mar. 1996.

58. "VCU School Plan Grows"; "The Future of Engineering and Fine Arts," *VCU Voice*, 25 Mar. 1996.

59. "University Begins Planning for Future Growth," *VCU Voice*, 26 Feb. 1996; "Broad Street Key to VCU Expansion—Architect Sees School's Growth Bringing New Activity Downtown," *TD*, 31 Mar. 1996.

60. "Revitalization Begins on Broad Street Corridor," *VCU Voice*, 6 May 1996.

61. "Grant to Back VCU Work in Carver Community," *TD*, 4 Sept. 1997. See also Howard and Allison, "Bringing All Partners."

62. BofV, Minutes, 17 May 1996, JBC; "VCU Approves Fine Arts Center Construction—Broad Street Site Will Be 'Showcase,'" *TD*, 18 May 1996.

63. "Bruegman Dedicates Career to Building University," *VCU Voice*, 10 June 1996; "Pharmacy Dean Leaves School Growth in His Wake" and "Dean Helped Build School of Allied Health Professions," *VCU Voice*, 6 May 1996.

64. "VCU Growth Plan Is Approved—Major Expansion along Broad Street Is Key Element," *TD*, 26 July 1996. On DePillars, see "Arts School Dean DePillars Leaving VCU," *TD*, 8 June 1995.

65. "Moving on Up?," *TD*, 6 Apr. 1996.

66. "Finance Secretary Paul Timmreck Resigns—He's Leaving Allen Cabinet for VCU Post," *TD*, 4 July 1996; "VCU Growth Plan Is Approved"; "Timmreck Named Vice President," *VCU Voice*, 19 Aug. 1996; Trani interviews, 10 March 2015.

67. On the Grace E. Harris Leadership Institute (and Dr. Harris), see the institute's website at https://gehli.vcu.edu/; on Jones, see "John E. Jones, Former VP of Health Sciences, Dies at 81," *VCU News*, 9 Dec. 2011; on Wyeth, see "Longtime Advancement Leader Set to Retire in March after Transformative Tenure," *VCU News*, 10 Feb. 2010; on Messmer, see "VCU Vice President for University Relations and Chief of Staff to Retire," *VCU News*, 22 Jan. 2010. Donald C. Gehring's low public profile belied his significance as an advocate for VCU with government officials and as a guide to VCU officials on dealings with government. He retired at the end of 2010 and was awarded the Presidential Medal at the May 2011 commencement ceremony. See "McDonnell: 'VCU Is Virginia,'" *TD*, 21 May 2011.

68. "Biotechnology Park Named Project of the Year—Award Notes Contribution to Downtown," *TD*, 17 Nov. 1996; "Biotechnology Park Readies for Opening," *VCU Voice*, 15 Jan. 1996 (on the opening, see also *VCU Voice*, 29 Jan. 1996); "Farinholt to Lead Research Park," *VCU Voice*, 25 Mar. 1996; "Better City for All, Better for All—Recent Investments throughout Region Attributed to Cooperation," *TD*, 30 Dec. 1996.

69. "Skunda Picked for Biotech Post," *TD*, 16 July 1997; "State Secretary to Head Biotech Park," *CT*, 22 Sept. 1997.

70. "VCU Policy Overrides Tenure in Incompetence Cases," *TD*, 20 Sept. 1996. See also "First-Year Applications Rise 15 Percent at VCU," *TD*, 21 Mar. 1997.

71. "VCU Advances with Initiatives Created by Strategic Plan," *VCU Voice*, 16 Jan. 1995; "VCU Begins Refocus of Strategic Plan," *VCU Voice*, 13 Jan. 1997; "Environmental Scan Shaping Refocus of VCU Strategic Plan," *VCU Voice*, 21 Apr. 1997.

72. "VCU Readies Strategic Plan for Review," *VCU Voice*, 10 Nov. 1997; "Open Forums Held on Strategic Plan," *VCU Voice*, 24 Nov. 1997; BofV, Minutes, 19 Jan. 1998, JBC; "Phase II of Strategic Plan Approved," *VCU Voice*, 26 Jan. 1998; *VCU Strategic Plan for the Future of Virginia Commonwealth University* (Richmond, VA: Office of Academic Affairs, 1998).

73. "Money Coming Back to Downtown—but the Shape of the Center City Is Changing," *TD*, 14 July 1996.

74. "Ethyl Won't Buy Shelter Property—Drops Plan to Renew Option on Building," *TD*, 27 Mar. 1996; "Donor's Money May Pull Strings—Daily Planet Gets Anonymous Offer," *TD*, 17 July 1996. Josephine Ensign, a VCU-educated nurse working at the Daily Planet later described her own fall into homelessness in Richmond in *Catching Homelessness*.

75. "Citation Remains in Force—Chuck Richardson Will Stay in Jail," *TD*, 5 Jan. 1997; "Conn Letter Said to List Misdeeds," *TD*, 20 Jan. 1997; "City Librarian Fired," *TD*, 10 Dec. 1996; "Joel Harris, Wife Plead Guilty," *TD*, 10 Sept. 1997; "Guilty Plea Will End a Flashy Career," *TD*, 31 Jan. 1999; "Bobb Takes Position in Oakland," *TD*, 14 Oct. 1997; "Townes Leaving Post in March," *TD*, 31 Dec. 1997.

76. "Chamber Members Invited Online," *TD*, 13 Aug. 1997; Peter Schmidt, "Engineering Complex at Va. Commonwealth U. Helps Lure Motorola," *Chronicle of Higher Education*, 6 June 1997.

77. "VCU Breaks Ground for New Fine Arts Center," *VCU Voice*, 23 Oct. 1997, 1. There were already signs of small-business development and residential housing making for a neighborhood along Broad between Belvidere on the west and the MCV Campus to the east. See "Two-Way Street—Transition Under Way on Broad," *TD*, 29 Sept. 1997.

78. "VCU Expresses Regret over SCHEV Decision," *VCU Voice*, 24 Nov. 1997; "Major in Black Studies Hits Snags for VCU," *WP*, 9 Oct. 1997.

79. "Engineering Students Get Boost—VCU Scholarships Aid New School," *TD*, 26 Aug. 1996; "$10 Million Needed for School," *TD*, 26 Aug. 1996; "Digging In," *TD*, 14 Nov. 1996.

80. "VCU Switches on Vow to Fund Project," *TD*, 30 Oct. 1997; "Renege by VCU Criticized," *TD*, 31 Oct. 1997; Trani, "VCU President Trani Answers Articles" and "The News Department Responds," *TD*, 9 Nov. 1997.

81. "Exponential Growth," *TD*, 23 June 1997; "North America's Most Improved Cities," *Fortune*, 24 Nov. 1997, 170–82. The *Fortune* article also reported that from 1990–96, the Richmond region's population increased by 8 percent and personal income increased by 24.5 percent. In 1987–96 the violent crime rate dropped by 40.3 percent.

82. "Building an Image," *Inside Business*, Dec. 1997, 16–19.

83. Trani, "1998: A Very Good Year at VCU," *VCU Voice*, 26 Jan. 1998; "Trani-Vision," *Style Weekly*, 5 Jan. 1999. "Trani Vision" was his term for his "ideas and goals for VCU," and those, he continued, involved "my belief—and our focus—that the university and the community are one." See "'Trani Vision' Focused on Cooperation between University and Community," *CT*, 1 Mar. 1999.

84. "McCarthy En Route to VCU?," *TD*, 4 Aug. 1997; "Will VCU Have to Create a Position for McCarthy?," *TD*, 5 Aug. 1997; "McCarthy Set as Heir to Smith," *TD*, 25 Aug. 1997.

85. "Serving Two Masters—VCU Gets Year of Co-Coaching," *TD*, 16 Nov. 1997; "Bidding Adieu to VCU: Smith Era Near End," *TD*, 23 Feb. 1998; "Whether Times Were Good or Bad, His Disposition Was Always Sonny," *TD*, 1 Mar. 1998; "1998 Top 10," *TD*, 27 Dec. 1998.

86. "VCU's Siegel Center a Site for Sore Eyes," *TD*, 16 Feb. 1999; "Siegel Center Marks Tradition of Aspirations," *TD*, 10 June 1999 (quotation). The *CT*, 1 Mar. 1999, carried an announcement to students that the recreational side of the Siegel Center would open on 15 March.

87. "Rams Right at Home—Siegel Center Gets Christened Today," *TD*, 19 Nov. 1999 (quotation); "After Slow Start Rams Rip Red Foxes for Weekend Split" (women's team), and "VCU Opens Siegel Center with Close Win over Louisville" (men's team), *CT*, 22 Nov. 1999.

10. Virginia's University, 2000–2004

1. See, for example, Wiewel, Carlson, and Friedman, "Planning the New Urban University," 129, 130, 131; Initiative for a Competitive Inner City and CEOs for Cities, *Leveraging Colleges and Universities*, 44–52; Rodin, *University and Urban Revival*, 16; Coalition of Urban Serving Universities, *Urban Universities*, 16. See also Trani, "Virginia Commonwealth University."

2. Trani, "Richmond at the Crossroads: The Greater Richmond Metropolitan Area and the Knowledge Based High Technology Economy of the 21st Century," supplement to *UniverCity News*, 31 Aug. 1998.

3. Ibid.; "Trip Sparks Trani's Vision for the Future; VCU President Sees Technology as Solution," *TD*, 10 Aug. 1998.

4. "Trip Sparks Trani's Vision"; "Old World Offers a High-Tech Example," *Inside Business*, 18 Aug. 1998.

5. "Bundling Regional Projects—Consultant Says Area Needs His MAPS to Chart Optimal Future," *TD*, 23 Apr. 1998. See also Horrow, *When the Game Is on the Line*, xxii, 118, 120,121, 133, 171.

6. "Metropolitan Area Project List Grows," *TD*, 31 Oct. 1998; "Picking Up the Check," *Style Weekly*, 23 July 2003.

7. "Aid Sought for College Buildings," *TD*, 15 Aug. 1995; "In 1998–2000 Budget, VCU Gets Nearly $40 Million," *TD*, 21 Mar. 1998; "Capital Projects Funded for VCU in State Budget," *VCU Voice*, 6 Apr. 1998; "VCU Breaks Ground for Life Sciences Bldg.," *CT*, 21 Jan. 1999.

8. "VCU Launches Its News Center," *TD*, 7 Nov. 1998; "'Red Hot and Ready to Go' VCU Launches 21st Century News Center," *CT*, 9 Nov. 1998; "GPAB Renamed for Temple," *CT*, 26 Oct. 1998; "VCU School Still Looking for Leader," *TD*, 15 Aug. 1998; "Communications School Won't Seek Reaccreditation," *TD*, 3 Oct. 1998; "Mass Communications Not Applying for Reaccreditation," *CT*, 8 Oct. 1998.

9. "VCU Reorganizing School of Mass Communications," *TD*, 8 Apr. 1999; "VCU's News Center Chief Resigns," *TD*, 22 Oct. 1999; "Media Center Creator Resigns," *CT*, 25 Oct. 1999.

10. "Mess Comm," *TD*, 13 Apr. 1999. As president of Northeastern University, in Boston, Richard Freeland found that the school's building program "conveyed a message of positive change more powerfully than any administrative initiative could possibly have done. The impact on recruitment of faculty and students cannot be overstated" (*Transforming the Urban University*, 87–88).

11. "VCU Shifts Adcenter Director," *TD*, 15 July 2000; "VCU Hires Mass Comm Director," *CT*, 30 Aug. 2001; "VCU Names Chief of Unit," *TD*, 1 Sept. 2001.

12. June O. Nicholson, the interim director in 1997–98, makes a good example. In addition to her work on the future of women in journalism (see her introduction in Nicholson et al., eds., *Edge of Change*, 1–26), she was director from 1985 through 2007 of the VCU Urban Journalism Workshop, a summer program to recruit minority high-school students into journalism careers. See "VCU Professor Honored for Commitment to Promoting Diversity in Newsrooms," *VCU News*, 6 Aug. 2008.

13. "VCU Sees Chance to Capitalize on Status as an Urban University," *TD*, 7 May 1989.

14. "Student Body at VCU Bigger and Brighter," *TD*, 16 Sept. 1992; "VCU Enrollment Dip Brings $2 Million Shortfall," *TD*, 23 Sept. 1994; "Slower Growth Is Projected for Colleges," *TD*, 12 Apr. 1995; "VCU Losing Students—Enrollment Drop Means Budget Cuts," *TD*, 24 Mar. 1995.

15. "Is Freshman Explosion Imminent?," *TD*, 14 June 1996; "Freshman Flood Overflows Dormitory Space," *TD*, 11 Aug. 1996; "VCU to Raise In-State Tuition 1 Percent for Undergraduates," *TD*, 17 May 1997; "VCU Is Expecting Record Numbers," *TD*, 17 Sept. 1998. See also Freeland, *Transforming the Urban University*, 36, 47.

16. "Gilmore Says Tuition Rollback Won't Be a Strain—Prosperity to Offset 20% Cut, He Says," *TD*, 15 Dec. 1998; "Enrollments Surge at Va. Colleges," *TD*, 22 Aug. 1999.

17. "VCU to Build $16 Million Apartment-Style Dorm," *TD*, 17 July 1999.

18. "Housing Demand Rising at VCU," *TD*, 14 Feb. 2002.

19. "VCU Will Enroll Record Number of Students," *UniverCity News*, 28 Sept. 1998.

20. "MCV Deal Means Health Agency Cuts," *TD*, 16 May 1998.

21. "VCU Requests $13.7 Million," *TD*, 18 Sept. 1998.

22. "VCU's Request," *TD*, 24 Sept. 1998.

23. "Funding Relief May Be on the Way to MCV—Treating Indigents, Managed Care Costly," *TD*, 17 Feb. 1999; "MCV: Cash Cow No More—Uninsured Indigents, Medical School, Doctors All Tug at Purse Strings," *TD*, 11 Apr. 1999.

24. "MCV Arm Enters Financing Venture," *TD*, 17 Oct. 1995; "Hospitals Apply for New Centers," *TD*, 4 Aug. 1995; "Health-Care Shift Hits Bumps," *TD*, 3 Oct. 1996; "HMO Cards Necessity for Many," *TD*, 29 Mar. 1999; "HMO Sale Set," 7 Oct. 1998.

25. Retchin, "Three Strategies" (the quoted phrases are from pp. 15, 16, 17, 22, 17, 22). See also Retchin, "Variations in Medicare." In October 1998 the *Times-Dispatch* published a series of articles, titled "Doctors' Cures," by health professionals about the economic pressures they felt, especially from HMOs. Retchin, with Harold Young, the chair of neurosurgery, provided the final essay in the series, in which they laid out the argument Retchin made in the professional journals cited above. See Retchin and Young, "Market Pressures Buffet Academic Medical Centers," *TD*, 24 Oct. 1998. The series was summarized in the *Scarab*, too; see "Doctors' Cures," *Scarab* 48 (Summer 1999): 18–21.

26. "VCU Starts Managed-Care Plan," *TD*, 22 Dec. 2000; Retchin, Garland, and Anum, "Transfer of Uninsured Patients," 245–52; Neimeyer, "Effect of a Coordinated Care Program," 6–7, 190 (the quoted phrase appears on p. 6).

27. "Enrollment in Clinical Trials Halted," *TD*, 9 Jan. 2000; "Agency Halts VCU Research on Humans," *CT*, 13 Jan. 2000; "VCU Moves to Shape Research Plan," *TD*, 15 Jan. 2000.

28. "Research Official at VCU Resigns," *TD*, 22 Jan. 2000; "Research Official Resigns, Will Stay as MCV Professor," *CT*, 24 Jan. 2000.

29. "Fixing Trials Costly," *TD*, 11 Feb. 2000. The mandated new research procedures even led to nervous (and temporary) orders prohibiting student journalists from conducting interviews. See "Communications Students Exempt," *TD*, 8 Feb. 2000, and "Interviewing Cleared from Research Suspension," *CT*, 17 Feb. 2000.

30. "VCU Research Losing Ground?," *TD*, 27 Aug. 2000. Vice President for Governmental Relations Donald Gehring and Acting Vice President for Research Francis Macrina responded with a letter to the editor stating that the paper's article considered only research funded by the National Institutes of Health, and by a more inclusive standard, VCU's research record showed growth and a higher ranking (see "VCU Supports Vital Research," *TD*, 1 Oct. 2000).

31. "MCV Entities Merging," *TD*, 25 June 2000.

32. Trani, "VCU Bracing for Gilmore's Budgetary Ax," *CT*, 1 Mar. 2001. The maneuver to fund indigent care was discussed in "Hospitals' Funding Seems Safe," *TD*, 14 Mar. 2001. See also Trani interview, May 2010.

33. "VCU Health System Trims Some Services," *TD*, 13 June 2001; "Housing Demand Rising at VCU."

34. Gov. Jim Gilmore, "Legislators Reminded of Car-Tax Mandate" (guest editorial), *CT*, 22 Feb. 2001; "VCU Tops $167 Million in Fund Drive," *TD*, 15 Sept. 1999. See also "Gilmore Declares a 'Digital Dominion,'" *Washington Times*, 7 Sept. 2000. On the dot-com bubble and bust, see, for example, Lowenstein, *Origins of the Crash*.

35. "Campus Projects May Feel State Budget Pinch," *CT*, 1 Mar. 2000; Trani, "VCU Bracing"; "Budget Scheme Yields Optimism among State Lawmakers," *CT*, 9 Apr. 2001.

36. Payne, *Mark Warner the Dealmaker*, 128–56 (quotation on p. 156).

37. "Dorm Cable Fiasco," "VCU's Identity Crisis," and "Trani Honors Faculty Standouts," *CT*, 10 Sept. 2001.

38. "Students 'Imagine' a Safer World," "Classes Canceled, Campus Consoled," and "MCVH Preps for Pentagon Patients," *CT*, 13 Sept. 2001.

39. "University Breaks Ground for Life Sciences Building," and Trani, "Defining Life Sciences," *UniverCity News*, 25 Jan. 1999.

40. "Flames Damage Life Sciences Building," and "Researchers Map Out Human Genome," *CT*, 10 Apr. 2000.

41. "VCU Names Huff New Interim Vice Provost for Life Sciences," *TD*, 20 Apr. 2000; "Symbiosis," *Scarab* 49 (Fall 2000): 22. The Board of Visitors removed Huff's interim status in May 2001. See "VCU Revamps Its Image with Logo, Slogan," *TD*, 19 May 2001.

42. "Trani, Huff Reveal Plans for Changes in Life Sciences Program," *CT*, 2 Oct. 2000.

43. "Radical Science: Beyond Biology 101," 11–13, 15, "Physical Plant: The Center for the Life Sciences," 12–13, and "The Rice Center," 14, *Shafer Court Connections*, Summer 2001.

44. "Trani Marks His VCU Legacy," *CT*, 15 Nov. 2001; "New Life Sciences Building Named for Dr. and Mrs. Trani," *Scarab* 50 (Sept. 2001): 19 (quoted phrase).

45. "Doctors, Lab Cited for Anthrax Work," *TD*, 16 Nov. 2001; "Study Looks at Outbreaks of Smallpox," *TD*, 16 Dec. 2001; "Caution Urged on Vaccine," *TD*, 29 Mar. 2002; Wenzel, "Exposure Dangers Too Great for Vaccination to Be Voluntary," *TD*, 10 July 2002 (quotation); "1 Million People, 10 Days," *TD*, 24 Sept. 2002; "VCU's Vaccine Stance Won't Affect State Plan," *TD*, 24 Dec. 2002; "MCVH Reluctant to Vaccinate Staff," *CT*, 16 Jan. 2003.

46. VCU-Qatar, *Leaving a Mark*, 17. See also "VCU Plans Arts Program with Qatar," *TD*, 27 June 1998; "VCU Will Establish Arts College in Qatar," *TD*, 23 July 1998; Bains, "Virginia Commonwealth University."

47. "VCU Wants Upgrade of Qatar Program," *TD*, 9 Feb. 2001; "VCU Plan for Qatar Advances," *TD*, 18 Apr. 2001; "VCU Staff to Stay in Qatar," *TD*, 29 Sept. 2001; "VCU Weighs Value, Risks of Campus in Qatar," *TD*, 12 Oct. 2001; "VCU Says Its Qatar Staff Members Safe," *TD*, 2 Nov. 2001; "VCU Qatar Campus Measure Advances," *TD*, 17 Jan. 2002; "VCU-Qatar in Hot Spot," *TD*, 26 Sept. 2002; "Schools Dissolve International Borders," *TD*, 13 Oct. 2002; "VCU Does Not Plan to Evacuate in Qatar," *TD*, 18 Mar. 2003; "Threat Shuts Down U.S. Embassy but VCU Official Says 'All of Our Information Indicates Things are Normal' at University's Qatar Campus," *CT*, 25 Mar. 2004; "Qatar Campus Opens Door for Cultural Exchange," *CT*, 22 Nov. 2004; "The Art of Expansion," *TD*, 16 Mar. 2005.

48. "VCU Chemist Wins the Nobel Prize," *CT*, 10 Oct. 2002. See also "VCU Raises Balloons and Whole Campus Is Afloat," *TD*, 10 Oct. 2002; "Nobel Raises Profile of VCU," *TD*, 14 Oct. 2002.

49. "Bullet Taken from Ashland Victim," *TD*, 21 Oct. 2002; "Trauma Team on Alert," *TD*, 30 Oct. 2002; "Sniper Victim in Ashland Improves," *TD*, 8 Nov. 2002; "Oct. 19 Sniper Victim Leaves MCV," *TD*, 21 Nov. 2002.

50. "Bond-Issue Vote Critical to Colleges," *TD*, 27 Oct. 2002; "Warner Discusses State Budget, Possible Higher Education Cuts" (quotation), and "Early Lights Out Frustrates Students," *CT*, 10 Oct. 2002; "Warner Addresses Commonwealth Focusing on Education, Budget," *CT*, 13 Jan. 2003; Payne, *Mark Warner the Dealmaker*, 188, 192–93; "A Governor's Hard Sell: Higher Taxes in Virginia," *NYT*, 20 Jan. 2004.

51. BofV, Minutes, 14 Aug. 2003 and 16 May 2003, JBC.

52. "AdCenter Director to Step Down," *TD*, 12 Apr. 2002; "AdCenter Lures 'Star' to Direct," *TD*, 7 Nov. 2002.

53. "Proposal Urges VCU to Elevate Its Quality, Status," *TD*, 9 Aug. 2001; "African-American Studies to Become Major Next Semester," *CT*, 24 Apr. 2003; "VCU to Offer Major in African-American Studies," VCU press release, 13 June 2003 (other founding faculty members were anthropologist Christopher Brooks; Mark Wood, religious studies; and Rose Landrum-Lee, women's studies);

"Around the Globe, Inside the Classroom—Programs Add Flavor to Academic Life," *TD*, 12 Oct. 2003.

54. "MCV Gateway to Unlock Maze," *TD*, 16 Sept. 2000; "New MCV Building Expands Services," *TD*, 16 Feb. 2002.

55. "Financial Health Check Planned," *TD*, 13 Apr. 2002; "Bitter Pills for Ailing Hospitals," *NYT*, 31 Oct. 1999.

56. "MCV to End Year with Profit," *TD*, 25 June 2002.

57. "MCV Executive Leaving," *TD*, 1 Aug. 2002; "Consultant's Role Grows at VCU Health System," *TD*, 1 Aug. 2002.

58. "A. D. Williams Clinic Not Closing," *TD*, 30 Aug. 2002; "VCU Official to Retire," *TD*, 10 Sept. 2002.

59. "Report: $130 Million in Adjustments Needed," *TD*, 11 Sept. 2002.

60. "Arizona Executive Named MCV Chief," *TD*, 5 Apr. 2003; "VCU Health System Expects Profit," *TD*, 16 May 2003; "VCU Health System Profits Rise," *TD*, 18 June 2003; "Profit News Is 'Good News,'" *TD*, 20 Aug. 2003.

61. "Profit for Health System," *TD*, 17 Mar. 2004; "System Cures Records Woes," *TD*, 4 July 2004 (Retchin quotation).

62. *VCUArts*. Another sign of the changed environment in Richmond, thanks in part to VCU's proximity, was the rise since 2000 of "First Fridays," a monthly event sponsored by the growing community of art galleries, restaurants, and other cultural venues, centered on the once decrepit blocks of Broad Street east of Belvidere Street. See "First Fridays," *Shafer Court Connections*, Spring 2008, 14–17.

63. "VCU Projects Provided Spark for Downtown," *TD*, 20 Nov. 2005.

64. "Sports Medicine Facility Established by VCU, Hospitals," *TD*, 4 Feb. 1987; "On Richmond's Horizon—VCU's Growing Footprint," *TD*, 20 Nov. 2005.

65. "New Boom at VCU—Apartment Swell Linked to College's Growth," *TD*, 27 July 2003.

66. "VCU Plans Growth in a New Direction," *TD*, 11 May 2003.

67. For the AP story, see, for example, "Nadeau Injured Critically," *Louisville Courier-Journal*, 3 May 2003. See also "A Hunt for a Sniper," *NYT*, 21 Oct. 2002; "A River's Long Way Back," *NYT*, 16 May 2004. The *TD*'s identification was a little better: "Virginia Commonwealth University's Medical College of Virginia Hospitals" (see "Nadeau Hurt in Crash," *TD*, 3 May 2003). As 2003 began, *USA Today* had given national front-page coverage to MCV Hospitals' influential decision not to participate in the Bush administration's fearful program of smallpox vaccinations, quoting Richard Wenzel, chairman of internal medicine, on why the issue involved "medical risk-benefit," not "patriotism." The problem was that the article identified Wenzel as chairman at "Virginia Medical College, the teaching arm of the University of Virginia." Here was the national spotlight, and deserved, too, thirty-five

years after the creation of VCU, yet the University of Virginia got the credit. "Hospitals Balk at Smallpox Vaccine," *USA Today*, 21 Jan. 2003.

68. "Drug Sales Bring Huge Profits, and Scrutiny, to Cancer Doctors," *NYT*, 26 Jan. 2003; "What's in a Name? Some at University Say New VCU Medical Center Moniker Is a Rose That Smells Less Sweet," *TD*, 9 Nov. 2003; "Judge Rejects Bid to Keep 'MCV' Label," *TD*, 8 Nov. 2003; Editorial, *TD*, 21 Nov., 7 Dec. 2003. On Nadeau's return to the VCU Medical Center, see "Nadeau to Visit MCV," *TD*, 5 Sept. 2003. See also "'We Can't Be More Thankful,'" *Shafer Court Connections*, Fall 2003, 5.

69. "Plan for Campus Backed, VCU Says," *TD*, 14 Nov. 2003; "More Growth for University?," *CT*, 20 Nov. 2003.

70. "VCU Renames Academic Campus," *TD*, 16 June 2004; "VCU's Identity Crisis," *CT*, 10 Sept. 2001.

71. "City Park near VCU in Line for Some TLC," *TD*, 6 May 2004.

72. "VCU Spruces Up Its 'Front Porch'—Monroe Park on Way to Becoming Integral Part of the University," *TD*, 5 July 2004; "Park's Fountain Has City Bubbling," *TD*, 23 Oct. 2004.

73. *VCU 2020 Master Site Plan*, 3–4. See also "VCU Adopts 15-Year Site Plan," *TD*, 13 Aug. 2004.

74. *VCU 2020 Master Site Plan*, 7, 25–26, 31. The plan noted that if the student body had become more traditional in seeking a residential university-community experience, it remained highly diverse in backgrounds (26).

75. Ibid., 9, 32, 37, 42, 62. The plan promised to replace West Hospital with a "similarly distinguished landmark piece of architecture" (62).

76. Ibid., 25.

11. OPPORTUNITY UNIVERSITY, 2005–2009

1. "VCU Making Large Strides toward Institutional Pride," *TD*, 29 Feb. 2004.

2. "McCarthy Out—Capel In," *TD*, 6 Mar. 2002; "Will Someone Different Make Difference for VCU?," *TD*, 7 Mar. 2002.

3. "After Eight-Year Drought, Joy Washes over VCU," *TD*, 9 Mar. 2004; "One Upped!," *CT*, 25 Mar. 2004.

4. "Wilder, Bliley Join Forces—Goal: Strong Mayor for City by 2005," *TD*, 26 July 2002. In his memoir, *Son of Virginia*, Wilder described conditions in Richmond then in terms more akin to descriptions of the city decades earlier: "Richmond seemed to be crumbling in on itself; decay was all around us" (149). The campaign for a strong mayor, however, focused on failures of leadership more than on other bad conditions in Richmond. Two VCU political scientists concluded that the election of that type of black mayor in both Washington and Richmond resulted in large part from "the

political corruption scandals that plagued both cities in the 1990s" (Jackson and Banks, "Redefining the Role of City Government," 57).

5. "Seeing Need for At-Large Mayor Is Just First Step," *TD*, 31 July 2002. Hayter, *Dream Is Lost*, credits the revitalization of Richmond less to VCU than to Richmond Renaissance and, especially, to "local people's resilience" (243).

6. "Group Seeks to Amend Wilder Plan," *TD*, 5 Aug. 2002; "Group Blasts Mayor Plan," *TD*, 10 Aug. 2002.

7. "Trani to Lead Richmond Renaissance," *TD*, 29 Aug. 2001; "Wilder Talk Draws Fire," *TD*, 1 Oct. 2002.

8. "Council Not Included in Panel," *TD*, 19 Sept. 2002; "City Creates Study Panel," *TD*, 15 Oct. 2002; "Businesses Give to Wilder Panel," *TD*, 3 Jan. 2003; "Elected Mayor Proposed," *TD*, 29 Jan. 2003; "Mayor Issue on Ballot," *TD*, 23 Aug. 2003; "Richmonders Debate Mayoral Selection Proposal," *CT*, 20 Oct. 2003; "City Voters Embrace At-Large Mayor Plan," *TD*, 5 Nov. 2003; "Our Town," *TD*, 16 Mar. 2004; "Wilder by a Landslide," *TD*, 3 Nov. 2004; "L. Douglas Wilder School of Government and Public Affairs," *Shafer Court Connections*, Summer 2004, 3.

9. "Wilder's Priority Is Police Business," *TD*, 25 Nov. 2004 (quotations); "New Police Chief Has Big-City Experience," *TD*, 25 Jan. 2005.

10. "VCU Ponders Razing Old Hospital Buildings," *TD*, 4 Aug. 2004.

11. Ibid.

12. "Save the West Hospital," *Style Weekly*, 11 Aug. 2004; "Buildings That May Be Razed to Be Subject of Walking Tour," *TD*, 11 Aug. 2004; "VCU Adopts 15-Year Site Plan," *TD*, 13 Aug. 2004; "Power Player: If You Take on VCU President Eugene Trani, You'd Better Be Prepared," *Style Weekly*, 25 Aug. 2004.

13. "Mayor Seeks Demolition Freeze," *TD*, 16 Sept. 2004.

14. On historic preservation in Richmond, see also "The Continuing Legacy of Historic Preservation," National Park Service, accessed 19 Feb. 2020, https://www.nps.gov/nr/travel/richmond/ContinuingLegacy.html. Allied with the historic preservationists were Richmonders who believed that confronting the city's history of slavery and racism was the way forward to reconciliation, which resulted in the city-sponsored Slave Trail Commission in 1998. See Corcoran, *Trustbuilding*, 57-69.

15. "City Will Seek Sites for VCU Expansion," *TD*, 30 Sept. 2004; "Wilder's Mayoral Triumph Raises More Questions Than Answers," *TD*, 7 Nov. 2004; "Wilder's Dual Role Raises Questions," *Style Weekly*, 8 Dec. 2004; "'Governor Wilder Is His Own Man'—Some See VCU Connection as a Conflict," *TD*, 12 Dec. 2004; "The Provocateur," *Style Weekly*, 5 Jan. 2005.

16. "Project on Broad Street Will Reroute Some Traffic," *TD*, 6 July 2003; "Gov. Warner, NCI Director Help Launch VCU Massey Cancer Center Research

Addition," *VCU News*, 24 Sept. 2003. On the Goodwins and other donors, see "VCU Gets Big Boost from Non-Alumni," *TD*, 10 Apr. 2005.

17. "New VCU Cancer Lab Has Been Named for Goodwins," *TD*, 6 May 2006; "New Lab Adds Cutting Edge to Cancer Research Center," *TD*, 7 May 2006; "Medical Center Builds on Past, Plan for Future," and "On Richmond's Horizon—Biotech and Medical," *TD*, 4 June 2006. A photo of the vista from Church Hill published in this book also appeared in *Scarab* 53 (Summer 2004): 21, and in Bonis, Koste, and Lyons, *Virginia Commonwealth University*, 119. On Trani's Saturday postbrunch tours with his grandchildren, see also "The City That Grandpa Rebuilt," *Richmond Magazine*, Oct. 2004.

18. "Confederate Museum Mulls Move," *TD*, 9 Oct. 2004. On the MOC's slavery exhibition, see Naile, "'Like Nixon Going to China.'"

19. "Confederate Landmark under Siege," *TD*, 28 Jan. 2005; "Hearings Set on Moving Key Confederate Sites Squeezed by VCU," *TD*, 14 June 2005; "Moving White House Is Delicate Subject," *TD*, 8 Oct. 2005; "ACORN Threatens VCU, State with Lawsuit," *Style Weekly*, 30 Nov. 2005; "Museum of the Confederacy—Collection to Leave VCU's Shadow," *TD*, 17 Oct. 2006; "Name Chosen for Combined Civil War Museums," *TD*, 16 Jan. 2014. The long story's conclusion came several years later. See "American Civil War Museum Sells Building to VCU Health System," VCU News Service, 30 June 2017.

20. "Philip Morris a Shot in the Arm for Park," *TD*, 23 May 2005; "VCU Starts Its New Nursing Building," *TD*, 15 June 2005; "Ground Broken for Hospital," *TD*, 16 Nov. 2005; "VCU Breaks Ground on $228 Million Addition," *TD*, 2 Nov. 2005.

21. "VCU Gets Big Boost," *TD*, 10 Apr. 2005; "Couple Smile on VCU," *TD*, 27 May 2005; "VCU Breaks Ground"; "VCU's $82 Million in Gifts Is Best Year," *TD*, 14 July 2005.

22. "VCU Names New Dean for Medical School," *TD*, 15 June 2005; "VCU's Mover and Shaper Moving On," *TD*, 30 June 2005; "30 Years of Public Service; VCU's Timmreck to Retire in 2006," *TD*, 7 July 2005; "State Finance Secretary Will Leave for a Top Post at VCU," *TD*, 5 Nov. 2005; "VCU's Sander Ready to Move On," *TD*, 19 Aug. 2005.

23. Courturier, "Checks and Balances," 1–9 (quotation from p. 9). See also Blake, "Restructuring Relationships in Virginia," and Leslie and Berdahl, "Politics of Restructuring Higher Education."

24. Courturier, "Checks and Balances"; "Three State Colleges Seek Charter Status," *TD*, 7 Jan. 2004; "Schools Delay Charter Request," *TD*, 24 Jan. 2004; "Colleges Aim to Revamp System," *TD*, 10 Sept. 2004; "Leaders Contest Charter Proposal at a VCU Forum," *TD*, 26 Oct. 2004.

25. "Leaders Contest Charter Proposal"; Timothy J. Sullivan (W&M), "Initiative Would Address Intractable Funding Problem," *TD*, 20 Dec. 2004; John T.

Casteen III (UVA), "Students, Parents Need Fiscal Predictability to Plan for College," *TD*, 21 Dec. 2004; Charles W. Steger (VT), "Entrepreneurial Schools Will Fuel State's Economy," *TD*, 22 Dec. 2004.

26. "Colleges Aim to Be in Different Class," *TD*, 9 Jan. 2005 (quotation); Blake, "Restructuring Relationships in Virginia," 31–32; Courturier, "Checks and Balances," 44.

27. Courturier, "Checks and Balances," 54 (boards of visitors); Leslie and Berdahl, "Politics of Restructuring Higher Education" 316–18; Trani, "Creating a Broader Model." Trani perceived that the Board of Visitors became in the last year or so of his presidency "an activist Board," which in part came from "the governor and the State Council and the legislature saying, 'by God, you're accountable'" (Trani interview, "Oregon Hill," 2009).

28. "Trani Extends His Stay at VCU," *TD*, 21 May 2005; "Philip Morris Will Add Jobs Here," *TD*, 5 Apr. 2005; "BioTech Park, City Welcome Big Catch," *TD*, 6 Apr. 2005 (quotation); "Philip Morris a Shot in the Arm."

29. "Wielding the Influence to Make Visions Reality" (first quotation), "4 Power Brokers Help Shape City's Landscape," and "VCU Transforming Richmond's Core" (second quotation), *TD*, 14 Aug. 2005.

30. "Police Continue July Murder Investigation," and "What Students Say about VCU Mail Anywhere," *CT*, 28 Aug. 2005; "Katrina's Wake," and "Largest Freshman Class in VCU History," *CT*, 1 Sept. 2005.

31. Pelasara, *Love You More*, 11–12; "Freshman at VCU Missing, Officials Say," *TD*, 9 Sept. 2005; "Search for Missing VCU Student Now a Criminal Investigation," VCU News, 15 Sept. 2005; "Statement from VCU President Eugene P. Trani," VCU News, 6 Oct. 2005. See also "Community Gathers to Remember Behl," *CT*, 10 Oct. 2005.

32. "30-Year Sentence in Slaying of Student," *WP*, 10 Aug. 2006. The local media coverage was equally intense, as evidenced by *Style Weekly*'s cover story, "My Roommate, Ben Fawley," 1 Feb. 2006.

33. "Kids Hang Out at MySpace.com—Maybe Parents Should Check In," *TD*, 15 Sept. 2005. VCU students were quick to go to Behl's MySpace and Facebook pages for information about her (see "Missing Student," *CT*, 12 Sept. 2005).

34. "VCU Breaks Ground"; "Ground Broken for Hospital"; "On Richmond's Horizon."

35. "VCU Expects Smooth Ride toward General Assembly Funding," *CT*, 19 Jan. 2006; "Medical Center Builds on Past"; "VCU Dedicates Research Building," *TD*, 25 Apr. 2009.

36. "VCU At Large," *CT*, 28 Aug. 2006; "A Huge Void to Fill—Capel's Departure Leaves Another Hole for Rams," *TD*, 12 Apr. 2006; "Teague, 40, Brings Energy, Enthusiasm and Vision to Rams' Athletic Department," *TD*,

18 Apr. 2006; "'This Feels Good'—VCU Basketball Job Comes after 10 Years under Donavan at the University of Florida," *TD*, 19 Apr. 2006; "VCU Will Pass on Adding Football," *TD*, 22 Apr. 2006.

37. "Madness of Leigh Street," *TD*, 6 Mar. 2007; "Maynor Sinks Duke," *TD*, 16 Mar. 2007; "Overtime and Out," *TD*, 18 Mar. 2007; "Grant Staying Put," *TD*, 6 Apr. 2007.

38. Trani interview, 24 Mar. 2015; "VCU Said to Set Up Ties to Indian Schools," *TD*, 13 Oct. 2006; Wilder, "Overseas Trip Highlighted the Necessity of Education," *TD*, 2 July 2006.

39. Trani interview, 24 Mar. 2015; "Group Pays for Wilder's India Trip," *TD*, 14 Oct. 2006 (first quotation); Trani, "Take Note, America: India Is Coming," *TD*, 19 Nov. 2006; "Trani: Universities Need to Embrace Global Strategies," *TD*, 8 Nov. 2007; "VCU Adds Partnership to Its List," *TD*, 20 Nov 2007 (second quotation). *Shafer Court Connections*, Spring 2006, was a special issue on VCU's new and abundant international connections.

40. "Oregon Hill Fights VCU Plan," *TD*, 9 Apr. 2007; "VCU's Rec Center Push Heats Up," *TD*, 29 May 2007; "VCU Oregon Hill Facility Advances," *TD*, 27 June 2007; Todd Woodson, "The Question Is Not Whether to Build, but Where," *TD*, 15 July 2007 (Woodson, then head of the Oregon Hill Home Improvement Council, suggested a spot on Broad Street for the new gym); Trani, "Athletic Facilities Fill a Serious Need for Students," *TD*, 15 July 2007; "VCU Gym Proposal Gains Key Approval," *TD*, 29 Sept. 2007. On enrollment, see "VCU Expects Enrollment This Fall to Top 31,000—Its Student Body Has Grown 44.4 Percent from 21,681 in 1996," *TD*, 10 Aug. 2007.

41. "Honoring Business Diversity," *TD*, 5 Dec. 2007.

42. Drake and Holsworth in *Affirmative Action and the Stalled Quest for Black Progress* argue that the *Croson* decision created consternation because "set-aside ordinances had simply become a routine (and sometimes essential) instrument by which urban leaders conducted politics" (138). See also Chambers, "Looking Back," esp. 1656.

43. Gustave R. Thomas (director, Virginia Regional Minority Supplier Development Council), "Minority Business Empowerment Must Start at Top," *TD*, 12 Mar. 1990; Joint Legislative Audit and Review Commission of the Virginia General Assembly, "Minority-Owned Business Participation in State Contracts," House Document No. 53 (1996 Session), 1; "VCU to Sponsor Networking Event for Minority Firms," *TD*, 25 May 1992; Benjamin J. Lambert, "Biotech Center Will Be a Social Plus," *TD*, 2 Oct. 1993. Lambert was a state senator from Richmond.

44. Trani interview, 15 Dec. 2015; Ohlinger interview, 22 Aug. 2014. Scholarship on universities and urban development ignores the issue of set-asides and minority contracts, despite the attention those issues received from

politicians and the media in the 1990s and after. See, for instance, Perry and Wiewel, eds., *University as Urban Developer*; Gilderbloom and Mullins, eds., *Promise and Betrayal*; and Trani and Holsworth, *Indispensable University*.

45. "Candid Report on Region out Today," *TD*, 19 Nov. 2007; "Report Criticizes Region's Direction," *TD*, 20 Nov. 2007; "Vision Thing," *TD*, 20 Nov. 2007; "A Conversation with the *Times-Dispatch*," *TD*, 20 Jan. 2008; Crupi, "Putting the Future Together," 49–54.

46. "For the Love of VCU," *Shafer Court Connections*, Spring 2008, 18–19; "VCU Brandcenter," *Shafer Court Connections*, Spring 2008, 6.

47. BofV, Minutes, 14 Feb. and 16 May 2008, JBC; "VCU Moves Up in College Rankings," *TD*, 29 Mar. 2008; "VCU Keeps Grant," *TD*, 25 Apr. 2008; "Kostin: 800 Wins and Counting" and "Quidditch Comes to VCU," *CT*, 1 May 2008. For different views of the *U.S. News & World Report* rankings, see Tuchman, *Wannabe U*, 117–29, and Freeland, *Transforming the Urban University*, 45–47.

48. "Kaine, Wilder, Trani Unveil VCU Building," *CT*, 10 Apr. 2008; "VCU Dedicates Its Newest Buildings," *TD*, 10 Apr. 2008. See also "Bold Transformation: How VCU Is Bringing Life to the Historically Dingy and Depressing Monroe Ward Neighborhood," *Style Weekly*, 27 Feb. 2008.

49. Trani, "Master Plans Acknowledge Symbiotic Relationship" and "Raising Downtown," *TD*, 27 Apr. 2008. On Level 3 status, see "VCU Expects More Students, Independence," *TD*, 7 Mar. 2007 (quotations); "VCU Granted Greater Autonomy," *TD*, 22 Mar. 2008.

50. "Charlotte, N.C. Woos Monroe for Police Chief," *TD*, 6 May 2008; "Council, Wilder Spar over Praise for Police Chief's Work," *TD*, 7 May 2008; "Don't Go!," *TD*, 11 May 2008; "Council Resolution Urges Monroe to Stay," *TD*, 13 May 2008; "Monroe Accepts Charlotte Job," *TD*, 16 May 2008; "Wilder Will Not Run for Re-Election," *TD*, 17 May 2008.

51. "VCU Degree Probe Expected by July 1," *TD*, 3 June 2008; "Degree of Separation," *Style Weekly*, 7 Jan. 2009. On Monroe's graduation, see "Monroe's Degree of Difficulty," *TD*, 18 May 2007.

52. "VCU Looking into Bogus Degree Case," *TD*, 23 May 2008.

53. Agenda, Vice Presidents' Meeting, 27 May 2008, Trani Papers, JBC; "At One University, Tobacco Money Is a Secret," *NYT*, 22 May 2008. On the historic relationship between MCV and tobacco companies, see Proctor, *Golden Holocaust*, which states that the relationship grew less close after the merger and creation of VCU in 1968, but previously "this cozy relationship meant that it was sometimes hard even to say where the company left off and the college began" (187).

54. "VCU, Philip Morris Partners in Research," *TD*, 23 May 2008.

55. "VCU Degree Probe"; Holsworth, "Subject: Request to Add Information," *TD*, 3 Aug. 2008 (first quotation); "Rules Broken for Monroe," *TD*, 6 Sept. 2008 (summarizes the report to SACS, dated 5 Sept. 2008); "Monroe Can Keep Degree from VCU" and "Flunked" (second quotation), *TD*, 28 June 2008.

56. "VCU Chief Orders Review of Policies," *TD*, 30 June 2008 (see also "VCU Will Review Research Pacts," *TD*, 5 June 2008); "VCU Sets Meeting on Research Setup," *TD*, 14 July 2008; "VCU President Healing after Bypass Surgery," *TD*, 15 July 2008.

57. "Rules Broken for Monroe"; "Trani Released from Hospital" and "Four VCU Leaders Resign Key Posts," *TD*, 23 July 2008.

58. "VCU Holds Forum on Research Ties," *TD*, 17 July 2008. See James A. Bacon, "A Tale of Two Outrages," *Bacon's Rebellion* (blog), 24 July 2008, http://baconsrebellion.com/tale-of-two-outrages/; James A. Bacon, "Scandal Reaches Critical Mass at VCU," *Bacon's Rebellion* (blog), 24 July 2008, https://www.baconsrebellion.com/wp/scandal-reaches-critical-mass-at-vcu/; James A. Bacon, "Has Gene Trani Stayed on Too Long," *Bacon's Rebellion* (blog), 24 July 2008, http://baconsrebellion.com/has-gene-trani-stayed-on-too-long/; "writedit" [Michelle Kienholz], "Secret Smoke-Filled Agreements," *Medical Writing, Editing & Grantsmanship* (blog), 22 May 2008, https://writedit.wordpress.com/2008/05/22/secret-smoke-filled-agreements/; "writedit" [Michelle Kienholz], "VCU-Philip Morris Agreement Researched," *Medical Writing, Editing & Grantsmanship* (blog), 1 June 2008, https://writedit.wordpress.com/2008/06/01/vcu-philip-morris-agreement-researched/; Roy M. Poses, "A Worse Variant of a New Species of Conflict of Interest," *Health Care Renewal* (blog), 28 May 2008, http://hcrenewal.blogspot.com/2008/05/worse-variant-of-new-species-of.html; Roy M. Poses, "Linking the Anechoic Effect and Suppression of Research to Conflicts of Interest and Mission-Hostile Management: The VCU Case," *Health Care Renewal* (blog), 4 June 2008, http://hcrenewal.blogspot.com/2008/06/linking-anechoic-effect-and-suppression.html; Roy M. Poses, "VCU, Philip Morris, and the 'Recent Unpleasantness,'" *Health Care Renewal* (blog), 15 July 2008, http://hcrenewal.blogspot.com/2008/07/vcu-philip-morris-and-recent.html; Roy M. Poses, "Courting Tobacco Money," *Health Care Renewal* (blog), 6 Aug. 2008, http://hcrenewal.blogspot.com/2008/08/courting-tobacco-money.html.

59. Holsworth, "Subject"; "VCU Panel Member Wants Study," *TD*, 13 Aug. 2008

60. "Trani Era Nears an End" and "VCU's Growth Will Be Legacy of Trani's Tenure," *TD*, 15 Aug. 2008.

61. Birnbaum and Eckel, "Dilemma of Presidential Leadership," 340–68 (second quotation, p. 340); Trachtenberg, Kauvar, and Bogue, *Presidencies*

Derailed, vii, 141 (third quotation). See also Harris and Ellis, "Exploring Involuntary Presidential Turnover," in which the authors conclude that the rate of involuntary turnover has increased from 1988 to 2016 (13). Gerhard Casper, former president of Stanford University, states that, unlike a corporation's CEO, the university president is "an authority with limited direct power" (*Winds of Freedom*, 5).

62. "VCU Learns Growth Doesn't Mean Prestige," *TD*, 23 Aug. 2008; Trani, "School Promotes Academic Excellence," *TD*, 31 Aug. 2008.

63. "Rules Broken for Monroe," *TD*, 6 Sept. 2008; "How VCU Flunked on Degree," *TD*, 7 Sept. 2008; "JLARC to Study Monroe Case," *TD*, 10 Sept. 2008. See also "VCU Releases Details on Improper Degree," *Inside Higher Ed*, 8 Sept. 2008. In 2018 Eugene Trani prepared for this book the following statement on the Rodney Monroe degree situation:

> I became president of VCU on July 1, 1990, and shortly thereafter headed to our Medical Center for my first meeting on that campus. I could not find a parking place and returned to my office at 910 West Franklin Street without going to the meeting. I asked my staff what I should do the next time I went to the MCV Campus. They told me I should go to the small parking lot behind the Putney House and when I did go, I saw a reserved parking spot marked, "Parking for VCU President, 24 hours a day. Towing enforced." It was a lesson for me to learn: staff will do everything they can to make happen what they believe will please their boss. I believe that is what happened in the Monroe case. I know how delighted I was that Chief Monroe was going to graduate and so were Governor Wilder and Dean Holsworth, but none of the three of us told anybody that this should happen, but I believe staff presumed we wanted it to occur, whether or not all of VCU's policies were being strictly followed. There was no evidence that any of the three of us told anybody to make the awarding of the degree happen, but we all, no doubt, expressed our admiration for Monroe and his persistence to get the degree. In fact, Dean Jon Steingass later said to the *Richmond Times-Dispatch* that there was "implied pressure." So I believe that VCU, through its Board of Visitors, overreacted and some Board members really did believe there was a high-level conspiracy, when, in fact, that was not the case. VCU's reputation, and those of some of its most senior administrators, took a hit, but in the end, the accreditation organization, SACS, correctly decided that no significant missteps had occurred.

64. "Ex-VCU Dean: 'Implied Pressure,'" *TD*, 16 Sept. 2008 (this story ran on p. 1, above the headline "Wall Street Sent Reeling"); Trani, "Even in Hard Times."

65. "VCU Panel Critiques Deals," *TD*, 2 Oct. 2008; "Budget Cuts Could Cost Jobs at VCU," *TD*, 7 Oct. 2008; "Protecting the Patient Is Hospital's Cornerstone," *TD*, 7 Oct. 2008; "Designer Is Chosen for Medical School," *TD*, 7 Oct. 2008.

66. "Revoke Degree, VCU Told," *TD*, 21 Oct. 2008; "VCU Revises Degree Policy," *TD*, 21 Nov. 2008.

67. "VCU Letting Public Pick Festival Bands," *TD*, 27 July 2008; "RPI Artwork Plants VCU's Roots in Stone," *TD*, 31 July 2008.

68. "Festival Will Be a Family Event and Tribute to Monroe Park," *TD*, 20 Oct. 2008; "Party in Monroe Park," *TD*, 26 Oct. 2008; "University Dedicates First Historic Markers on Both Campuses," *VCU News*, 24 Oct. 2008; "Richmond's Own," *TD*, 25 Oct. 2008.

69. "Obama Speak [*sic*] at Coliseum," *CT*, 23 Oct. 2008; "'Tears, Cheers, No More Fears'—Crowd Fills Broad Street to Celebrate Election of Obama," *TD*, 5 Nov. 2008; "Obama Supporters Take to the Streets," *CT*, 6 Nov. 2008.

70. "Not Just Maynor," *TD*, 5 Dec. 2008; "'Value Yourself,' Cosby Says at VCU," *TD*, 6 Dec. 2008; "Cosby Disclosures Call Degrees into Question," *TD*, 14 Aug. 2015.

71. "Degree of Separation," *Style Weekly*, 7 Jan. 2009; "VCU to Set Up Private Tip Line," *TD*, 14 Jan. 2009 (quotation); "Confidential Tip Line New at VCU," *CT*, 22 Jan. 2009.

72. "Newsmakers: Gov. Timothy M. Kaine," *TD*, 13 Jan. 2009; "More Saturday Classes Likely at VCU" (quotation), and "What's Happening at the Legislature?," *TD*, 13 Feb. 2009. Jon McGee declares in *Breakpoint* that "the Great Recession converged with long-brewing demographic change to fundamentally alter the postsecondary marketplace" (2). See also, for example, Barr and Turner, "Expanding Enrollments"; Brown and Hoxby, *How the Financial Crisis*, and Grawe, *Demographics*.

73. "VCU Names Next Leader," *TD*, 21 Feb. 2009 (quotation). See also "Michael Rao to Be VCU's Fifth President," *CT*, 23 Feb. 2009.

74. "Era Ends at VCU as Grant Departs," *TD*, 28 Mar. 2009; "Rams Hire Smart," 1 Apr. 2009; "Mutual Admiration," *TD*, 3 Apr. 2009 (quotations).

75. Goodwin, "Trani Built a Better VCU," Woodson, "VCU Hurt Historic Neighborhoods," Munro, "Trani's Complex Academic Legacy," "VCU's Trani Helped Transform School, City, and Lives" (first quotation), "Legacy," *TD*, 19 Apr. 2009; "The Man Behind the Curtain: A Q and A with Trani," *CT*, 27 Apr. 2009. The *Times-Dispatch* provided a positive assessment of the Biotechnology Research Park, with a history, in "Business of Life" and "Park Timeline," *TD*, 12 Jan. 2009. See also "Presidential Perspective," *Shafer Court Connections*, Spring 2009, 8–11, and "The End of an Era: VCU's Fourth President Retires," *Scarab* 58 (Summer 2009): 22. For VCU's role in

Richmond's economic development after 1990, see also Porter and Grogan, "Richmond Citizens Benefit," 164–70.

76. "VCU Graduates 4,000," *TD*, 17 May 2009.

77. Ibid.

78. "Trani Statue Unveiled at Life Sciences Building," *TD*, 30 May 2009; "Trani Steps Down at VCU," *TD*, 30 June 2009.

79. "VCU Exceeds Goal, Raises $410 Million," *TD*, 28 Sept. 2007; email, Peter L. Wyeth to Trani, 19 Aug. 2009, Trani Papers, JBC; "Dental Building Opening at VCU," TD, 18 June 2009.

Epilogue

1. "How VCU's Footprint Is Expanding in Richmond," *TD*, 28 Jan. 2009; "VCU President Highlights School's Diversity in State of the University Address," *TD*, 25 Jan. 2018. On universities as "anchor institutions," see, for example, CEOs for Cities, "How to Behave Like an Anchor Institution"; Perry and Menendez, "Urban Universities as Anchor Institutions"; Birch, Perry, and Taylor, "Universities as Anchor Institutions"; Diner, *Universities and Their Cities*, 112–13. The term "eds and meds" comes from Harkavy and Zuckerman, "Eds and Meds," See also "The City's Anchor: VCU Has Been a Big Factor in Richmond's Revival," *Virginia Business*, 27 Mar. 2015; Rao, "Talent, Innovation, and Place."

2. Trani and Holsworth, *Indispensable University*, 215. That same year, Trani announced formation of a nonprofit think tank named Richmond's Future, to help with regional planning, which he would head. See "Ex-VCU Chief to Lead Think Tank," *TD*, 28 June 2010. Richmond's Future's final report appeared in the *TD*, 21 Feb. 2016.

3. Wikipedia, accessed 19 Feb. 2020: "College Basketball Invitational," https://en.wikipedia.org/wiki/College_Basketball_Invitational, "2010 College Basketball Invitational," https://en.wikipedia.org/wiki/2010_College_Basketball_Invitational, and "VCU Rams Men's Basketball: Shaka Smart Era," https://en.wikipedia.org/wiki/VCU_Rams_men%27s_basketball#Shaka_Smart_era.

4. "CAA Final: ODU Beats VCU 70–65," *TD*, 7 Mar. 2011; "NCAA Right to Reject Tech, Select VCU," *TD*, 14 Mar. 2011; "VCU Drops USC, Faces Georgetown on Friday," *TD*, 16 Mar. 2011; "VCU Blows Past Georgetown," *TD*, 18 Mar. 2011.

5. "Richmond, Center of the College Hoops Universe," *TD*, 22 Mar. 2011; "Sweet: Two in the 16," *Roanoke Times*, 25 Mar. 2011.

6. "VCU and Richmond Pep Rallies Fuel Friendly Competition," *CT*, 24 Mar. 2011; "Richmond Must Bottle Its Sweet 16 Success beyond Basketball," *TD*, 25 Mar. 2011. See also "City of Richmond—with Rams and Spiders—Is Center of College Hoops," *Washington Times*, 23 Mar. 2011.

7. "VCU Fans Send Men's Basketball Team on Road to Sweet 16," *VCU News*, 23 Mar. 2011; "VCU Is Ram Tough in Overtime Win over Florida State," *WP*, 26 Mar. 2011; "March Madness Boosts VCU, UR and Richmond," *TD*, 27 Mar. 2011.

8. "Dancing with the Stars: VCU Rams Head to Final Four," *TD*, 28 Mar. 2011; "UPDATE: VCU to Welcome Team Home at Midnight," *TD*, 27 Mar. 2011; "Upstart VCU Crashes Final Four Gate," *WP*, 28 Mar. 2011; "Shooting Stars," *Style Weekly*, 29 Mar. 2011 (quotation). See also "First Four to Final Four: V.C.U. Stuns Kansas," *NYT*, 28 Mar. 2011. The statistical expert Nate Silver declared that VCU had overcome 820–1 odds to make the Final Four. See Nate Silver, "In Tournament of Upsets, V.C.U. Has Overcome Longest Odds," *NYT*, 28 Mar. 2011.

9. "VCU's Final Four Foray Brings Record-Levels of Attention," *WP*, 2 Apr. 2011; "A Win-Win at the NCAA Tourney," *WP*, 24 Mar. 2011 (Rao quotations).

10. "VCU Celebrates and Waits," *TD*, 29 Mar. 2011; "Update: McDonnell, Cantor to Watch VCU in Houston," *TD*, 29 Mar. 2011; "Transition Game for VCU: Celebration to Final Four Preparation," *USA Today*, 29 Mar. 2011.

11. "Reliving the Run: A Student's Perspective," 14 Apr. 2011, https://www.vcuathletics.com/sports/mbkb/2010-11/releases/20110414lsboos; "The Run Revisited: An Insider's Perspective," 18 April 2011, https://www.vcuathletics.com/sports/mbkb/2010-11/releases/20110418qgdgx5.

12. "Police, VCU Praise Restraint," *TD*, 5 Apr. 2011. University officials expressed regret that one of the six persons charged with disorderly conduct was a VCU student.

13. "Rams' Historic Run Comes to Close with 70–62 Loss to Butler in National Semifinal," http://www.vcuathletics.com/sports/mbkb/2010–11/releases/20110414lsboos. There was some salve in the final *USA Today* Coaches' Poll, which ranked VCU sixth in the nation (see http://www.espn.com/mens-college-basketball/rankings/_/year/2011).

14. Clare F. Anderson in "Correspondent of the Day," *TD*, 31 Mar. 2011; Adele McClure, Drew Tolley, Chris Peck, Taylor Early, and Bill Schwartz, in "VCU Celebrates Final Four Berth," *VCU News*, 28 Mar. 2011; Geral Staten in "VCU Ram Nation Catches Final Four Fever," NBC 12, 28 Mar. 2011, http://www.nbc12.com/story/14332283/vcu-ram-nation-catches-final-four-fever; Joe Bradford and Chris Grubb in "Local Fans Ready for Final Four," *Albany Times-Union* (Albany, NY), 2 Apr. 2011; Melissa Harreld and Dee Anderson in "VCU Celebrates and Waits," *TD*, 29 Mar. 2011; Asha Patel and Chelse Greaux in "Students Are Drawn to VCU's Diversity," *TD*, 31 Mar. 2011; Brian Gresca, Alaina Jacoby, and Jessica Oberholtzer in "Looking at Final Four Matchups," *All Things Considered*, National Public Radio, 28 Mar. 2011. University officials concluded afterward that VCU "lacked a memorable,

emotional, and unique brand voice." The VCU logo remained in the new "brand mark," but now it was a seal depicting the Egyptian Building with the founding date of 1838. Unlike the original VCU logo, which turned its back on the past, this brand mark embraced the university. With it came a new slogan for VCU: "Make It Real." See "Communications, Sustained Messaging, and Team Effort Put VCU on the Map," *PRweek*, Dec. 2012, 17.

15. "VCU Graduates 4,000."

16. "Dika Newlin, 82, Punk-Rock Schoenberg Expert, Dies," *NYT*, 28 July 2006; Video, *VCU Confidential*, VCU Athletics, 2011, at 4:10.

BIBLIOGRAPHY

Primary Sources

ARCHIVAL SOURCES

Governor Gerald Baliles Executive Papers, LVA
Board of Visitors Minutes, JBC
Betsy Brinson Papers, VHS
Virginius Dabney Papers, University of Virginia Library
William V. Daniels Papers, VHS
Papers of the Gay Alliance of Students, 1974–1977, M357, JBC
Governor Mills Edwin Godwin Jr. Executive Papers, LVA
James Edward Grimsley Papers, University of Virginia Library
Governor Albertis Sydney Harrison Jr. Executive Papers, LVA
Governor Linwood Holton Executive Papers, LVA
Stephen Michael Lenton Papers, VHS
Metropolitan Economic Development Council Archives, JBC
Edward H. Peeples Papers, JBC
J. Sargeant Reynolds Papers, VHS
Richmond Renaissance Papers, JBC
Richmond Urban Institute Papers, JBC
Fred O. Wygal Papers, M154, JBC

ORAL HISTORY INTERVIEWS

Ackell, Edmund F., 30 June 1995, with John Andrako, TMC
Blake, William E., 1 Oct. 2012, with John Kneebone
Blanton, Wyndham B., Jr., 2001, TMC
Brandt, Warren E., 18 Sept. 2007, with Betsy Brinson, JBC
Briceland, Alan, 2 Aug. 2011, with John Kneebone
Brinson, Betsy, 6 Sept. 2016, with John Kneebone
Brumfield, Dale, 14 July 2014, with John Kneebone
Coppedge, Walter, 2 July 2015, with John Kneebone
Davies, Gordon, 16 Aug. 2010, with John Kneebone
Gehring, Donald, 8 Aug. 2010, with John Kneebone
Harris, Grace, 28 July 2010, with John Kneebone
Holsworth, Robert D., 6 July 2010, with John Kneebone
Kelso, Jeff, 26 June 2012, with John Kneebone

Kontos, Hermes, 16 Aug. 2011, with John Kneebone
Lawrence, Walter, 25 Apr. 1996, TMC
McGuire, Hunter, 30 July 1996, TMC
McLeod, Charles, 11 May 2011, with John Kneebone
Messmer, Sue Ann, 18, 20 Aug. 2010, with John Kneebone
Neal, Pinson M., 23 Mar. 1995, TMC
Ohlinger, Brian, 22 Aug. 2014, with John Kneebone
Peeples, Edward H., 15 July 2010, with John Kneebone
Ruffin, Alexis, Aug. 2015, with John Kneebone
Temple, T. Edward, 2 Mar. 1976, College of William and Mary
Townes, Clarence, 3 June 2014, with John Kneebone
Trani, Eugene P., 2009, 2010, 2015, with John Kneebone
Valentine, Henry L., 8 July, 5 Aug. 2011, JBC
Ware, Ralph M., Jr., 28 Mar. 1994, TMC
Watts, Daniel T., 17 Mar. 1994, TMC
Woodlief, Ann, 3 Aug. 2010, with John Kneebone
Wyeth, Peter, 11 Jan. 2012, with John Kneebone

NEWSPAPERS AND PERIODICALS

Inside Business

Medicovan

New York Times

Proscript

Reflections in Ink

Richmond Afro-American

Richmond Magazine

Richmond Mercury

Richmond News Leader

Richmond Times-Dispatch

Scarab

Shafer Court Connections

Style Weekly

VCU Magazine

VCU News

VCU Today

Virginia Dental Journal

Washington Post

X-Ray

Secondary Sources

Acolin, Arthur, Richard Voith, and Susan Wachter. "City and Suburbs: Has There Been a Regime Change?" Penn Institute for Urban Research, Philadelphia, 2016. https://penniur.upenn.edu/uploads/media/City_and_Suburbs_%E2%80%93 _Has_There_Been_a_Regime_Change.pdf.

Allen, Jody, and Brian Daugherity. "Recovering a 'Lost' Story Using Oral History: The United States Supreme Court's Historic *Green v. New Kent County, Virginia,* Decision." *Oral History Review* 33 (Summer 2006): 25–44.

Alley, Reuben E. *History of the University of Richmond, 1830–1971.* Charlottesville: University Press of Virginia, 1977.

Altbach, Philip G., Robert O. Berdahl, and Patricia J. Gumport, eds. *American Higher Education in the Twenty-First Century: Social, Political, and Economic Challenges*. 2nd ed. Baltimore: Johns Hopkins University Press, 2005.

Atkinson, Frank B. *The Dynamic Dominion: Realignment and the Rise of Two-Party Competition in Virginia, 1945–1980*. 2nd rev. ed. Lanham, MD: Rowman and Littlefield, 2006.

———. *Virginia in the Vanguard: Political Leadership in the 400-Year-Old Cradle of American Democracy, 1981–2006*. Lanham, MD: Rowman and Littlefield, 2006.

Axtell, James. *The Making of Princeton University: From Woodrow Wilson to the Present*. Princeton, NJ: Princeton University Press, 2006.

Azziz, Ricardo. "What Is the Value and Role of Academic Medicine in the Life of Its University?" *Academic Medicine* 89 (February 2014): 208–11.

Azziz, Ricardo, Guilbert C. Hentschke, Bonita C. Jacobs, et al. *Strategic Mergers in Higher Education*. Baltimore: Johns Hopkins University Press, 2019.

Bains, Elizabeth. "Virginia Commonwealth University: The U.S. Arts School Was the First University to Set Up a Branch at Qatar's Education City Site." *MEED Middle East Economic Digest*, 18 September 2009, 13–14.

Baker, Donald P. *Wilder: Hold Fast to Dreams*. Cabin John, MD: Seven Locks Press, 1989.

Baldwin, Roger G., and Jay L. Chronister. *Teaching without Tenure: Policies and Practices for a New Era*. Baltimore: Johns Hopkins University Press, 2001.

Barr, Andrew, and Sarah E. Turner. "Expanding Enrollments and Contracting State Budgets: The Effect of the Great Recession on Higher Education." *Annals of the American Academy of Political and Social Sciences* 650 (November 2013): 168–93.

Bayer, Ronald. *Homosexuality and American Psychiatry: The Politics of Diagnosis*. New York: Basic Books, 1981.

Bazin, Nancy Topping. "The Gender Revolution." In *The Politics of Women's Studies: Testimony from Thirty Founding Mothers*, edited by Florence Howe, 57–68. New York: Feminist Press, 2000.

Beach, Marie, ed. *The Only Complete Guide to Richmond*. Midlothian, VA: Guide to Richmond, 1981.

Biondi, Martha. *The Black Revolution on Campus*. Berkeley: University of California Press, 2012.

Birch, Eugenie, David C. Perry, and Henry Louis Taylor Jr. "Universities as Anchor Institutions." *Journal of Higher Education Outreach and Engagement* 17 (2013): 7–15.

Birnbaum, Robert, and Peter D. Eckel. "The Dilemma of Presidential Leadership." In *American Higher Education in the Twenty-First Century: Social, Political, and*

Economic Challenges, 2nd ed., edited by Philip G. Altbach, Robert O. Berdahl, and Patricia J. Gumport, 340–68. Baltimore: Johns Hopkins University Press, 2005.

Blake, Peter. "Restructuring Relationships in Virginia: The Changing Compact between Higher Education Institutions and the State." *Change*, January–February 2006, 27–33.

Bloom, Nicholas Dagen. *Merchant of Illusion: James Rouse, America's Salesman of the Businessman's Utopia.* Columbus: Ohio State University Press, 2004.

Bonis, Ray, Jodi L. Koste, and Curtis Lyons. *Virginia Commonwealth University.* Charleston, SC: Arcadia, 2006.

Bowen, William G., and Eugene M. Tobin. *Locus of Authority: The Evolution of Faculty Roles in the Governance of Higher Education.* Princeton, NJ: Princeton University Press and Ithaka, 2015.

Breo, Dennis L. "E. Grey Dimond, M.D.: The 'Counterculture' Medical Educator." *Journal of the American Medical Association* 266 (21 August 1991): 1019–22.

Brinson, Betsy, and Carol Hampton. "Women in Medicine at the Medical College of Virginia of Virginia Commonwealth University." *Virginia Medical Quarterly* 125 (Winter 1998): 50.

Brown, Jeffrey R., and Caroline M. Hoxby. *How the Financial Crisis and Great Recession Affected Higher Education.* Chicago: University of Chicago Press, 2015.

Brumfield, Dale. *The Richmond Independent Press: A History of the Underground Zine Scene.* Charleston, SC: History Press, 2013.

Bugg, James L., Jr., "Mills Edwin Godwin, Jr.: A Man for All Seasons." In *The Governors of Virginia, 1860–1978*, edited by Edward Younger and James Tice Moore, 373–92. Charlottesville: University Press of Virginia, 1982.

Byng, Michelle D. "The Clash of Government Structure and Racial Politics in *The City of Richmond v. J. A. Croson.*" *Race and Society* 1 (1998): 77–91.

Caravati, Charles M. *Medicine in Richmond, 1900–1975.* Richmond, VA: Richmond Academy of Medicine, 1975.

Carruth, Ricki D. *A Medical College of Virginia Story.* Richmond, VA: n.p., 1988.

Carter, Rob, Libby Meggs, and Sandra Wheeler, eds. *Meggs: Making Graphic Design History.* Hoboken, NJ: John Wiley and Sons, 2008.

Casper, Gerhard. *The Winds of Freedom: Addressing Challenges to the University.* New Haven CT: Yale University Press, 2014.

CEOs for Cities. "How to Behave Like an Anchor Institution." White paper, CEOs for Cities with Living Cities, Washington, DC, June 2010. https://community -wealth.org/content/how-behave-anchor-institution.

Chambers, Bryan B. "Looking Back at *City of Richmond v. J. A. Croson Co.*: Its Effects on State and Local Set-Aside Programs." *Brigham Young University Law Review* 4 (1991): 1633–56.

Cheit, Earl F. *The New Depression in Higher Education: A Study of Financial Conditions at 41 Colleges and Universities*. New York: McGraw-Hill, 1971.

Clark, Burton. *The Distinctive College: Antioch, Reed, and Swarthmore*. Chicago: Aldine, 1970.

Clifford, J. Garry, and Theodore A. Wilson, eds. *Presidents, Diplomats, and Other Mortals*. Columbia: University of Missouri Press, 2007.

Coalition of Urban Serving Universities. *Urban Universities: Anchors Generating Prosperity for America's Cities*. Washington, DC: Coalition of Urban Serving Universities, 2010.

Commission on the Future of the University. *Strategic Plan for the Future of Virginia Commonwealth University*. Richmond: Virginia Commonwealth University, 1993.

Corcoran, Rob. *Trustbuilding: An Honest Conversation on Race, Reconciliation, and Responsibility*. Charlottesville: University of Virginia Press, 2010.

Courturier, Lara K. "Checks and Balances at Work: The Restructuring of Virginia's Public Higher Education System." Report 06-3, National Center for Public Policy and Higher Education, San Jose, CA, June 2006, 1–9.

Crupi, James A. *Back to the Future: Richmond at the Crossroads*. N. p.: Strategic Leadership Solutions, 1993.

———. "Putting the Future Together." Strategic Leadership Solutions, Plano, TX, 2007. https://lmrcommunity.files.wordpress.com/2007/11/putting_the_future _together_final.pdf.

Cushing, Nathan. "Sticking It to Richmond: The Origin and Future of the 'RVA' Sticker." *RVANews*, 13 February 2012. https://rvanews.com/news/sticking-it-to -richmond-the-origin-and-future-of-the-rva-sticker/56426.

Dabney, Virginius. *Across the Years: Memories of a Virginian*. Garden City, NY: Doubleday, 1978.

———. "Albertis S. Harrison, Jr.: Transition Governor." In *The Governors of Virginia, 1860–1978*, edited by Edward Younger and James Tice Moore, 361–72. Charlottesville: University Press of Virginia, 1982.

———. *Mr. Jefferson's University: A History*. Charlottesville: University Press of Virginia, 1981.

———. *Richmond: The Story of a City*. Garden City, NY: Doubleday, 1976.

———. *Virginia Commonwealth University: A Sesquicentennial History*. Charlottesville: University Press of Virginia, 1987.

D'Emilio, John. "Cycles of Change, Questions of Strategy: The Gay and Lesbian Movement after Fifty Years." In *The Politics of Gay Rights*, edited by Craig A. Rimmerman, Kenneth D. Wald, and Clyde Wilcox, 31–53. Chicago: University of Chicago Press, 2000.

Deslippe, Dennis. *Protesting Affirmative Action: The Struggle over Equality after the Civil Rights Revolution*. Baltimore: Johns Hopkins University Press, 2012.

Dimond, E. Grey. *Inside China Today: A Western View*. New York: Norton, 1983.

Diner, Steven D. *Universities and Their Cities: Urban Higher Education in America*. Baltimore: Johns Hopkins University Press, 2017.

Diner, Steven J. "How Universities Migrated into Cities and Democratized Higher Education." *Zócalo Public Square*, 31 August 2017. https://www.zocalopublic square.org/2017/08/31/universities-migrated-cities-democratized-higher -education/ideas/nexus/.

Donoghue, Frank. *The Last Professors: The Corporate University and the Fate of the Humanities*. New York: Fordham University Press, 2008.

Dorn, Charles. *For the Common Good: A New History of Higher Education in America*. Ithaca, NY: Cornell University Press, 2017.

Drake, W. Avon, and Robert D. Holsworth. *Affirmative Action and the Stalled Quest for Black Progress*. Urbana: University of Illinois Press, 1996.

Dunford, Earle, and George Bryson. *Under the Clock: The Story of Miller and Rhoads*. Charleston, SC: History Press, 2008.

Dunning, James Morse. *The Principles of Dental Public Health*. 4th ed. Cambridge, MA: Harvard University Press, 1986.

Edds, Margaret. *Claiming the Dream: The Victorious Campaign of Douglas Wilder of Virginia*. Chapel Hill, NC: Algonquin Books, 1990.

———. *Free at Last: What Really Happened When Civil Rights Came to Southern Politics*. Bethesda, MD: Adler and Adler, 1987.

Ensign, Josephine. *Catching Homelessness: A Nurse's Story of Falling through the Safety Net*. Berkeley, CA: She Writes Press, 2016.

Epps, Rozanne Garrett. *Community of Interest, an Analysis of Virginia Commonwealth University Evening College*. Richmond: n. p., 1974.

Flexner, Abraham. *Medical Education in the United States and Canada*. New York: Carnegie Foundation for the Advancement of Teaching, 1910.

Freeland, Richard M. *Transforming the Urban University: Northeastern, 1996–2006*. Philadelphia: University of Pennsylvania Press, 2019.

Gates, Henry Louis, Jr. *Loose Canons: Notes on the Culture Wars*. New York: Oxford University Press, 1992.

Geiger, Roger L. "The Student Protest Movement in the *1968 Era* in Three Acts: Inception, Confrontations, and Legacies." In *American Higher Education in the Postwar Era, 1945–1970*, edited by Roger L. Geiger, Nathan M. Sorber, and Christian K. Anderson, 170–200. New York: Routledge, 2018.

Geiger, Roger L., Nathan M. Sorber, and Christian K. Anderson, eds. *American Higher Education in the Postwar Era, 1945–1970*. New York: Routledge, 2018.

Gilderbloom, John I., and R. L. Mullins Jr., eds. *Promise and Betrayal: Universities and the Battle for Sustainable Urban Neighborhoods*. Albany: State University of New York Press, 2005.

Ginsberg, Benjamin. *The Fall of the Faculty: The Rise of the All-Administrative University and Why It Matters*. Oxford: Oxford University Press, 2011.

Grawe, Nathan D. *Demographics and the Demand for Higher Education*. Baltimore: Johns Hopkins University Press, 2018.

Gray, Hanna Holborn. *Searching for Utopia: Universities and Their Histories*. Berkeley: University of California Press, 2012.

Griggs, Walter S., Jr. "A History of the Virginia Commonwealth University School of Business." Unpublished typescript, copy in possession of Kneebone.

———. "The Influence of Accreditation on the Development of the Medical College of Virginia into an Institution with University Affiliation." EdD diss., College of William and Mary, 1979.

Gutek, Gerald L. *Education in the United States: An Historical Perspective*. Englewood Cliffs, NJ: Prentice-Hall, 1986.

Hamilton, Philip. *Serving the Old Dominion: A History of Christopher Newport University, 1958–2011*. Macon, GA: Mercer University Press, 2011.

Harkavy, Ira, and Harmon Zuckerman. "Eds and Meds: Cities' Hidden Assets." Brookings Institution, Washington, DC, 1999. https://www.brookings.edu/research/eds-and-meds-cities-hidden-assets/.

Harper, Robert A. *The University That Shouldn't Have Happened, but Did: Southern Illinois during the Morris Years, 1948–1970*. Carbondale: Southern Illinois University Press, 1998.

Harris, Michael S., and Molly K. Ellis. "Exploring Involuntary Presidential Turnover in American Higher Education." *Journal of Higher Education* 88 (November 2017): 1–24.

Harris, Ron. "Richmond: The Confederate Capital Finally Falls to Blacks." *Ebony* 34 (June 1980): 46–52.

Hayter, Julian Maxwell. *The Dream Is Lost: Voting Rights and the Politics of Race in Richmond, Virginia*. Lexington: University Press of Kentucky, 2017.

Heilig, Peggy, and Robert J. Mundt. *Your Voice at City Hall: The Politics, Procedures, and Policies of District Representation*. Albany: State University of New York Press, 1984.

Heller, Donald E. "Introduction: Affordability, Access, and Accountability in Twenty-First Century Public Higher Education." In *The States and Public Higher Education Policy*, 2nd ed., edited by Donald E. Heller, 1–9. Baltimore: Johns Hopkins University Press, 2011.

———, ed. *The States and Public Higher Education Policy: Affordability, Access, and Accountability*. 2nd ed. Baltimore: Johns Hopkins University Press, 2011.

Helms, Frances. "Visions of Change." *Richmond Surroundings* 7 (November 1992): 7–10.

Herbert, Paul. *The Jefferson Hotel: The History of a Richmond Landmark*. Charleston, SC: History Press, 2012.

Hershman, James H., Jr. "A. Linwood Holton (1923–)." *Encyclopedia Virginia*, 24 March 2014. http://www.EncyclopediaVirginia.org/Holton_A_Linwood _1923-.

Hibbs, Henry H. *A History of the Richmond Professional Institute*. Richmond, VA: RPI Foundation, 1973.

Hitz, Mary Buford. *Never Ask Permission: Elizabeth Scott Bocock of Richmond, A Memoir*. Charlottesville: University of Virginia Press, 2012.

Hoekema, David A. *Campus Rules and Moral Community: In Place of* In Loco Parentis. Lanham, MD: Rowman and Littlefield, 1994.

Hoffman, Beatrix. "Emergency Rooms: The Reluctant Safety Net." In *History and Health Policy in the United States: Putting the Past Back In*, edited by Rosemary A. Stevens, Charles E. Rosenberg, and Lawton R. Burns, 250–72. New Brunswick, NJ: Rutgers University Press, 2006.

[Hoke, Thelma Vain]. "The First 125 Years, 1838–1963." *Medical College of Virginia Bulletin* 61 (Sept. 1963).

Holton, Linwood. *Opportunity Time: A Memoir*. Charlottesville: University of Virginia Press, 2008.

Horowitz, Helen Lefkowitz. *Campus Life: Undergraduate Cultures from the End of the Eighteenth Century to the Present*. New York: Alfred A. Knopf, 1987.

Horrow, Rick, with Lary Bloom. *When the Game Is on the Line: From the Man Who Brought the Heat to Miami and the Browns Back to Cleveland, an Inside Look at the High-Stakes World of Sports Deal-Making*. New York: Morgan James, 2011.

Howard, Catherine W., and Kevin W. Allison. "Bringing All Partners to the Table: The Virginia Commonwealth University and Carver Community Partnership." *Metropolitan Universities* 15 (2004): 57–76.

Howard, Vicki. *From Main Street to Mall: The Rise and Fall of the American Department Store*. Philadelphia: University of Pennsylvania Press, 2015.

Howe, Florence, ed. *The Politics of Women's Studies: Testimony from Thirty Founding Mothers*. New York: Feminist Press, 2000.

Initiative for a Competitive Inner City and CEOs for Cities. *Leveraging Colleges and Universities for Urban Economic Revitalization: An Action Agenda*. Boston: ICIC and CEOs for Cities, 2002.

Jablonski, Rita A. Seeger. "Sparks to Wildfires: The Emergence and Impact of Nurse Practitioner Education at Virginia Commonwealth University, 1974–1991."*Nursing History Review* 11 (2003): 167–85.

Jackson, Melanie Njeri, and Manley Elliott Banks II. "Redefining the Role of City Government: Neoconservative Black Urban Regimes in Richmond, Virginia, and Washington, D.C., 1998–2008." *Journal of Race and Policy* 5 (Spring 2009): 54–66.

Jeffries, J. L. *Virginia's Native Son: The Elections and Administration of Governor L. Douglas Wilder.* West Lafayette, IN: Purdue University Press, 2000.

Jones, Stacey. "Dynamic Social Norms and the Unexpected Transformation of Women's Higher Education, 1965–1975." *Social Science History* 33 (Fall 2009): 247–91.

Kemp, Roger L., ed. *Town and Gown Relations: A Handbook of Best Practices.* Jefferson, NC: McFarland, 2013.

Kennedy, Susan Estabrook. *America's White Working-Class Women: A Historical Bibliography.* New York: Garland, 1981.

———. *The Banking Crisis of 1933.* Lexington: University Press of Kentucky, 1973.

———. *If All We Did Was to Weep at Home: A History of White Working-Class Women in America.* Bloomington: Indiana University Press, 1979.

Kierner, Cynthia A., Jennifer R. Loux, and Megan Taylor Shockley. *Changing History: Virginia Women through Four Centuries.* Richmond: Library of Virginia, 2012.

Kirp, David L. *Shakespeare, Einstein, and the Bottom Line: The Marketing of Higher Education.* Cambridge, MA: Harvard University Press, 2003.

Kistler, Ashley. *Anderson Gallery: 45 Years of Art on the Edge.* Richmond: VCU School of the Arts, 2016.

Kollatz, Harry, Jr. *True Richmond Stories.* Charleston, SC: History Press, 2007.

Kors, Alan Charles, and Harvey A. Silvergate. *The Shadow University: The Betrayal of Liberty on America's Campuses.* New York: Free Press, 1998.

Lederer, Susan E. *Flesh and Blood: Organ Transplantation and Blood Transfusion in Twentieth-Century America.* New York: Oxford University Press, 2008.

Lee, H. M. "David M. Hume." In *History of Transplantation: Thirty-Five Recollections,* edited by Paul I. Terasaki, 111–19. Los Angeles: UCLA Tissue Typing Laboratory, 1991.

Leffler, Phyllis. "Mr. Jefferson's University: Women in the Village." *Virginia Magazine of History and Biography* 115 (2007): 56–87.

Leslie, David W., and Robert Oliver Berdahl. "The Politics of Restructuring Higher Education in Virginia: A Case Study." *Review of Higher Education* 31 (Spring 2008): 309–28.

Link, William A. *William Friday: Power, Purpose, and American Higher Education.* Chapel Hill: University of North Carolina Press, 1995.

Lowenstein, Roger. *Origins of the Crash: The Great Bubble and Its Undoing.* New York: Penguin Books, 2004.

Ludmerer, Kenneth M. *A Time to Heal: American Medical Education from the Turn of the Century to the Era of Managed Care.* New York: Oxford University Press, 1999.

Macrina, Francis L. *Scientific Integrity: Text and Cases in Responsible Conduct of Research*. 3rd ed. Washington, DC: American Society for Microbiology Press, 2005.

Mattingly, Paul H. "Introduction: Renegotiating the Historical Narrative: The Case of American Higher Education." *History of Higher Education Quarterly* 44 (Winter 2004): 577–86.

May, Walter P. "The History of Student Governance in Higher Education." *College Student Affairs Journal* 28 (2010): 207–20.

Mazurek, Jan. *Making Microchips: Policy, Globalization, and Economic Restructuring in the Semiconductor Industry*. Cambridge, MA: MIT Press, 1999.

McCormick, Richard P. *The Black Student Protest Movement at Rutgers*. New Brunswick, NJ: Rutgers University Press, 1990.

McGee, Jon. *Breakpoint: The Changing Marketplace for Higher Education*. Baltimore: Johns Hopkins University Press, 2015.

McRae, Donald. *Every Second Counts: The Race to Transplant the First Human Heart*. New York: G. P. Putnam's Sons, 2006.

Michie, Thomas J., Jr., and Marcia S. Mashaw. "Annexation and State Aid to Localities: A Compromise Is Reached." *University of Virginia News Letter* 55 (July 1979): 43.

Mills, Linda, ed. *A Proud Heritage: 100 Years of Nursing Education*. Richmond: Virginia Commonwealth University, 1992.

Mitchell, Betty. *Delyte Morris of SIU*. Carbondale: Southern Illinois University Press, 1988.

Moeser, John V., and Rutledge H. Dennis. *The Politics of Annexation: Oligarchic Power in a Southern City*. Cambridge, MA: Schenkman, 1982.

Musick, Mark D., and Jeffrey S. Cribbs. *Virginia Higher Education/The 1974 General Assembly: A Summary of Legislation and Appropriations*. Richmond: State Council of Higher Education for Virginia, 1974.

Naile, Meghan Theresa. "'Like Nixon Going to China': The Exhibition of Slavery in the Valentine Museum and the Museum of the Confederacy." MA thesis, Virginia Commonwealth University, 2009.

Neimeyer, Jennifer Christine Mills. "The Effect of a Coordinated Care Program on Uninsured, Chronically Ill Patients." PhD diss., Virginia Commonwealth University, 2010.

Nicholson, June O., Pamela J. Creedon, Wanda S. Lloyd, and Pamela J. Johnson, eds. *The Edge of Change: Women in the Twenty-First-Century Press*. Urbana: University of Illinois Press, 2009.

Ogren, Christine A. "Sites, Students, Scholarship, and Structures: The Historiography of American Higher Education in the Post-Revisionist Era." In *Rethinking the History of American Education*, edited by William J. Reese and John L. Rury, 187–222. New York: Palgrave Macmillan, 2008.

Olscamp, Paul J. *Moral Leadership: Ethics and the College Presidency.* Lanham, MD: Rowman and Littlefield, 2003.

O'Mara, Margaret Pugh. *Cities of Knowledge: Cold War Science and the Search for the Next Silicon Valley.* Princeton, NJ: Princeton University Press, 2005.

Owens, Ann. "Urban Revitalization in U.S. Cities and Neighborhoods, 1990 to 2010." Paper prepared for the 21st Century Cities Initiative Symposium, Johns Hopkins University, 2016. owens_21cc_neighborhood_transformation_final. pdf.

Ozmon, Howard, and Sam Craver. *Busing: A Moral Issue.* Bloomington, IN: Phi Delta Kappa Educational Foundation, 1972.

Parkhurst, Kathryn S. "Expansion and Exclusion: A Case Study of Gentrification in Church Hill." MA thesis, Virginia Commonwealth University, 2016.

Payne, Will. *Mark Warner the Dealmaker: From Business Success to the Business of Governing.* Charleston, SC: History Press, 2015.

Pearsall, Tricia. "Ellen Glasgow's Richmond." In *Regarding Ellen Glasgow: Essays for Contemporary Readers,* edited by Welford D. Taylor and George C. Longest, 139–154. Richmond: Library of Virginia, 2001.

Pelasara, Janet. *Love You More: My Fight for Justice for My Daughter.* New York: HarperCollins, 2006.

Perry, David, and Carrie Menendez. "Urban Universities as Anchor Institutions: A Report of National Data and Survey Findings." Coalition of Urban Serving Universities, Washington, DC, 2010. https://community-wealth.org/content /urban-universities-anchor-institutions-report-national-data-and-survey -findings.

Perry, David C., and Wim Wiewel, eds. *The University as Urban Developer: Case Studies and Analysis.* Armonk, NY: M. E. Sharpe, 2005.

Perry, Huey L., ed. *Race, Politics, and Governance in the United States.* Gainesville: University Press of Florida, 1996.

Pollak, Theresa. *An Art School: Some Reminiscences.* Richmond: Virginia Commonwealth University, 1969.

Pool, Charles, and Dulaney Ward. "Plainly Significant: The Jacob House Is a Window on Richmond through the Centuries." *Richmond Journal of History and Architecture* 2 (Spring 1995): 1, 3–9.

Porter, Michael, and Paul Grogan. "Richmond Citizens Benefit from Virginia Commonwealth University's Investments." In *Town and Gown Relations: A Handbook of Best Practices,* edited by Roger L. Kemp, 164–70. Jefferson, NC: McFarland, 2013.

Pratt, Robert A. *The Color of Their Skin: Education and Race in Richmond, Virginia, 1954–89.* Charlottesville: University Press of Virginia, 1992.

Proctor, Robert N. *Golden Holocaust: Origins of the Cigarette Catastrophe and the Case for Abolition.* Berkeley: University of California Press, 2011.

Randolph, Lewis A., and Gayle T. Tate. *Rights for a Season: The Politics of Race, Class, and Gender in Richmond, Virginia*. Knoxville: University of Tennessee Press, 2003.

Rao, Michael. "Talent, Innovation, and Place: A More Relevant Research University of the 21st Century." *Journal on Anchor Institutions and Communities* 1 (2016): 49–52.

Reese, William J., and John L. Rury, eds. *Rethinking the History of American Education*. New York: Palgrave Macmillan, 2008.

Retchin, Sheldon M. "Three Strategies Used by Academic Health Centers to Expand Primary Care Capacity." *Academic Medicine* 75 (January 2000): 15–22.

———. "Variations in Medicare Health Maintenance Organizations." *Journal of the American Medical Association* 281 (24 February 1999): 755–56.

Retchin, Sheldon M., Sheryl L. Garland, and Emmanuel A. Anum. "The Transfer of Uninsured Patients from Academic to Community Primary Care Settings." *American Journal of Managed Care* 15 (April 2009): 245–52.

Richmond Tomorrow. *Citizens' Report: A Strategic Plan for Richmond's Future*. Richmond, VA: Richmond City Council, 1991.

Rimmerman, Craig A., Kenneth D. Wald, and Clyde Wilcox, eds. *The Politics of Gay Rights*. Chicago: University of Chicago Press, 2000.

Rodesch, Jerrold C., and Eugene P. Trani. "Paul Simon, Midwestern Progressive: A Review Essay." *Wisconsin Magazine of History* 73 (Winter 1989–1990): 134–41.

Rodin, Judith. *The University and Urban Renewal: Out of the Ivory Tower and into the Streets*. Philadelphia: University of Pennsylvania Press, 2007.

Rosenzweig, Roy. "Scarcity or Abundance? Preserving the Past in a Digital Era." *American Historical Review* 108 (June 2003): 735–62.

Rothchild, John. *Going for Broke: How Robert Campeau Bankrupted the Retail Industry, Jolted the Junk Bond Market, and Brought the Booming Eighties to a Crashing Halt*. New York: Simon and Schuster, 1991.

Rothstein, William G. *American Medical Schools and the Practice of Medicine: A History*. New York: Oxford University Press, 1987.

Russell, John Dale. *Report of the Higher Education Study Commission*. Richmond, VA: n.p., 1965.

Ryan, James E. *Five Miles Away, a World Apart: One City, Two Schools, and the Story of Educational Opportunity in America*. New York: Oxford University Press, 2010.

Sample, Steven B. *The Contrarian's Guide to Leadership*. San Francisco: Jossey-Bass, 2002.

Sawyer, Charles. *Concerns of a Conservative Democrat*. Carbondale: Southern Illinois University Press, 1968.

Schexnider, Alvin. "Analyzing the Wilder Administration through the Construct of Deracialization Politics." In *Race, Politics, and Governance in the United*

States, edited by Huey L. Perry, 15–28. Gainesville: University Press of Florida, 1996.

Schill, Michael H., and Richard P. Nathan. *Revitalizing America's Cities: Neighborhood Reinvestment and Displacement.* Albany: State University of New York Press, 1983.

Scully, Diana. "Overview of Women's Studies: Organization and Institutional Status in U.S. Higher Education." *National Women's Studies Association Journal* 8 (Autumn 1996): 122–28.

Shaw, Kenneth A. *The Successful President: "Buzz Words" on Leadership.* Phoenix, AZ: American Council on Education and Orynx Press, 1999.

Shields, Jon A., and Joshua M. Dunn Sr. *Passing on the Right: Conservative Professors in the Progressive University.* New York: Oxford University Press, 2016.

Silver, Christopher. *Twentieth-Century Richmond: Planning, Politics, and Race.* Knoxville: University of Tennessee Press, 1984.

Simon, Paul. *P. S.: The Autobiography of Paul Simon.* Chicago: Bonus Books, 1999.

Smartt, Elizabeth Thalhimer. "Thalhimers Department Store: Story, History, and Theory." MA thesis, Virginia Commonwealth University, 2005.

Smartt, Steven H. *Urban Universities in the Eighties: Issues in Statewide Planning.* Atlanta, GA: Southern Regional Education Board, 1981.

Smith, Wilson, and Thomas Bender, eds. *American Higher Education Transformed, 1940–2005: Documenting the National Discourse.* Baltimore: Johns Hopkins University Press, 2008.

Snow, Charlotte. "Another Slice of the Pie: Virginia Hospital Adds Affiliation with Bon Secours." *Modern Healthcare* 27 (20 January 1997): 14.

———. "For Va.'s MCV, Independence Day is July 1." *Modern Healthcare* 27 (30 June 1997): 32.

Soffee, Anne Thomas. *Snake Hips: Belly Dancing and How I Found True Love.* Chicago: Chicago Review Press, 2002.

Sorrell, Andrew V., and Bruce A. Vlk. "Virginia's Never-Ending Moratorium on City–County Annexations." *Virginia Newsletter* 88 (January 2012): 1–8.

Starr, Paul. *Remedy and Reaction: The Peculiar American Struggle over Health Care Reform.* New Haven, CT: Yale University Press, 2011.

———. *The Social Transformation of American Medicine: The Rise of a Sovereign Profession and the Making of a Vast Industry.* New York: Basic Books, 1982.

Stevens, Rosemary A., Charles E. Rosenberg, and Lawton R. Burns, eds. *History and Health Policy in the United States: Putting the Past Back In.* New Brunswick, NJ: Rutgers University Press, 2006.

Strother, Warren H., and Peter Wallenstein. *From VPI to State University: President T. Marshall Hahn and the Transformation of Virginia Tech, 1962–1974.* Macon, GA: Mercer University Press, 2004.

Students of English 102-38, 102-50, and 102-75. *The Works: An Inside Look at Virginia Commonwealth University.* Richmond: VCU Print Shop, 1983.

Tarter, Brent. "Lloyd Campbell Bird." In *Dictionary of Virginia Biography,* edited by John T. Kneebone et al., vol. 1, 501–2. Richmond: Library of Virginia, 1998.

Thelin, John R. *Games Colleges Play: Scandal and Reform in Intercollegiate Athletics.* Baltimore: Johns Hopkins University Press, 1994.

———. *Going to College in the Sixties.* Baltimore: Johns Hopkins University Press, 2018.

———. *A History of American Higher Education.* 2nd ed. Baltimore: Johns Hopkins University Press, 2011.

———. "The New 'A&M.'" *Inside Higher Education,* 16 June 2009.

———. "Success and Excess: The Contours and Character of American Higher Education since 1960." *Society* 50 (2013): 106–14.

Tossell, Chad C., Philip Kortum, Clayton Shepard, et al. "You Can Lead a Horse to Water but You Cannot Make Him Learn: Smartphone Use in Higher Education." *British Journal of Educational Technology* 46 (July 2015): 713–24.

Trachtenberg, Stephen Joel, Gerald B. Kauvar, and E. Grady Bogue. *Presidencies Derailed: Why University Leaders Fail and How to Prevent It.* Baltimore: Johns Hopkins University Press, 2013.

Trani, Eugene P. "Creating a Broader Model of Shared Governance." *Chronicle of Higher Education,* 10 January 1997. Reprinted in *Moral Leadership: Ethics and the College Presidency,* edited by Paul J. Olscamp (Lanham, MD: Rowman and Littlefield, 2003), 147–51.

———. "The Distorted Landscape of Intercollegiate Sports." *Chronicle of Higher Education,* 17 March 1995.

———. "Even in Hard Times, Colleges Should Help Their Communities." *Chronicle of Higher Education,* 16 May 2008.

———. "The Man and the Land: The Politics of Paul Simon and Southern Illinois, 1950–1973." Working paper 21, *The Simon Review* (Occasional papers of the Paul Simon Public Policy Institue), July 2010. Originally published 1975.

———. "A 'Metroversity' for a New Millenium." In *University Leadership in Urban School Renewal,* edited by Nancy L. Zimpher and Kenneth R. Howey, 285–304. Westport, CT: American Council on Education and Praeger, 2004.

———. "Richmond at the Crossroads: The Greater Richmond Metropolitan Area and the Knowledge Based High Technology Economy of the 21st Century." Richmond: Greater Richmond Chamber of Commerce and Virginia Commonwealth University, 1998.

———. *The Treaty of Portsmouth: An Adventure in American Diplomacy.* Lexington: University Press of Kentucky, 1969.

———. "Virginia Commonwealth University: A Partner in Richmond's Revitalization." *Economic Development Association Newsletter,* November 2004, 9–11.

Trani, Eugene P., and Donald E. Davis. "A Tale of Two Kennans: American-Russian Relations in the Twentieth Century." In *Presidents, Diplomats, and Other Mortals*, edited by J. Garry Clifford and Theodore A. Wilson, 31–55. Columbia: University of Missouri Press, 2007.

Trani, Eugene P., and Robert D. Holsworth. *The Indispensable University: Higher Education, Economic Development, and the Knowledge Economy*. Lanham, MD: Rowman and Littlefield, 2010.

Trani, Eugene P., and David L. Wilson. *The Presidency of Warren G. Harding*. Lawrence: Regents Press of Kansas, 1977.

Tuchman, Gaye. *Wannabe U: Inside the Corporate University*. Chicago: University of Chicago Press, 2009.

Tyler-McGraw, Marie. *At the Falls: A History of Richmond, Virginia, and Its People*. Chapel Hill: University of North Carolina Press, 1994.

U.S. Commission on Civil Rights. *The Black/White Colleges: Dismantling the Dual System of Higher Education*. Washington, DC: U.S. Commission on Civil Rights, 1981.

VCUArts. Richmond: Virginia Commonwealth University School of the Arts, 2005.

VCU-Qatar. *Leaving a Mark: A Decade of Design: 10 Years of VCU School of the Arts in Qatar*. Doha: Virginia Commonwealth University School of the Arts in Qatar, 2008.

VCU 2020 Master Site Plan. Richmond: Virginia Commonwealth University, 2004.

Virginia Commonwealth University Faculty Handbook. Richmond: Virginia Commonwealth University, [1978].

Virginia Commonwealth University Self-Study. Richmond: Virginia Commonwealth University, 1972.

Virginia Commonwealth University Self Study. Richmond: Virginia Commonwealth University, 1983.

Wallenstein, Peter. "Black Southerners and Nonblack Universities: The Process of Desegregating Southern Higher Education, 1935–1965." In *Higher Education and the Civil Rights Movement: White Supremacy, Black Southerners, and College Campuses*, edited by Peter Wallenstein, 17–59. Gainesville: University Press of Florida, 2008.

———. *Cradle of America: Four Centuries of Virginia History*. Lawrence: University Press of Kansas, 2007.

———. "Desegregation in Higher Education in Virginia." *Encyclopedia Virginia*, 7 April 2011. http://www.EncyclopediaVirginia.org/Desegregation_in_Higher_Education.

———, ed. *Higher Education and the Civil Rights Movement: White Supremacy, Black Southerners, and College Campuses*. Gainesville: University Press of Florida, 2008.

Wiewel, Wim, Virginia Carlson, and Suzanne Friedman. "Planning the New Urban University: The Role of Planning Departments." *Journal of Planning Education and Research* 16 (1996): 127–35.

Wilder, L. Douglas. *Son of Virginia: A Life in America's Political Arena*. Guilford, CT: Lyons Press, 2015.

Wilkinson, J. Harvie. *Harry Byrd and the Changing Face of Virginia Politics, 1945–1966*. Charlottesville: University Press of Virginia, 1968.

Williams, Ann Laurens. "In Search of a Home: An Historical Analysis of the Major Factors concerning the Location of Virginia Commonwealth University." PhD diss., College of William and Mary, 1985.

Woodlief, Ann. *In River Time: The Way of the James*. Chapel Hill, NC: Algonquin Books, 1985.

Yancey, Dwayne. *When Hell Froze Over: The Untold Story of Doug Wilder: A Black Politician's Rise to Power in the South*. Dallas, TX: Taylor, 1988.

Younger, Edward, and James Tice Moore, eds. *The Governors of Virginia, 1860–1978*. Charlottesville: University Press of Virginia, 1982.

Zacharias, Lee. "The End of the Counterculture." *Southern Quarterly* 34 (Spring 1996): 137–47.

———. *Lessons*. Boston: Houghton Mifflin, 1981.

Zimpher, Nancy L., and Kenneth R. Howey. "The President's Role in Educational Reform: Concluding Observations." In *University Leadership in Urban School Renewal*, edited by Nancy L. Zimpher and Kenneth R. Howey, 305–22. Westport, CT: American Council on Education and Praeger Publishers, 2004.

———, eds. *University Leadership in Urban School Renewal*. Westport, CT: American Council on Education and Praeger Publishers, 2004.

INDEX

Italicized page numbers refer to illustrations.

State Council of Higher Education for
  Virginia (SCHEV) (continued)
  budgets, 93, 196–197; and Shaner
  Report, 4; and urban universities, 103;
  and VCU-Qatar, 265; and *The
  Virginia Plan for Higher Education*,
  121; and women's studies program, 165
Steinfeld, Jesse L., 94, 137
Steingass, Jon, 296–300, 376n63
Stepka, William, 115
Sterling, Wayne, 235
St. Paul's Episcopal Church, 131
*Strategic Plan for the Future of Virginia
  Commonwealth University*, 198–203
Strauss, Jerome F., III, 285
streaking, 74
Student Affairs Committee, 105
Student Bill of Rights, 30
Student Government Association
  (SGA): abolishment of, 79, 104; and
  African American president of, 53;
  constitutional convention, 40;
  representation of in governing bodies,
  48–49; and SLG, 30–32; student
  strike, 54–59; on tuition and fees,
  214–215; and Wright controversy,
  61–62
student protest movements, 29, 30–32,
  36–39, 54–59
Students for a Democratic Society, 30
Study Commission on Higher Education, 80
Sun Belt Conference, 102, 119–120, 147,
  166, 188–189
Swain, Donald, 189
Swift, Harley "Skeeter," 96–97

Taubman Center for State and Local
  Government at Harvard University, 295
Teague, Norwood, 290, 303–304
Teams of Progress, 53
Temple, Polly D., 97
Temple, T. Edward: administrative
  reorganization of VCU, 86–87; on

affirmative action in hiring, 90;
  appointment and inauguration of,
  79–80, 83–84; on basketball team, 97;
  on campus identities, 80–81; career
  before VCU, 16–17, 55–56, 76–77, 80,
  329n76; death of, 99; and Interim
  Administrative Committee, 75–77;
  and MCV Hospitals bond issue,
  82–84, 86–87; photograph of, *80*; and
  Polly's death, 97; and Richmond
  annexation, 73; and unity of univer-
  sity, 78; on VCU funding and
  finances, 87–89
Thalhimer, Charles G., 148, 158
Thalhimer, Rhoda, 148
Thalhimer, William B., 188
Thalhimers department store, 188, 191
Thompson, Taliaferro, 64
Throttle, 136
Times-Dispatch, 243
Timmreck, Paul, 241, 261, 281, 285, 286
Toppin, Edgar A., 34–35
Topping, Nancy Bazin, 164
Torgersen, Paul E., 208–209, 221
Toscan, Richard, 240, 245, 265
Townes, Clarence L., Jr., 139, 147, 242,
  245, 278
Townsend, J. Ives, 329n91
Training in Expanded Auxiliary
  Management (TEAM), 84–86, 87
Trani, Anne, 175–176
Trani, Eugene P.: and AdCenter,
  230–232; and administrative organ-
  ization, 183–184; appointment and
  inauguration of, 178–179, 189–190; and
  athletic program, 189, 215–216,
  221–222, 276, 290, 312; on Behl, 288;
  biographical information, 71, 174–178;
  and Biotechnology Research Park,
  194, 203; on Board of Visitors, 372n27;
  "Burning Secrets," response to,
  218–219; and Cambridge sabbatical,
  250–251; and China, trip to, 232; and
  communication, 178, 194–195; on